Juxtapositions

Juxtapositions

Connections and Contrasts

William Vesterman
Rutgers University

MAYFIELD PUBLISHING COMPANY
Mountain View, California
London • Toronto

Library of Congress Cataloging-in-Publication Data

Vesterman, William
   Juxtapositions : connections and contrasts / William Vesterman.
     p. cm.
   Includes index.
    ISBN 1–55934–449–0
    1. College readers. 2. English language—Rhetoric. 3. Critical thinking
    I.   Title.
PE1417.V487   1995
808′.0427—dc20   95-34508
                                               CIP

Manufactured in the United States of America
10 9 8 7 6 5 4 3 2 1

Mayfield Publishing Company
1280 Villa Street
Mountain View, CA 94041

Sponsoring editor, Thomas V. Broadbent; production editor, Julianna Scott Fein; manuscript editor, Loralee Windsor; art director, Jeanne M. Schreiber; text and cover designer, Linda Robertson; manufacturing manager, Randy Hurst. The text was set in 11/12 Bembo by G & S Typesetters, Inc. and printed on 50# Butte des Mortes by Banta Book Group.

Acknowledgments and copyrights continue at the back of the book on pages 441–444, which constitute an extension of the copyright page.

 This book is printed on acid-free, recycled paper.

Preface

Juxtapositions is an anthology aimed at stimulating critical thinking in readers and writers through the proven powers of comparison and contrast. I long ago found in my own writing classes something very simple and potentially effective: Given one essay or one topic to consider, some students invariably felt they could find nothing interesting to say. Yet students presented with two or more pieces of writing—especially when the selections made an easy taking of sides impossible—were always able to find ideas they believed were worth thinking and writing about. These ideas are as often remarkable for their diversity as for what they have in common, and they make for real discussions rather than ritualized "debates" in class.

Accordingly the juxtapositions in this book are of many kinds, some of them unexpected and some undoubtedly not recognized by me but awaiting discovery by alert readers. All, I hope, will be stimulating for students and instructors.

In any given cluster readers may find interesting differences or similarities of cultural context, purpose, genre, gender, and historical circumstances, to name just a few possibilities. Theory may be juxtaposed with practice, physical with imagined reality, contemporary life with the life of the past, and so on. The editorial aim is to start students thinking about all these matters as natural aspects of writing by inviting them to attend to differences rather than to adjudicate among them. Thus, for example, students are invited to become alert to the ways differing cultural contexts may inform essays on the same topic. Taking account of such differences may be seen as one of the normal requirements of reading by educated people in contemporary America. That is, differences among cultural contexts do not necessarily suggest a "problem" to be "solved" or a "political agenda" to be discovered for denunciation or approval.

In addition to the illumination provided by the juxtapositions themselves, some further ordering seemed necessary to make the book a practical tool for classroom use. Like many composition courses, the book begins with materials that call most obviously for expressive writing and for the student writer's engagement with questions of personal identity. As the juxtapositions go on to emphasize more explicitly the modes of analysis and argumentation, the individual selections focus on more public issues. The critical apparatus for each set of selections has been organized with a single class period in mind, although many units and many individual selections may be usefully compared and contrasted with others in the book, and instructors will soon find many innovative ways of approaching the book's materials.

The discussion questions and suggestions for writing focus not only on the thematic and rhetorical issues raised by particular readings but also on the common concerns of writing courses, such as strategies and structures for introductory paragraphs, the nature of metaphor, and the uses and misuses of irony. The explicit attention paid to such matters within the book should enrich class discussion and give those charged with supervising many sections of a common course ways to ensure a minimum set of testable skills. The accompanying *Instructor's Resource Guide* offers still more practical help in making the most of the book.

I am happy to acknowledge the debt this book owes to Robert Atwan, who gave me much selfless and effective aid in conceiving and designing it. Tom Broadbent, my editor at Mayfield, encouraged and helped to develop the project with all his experience, skill, and good nature. Marianne Cotugno followed out the mazes of permissions paths with intelligence and patience. Dan Moran, author of the accompanying *Instructor's Resource Guide,* brought his admirable talents and energies as a teacher to the task and has produced one of the best examples of that form I have seen.

Many other teachers from across the country have helped to shape the book's final form and content. M. Thomas Inge of Randolph-Macon College sent me Walt Disney's "The Story of Mickey Mouse." I thank Vincent Casaregola, Saint Louis University; Gilbert Gigliotti, Central Connecticut State University; Dana Goodrich, Metropolitan Community College; John Hanes, Duquesne University; Martha L. Hemming, Portland Community College; Kathryn Henkins, Mt. San Antonio College; Priscilla Kelly, Slippery Rock University of Pennsylvania; James C. McDonald, University of Southwestern Louisiana; David Rollison, College of Marin; Susan A. Schiller, Central Michigan University; William E. Smith, Western Washington University; Mark Wiley, California State University, Long Beach; Holly Zaitchik, Boston University; and Richard J. Zbaracki, Iowa State University.

Contents

Preface *v*

Personal Observation and Narration *1*

1 *Facing Social Pressure* 2

Langston Hughes, "Salvation" 4
George Orwell, "Shooting an Elephant" 7
Anna Quindlen, "The Name Is Mine" 13

> Social pressure often makes us act in ways we later regret. Three widely differing experiences illuminate a pervasive problem for self-definiton.

2 *Three Diaries from States of Siege* 16

Anne Frank, from *The Diary of a Young Girl* 18
Zlata Filipovic, from *Zlata's Diary: A Child's Life in Sarajevo* 27
LaToya Hunter, from *The Diary of LaToya Hunter* 37

> Three young women describe the process of coming of age in worlds that threaten to destroy them, not because of anything they have done but simply because of who they are.

3 *Fathers* 42

E. B. White, "Once More to the Lake" 44
Sylvia Plath, "Daddy" 50
Raymond Carver, "Photograph of My Father in His Twenty-Second Year" 53
Theodore Roethke, "My Papa's Waltz" 54

> A great essayist fondly turns a summer home on a lake into a metaphor for the generational links between his father, himself, and his son. Two modern poets and a novelist evoke equally deep but more painful feelings.

4 *From Story to Film: "Paul's Case"* 56

Willa Cather, "Paul's Case: A Study in Temperament" 58
Ron Cowen, screenplay excerpt from *Paul's Case* 74

"Paul's Case" is the story of a teenager who is determined to give his fantasies life, even if he has to die for it. Two media illuminate differing artistic possibilities for the expression of the same theme.

5 *To Die by Law* 82

Charles Dickens, "Among the Condemned" 85
George Orwell, "A Hanging" 88
H. L. Mencken, "Hangings I Have Known" 92
Norman Mailer, "Let's Do It" 94

The process of finding language to describe the lives of strangers faced with execution reflects and dramatizes what death and justice mean to the lives of the writers.

6 *Mothers* 98

Alice Walker, "In Search of Our Mothers' Gardens" 100
David James Duncan, "Ma" 108
Maxine Hong Kingston, "Photographs of My Mother" 112
Jamaica Kincaid, "Girl" 116
Carolyn Kizer, from "The Blessing" 118

In essays, fiction, and poetry, five writers attempt to come to terms with the values of the women who gave them life.

7 *Fact and Fiction: Two Accounts of One Disaster* 120

Stephen Crane, "News Account of the Disaster" 122
Stephen Crane, "The Open Boat" 130

Fact turns into fiction for an American novelist who was also a reporter. The differences in focus and technique show some of the many ways in which writers seek to express the meanings of a single personal disaster.

8 *An Ancient Story Told and Retold* 150

King James Bible, "The Book of Ruth" 152
Thomas Hood, "Ruth" 158
lucille clifton, "naomi watches as ruth sleeps" 160

Some of the ways in which ancient stories continue to influence and stimulate later lives become clear when the same tale is seen through the eyes and styles of different historical periods.

9 *Immigrants: Horror and Hope* 162

Charles Ball, "Slave Ship" 164
Mary Gordon, "More Than Just a Shrine: Paying Homage to the Ghosts of Ellis Island" 166
Vo Thi Tam, "A Boat Person's Story" 170

These accounts by a slave, a novelist, and a refugee show us some of the many paths of horror and hope that have led to the present population of the United States.

Analysis and Explanation *175*

10 *Twentieth-Century Homelessness* 176

Jack London, "Among the London Poor" 178
Scott Shuger, "Who Are the Homeless?" 186

Here are two accounts of modern urban poverty and homelessness—one written at the beginning of the twentieth century and one at that century's end.

11 *Imagining the End of the World* 202

Robert Frost, "Fire and Ice" 204
Sir Frederick Hoyle, "The Next Ice Age" 206
Carl Sagan, "The Warming of the World" 212

"Some say the world will end in fire / Some say in ice. . . ." So begins Robert Frost's metaphoric and moral appreciation of what is also a literal and scientific controversy explored by two eminent scientists.

12 *Thought for Food* 218

M. F. K. Fisher, "The Indigestible: The Language of Food" 220
William Safire, "A Bottle of Ketchup" 229

For humans, language makes food more than the basic need we share with other forms of life. How food feeds the imagination makes a common theme for two very different sensibilities.

13 *Mickey Mouse: An American Myth* 234

Walt Disney, "The Story of Mickey Mouse" 236
Stephen Jay Gould, "A Biological Homage to Mickey Mouse" 240
John Updike, "The Mystery of Mickey Mouse" 250
George Vlahogiannis, "Weird World of Disney" 256

Mickey Mouse is an American mythical figure who has come to worldwide recognition. Here is Mickey from four points of view.

14 *Why Is Weight So Weighty?* 260

Anne Hollander, "Why It's Fashionable to Be Thin" 262
Sallie Tisdale, "A Weight That Women Carry" 265
Joseph Epstein, "A Fat Man Struggles to Get Out" 275

Why is weight so weighty an issue in contemporary life? Three essayists discuss some ways in which the imagination and physical reality interact on this topic.

15 *Meaning on the Mall* 280

Bob Greene, "15"   282
Joyce Carol Oates, "Shopping"   288
William Geist, "Sport Shopping in Suburbia"   298

> The mall is the village green of the present generation of American young people. What layers of meaning does materialism add to the age-old desire of young people to get together?

16 *Reimagining a Fairy Tale* 304

Jakob and Wilhelm Grimm, "Red Riding Hood"   306
James Finn Garner, "Little Red Riding Hood"   309
Russell Baker, "Little Red Riding Hood Revisited"   312
Bruno Bettelheim, "Fairy Tale versus Myth: Optimism versus Pessimism"   315

> Fairy tales continue to illuminate contemporary life and in this sense may be said to be timeless. Three modern sensibilities examine the subject.

Advocacy and Argument   323

17 *Language and Manners* 324

Thomas H. Middleton, "Freshman Class?"   326
Ellen Goodman, "Vulgarity May Be Common, but It's Not Okay"   329
Barbara Lawrence, "Four-Letter Words Can Hurt You"   331

> Public manners are largely a matter of language—particularly of word choice. On what basis should people choose their words when they enter the public world?

18 *The Power of Naming* 334

Itabari Njeri, "What's in a Name?"   336
Richard Crasta, "What's in a Name?"   342

> "A rose by any other name would smell as sweet" is the answer Juliet gives to Shakespeare's famous question. Here are some other answers of today.

19 *Two Visions of Freedom* 346

Martin Luther King, Jr., "I Have a Dream"   348
Malcolm X, "The Ballot or the Bullet"   352

> The historic arguments of two leaders of the 1960s illuminate issues still debated today.

20 *Einstein's Brain* 356

Steven Levy, "My Search for Einstein's Brain"   358
Roland Barthes, "The Brain of Einstein"   371

> Mind and brain are words often used synonymously. What are the implications of treating the physical and the metaphysical aspects of human beings as if they were the same thing?

21 *When the Earth Shook* 374

William James, "On Some Mental Effects of the Earthquake" 376
Susanna Styron, "Risk Management: Men versus Women in the
  L. A. Earthquake" 383
Isak Dinesen, "The Earthquake" 386

> Similar natural disasters beyond personal control stimulate widely differing
> personal reflections on the relation of human life to the natural world.

22 *Regulating Speech* 388

Russell Baker, "Don't Mention It" 390
David G. Savage, "Forbidden Words on Campus" 393
Gloria Naylor, "A Question of Language" 398

> What are the proper relations between freedom of speech and the right
> not to be harassed and insulted? A current issue for American campuses
> is examined from three points of view.

23 *Language as Power* 402

Frederick Douglass, "Learning to Read and Write" 404
Amy Tan, "Mother Tongue" 409
Leonard Q. Ross, "Mr. K★A★P★L★A★N, the Comparative,
  and the Superlative" 414

> The ability to read and write is easy to take for granted, but a former
> American slave, a first-generation Chinese American, and a fictional
> Jewish immigrant remind us that power of language is power over life.

24 *Mirror, Mirror* 418

Nathaniel Hawthorne, "The Birth-Mark" 420
Molly O'Neill, "The Anatomy Lesson" 433
Marjorie Rosen, "New Face, New Body, New Self" 435

> What happens when the desire for beauty becomes an obsession? A
> classic American short story and two contemporary essays explore
> some of the answers.

Acknowledgments 441

Index to the Readings by Type 445

Index of Authors and Titles 447

Personal Observation and Narration

1 Facing Social Pressure

Langston Hughes, "Salvation"
George Orwell, "Shooting an Elephant"
Anna Quindlen, "The Name Is Mine"

The three essays that follow provide examples of individuals struggling with worlds that both surround and exclude them. As you read the different responses of the individual writers, consider the following questions:

1. In what ways do the examples of "social pressure" dramatized in the essays differ? In what ways do they appear the same? "Social custom," for example, might describe a source of pressure for each writer, but in what ways do the natures and instrumentalities of the "customs" differ?

2. Each essay is both a confession of weakness and an affirmation of strength. What each writer considered to be his or her weakness seems easy enough to say, but how would you characterize the strengths dramatized by each writer?

3. Each writer seems clear about his or her final stance with regard to the issues faced. Through what similar means do the authors present the *unclearness* and complexity of those issues? In what distinct ways does each do so?

4. What attitudes in the reader does each writer seem to assume? Compassion? Disdain? Find a moment in each essay when the writer seems to anticipate and deal with a response from the reader, and describe the dynamics of the situation.

SALVATION

Langston Hughes

Langston Hughes (1902–1967) was a leading poet of what came to be known as the Harlem Renaissance in the 1920s. He attended Columbia University but left after a year to work as a merchant seaman before being published, first in periodicals and later in anthologies and books of his own. In the following selection he recalls a crucial moment in his childhood.

I was saved from sin when I was going on thirteen. But not really saved. 1
It happened like this. There was a big revival at my Auntie Reed's church. Every night for weeks there had been much preaching, singing, praying, and shouting, and some very hardened sinners had been brought to Christ, and the membership of the church had grown by leaps and bounds. Then just before the revival ended, they held a special meeting for children, "to bring the young lambs to the fold." My aunt spoke of it for days ahead. That night I was escorted to the front row and placed on the mourners' bench with all the other young sinners, who had not yet been brought to Jesus.

My aunt told me that when you were saved you saw a light, and something happened to you inside! And Jesus came into your life! And God was with you from then on! She said you could see and hear and feel Jesus in your soul. I believed her. I had heard a great many old people say the same thing and it seemed to me they ought to know. So I sat there calmly in the hot, crowded church, waiting for Jesus to come to me.

The preacher preached a wonderful rhythmical sermon, all moans and shouts and lonely cries and dire pictures of hell, and then he sang a song about the ninety and nine safe in the fold, but one little lamb was left out in the cold. Then he said: "Won't you come? Won't you come to Jesus? Young lambs, won't you come?" And he held out his arms to all us young sinners there on the mourners' bench. And the little girls cried. And some of them jumped up and went to Jesus right away. But most of us just sat there.

A great many old people came and knelt around us and prayed, old women with jet-black faces and braided hair, old men with work-gnarled hands. And the church sang a song about the lower lights are burning, some poor sinners to be saved. And the whole building rocked with prayer and song.

Still I kept waiting to *see* Jesus. 5

Finally all the young people had gone to the altar and were saved, but one boy and me. He was a rounder's son named Westley. Westley and I were surrounded by sisters and deacons praying. It was very hot in the church, and getting late now. Finally Westley said to me in a whisper: "God damn!

I'm tired o' sitting here. Let's get up and be saved." So he got up and was saved.

Then I was left all alone on the mourners' bench. My aunt came and knelt at my knees and cried, while prayers and song swirled all around me in the little church. The whole congregation prayed for me alone, in a mighty wail of moans and voices. And I kept waiting serenely for Jesus, waiting, waiting—but he didn't come. I wanted to see him, but nothing happened to me. Nothing! I wanted something to happen to me, but nothing happened.

I heard the songs and the minister saying: "Why don't you come? My dear child, why don't you come to Jesus? Jesus is waiting for you. He wants you. Why don't you come? Sister Reed, what is this child's name?"

"Langston," my aunt sobbed.

"Langston, why don't you come? Why don't you come and be saved? Oh, Lamb of God! Why don't you come?"   *10*

Now it was really getting late. I began to be ashamed of myself, holding everything up so long. I began to wonder what God thought about Westley, who certainly hadn't seen Jesus either, but who was now sitting proudly on the platform, swinging his knickerbockered legs and grinning down at me, surrounded by deacons and old women on their knees praying. God had not struck Westley dead for taking his name in vain or for lying in the temple. So I decided that maybe to save further trouble, I'd better lie, too, and say that Jesus had come, and get up and be saved.

So I got up.

Suddenly the whole room broke into a sea of shouting, as they saw me rise. Waves of rejoicing swept the place. Women leaped in the air. My aunt threw her arms around me. The minister took me by the hand and led me to the platform.

When things quieted down, in a hushed silence, punctuated by a few ecstatic "Amens," all the new young lambs were blessed in the name of God. Then joyous singing filled the room.

That night, for the last time in my life but one—for I was a big boy   *15* twelve years old—I cried. I cried, in bed alone, and couldn't stop. I buried my head under the quilts, but my aunt heard me. She woke up and told my uncle I was crying because the Holy Ghost had come into my life, and because I had seen Jesus. But I was really crying because I couldn't bear to tell her that I had lied, that I had deceived everybody in the church, that I hadn't seen Jesus, and that now I didn't believe there was a Jesus any more, since he didn't come to help me.

Questions of Subject and Theme

1. Explain what you understood Hughes' first two sentences to mean when you first read them. What do they mean on re-reading them in the context of the essay as a whole? In what sense do you finally understand the author's use of the title "Salvation"?

2. For most of the revival meeting Hughes describes himself as calm. What kind of faith produced this calm? Explain what happens to that faith and what, if anything, replaces it in the author by the end of the essay.

Questions of Method and Strategy

1. Until the end of his experience, Hughes the child held himself aloof in many senses from those around him. How does Hughes the writer feel about his relation to the others? Explain some of the ways in which he creates an emotional relation to the events of his past. For example, is he ever ironic about them? What emotional relation to its subject does irony create?
2. What effects on his reader does Hughes create by describing and quoting Westley? How does Hughes dramatize his own feelings through the example of Westley by comparison and contrast?

SHOOTING AN ELEPHANT

George Orwell

George Orwell was the pen name of Eric Arthur Blair (1903–1950), an Englishman perhaps most known for *1984,* his futuristic novel about totalitarianism. Educated at the famous secondary school Eton, the young Orwell went on to serve with the Indian Imperial Police in Burma from 1922 through 1927. He became convinced of the basic evil of imperialism, though he never concealed his doubts about the abilities for self-rule among the people he helped to govern. "Shooting an Elephant" comes out of Orwell's Burmese experience, as does the essay "A Hanging," which appears in Juxtaposition 5 (p. 88).

In Moulmein, in lower Burma, I was hated by large numbers of people— *1* the only time in my life that I have been important enough for this to happen to me. I was sub-divisional police officer of the town, and in an aimless, petty kind of way anti-European feeling was very bitter. No one had the guts to raise a riot, but if a European woman went through the bazaars alone somebody would probably spit betel juice over her dress. As a police officer I was an obvious target and was baited whenever it seemed safe to do so. When a nimble Burman tripped me up on the football field and the referee (another Burman) looked the other way, the crowd yelled with hideous laughter. This happened more than once. In the end the sneering yellow faces of young men that met me everywhere, the insults hooted after me when I was at a safe distance, got badly on my nerves. The young Buddhist priests were the worst of all. There were several thousands of them in the town and none of them seemed to have anything to do except stand on street corners and jeer at Europeans.

All this was perplexing and upsetting. For at that time I had already made up my mind that imperialism was an evil thing and the sooner I chucked up my job and got out of it the better. Theoretically—and secretly, of course—I was all for the Burmese and all against their oppressors, the British. As for the job I was doing, I hated it more bitterly than I can perhaps make clear. In a job like that you see the dirty work of Empire at close quarters. The wretched prisoners huddling in the stinking cages of the lock-ups, the grey, cowed faces of the long-term convicts, the scarred buttocks of the men who had been flogged with bamboos—all these oppressed me with an intolerable sense of guilt. But I could get nothing into perspective. I was young and ill-educated and I had had to think out my problems in the utter silence that is imposed on every Englishman in the East. I did not even know that the British Empire is dying, still less did I know that it is a great deal better than the younger empires that are going to supplant it. All I knew was that I was stuck between my hatred of the empire I served and my rage against the evil-spirited little beasts who tried to make my job impossible. With one part of my mind I thought of the British Raj as an unbreakable tyranny, as something clamped down, in *saecula saeculorum,* upon the will of prostrate peoples; with another part I thought that the greatest joy in the world would be to drive a bayonet into a Buddhist priest's guts. Feelings like these are the normal by-products of imperialism; ask any Anglo-Indian official, if you can catch him off duty.

One day something happened which in a roundabout way was enlightening. It was a tiny incident in itself, but it gave me a better glimpse than I had had before of the real nature of imperialism—the real motive for which despotic governments act. Early one morning the sub-inspector at a police station the other end of the town rang me up on the 'phone and said that an elephant was ravaging the bazaar. Would I please come and do something about it? I did not know what I could do, but I wanted to see what was happening and I got on to a pony and started out. I took my rifle, an old .44 Winchester and much too small to kill an elephant, but I thought the noise might be useful *in terrorem.* Various Burmans stopped me on the way and told me about the elephant's doings. It was not, of course, a wild elephant, but a tame one which had gone "must." It had been chained up, as tame elephants always are when their attack of "must" is due, but on the previous night it had broken its chain and escaped. Its mahout, the only person who could manage it when it was in that state, had set out in pursuit, but had taken the wrong direction and was now twelve hours' journey away, and in the morning the elephant had suddenly reappeared in the town. The Burmese population had no weapons and were quite helpless against it. It had already destroyed somebody's bamboo hut, killed a cow and raided some fruit-stalls and devoured the stock; also it had met the municipal rubbish van and, when the driver jumped out and took to his heels, had turned the van over and inflicted violences upon it.

The Burmese sub-inspector and some Indian constables were waiting for me in the quarter where the elephant had been seen. It was a very poor quarter, a labyrinth of squalid bamboo huts, thatched with palm-leaf, winding all over a steep hillside. I remember that it was a cloudy, stuffy morning at the beginning of the rains. We began questioning the people as to where the elephant had gone and, as usual, failed to get any definite information. That is invariably the case in the East; a story always sounds clear enough at a distance, but the nearer you get to the scene of events the vaguer it becomes. Some of the people said that the elephant had gone in one direction, some said that he had gone in another, some professed not even to have heard of any elephant. I had almost made up my mind that the whole story was a pack of lies, when we heard yells a little distance away. There was a loud, scandalized cry of "Go away, child! Go away this instant!" and an old woman with a switch in her hand came round the corner of a hut, violently shooing away a crowd of naked children. Some more women followed, clicking their tongues and exclaiming; evidently there was something that the children ought not to have seen. I rounded the hut and saw a man's dead body sprawling in the mud. He was an Indian, a black Dravidian coolie, almost naked, and he could not have been dead many minutes. The people said that the elephant had come suddenly upon him round the corner of the hut, caught him with its trunk, put its foot on his back and ground him into the earth. This was the rainy season and the ground was soft, and his face had scored a trench a foot deep and a couple of yards long. He was lying on his belly with arms crucified and head sharply twisted to one side. His face was coated with mud, the eyes wide open, the teeth bared and grinning with an expression of unendurable agony. (Never tell me, by the way, that the dead look peaceful. Most of the corpses I have seen looked devilish.) The friction of the great beast's foot had stripped the skin from his back as neatly as one skins a rabbit. A soon as I saw the dead man I sent an orderly to a friend's house nearby to borrow an elephant rifle. I had already sent back the pony, not wanting it to go mad with fright and throw me if it smelt the elephant.

The orderly came back in a few minutes with a rifle and five cartridges, 5 and meanwhile some Burmans had arrived and told us that the elephant was in the paddy fields below, only a few hundred yards away. As I started forward practically the whole population of the quarter flocked out of the houses and followed me. They had seen the rifle and were all shouting excitedly that I was going to shoot the elephant. They had not shown much interest in the elephant when he was merely ravaging their homes, but it was different now that he was going to be shot. It was a bit of fun to them, as it would be to an English crowd; besides they wanted the meat. It made me vaguely uneasy. I had no intention of shooting the elephant—I had merely sent for the rifle to defend myself if necessary—and it is always unnerving to have a crowd following you. I marched down the hill, looking and feeling a fool, with the rifle over my shoulder and an ever-growing army of people jostling at my heels. At the bottom, when you got away from the huts, there was a metalled road and beyond that a miry waste of paddy fields a thousand yards across, not yet ploughed but soggy from the first rains and dotted with coarse grass. The elephant was standing eight yards from the road, his left side towards us. He took not the slightest notice of the crowd's approach. He was tearing up branches of grass, beating them against his knees to clean them and stuffing them into his mouth.

I had halted on the road. As soon as I saw the elephant I knew with perfect certainty that I ought not to shoot him. It is a serious matter to shoot a working elephant—it is comparable to destroying a huge and costly piece of machinery—and obviously one ought not to do it if it can possibly be avoided. And at that distance, peacefully eating, the elephant looked no more dangerous than a cow. I thought then and I think now that his attack of "must" was already passing off; in which case he would merely wander harmlessly about until the mahout came back and caught him. Moreover, I did not in the least want to shoot him. I decided that I would watch him for a little while to make sure that he did not turn savage again, and then go home.

But at that moment I glanced round at the crowd that had followed me. It was an immense crowd, two thousand at the least and growing every minute. It blocked the road for a long distance on either side. I looked at the sea of yellow faces above the garish clothes—faces all happy and excited over this bit of fun, all certain that the elephant was going to be shot. They were watching me as they would watch a conjurer about to perform a trick. They did not like me, but with the magical rifle in my hands I was momentarily worth watching. And suddenly I realized that I should have to shoot the elephant after all. The people expected it of me and I had got to do it; I could feel their two thousand wills pressing me forward, irresistibly. And it was at this moment, as I stood there with the rifle in my hands, that I first grasped the hollowness, the futility of the white man's dominion in the East. Here was I, the white man with his gun, standing in front of the unarmed native crowd—seemingly the leading actor of the piece; but in reality I was only an absurd puppet pushed to and fro by the will of those yellow faces behind. I perceived in this moment that when the white man turns tyrant it is his own freedom that he destroys. He becomes a sort of hollow, posing dummy, the conventionalized figure of a sahib. For it is the condition of his rule that he shall spend his life in trying to impress the "natives," and so in every crisis he has got to do what the "natives" expect of him. He wears a mask, and his face grows to fit it. I had got to shoot the elephant. I had committed myself to doing it when I sent for the rifle. A sahib has got to act like a sahib; he has to appear resolute, to know his own mind and do definite things. To come all that way, rifle in hand, with two thousand people marching at my heels, and then to trail feebly away, having done nothing—no, that was impossible. The crowd would laugh at me. And my whole life, every white man's life in the East, was one long struggle not to be laughed at.

But I did not want to shoot the elephant. I watched him beating his bunch of grass against his knees, with that preoccupied grandmotherly air that elephants have. It seemed to me that it would be murder to shoot him. At that age I was not squeamish about killing animals, but I had never shot an elephant and never wanted to. (Somehow it always seems worse to kill a *large* animal.) Besides, there was the beast's owner to be considered. Alive, the elephant was worth at least a hundred pounds; dead, he would only be worth the value of his tusks, five pounds, possibly. But I had got to act quickly. I turned to some experienced-looking Burmans who had been there when we arrived, and asked them how the elephant had been behaving. They all said the same thing: he took no notice of you if you left him alone, but he might charge if you went too close to him.

It was perfectly clear to me what I ought to do. I ought to walk up to within, say, twenty-five yards of the elephant and test his behavior. If he charged, I could shoot; if he took no notice of me, it would be safe to leave him until the mahout came back. But also I knew that I was going to do no such thing. I was a poor shot with a rifle and the ground was soft mud into which one would sink at every step. If the elephant charged and I missed him, I should have about as much chance as a toad under a steam-roller. But even then I was not thinking particularly of my own skin, only of the watchful yellow faces behind. For at that moment, with the crowd watching me, I was not afraid in the ordinary sense, as I would have been if I had been alone. A white man mustn't be frightened in front of "natives"; and so, in general, he isn't frightened. The sole thought in my mind was that if anything went wrong those two thousand Burmans would see me pursued, caught, trampled on and reduced to a grinning corpse like that Indian up the hill. And if that happened it was quite probable that some of them would laugh. That would never do. There was only one alternative. I shoved the cartridges into the magazine and lay down on the road to get a better aim.

The crowd grew very still, and a deep, low, happy sigh, as of people   *10* who see the theatre curtain go up at last, breathed from innumerable throats. They were going to have their bit of fun after all. The rifle was a beautiful German thing with cross-hair sights. I did not then know that in shooting an elephant one would shoot to cut an imaginary bar running from ear-hole to ear-hole. I ought, therefore, as the elephant was sideways on, to have aimed straight at his ear-hole; actually I aimed several inches in front of this, thinking the brain would be further forward.

When I pulled the trigger I did not hear the bang or feel the kick—one never does when a shot goes home—but I heard the devilish roar of glee that went up from the crowd. In that instant, in too short a time, one would have thought, even for the bullet to get there, a mysterious, terrible change had come over the elephant. He neither stirred nor fell, but every line of his body had altered. He looked suddenly stricken, shrunken, immensely old, as though the frightful impact of the bullet had paralysed him without knocking him down. At last, after what seemed a long time—it might have been five seconds, I dare say—he sagged flabbily to his knees. His mouth slobbered. An enormous senility seemed to have settled upon him. One could have imagined him thousands of years old. I fired again into the same spot. At the second shot he did not collapse but climbed with desperate slowness to his feet and stood weakly upright, with legs sagging and head drooping. I fired a third time. That was the shot that did for him. You could see the agony of it jolt his whole body and knock the last remnant of strength from his legs. But in falling he seemed for a moment to rise, for as his hind legs collapsed beneath him he seemed to tower upward like a huge rock toppling, his trunk reaching skywards like a tree. He trumpeted, for the first and only time. And then down he came, his belly towards me, with a crash that seemed to shake the ground even where I lay.

I got up. The Burmans were already racing past me across the mud. It was obvious that the elephant would never rise again, but he was not dead. He was breathing very rhythmically with long rattling gasps, his great mound of a side painfully rising and falling. His mouth was wide open—I could see far down into caverns of pale pink throat. I waited a long time for him to die, but his breathing did not weaken. Finally I fired my two remaining shots into the spot where I thought his heart must be. The thick blood welled out of him like red velvet, but still he did not die. His body did not even jerk when the shots hit him, the tortured breathing continued without a pause. He was dying, very slowly and in great agony, but in some world remote from me where not even a bullet could damage him further. I felt that I had got to put an end to that dreadful noise. It seemed dreadful to see the great beast lying there, powerless to move and yet powerless to die, and not even to be able to finish him. I sent back for my small rifle and poured shot after shot into his heart and down his throat. They seemed to make no impression. The tortured gasps continued as steadily as the ticking of a clock.

In the end I could not stand it any longer and went away. I heard later that it took him half an hour to die. Burmans were bringing dahs and baskets even before I left, and I was told they had stripped his body almost to the bones by the afternoon.

Afterwards, of course, there were endless discussions about the shooting of the elephant. The owner was furious, but he was only an Indian and could do nothing. Besides, legally I had done the right thing, for a mad elephant has to be killed, like a mad dog, if its owner fails to control it. Among the Europeans opinion was divided. The older men said I was right, the younger men said it was a damn shame to shoot an elephant for killing a coolie, because an elephant was worth more than any damn Coringhee coolie. And afterwards I was very glad that the coolie had been killed; it put me legally in the right and it gave me a sufficient pretext for shooting the elephant. I often wondered whether any of the others grasped that I had done it solely to avoid looking a fool.

Questions of Subject and Theme

1. According to the essay as a whole, who exactly is oppressed by imperialism? Find some examples that suggest differing kinds of oppression, and explain the differing ways in which they are shown to work.
2. At the end of the essay Orwell says that he was glad the coolie was killed. Why was he glad at the time of the events? Does the essay as a whole make it seem that he was glad at the time he *wrote* about the events? Find evidence to support your answers.

Questions of Method and Strategy

1. In what ways does Orwell's description of the *manner* of the elephant's death symbolize the complicated human relations dramatized in the essay?
2. Orwell's general tone is often very bitter. What are the ways in which he uses language to create that sense of bitterness? Find examples of bitterness directed both at himself and at others. How are the examples similar, and how do they differ?

THE NAME IS MINE

Anna Quindlen

Now a full-time novelist, Anna Quindlen retired from the *New York Times* where she served as deputy metropolitan editor and long-standing columnist. In the following essay, she reflects on the part names have played in her complex identity as an individual, family member, and mother.

I am on the telephone to the emergency room of the local hospital. My elder son is getting stitches in his palm, and I have called to make myself feel better, because I am at home, waiting, and my husband is there, holding him. I am 34 years old, and I am crying like a child, making a slippery mess of my face. "Mrs. Krovatin?" says the nurse, and for the first time in my life I answer "Yes."

This is a story about a name. The name is mine. I was given it at birth, and I have never changed it, although I married. I could come up with lots of reasons why. It was a political decision, a simple statement that I was somebody and not an adjunct of anybody, especially a husband. As a friend of mine told her horrified mother, "He didn't adopt me, he married me."

It was a professional and a personal decision, too. I grew up with an ugly dog of a name, one I came to love because I thought it was weird and un-lovable. Amid the Debbies and Kathys of my childhood, I had a first name only my grandmothers had and a last name that began with a strange letter. "Sorry, the letters I, O, Q, U, V, X, Y and Z are not available," the cata-logues said about monogrammed key rings and cocktail napkins. Seeing my name in black on white at the top of a good story, suddenly it wasn't an ugly dog anymore.

But neither of these are honest reasons, because they assume rational consideration, and it so happens that when it came to changing my name, there was no consideration, rational or otherwise. It was mine. It belonged to me. I don't even share a checking account with my husband. Damned if I was going to be hidden beneath the umbrella of his identity.

It seemed like a simple decision. But nowadays I think the only simple decisions are whether to have grilled cheese or tuna fish for lunch. Last week, my older child wanted an explanation of why he, his dad and his brother have one name, and I have another.

My answer was long, philosophical and rambling—that is to say, unsat-isfactory. What's in a name? I could have said disingenuously. But I was talking to a person who had just spent three torturous, exhilarating years learning names for things, and I wanted to communicate to him that mine meant something quite special to me, had seemed as form-fitting as my skin, and as painful to remove. Personal identity and independence, however, were not what he was looking for; he just wanted to make sure I was one of them. And I am—and then again, I am not. When I made this decision, I was part of a couple. Now, there are two me's, the me who is the individual and the me who is part of a family of four, a family of four in which, in a small way, I am left out.

A wise friend who finds herself in the same fix says she never wants to change her name, only to have a slightly different identity as a family member, an identity for pediatricians' offices and parent-teacher conferences. She also says that the entire situation reminds her of the women's movement as a whole. We did these things as individuals, made these decisions about ourselves and what we wanted to be and do. And they were good decisions, the right decisions. But we based them on individual choice, not on group dynamics. We thought in terms of our sense of ourselves, not our relationships with others.

Some people found alternative solutions: hyphenated names, merged names, matriarchal names for the girls and patriarchal ones for the boys, one name at work and another at home. I did not like those choices; I thought they were middle grounds, and I didn't live much in the middle ground at the time. I was once slightly disdainful of women who went all the way and changed their names. But I now know too many smart, independent, terrific women who have the same last names as their husbands to be disdainful anymore. (Besides, if I made this decision as part of a feminist world view, it seems dishonest to turn around and trash other women for deciding as they did.)

I made my choice. I haven't changed my mind. I've just changed my life. Sometimes I feel like one of those worms I used to hear about in biology, the ones that, chopped in half, walked off in different directions. My name works fine for one half, not quite as well for the other. I would never give it up. Except for that one morning when I talked to the nurse at the hospital, I always answer the question "Mrs. Krovatin?" with "No, this is Mr. Krovatin's wife." It's just that I understand the down side now.

Questions of Subject and Theme

1. Quindlen describes several attitudes she has taken toward her name during the course of her life. How would you describe some of these attitudes? Locate some examples and name the attitudes.
2. Toward the end of her essay Quindlen distinguishes between issues of "individual choice" and issues of "group dynamics." In what ways are those issues both present in the beginning of her essay?

Questions of Method and Strategy

1. Quindlen says around the middle of her essay that keeping her name "seemed like a simple decision." Her essay as a whole suggests otherwise. Find a moment when you feel her sense of the issue's complexity, and point to the uses of language that express that complexity to you.

2. What emotional effects does Quindlen create by the image or metaphor of "my husband's umbrella?" By the image or metaphor of the severed worm? Explain how these verbal devices concentrate the expressions of issues also treated in more abstract language.

———

Suggestions for Writing on the Juxtapositions

1. Pick a moment from your own life when you have acted in a way you later regretted. Write about that moment in an essay that takes advantage of at least some of the techniques of expression that you admire in the authors represented here.
2. Each writer describes the operation of what Emerson calls a "double consciousness." Anna Quindlen, for example, refers to "two me's" and to the severed halves of a worm. Write an essay that shows how each writer creates through his or her use of language a sense of double consciousness.
3. In your view, which writer seems most ashamed of what he or she has done? Which least ashamed? Write an essay in which you explain and defend your views by pointing to and analyzing evidence.
4. Orwell says that the basis of imperialism is "one long struggle not to be laughed at." Pick another ostensibly political or social theme, and write an essay in which you explore its personal and psychological roots.

2 Three Diaries from States of Siege

Anne Frank, from *The Diary of a Young Girl*

Zlata Filipovic, from *Zlata's Diary: A Childs Life in Sarajevo*

LaToya Hunter, from *The Diary of LaToya Hunter*

The following selections are from diaries written by young girls, each embattled in a different time and culture, each faced not only with the problems of growing up but also with outside forces that threaten to destroy them. As you read, consider the following questions:

1. Each writer lives in the midst of a family. What does her family mean to each girl? Discuss the range of relations to her family expressed and implied by each writer.

2. Each girl writes in the midst of potential danger. Compare and contrast the ways in which each faces the issue.

3. Each diarist lives in a different culture, but each faces common issues such as danger. What other aspects of life seem to make the girls most alike? What aspects of life seem to make them most different?

4. Part of the appeal of each writer is the combination of innocence and experience she expresses. Compare and contrast the childlike and mature qualities that each writer displays.

FROM THE DIARY OF A YOUNG GIRL

Anne Frank

After the German invasion of Holland during World War II, Anne Frank, with her own family and another family of Jews, lived for two years in a secret hiding place attached to a business building in Amsterdam. In 1944 they were discovered and sent to Nazi concentration camps, in one of which Anne died. Her father survived and found her diary on his return to Amsterdam, where he published it in 1952.

Thursday, 6 April, 1944

Dear Kitty,

You asked me what my hobbies and interests were, so I want to reply. I *1*
warn you, however, that there are heaps of them, so don't get a shock!

First of all: writing, but that hardly counts as a hobby.

Number two: family trees. I've been searching for family trees of the French, German, Spanish, English, Austrian, Russian, Norwegian, and Dutch royal families in all the newspapers, books, and pamphlets I can find. I've made great progress with a lot of them, as, for a long time already, I've been taking down notes from all the biographies and history books that I read; I even copy out many passages of history.

My third hobby then is history, on which Daddy has already bought me a lot of books. I can hardly wait for the day that I shall be able to comb through the books in a public library.

Number four is Greek and Roman mythology. I have various books *5*
about this too.

Other hobbies are film stars and family photos. Mad on books and reading. Have a great liking for history of art, poets and painters. I may go in for music later on. I have a great loathing for algebra, geometry, and figures.

I enjoy all the other school subjects, but history above all!

Yours, Anne

Tuesday, 11 April, 1944

Dear Kitty,

My head throbs, I honestly don't know where to begin.

On Friday (Good Friday) we played Monopoly, Saturday afternoon too. These days passed quickly and uneventfully. On Sunday afternoon, on my invitation, Peter came to my room at half past four; at a quarter past five we went to the front attic, where we remained until six o'clock. There was a beautiful Mozart concert on the radio from six o'clock until a quarter past seven. I enjoyed it all very much, but especially the "Kleine Nachtmusik." I can hardly listen in the room because I'm always so inwardly stirred when I hear lovely music.

On Sunday evening Peter and I went to the front attic together and, in order to sit comfortably, we took with us a few divan cushions that we were able to lay our hands on. We seated ourselves on one packing case. Both the case and the cushions were very narrow, so we sat absolutely squashed together, leaning against other cases. Boche kept us company too, so we weren't unchaperoned.

Suddenly, at a quarter to nine, Mr. Van Daan whistled and asked if we had one of Dussel's cushions. We both jumped up and went downstairs with cushion, cat, and Van Daan.

A lot of trouble arose out of this cushion, because Dussel was annoyed that we had one of his cushions, one that he used as a pillow. He was afraid that there might be fleas in it and made a great commotion about his beloved cushion! Peter and I put two hard brushes in his bed as a revenge. We had a good laugh over this little interlude!

Our fun didn't last long. At half past nine Peter knocked softly on the door and asked Daddy if he would just help him upstairs over a difficult English sentence. "That's a blind," I said to Margot, "anyone could see through that one!" I was right. They were in the act of breaking into the warehouse. Daddy, Van Daan, Dussel, and Peter were downstairs in a flash. Margot, Mummy, Mrs. Van Daan, and I stayed upstairs and waited.

Four frightened women just have to talk, so talk we did, until we heard a bang downstairs. After that all was quiet, the clock struck a quarter to ten. The color had vanished from our faces, we were still quiet, although we were afraid. Where could the men be? What was that bang? Would they be fighting the burglars? Ten o'clock, footsteps on the stairs: Daddy, white and nervous, entered, followed by Mr. Van Daan. "Lights out, creep upstairs, we expect the police in the house!"

There was no time to be frightened: the lights went out, I quickly grabbed a jacket, and we were upstairs. "What has happened? Tell us quickly!" There was no one to tell us, the men having disappeared downstairs again. Only at ten past ten did they reappear; two kept watch at Peter's open window, the door to the landing was closed, the swinging cupboard shut. We hung a jersey round the night light, and after that they told us:

Peter heard two loud bangs on the landing, ran downstairs, and saw there was a large plank out of the left half of the door. He dashed upstairs, warned the "Home Guard" of the family, and the four of them proceeded downstairs. When they entered the warehouse, the burglars were in the act of enlarging the hole. Without further thought Van Daan shouted: "Police!"

A few hurried steps outside, and the burglars had fled. In order to avoid the hole being noticed by the police, a plank was put against it, but a good hard kick from outside sent it flying to the ground. The men were perplexed at such impudence, and both Van Daan and Peter felt murder welling up within them; Van Daan beat on the ground with a chopper, and all was quiet again. Once more they wanted to put the plank in front of the hole.

Disturbance! A married couple outside shone a torch through the opening, lighting up the whole warehouse. 'Hell!' muttered one of the men, and now they switched over from their role of police to that of burglars. The four of them sneaked upstairs, Peter quickly opened the doors and windows of the kitchen and private office, flung the telephone onto the floor, and finally the four of them landed behind the swinging cupboard.

End of Part One

The married couple with the torch would probably have warned the police: it was Sunday evening, Easter Sunday, no one at the office on Easter Monday, so none of us could budge until Tuesday morning. Think of it, waiting in such fear for two nights and a day! No one had anything to suggest, so we simply sat there in pitch-darkness, because Mrs. Van Daan in her fright had unintentionally turned the lamp right out; talked in whispers, and at every creak one heard "Sh! sh!"

It turned half past ten, eleven, but not a sound; Daddy and Van Daan joined us in turns. Then a quarter past eleven, a bustle and noise downstairs. Everyone's breath was audible, otherwise no one moved. Footsteps in the house, in the private office, kitchen, then . . . on our staircase. No one breathed audibly now, footsteps on our staircase, then a rattling of the swinging cupboard. This moment is indescribable. "Now we are lost!" I said, and could see us all being taken away by the Gestapo that very night. Twice they rattled at the cupboard, then there was nothing, the footsteps withdrew, we were saved so far. A shiver seemed to pass from one to another, I heard someone's teeth chattering, no one said a word.

There was not another sound in the house, but a light was burning on our landing, right in front of the cupboard. Could that be because it was a secret cupboard? Perhaps the police had forgotten the light? Would someone come back to put it out? Tongues loosened, there was no one in the house any longer, perhaps there was someone on guard outside.

Next we did three things: we went over again what we supposed had happened, we trembled with fear, and we had to go to the lavatory. The buckets were in the attic, so all we had was Peter's tin wastepaper basket. Van Daan went first, then Daddy, but Mummy was too shy to face it. Daddy brought the wastepaper basket into the room, where Margot, Mrs. Van Daan, and I gladly made use of it. Finally Mummy decided to do so too. People kept on asking for paper—fortunately I had some in my pocket!

The tin smelled ghastly, everything went on in a whisper, we were tired, it was twelve o'clock. "Lie down on the floor then and sleep." Margot and I were each given a pillow and one blanket; Margot lying just near the store cupboard and I between the table legs. The smell wasn't quite so bad when one was on the floor, but still Mrs. Van Daan quietly brought some chlorine, a tea towel over the pot serving as a second expedient.

Talk, whispers, fear, stink, flatulation, and always someone on the pot; then try to go to sleep! However, by half past two I was so tired that I knew no more until half past three. I awoke when Mrs. Van Daan laid her head on my foot.

"For heaven's sake, give me something to put on!" I asked. I was given something, but don't ask what—a pair of woolen knickers over my pajamas, a red jumper, and a black skirt, white oversocks and a pair of sports stockings full of holes. Then Mrs. Van Daan sat in the chair and her husband came and lay on my feet. I lay thinking till half past three, shivering the whole time, which prevented Van Daan from sleeping. I prepared myself for the return of the police, then we'd have to say that we were in hiding; they would either be good Dutch people, then we'd be saved, or N.S.B.-ers,[1] then we'd have to bribe them!

"In that case, destroy the radio," sighed Mrs. Van Daan. "Yes, in the stove!" replied her husband. "If they find us, then let them find the radio as well!"

"Then they will find Anne's diary," added Daddy. "Burn it then," suggested the most terrified member of the party. This, and when the police rattled the cupboard door, were my worst moments. "Not my diary; if my diary goes, I go with it!" But luckily Daddy didn't answer.

There is no object in recounting all the conversations that I can still remember; so much was said. I comforted Mrs. Van Daan, who was very scared. We talked about escaping and being questioned by the Gestapo, about ringing up, and being brave.

"We must behave like soldiers, Mrs. Van Daan. If all is up now, then let's go for Queen and Country, for freedom, truth, and right, as they always say on the Dutch News from England. The only thing that is really rotten is that we get a lot of other people into trouble too."

Mr. Van Daan changed places again with his wife after an hour, and Daddy came and sat beside me. The men smoked non-stop, now and then there was a deep sigh, then someone went on the pot and everything began all over again.

Four o'clock, five o'clock, half past five. Then I went and sat with Peter by his window and listened, so close together that we could feel each other's bodies quivering; we spoke a word or two now and then, and listened attentively. In the room next door they took down the blackout. They wanted to call up Koophuis at seven o'clock and get him to send someone around. Then they wrote down everything they wanted to tell Koophuis over the phone. The risk that the police on guard at the door, or in the warehouse, might hear the telephone was very great, but the danger of the police returning was even greater.

The points were these:

Burglars broken in: police have been in the house, as far as the swinging cupboard, but no further.

Burglars apparently disturbed, forced open the door in the warehouse and escaped through the garden.

---

1. The Dutch National Socialist Movement.

Main entrance bolted, Kraler must have used the second door when he left. The typewriters and adding machine are safe in the black case in the private office.

Try to warn Henk and fetch the key from Elli, then go and look round the office—on the pretext of feeding the cat.

Everything went according to plan. Koophuis was phoned, the type-   35
writers which we had upstairs were put in the case. Then we sat around the table again and waited for Henk or the police.

Peter had fallen asleep and Van Daan and I were lying on the floor, when we heard loud footsteps downstairs. I got up quietly: "That's Henk."

"No, no, it's the police," some of the others said.

Someone knocked at the door, Miep whistled. This was too much for Mrs. Van Daan, she turned as white as a sheet and sank limply into a chair; had the tension lasted one minute longer she would have fainted.

Our room was a perfect picture when Miep and Henk entered, the table alone would have been worth photographing! A copy of *Cinema and Theater,* covered with jam and a remedy for diarrhea, opened at a page of dancing girls, two jam pots, two started loaves of bread, a mirror, comb, matches, ash, cigarettes, tobacco, ash tray, books, a pair of pants, a torch, toilet paper, etc., etc., lay jumbled together in variegated splendor.

Of course Henk and Miep were greeted with shouts and tears. Henk   40
mended the hole in the door with some planks, and soon went off again to inform the police of the burglary. Miep had also found a letter under the warehouse door from the night watchman Slagter, who had noticed the hole and warned the police, whom he would also visit.

So we had half an hour to tidy ourselves. I've never seen such a change take place in half an hour. Margot and I took the bedclothes downstairs, went to the W.C., washed, and did our teeth and hair. After that I tidied the room a bit and went upstairs again. The table there was already cleared, so we ran off some water and made coffee and tea, boiled the milk, and laid the table for lunch. Daddy and Peter emptied the potties and cleaned them with warm water and chlorine.

At eleven o'clock we sat round the table with Henk, who was back by that time, and slowly things began to be more normal and cozy again. Henk's story was as follows:

Mr. Slagter was asleep, but his wife told Henk that her husband had found the hole in our door when he was doing his tour round the canals, and that he had called a policeman, who had gone through the building with him. He would be coming to see Kraler on Tuesday and would tell him more then. At the police station they knew nothing of the burglary yet, but the policeman had made a note of it at once and would come and look round on Tuesday. On the way back Henk happened to meet our green-grocer at the corner, and told him that the house had been broken into. "I know that," he said quite coolly. "I was passing last evening with my wife and saw the hole in the door. My wife wanted to walk on, but I just had a look in with my torch; then the thieves cleared at once. To be on the safe side, I didn't ring up the police, as with you I didn't think it was the thing to do. I don't know anything, but I guess a lot."

Henk thanked him and went on. The man obviously guesses that we're here, because he always brings the potatoes during the lunch hour. Such a nice man!

It was one by the time Henk had gone and we'd finished doing the   *45*
dishes. We all went for a sleep. I awoke at a quarter to three and saw that Mr. Dussel had already disappeared. Quite by chance, and with my sleepy eyes, I ran into Peter in the bathroom; he had just come down. We arranged to meet downstairs.

I tidied myself and went down. "Do you still dare to go to the front attic?" he asked. I nodded, fetched my pillow, and we went up to the attic. It was glorious weather, and soon the sirens were wailing; we stayed where we were. Peter put his arm around my shoulder, and I put mine around his and so we remained, our arms around each other, quietly waiting until Margot came to fetch us for coffee at four o'clock.

We finished our bread, drank lemonade and joked (we were able to again), otherwise everything went normally. In the evening I thanked Peter because he was the bravest of us all.

None of us has ever been in such danger as that night. God truly protected us; just think of it—the police at our secret cupboard, the light on right in front of it, and still we remained undiscovered.

If the invasion comes, and bombs with it, then it is each man for himself, but in this case the fear was also for our good, innocent protectors. "We are saved, go on saving us!" That is all we can say.

This affair has brought quite a number of changes with it. Mr. Dussel   *50*
no longer sits downstairs in Kraler's office in the evenings, but in the bathroom instead. Peter goes round the house for a checkup at half past eight and half past nine. Peter isn't allowed to have his window open at nights any more. No one is allowed to pull the plug after half past nine. This evening there's a carpenter coming to make the warehouse doors even stronger.

Now there are debates going on all the time in the "Secret Annexe." Kraler reproached us for our carelessness. Henk, too, said that in a case like that we must never go downstairs. We have been pointedly reminded that we are in hiding, that we are Jews in chains, chained to one spot, without any rights, but with a thousand duties. We Jews mustn't show our feelings, must be brave and strong, must accept all inconveniences and not grumble, must do what is within our power and trust in God. Sometimes this terrible war will be over. Surely the time will come when we are people again, and not just Jews.

Who has inflicted this upon us? Who has made us Jews different from all other people? Who has allowed us to suffer so terribly up till now? It is God that has made us as we are, but it will be God, too, who will raise us up again. If we bear all this suffering and if there are still Jews left, when it is over, then Jews, instead of being doomed, will be held up as an example. Who knows, it might even be our religion from which the world and all peoples learn good, and for that reason and that reason only do we have to suffer now. We can never become just Netherlanders, or just English, or representatives of any country for that matter, we will always remain Jews, but we want to, too.

Be brave! Let us remain aware of our task and not grumble, a solution will come, God has never deserted our people. Right through the ages there have been Jews, through all the ages they have had to suffer, but it has made them strong too; the weak fall, but the strong will remain and never go under!

During that night I really felt that I had to die, I waited for the police, I was prepared, as the soldier is on the battlefield. I was eager to lay down my life for the country, but now, now I've been saved again, now my first wish after the war is that I may become Dutch! I love the Dutch, I love this country, I love the language and want to work here. And even if I have to write to the Queen myself, I will not give up until I have reached my goal.

I am becoming still more independent of my parents, young as I am, I 55 face life with more courage than Mummy; my feeling for justice is immovable, and truer than hers. I know what I want, I have a goal, an opinion, I have a religion and love. Let me be myself and then I am satisfied. I know that I'm a woman, a woman with inward strength and plenty of courage.

If God lets me live, I shall attain more than Mummy ever has done, I shall not remain insignificant, I shall work in the world and for mankind!

And now I know that first and foremost I shall require courage and cheerfulness!

Yours, Anne

Wednesday, 3 May, 1944

Dear Kitty,

First, just the news of the week. We're having a holiday from politics; there is nothing, absolutely nothing to announce. I too am gradually beginning to believe that the invasion will come. After all, they can't let the Russians clear up everything; for that matter, they're not doing anything either at the moment.

Mr. Koophuis comes to the office every morning again now. He's got a new spring for Peter's divan, so Peter will have to do some upholstering, about which, quite understandably, he doesn't feel a bit happy.

Have I told you that Moffi has disappeared? Simply vanished—we 60 haven't seen a sign of her since Thursday of last week. I expect she's already in the cats' heaven, while some animal lover is enjoying a succulent meal from her. Perhaps some little girl will be given a fur cap out of her skin. Peter is very sad about it.

Since Saturday we've changed over, and have lunch at half past eleven in the mornings, so we have to last out with one cupful of porridge; this saves us a meal. Vegetables are still very difficult to obtain: we had rotten boiled lettuce this afternoon. Ordinary lettuce, spinach and boiled lettuce, there's nothing else. With these we eat rotten potatoes, so it's a delicious combination!

As you can easily imagine we often ask ourselves here despairingly: "What, oh, what is the use of the war? Why can't people live peacefully together? Why all this destruction?"

The question is very understandable, but no one has found a satisfactory answer to it so far. Yes, why do they make still more gigantic planes, still heavier bombs and, at the same time, prefabricated houses for reconstruction? Why should millions be spent daily on the war and yet there's not a penny available for medical services, artists, or for poor people?

Why do some people have to starve, while there are surpluses rotting in other parts of the world? Oh, why are people so crazy?

I don't believe that the big men, the politicians and the capitalists alone, are guilty of the war. Oh no, the little man is just as guilty, otherwise the peoples of the world would have risen in revolt long ago! There's in people simply an urge to destroy, an urge to kill, to murder and rage, and until all mankind, without exception, undergoes a great change, wars will be waged, everything that has been built up, cultivated, and grown will be destroyed and disfigured, after which mankind will have to begin all over again.

I have often been downcast, but never in despair; I regard our hiding as a dangerous adventure, romantic and interesting at the same time. In my diary I treat all the privations as amusing. I have made up my mind now to lead a different life from other girls and, later on, different from ordinary housewives. My start has been so very full of interest, and that is the sole reason why I have to laugh at the humorous side of the most dangerous moments.

I am young and I possess many buried qualities; I am young and strong and am living a great adventure; I am still in the midst of it and can't grumble the whole day long. I have been given a lot, a happy nature, a great deal of cheerfulness and strength. Every day I feel that I am developing inwardly, that the liberation is drawing nearer and how beautiful nature is, how good the people are about me, how interesting this adventure is! Why, then, should I be in despair?

Yours, Anne

Friday, 5 May, 1944

Dear Kitty,

Daddy is not pleased with me; he thought that after our talk on Sunday I automatically wouldn't go upstairs every evening. He doesn't want any "necking," a word I can't bear. It was bad enough talking about it, why must he make it so unpleasant now? I shall talk to him today. Margot has given me some good advice, so listen; this is roughly what I want to say:

"I believe, Daddy, that you expect a declaration from me, so I will give it you. You are disappointed in me, as you had expected more reserve from me, and I suppose you want me to be just as a fourteen-year-old should be. But that's where you're mistaken!

"Since we've been here, from July 1942 until a few weeks ago, I can assure you that I haven't had any easy time. If you only knew how I cried in the evenings, how unhappy I was, how lonely I felt, then you would understand that I want to go upstairs!

"I have now reached the stage that I can live entirely on my own, without Mummy's support or anyone else's for that matter. But it hasn't just happened in a night; it's been a bitter, hard struggle and I've shed many a tear, before I became as independent as I am now. You can laugh at me and not believe me, but that can't harm me. I know that I'm a separate individual and I don't feel in the least bit responsible to any of you. I am only telling you this because I thought that otherwise you might think that I was underhand, but I don't have to give an account of my deeds to anyone but myself.

"When I was in difficulties you all closed your eyes and stopped up your ears and didn't help me; on the contrary, I received nothing but warnings not to be so boisterous. I was only boisterous so as not to be miserable all the time. I was reckless so as not to hear that persistent voice within me continually. I played a comedy for a year and a half, day in, day out, I never grumbled, never lost my cue, nothing like that—and now, now the battle is over. I have won! I am independent both in mind and body. I don't need a mother any more, for all this conflict has made me strong.

"And now, now that I'm on top of it, now that I know that I've fought the battle, now I want to be able to go on in my own way too, the way that I think is right. You can't and mustn't regard me as fourteen, for all these troubles have made me older; I shall not be sorry for what I have done, but shall act as I think I can. You can't coax me into not going upstairs; *either* you forbid it, *or* you trust me through thick and thin, but then leave me in peace as well!"

Yours, Anne

Questions of Subject and Theme

1. In her entry for 3 May, Anne Frank says at age fourteen "I regard our hiding as a dangerous adventure, romantic and interesting at the same time. In my diary I treat all the privations as amusing." Find examples that show what you think Anne Frank means by her assessment of her writing as "amusing."
2. Anne defends her budding love affair at the end of this selection. Do you find her touching? Silly? Sensible? Naive? Discuss the character of the person you feel expressed through her writing here.

Questions of Method and Strategy

1. How does Anne Frank attempt to make her writing "amusing" on the subject of her privations? Pick one of your examples and show how her particular uses of language attempt to transform the conventional responses her subject might be expected to produce.
2. When does Anne's style seem most childlike? When most adult? Find an example of each manner and analyze what it is about her writing that produces a sense of her apparent level of maturity.

FROM ZLATA'S DIARY
A Child's Life in Sarajevo

Zlata Filipovic

When the thirteen-year-old Zlata Filipovic's diary became known to the world, she was very quickly called "the Anne Frank of Sarajevo." Recording her experiences during the siege of that city in 1991–1992, Zlata became a symbol of civilian suffering in a war, a war that continues at the present time.

Thursday, May 21, 1992

Dear Mimmy,

Mommy went to see Braco in the hospital today. He's alive. That's the most important thing. But he's badly wounded. It's his knee. Two hundred wounded were brought to the clinic that day. They were going to amputate his leg, but his friend Dr. Adnan Dizdar (the surgeon) recognized him, canceled the amputation and took him into the operating room. The operation lasted four-and-a-half hours and the doctors say it was a success. But he'll have to stay in bed for a long, long time. He has some rods, a cast, all sorts of things on his leg. Mommy is terribly worried and sad. So are Grandma and Granddad (that's what Mommy tells me, because I haven't seen them since April 12; I haven't been out of the house). In the end he was lucky. I hope it will turn out all right. Hold on there, Braco!!!

Your Zlata

Saturday, May 23, 1992

Dear Mimmy,

I'm not writing to you about me anymore. I'm writing to you about war, death, injuries, shells, sadness and sorrow. Almost all my friends have left. Even if they were here, who knows whether we'd be able to see one another. The phones aren't working, we couldn't even talk to one another. Vanja and Andrej have gone to join Srdjan in Dubrovnik. The war has stopped there. They're lucky. I was so unhappy because of that war in Dubrovnik. I never dreamed it could move to Sarajevo. Verica and Bojana have also left.

I now spend all my time with Bojana and Maja. They're my best friends now. Bojana is a year-and-a-half older than me, she's finished seventh grade and we have a lot in common. Maja is in her last year of school. She's much older than I am, but she's wonderful. I'm lucky to have them, otherwise I'd be all alone among the grownups.

On the news they reported the death of Silva Rizvanbegović, a doctor at the Emergency Clinic, who's Mommy's friend. She was in an ambulance.

They were driving a wounded man to get him help. Lots of people Mommy and Daddy know have been killed. Oh, God, what is happening here???

Love,
Zlata

Monday, May 25, 1992

Dear Mimmy,

Today the Zetra Hall, the Olympic Zetra, went up in flames. The whole world knew about it, it was the Olympic beauty, and now it's going up in flames. The firefighters tried to save it, and our Žika joined them. But it didn't stand a chance. The forces of war don't know anything about love and the desire to save something. They just know how to destroy, burn, take things away. So they wanted Zetra to disappear as well. It makes me sad, Mimmy.

I feel as though no one and nothing here will survive.

Your Zlata

Tuesday, May 26, 1992

Dear Mimmy,

I keep thinking about Mirna; May 13 was her birthday. I would love to see her so much. I keep asking Mommy and Daddy to take me to her. She left Mojmilo with her mother and father to go to her grandparents' place. Their apartment was shelled and they had to leave it.

There's no shooting, the past few days have been quiet. I asked Daddy to take me to Mirna's because I made her a little birthday present. I miss her. I wish I could see her.

I was such a nag that Daddy decided to take me to her. We went there, but the downstairs door was locked. We couldn't call out to them and I came home feeling disappointed. The present is waiting for her, so am I. I suppose we'll see each other.

Love,
Zlata

Wednesday, May 27, 1992

Dear Mimmy,

SLAUGHTER! MASSACRE! HORROR! CRIME! BLOOD! SCREAMS! TEARS! DESPAIR!

That's what Vaso Miškin Street looks like today. Two shells exploded in the street and one in the market. Mommy was nearby at the time. She ran to Grandma and Granddad's. Daddy and I were beside ourselves because she hadn't come home. I saw some of it on TV but I still can't believe what I actually saw. It's unbelievable. I've got a lump in my throat and a knot in my tummy. HORRIBLE. They're taking the wounded to the hospital. It's a madhouse. We kept going to the window hoping to see Mommy, but she wasn't back. They released a list of the dead and wounded. Daddy and I were tearing our hair out. We didn't know what had happened to her. Was she alive? At 4:00, Daddy decided to go and check the hospital. He got dressed, and I got ready to go to the Bobars', so as not to stay at home alone. I looked out the window one more time and . . . I SAW MOMMY RUNNING ACROSS THE BRIDGE. As she came into the house she started shaking and crying. Through her tears she told us how she had seen dismembered bodies. All the neighbors came because they had been afraid for her. Thank God, Mommy is with us. Thank God.

A HORRIBLE DAY. UNFORGETTABLE. HORRIBLE! HORRIBLE!

Your Zlata

Thursday, May 28, 1992

Dear Mimmy,

It started at around 10:00. First we went to Neda's. I put Saša to sleep and left the bedroom. I looked toward the bathroom, and then . . . BOOM. The window in the bathroom shattered into pieces and I was alone in the hall and saw it all. I began to cry hysterically. Then we went down into the cellar. When things calmed down we went up to Neda's and spent the night there. Today in Vaso Miškin Street people signed the book of mourning and laid flowers. They renamed the street and now it's called the Street of Anti-Fascist Resistance.

Zlata

Friday, May 29, 1992

Dear Mimmy,

I'm at Neda's. The result of last night's fascism is broken glass in Daddy's office and at the Bobars' shattered windows. A shell fell on the house across the way, and I can't even tell you how many fell nearby. The whole town was in flames.

Your Zlata

Saturday, May 30, 1992

Dear Mimmy,

The City Maternity Hospital has burned down. I was born there. Hundreds of thousands of new babies, new residents of Sarajevo, won't have the luck to be born in this maternity hospital now. It was new. The fire devoured everything. The mothers and babies were saved. When the fire broke out two women were giving birth. The babies are alive. God, people get killed here, they die here, they disappear, things go up in flames here, and out of the flames, new lives are born.

Your Zlata

Monday, June 1, 1992

Dear Mimmy,

Today is Maja's birthday. She's eighteen. She's an adult now. She's a grown-up. It's an important day in her life, but, what can you do, she's celebrating it in wartime. We all did our best to make this day special for her, but she was sad and moody. Why did this war have to ruin everything for her? Maja isn't even having her senior prom, or an evening gown. All there is here is war, war and more war.

Fortunately, there wasn't too much shooting, so we could sit in peace. Auntie Boda made a special lunch (how special can it be in wartime???). Mommy used the last walnuts in the house to make a cake (Maja and her eighteen years deserve it). We gave her a necklace and bracelet made of Ohrid pearls. She got a lot of valuable presents made of gold. Well, you're only eighteen once in your life. Happy birthday to you Maja on this big day, may all your other birthdays be celebrated in peace.

Zlata

Friday, June 5, 1992

Dear Mimmy,

There's been no electricity for quite some time and we keep thinking about the food in the freezer. There's not much left as it is. It would be a pity for all of it to go bad. There's meat and vegetables and fruit. How can we save it?

Daddy found an old wood-burning stove in the attic. It's so old it looks funny. In the cellar we found some wood, put the stove outside in the yard, lit it and are trying to save the food from the refrigerator. We cooked everything, and joining forces with the Bobars, enjoyed ourselves. There was veal and chicken, squid, cherry strudel, meat and potato pies. All sorts of things. It's a pity, though, that we had to eat everything so quickly. We even overate. WE HAD A MEAT STROKE.

We washed down our refrigerators and freezers. Who knows when we'll be able to cook like this again. Food is becoming a big problem in Sarajevo. There's nothing to buy, and even cigarettes and coffee are becoming a problem for grown-ups. The last reserves are being used up. God, are we going to go hungry to boot???

Zlata

20

Wednesday, June 10, 1992

Dear Mimmy,

At about eleven o'clock last night it started to thunder again. No, not the weather, the shells. We ran over to Nedo's. I fell asleep there, but Mommy and Daddy went back home.

There's no electricity. We're cooking on the wood stove in the yard. Everybody is. The whole neighborhood. What luck to have this old stove.

Daddy and Žika keep fiddling with the radio, listening to the news. They found RFI (Radio France Internationale) in our language. That's at nine o'clock in the evening and they listen to it regularly. Bojana and I usually play cards, word games or draw something.

Love,
Zlata

Sunday, June 14, 1992

Dear Mimmy,

There's still no electricity, so we're still cooking on the stove in the yard. Around 2:00, when we were doing something around the stove, a shell fell on the opposite corner of the street, destroying Zoka's wonderful jewelry shop. We ran straight to the cellar, waiting for the barrage. Luckily there was only that one shell, so we went back at around 4:00.

Your Zlata

Tuesday, June 16, 1992

Dear Mimmy,

Our windows are broken. All of them except the ones in my room.   25
That's the result of the revolting shell that fell again on Zoka's jewelry shop, across the way from us. I was alone in the house at the time. Mommy and Daddy were down in the yard, getting lunch ready, and I had gone upstairs to set the table. Suddenly I heard a terrible bang and glass breaking. I was terrified and ran toward the hall. That same moment, Mommy and Daddy were at the door. Out of breath, worried, sweating and pale they hugged me and we ran to the cellar, because the shells usually come one after the other. When I realized what had happened, I started to cry and shake. Everybody tried to calm me down, but I was very upset. I barely managed to pull myself together.

We returned to the apartment to find the rooms full of glass and the windows broken. We cleared away the glass and put plastic sheeting over the windows. We had had a close shave with that shell and shrapnel. I picked up a piece of shrapnel and the tail end of a grenade, put them in a box and thanked God I had been in the kitchen, because I could have been hit . . . HORRIBLE! I don't know how often I've written that word.

HORRIBLE. We've had too much horror. The days here are full of horror. Maybe we in Sarajevo could rename the day and call it horror, because that's really what it's like.

Love,
Zlata

Thursday, June 18, 1992

Dear Mimmy,

Today we heard some more sad, sad news. Our country house in Crnotina, a tower that's about 150 years old, has burned down. Like the post office, it disappeared in the flames. I loved it so much. We spent last summer there. I had a wonderful time. I always looked forward to going there. We had redone it so nicely, bought new furniture, new rugs, put in new windows, given it all our love and warmth, and its beauty was our reward. It lived through so many wars, so many years and now it's gone. It has burned down to the ground. Our neighbors Žiga, Meho and Bečir were killed. That's even sadder. Vildana's house also burned down. All the houses burned down. Lots of people were killed. It's terribly sad news.

I keep asking why? What for? Who's to blame? I ask, but there's no answer. All I know is that we are living in misery. Yes, I know, politics is to blame for it all. I said I wasn't interested in politics, but in order to find out the answer I have to know something about it. They tell me only a few things. I'll probably find out and understand much more one day. Mommy and Daddy don't discuss politics with me. They probably think I'm too young or maybe they themselves don't know anything. They just keep telling me: This will pass—"it has to pass"????????

Your Zlata

Saturday, June 20, 1992

Dear Mimmy,

Auntie Radmila (Mommy's friend from work) came today. She came from Vojničko polje (a new housing complex). Her apartment has been completely destroyed. Wiped out in the shelling. Everything in it has been destroyed. All that's left is a useless pile of furniture, clothes, pictures and all the other things that go into an apartment. She's sad, because her daughters Sunčica and Mirna aren't there (they're in Zagreb), but she's glad they didn't have to live through the hell of Vojničkopolje. Today we heard that Narmin Tulič, the actor at the Experimental Theater, lost both his legs. Awful! Awful! Awful!

Saša went to stay with his grandmother. But he'll probably be coming back.

Your Zlata

Monday, June 22, 1992

Dear Mimmy,

More blood on the streets of Sarajevo. Another massacre. In Tito Street. Three people killed, thirty-five wounded. Shells fell on Radič, Miss Irbin and Šenoa streets. About fifteen people were killed in the three streets. I'm worried that something may have happened to Marina's, Marijana's or Ivana's parents.

These people just go on killing. MURDERS!

I pity them for being so very, very stupid, so servile, for humiliating themselves so much in front of certain people. Terrible!!!!!!

Your Zlata

Tuesday, June 23, 1992

Dear Mimmy,

Cicko could have been killed today. He fell out of the kitchen window onto a tin roof. We ran downstairs into the yard and brought him in. He just lay there in the corner of his cage, blinking madly. I tried to cheer him up with a leaf of lettuce. Fortunately he survived.

A shell fell on the central market and the cathedral today.

The electricity went out at eight o'clock last night. It's now 11:30 and it's still not back.
HORRIBLE

Zlata

Wednesday, June 24, 1992

Dear Mimmy,

9:45—the water is back on. Still no electricity. 10:30—we've still got water. 12:00—no water, but we've got electricity. YESSS!

Mimmy, I've just realized that all my friends have left: Oga, Martina, Matea, Dejan, Vanja and Andrej. OHHHH!

They're shooting outside. Bojana and I aren't allowed to go out into the yard, so we're rollerskating in the lobby of their building. It's not bad!

These are the books I've read so far: *Mommy I Love You, Eagles Fly Early,* and the next book I'm going to read is *Little Toto.*

Your Zlata

Monday, June 29, 1992

Dear Mimmy,

BOREDOM!!! SHOOTING!!! SHELLING!!! PEOPLE BEING KILLED!!! DESPAIR!!! HUNGER!!! MISERY!!! FEAR!!!

That's my life! The life of an innocent eleven-year-old schoolgirl!! A schoolgirl without a school, without the fun and excitement of school. A child without games, without friends, without the sun, without birds, without nature, without fruit, without chocolate or sweets, with just a little powdered milk. In short, a child without a childhood. A wartime child. I now realize that I am really living through a war, I am witnessing an ugly, disgusting war. I and thousands of other children in this town that is being destroyed, that is crying, weeping, seeking help, but getting none. God, will this ever stop, will I ever be a schoolgirl again, will I ever enjoy my childhood again? I once heard that childhood is the most wonderful time of your life. And it is. I loved it, and now an ugly war is taking it all away from me. Why? I feel sad. I feel like crying. I am crying.

Your Zlata

Thursday, July 2, 1992

Dear Mimmy,

We gave ourselves a treat today. We picked the cherries off the tree in the yard and ate them all up. We had watched it blossom and its small green fruits slowly turn red and now here we were eating them. Oh, you're a wonderful cherry tree! The plum tree hasn't gotten any fruit so we won't even get to try it! I miss fruit a lot. In these days of war in Sarajevo, there is no basic food or any of the other things a person needs, and there is no fruit. But now I can say that I ate myself silly on cherries.

Braco, Mommy's brother, is getting better. He's even walking a bit now.

Zlata

Friday, July 3, 1992

Dear Mimmy,

Mommy goes to work at her new office. She goes if there's no shooting, but we never know when the shelling will start. It's dangerous to walk around town. It's especially dangerous to cross our bridge, because snipers shoot at you. You have to run across. Every time she goes out, Daddy and I go to the window to watch her run. Mommy says: "I didn't know the Miljacka (our river) was so wide. You run, and you run, and you run, and there's no end to the bridge." That's fear, Mommy, fear that you'll be hit by something.

Daddy doesn't go to work. The two of us stay at home, waiting for Mommy. When the sirens go off we worry about how and when and if she'll get home. Oh, the relief when she walks in!

Neda came for lunch today. Afterward we played cards. Neda said something about going to Zagreb. It made Mommy sad, because they've been friends since childhood. They grew up together, spent their whole lives together. I was sad too because I love her and I know she loves me.

Zlata

Sunday, July 5, 1992

Dear Mimmy,

I don't remember when I last left the house. It must be almost two months ago now. I really miss Grandma and Granddad. I used to go there every day, and now I haven't seen them for such a long time.

I spend my days in the house and in the cellar. That's my wartime childhood. And it's summer. Other children are vacationing on the seaside, in the mountains, swimming, sunbathing, enjoying themselves. God, what did I do to deserve being in a war, spending my days in a way that no child should. I feel caged. All I can see through the broken windows is the park in front of my house. Empty, deserted, no children, no joy. I hear the sound of shells, and everything around me smells of war. War is now my life. OOHHH, I can't stand it anymore! I want to scream and cry. I wish I could play the piano at least, but I can't even do that because it's in "the dangerous room," where I'm not allowed. How long is this going to go on???

Zlata

Tuesday, July 7, 1992

Dear Mimmy,

There was no water yesterday, the day before or the day before that. It came at around 8:30 this morning and now, at 10:30, it's slowly disappearing again.

We filled whatever we could find with water and now have to save on the precious liquid. You have to save on everything in this war, including water and food.

Mommy is at work, Daddy is reading something and I'm going to Bojana's because there's no shooting.

Saturday, July 11, 1992

Dear Mimmy,

Nedo brought us a little visitor today. A kitten. It followed him and he couldn't just leave it in the street so he picked it up and brought it home. We'll call it Skinny, Lanky, Kitty, Mikana, Persa, Cici . . . ???? It's orange, has white socks and a white patch on its chest. It's cute, but a little wild.

Zlata

Tuesday, July 14, 1992

Dear Mimmy,

On July 8 we got a UN package. Humanitarian aid. Inside were 6 cans of beef, 5 cans of fish, 2 boxes of cheese, 3 kilos of detergent, 5 bars of soap, 2 kilos of sugar and 5 liters of cooking oil. All in all, a super package. But Daddy had to stand in line for four hours to get it.

Dobrinja has been liberated. They received UN packages there too.   *55*

We're waiting to hear what the Security Council has decided about military intervention in B-H.

The water and electricity went off the day before yesterday, July 12, and still aren't back.

Ciao!
Zlata

Questions of Subject and Theme

1. Does Anne Frank's characterization of her life as a "dangerous adventure, romantic and interesting at the same time" also describe the spirit of Zlata's writing? Explain your answer using examples.
2. Like Anne Frank, Zlata demonstrates a capacity for affection and enjoyment in many entries. Pick one example and describe the kind of person who seems to be expressed during the moments when her writing attends to lighter topics.

Questions of Method and Strategy

1. Pick a moment of danger and show how Zlata's writing attempts to express her feelings. What particular uses of language seem most effective to you? Which least? Explain with examples.
2. When does Zlata's style seem most childlike? When most adult? Find an example of each manner and analyze what it is about her writing that produces a sense of her apparent level of maturity.

FROM THE DIARY OF LATOYA HUNTER

LaToya Hunter

A *New York Times* article on a sixth-grade class in the Bronx led to a publisher's offer to one of its exceptional students, LaToya Hunter. The young girl kept a diary of her life during her first year of junior high school, beginning in September 1990. Like the other writers in this section, LaToya writes as if corresponding with an intimate though imaginary friend.

January 7, 1991

Dear Janice,

Derek called after school today, he's nice to talk to. I like him. We talk naturally to each other like we've known each other for years and years. Anyways, my mom doesn't know he calls yet. I don't want her to answer the phone one day when he's calling. Who knows what she'll say. I don't want to find out. Rondah is already giving me a hard time about it. I know I'm in for a lot of arguments and maybe I'm just being stupid, but I'm not going to tell him to stop calling. I could be really stubborn sometimes and now is one of those times. I like him, is it a sin? I wish I had a family like my friend Teniesha has. She can even invite boys over to the house and she's younger than me. Her mother is so chill. They wear the same clothes, they go out a lot together, and they talk about anything together. I think Jamaican mothers are more strict about things like boys. Maybe I'm wrong. Maybe it's a universal thing. I don't know. Teniesha is so lucky! She's always so happy, she never seems to have any problems with her family. I really envy her.

January 9, 1991

Dear Janice,

Today gunshots echo in my head. They are the same gunshots that killed an innocent human being right across from my house last night. They are the same gunshots that have scarred me, I think, forever.

Late last night, I was in bed when I heard a man screaming for a police officer. I told myself, I didn't hear that. Later I told myself I didn't hear the four gunshots that followed his cry for help. I lay there in bed and it was like I was frozen. I didn't want to move an inch. I then heard hysterical crying. I ran to the window when I couldn't keep myself back any longer. What I saw outside were cops arriving. I ran into my parent's room and woke them up. By that time, tears were pouring unstoppably from my eyes. I couldn't stop shaking. My parents looked through the window and got dressed. They rushed outside and I followed them. It turned out that I knew the person who got shot. He worked at the store at the corner. He was always so nice to me, he was always smiling. He didn't know much English but we still managed a friendship.

I can't believe this happened. Things like this happen everyday in N.Y., but not in my neighborhood, not to people I know.

January 11, 1991

Dear Janice,

Today the store was closed. It was closed yesterday also. The blood stains are still across the street. In school I couldn't stop thinking about what happened, yesterday was the same thing. I don't think I'll get over this for a long while.

The whole neighborhood is talking about it, some say one thing and others say something else. They say the murderers were waiting for him in his van. He and his partner were going into the van when the murderers came out. That's all that has been said about it. I don't think drugs had anything to do with it—the guy was just too sweet. When I listen to them yapping away about it, I don't mention that I heard a thing when it happened. They're only interested in the facts of the matter. I'm interested in the heart of it. It really makes me think why did it happen to such a sweet, innocent guy? He didn't deserve it.

January 12, 1991

Dear Janice,

The store was opened today. There were a lot of people standing around in there. Not necessarily buying anything, they just stood around. Fernando, a young friendly guy who works in the store who was always very cheerful, was not as cheerful today. His eyes were red and swollen and he just kind of moped around. The funeral is Saturday and they're asking for donations. I wouldn't feel right going to his funeral. I think funerals should be for the really close family of the dead. Those whose goodbye would mean the most to him. I have nothing to donate so my parents donated some money. All I have is deep sympathy and sadness for the loss of a friendly person who always put a smile on my face.

January 14, 1991

Dear Janice,

I've been so caught up in the murder shock that I've forgotten to update you on school. A really good saxophone player came to school to perform. His name is Naji. The school loved him. He is really talented. I have a feeling he's going to make it big in the music industry.

You don't know this but when I was ten I used to play the drums at P.S. 94. It was really easy; as my music teacher said, you've just got to have rhythm. This year however, I'm stuck in vocals as you know.

January 15, 1991

Dear Janice,

Since the murder I haven't been particularly interested in going outside. *10*
Today I was thinking about everything. My friends have been doing things
and I haven't been there. They'll tell me what's happened the previous day,
and I'll feel left out. I was thinking I shouldn't spend so much time in the
house anymore. I think tomorrow I'll go outside for a while. This is going
to sound funny but for every car that passes me by while I'm walking down
the street, a thought comes to me. It says "I'm going to die now, the person
in the car is going to pull out a gun and shoot." The funny thing is when
that thought occurs, I don't feel scared that much. I feel calm and ready to
face my death. I've discovered about myself that when the day of my death
comes, I'll be ready and I'll have a calm soul.

January 16, 1991

Dear Janice,

I hung out with my friends today and must admit had a good time. I
think I'm not as conscious of simple things like cars driving by as I was just
24 hours ago. I'm still conscious of people who look suspicious but that's
natural for everyone I think. There's a guardian angel in the store at the
corner now. Guardian angels are guys who volunteer to protect people who
need protection. There are a lot of them in my neighborhood. Other neighborhoods have them too. They go out with taxi drivers in NYC. They
started when there was the string of killings of taxi drivers. My personal
opinion is the robber will just shoot the taxi driver and the guardian angel
and go on with their life.

January 17, 1991

Dear Janice,

Today was a particularly good day. School was fun especially Gym. We
played soccer and my team won 8 to 2. We are good!

At the homefront, Courtney and Michelle came over. It's always fun
when they come over. Courtney is funny as always and I find fun in bugging
Michelle. Dave has not been visiting too often lately. I understand he's busy
but he should try to make more time for his family. Especially his little sister
who's missing him very much.

January 21, 1991

Dear Janice,

Today someone who's in Mr. Pelka's sixth grade class this year told me
some terrible news. Mr. Pelka has pneumonia. He hasn't been working for
the past week. I hope it's not a severe case. I'd hate it if anything happened
to him.

January 23, 1991

Dear Janice,

Pneumonia is definitely in season. I just heard that my little cousin Larry   *15*
is in the hospital suffering from it. He's only 8 months old, I hope he can
fight it. He's been sick before. When he was around one month old, he was
in the hospital. I remember his mother (my cousin) was telling my sister and
me how many hours she spent in the hospital waiting room worrying. I pray
to God I never go through anything like that in my life. I pray my life doesn't
have any obstacles in it. I really don't think I'm the kind of person that can
cross obstacles.

February 1, 1991

Dear Janice,

It's the first day of February. I hate this month. It just seems so long. I
think it'll be really boring. It's getting closer to the wedding though. I'm
really happy about that. There's a girl in my school who actually had a baby
already. She's in the ninth grade, she's probably around 15. My friends were
talking about her today. I feel really sorry for her, it's too early! She is only
in Junior High! I wonder how it happened. I mean, I know how it happened, but how could she let it? Her mom must have been so upset. I would
never do that to my mother. This really makes me think about this whole
sex business. I wonder if that girl was ready. I know I talked about a person
feeling that they're ready and doing it. Maybe she thought she was and really
wasn't and maybe she knew she was and still knows she is but just isn't ready
for a child. I think being ready for sex and ready for a child are two different
things. To be ready for sex, you must have the ability to fall in love and feel
close to the maximum to the person you are with. To be ready for a baby,
you should be able to take care of yourself and the child and know what's
right and what's wrong. You should be able to devote yourself to the child
in every way possible. The thing I would say should have been taken care of
by that girl is protection. Ready or not ready, she should have thought
about that.

Questions of Subject and Theme

1. Early in the selection LaToya faces the existence of violent death. What
   details of the incident does she seem to focus on? What other matters
   seem to concern her less?
2. At the end of the selection, LaToya tries to come to terms with the implications of sex. Again, what details of the topic does she seem to focus
   on? What other matters seem to concern her less?

Questions of Method and Strategy

1. Pick a moment when LaToya worries about danger and show how her
   writing attempts to express her feelings. What particular uses of language

seem most effective to you? Which least? Explain your answers with examples.

2. When does LaToya's style seem most childlike? When most adult? Find an example of each manner and analyze what it is about her writing that produces a sense of her apparent level of maturity.

———

Suggestions for Writing on the Juxtapositions

1. Each girl writes her diary entries like letters to an imaginary friend who, of course, never replies. Write a friendly letter to the diarist of your choice and explain what you think and feel about what you have read of her life.

2. Pick a moment from your own life when you have faced the serious implications of love or death, and write about your experience using the diary form.

3. Write an essay in which you describe the major strengths and weaknesses of each girl as a writer. Organize your essay by comparing and contrasting particular examples.

4. Using examples from the selections here, write an essay in which you describe what seem to you to be the strengths and weaknesses of the diary form of writing.

3 Fathers

E. B. White, "Once More to the Lake"

Sylvia Plath, "Daddy"

Raymond Carver, "Photograph of My Father in His Twenty-Second Year"

Theodore Roethke, "My Papa's Waltz"

A famous essayist and three poets attempt to come to terms with their fathers through language. In considering the different efforts, keep in mind the following questions:

1. "Father," "Daddy," "Papa"—compare and contrast the ways in which each choice of name for the parent contributes to the general attitude the writer creates toward that parent.

2. Where do you find the first writer, E. B. White, to be most poetical? Where in any of the poems included do you find the poet least poetic? Using examples, discuss some of the values and assumptions that define the poetic to you.

3. Waiving your approval or disapproval of the man, which father is brought most fully to life for you through language? Which least? Use examples to discuss the differences.

4. Find an example from each selection in which the idea of time seems most crucial to the writer. Discuss some of the similarities and differences among the moments you select.

ONCE MORE TO THE LAKE

E. B. White

E. B. White (1899–1985) began his career as a professional writer with the newly founded *New Yorker* magazine in the 1920s. Over the years he produced nineteen books, including collections of essays, the famous children's books *Stuart Little* and *Charlotte's Web,* and the long-popular writing textbook *The Elements of Style.*

One summer, along about 1904, my father rented a camp on a lake in Maine and took us all there for the month of August. We all got ringworm from some kittens and had to rub Pond's Extract on our arms and legs night and morning, and my father rolled over in a canoe with all his clothes on; but outside of that the vacation was a success and from then on none of us ever thought there was any place in the world like that lake in Maine. We returned summer after summer—always on August 1st for one month. I have since become a salt-water man, but sometimes in summer there are days when the restlessness of the tides and the fearful cold of the sea water and the incessant wind which blows across the afternoon and into the evening make me wish for the placidity of a lake in the woods. A few weeks ago this feeling got so strong I bought myself a couple of bass hooks and a spinner and returned to the lake where we used to go, for a week's fishing and to revisit old haunts.

I took along my son, who had never had any fresh water up his nose and who had seen lily pads only from train windows. On the journey over to the lake I began to wonder what it would be like. I wondered how time would have marred this unique, this holy spot—the coves and streams, the hills that the sun set behind, the camps and the paths behind the camps. I was sure that the tarred road would have found it out and I wondered in what other ways it would be desolated. It is strange how much you can remember about places like that once you allow your mind to return into the grooves which lead back. You remember one thing, and that suddenly reminds you of another thing. I guess I remembered clearest of all the early mornings, when the lake was cool and motionless, remembered how the bedroom smelled of the lumber it was made of and of the wet woods whose scent entered through the screen. The partitions in the camp were thin and did not extend clear to the top of the rooms, and as I was always the first up I would dress softly so as not to wake the others, and sneak out into the sweet outdoors and start out in the canoe, keeping close along the shore in the long shadows of the pines. I remembered being very careful never to rub my paddle against the gunwale for fear of disturbing the stillness of the cathedral.

1

The lake had never been what you would call a wild lake. There were cottages sprinkled around the shores, and it was in farming country although the shores of the lake were quite heavily wooded. Some of the cottages were owned by nearby farmers, and you would live at the shore and eat your meals at the farmhouse. That's what our family did. But although it wasn't wild, it was a fairly large and undisturbed lake and there were places in it which, to a child at least, seemed infinitely remote and primeval.

I was right about the tar: it led to within half a mile of the shore. But when I got back there, with my boy, and we settled into a camp near a farmhouse and into the kind of summertime I had known, I could tell that it was going to be pretty much the same as it had been before—I knew it, lying in bed the first morning, smelling the bedroom, and hearing the boy sneak quietly out and go off along the shore in a boat. I began to sustain the illusion that he was I, and therefore, by simple transposition, that I was my father. This sensation persisted, kept cropping up all the time we were there. It was not an entirely new feeling, but in this setting it grew much stronger. I seemed to be living a dual existence. I would be in the middle of some simple act, I would be picking up a bait box or laying down a table fork, or I would be saying something, and suddenly it would be not I but my father who was saying the words or making the gesture. It gave me a creepy sensation.

We went fishing the first morning. I felt the same damp moss covering   *5* the worms in the bait can, and saw the dragonfly alight on the tip of my rod as it hovered a few inches from the surface of the water. It was the arrival of this fly that convinced me beyond any doubt that everything was as it always had been, that the years were a mirage and there had been no years. The small waves were the same, chucking the rowboat under the chin as we fished at anchor, and the boat was the same boat, the same color green and the ribs broken in the same places, and under the floor-boards the same freshwater leavings and débris—the dead helgramite, the wisps of moss, the rusty discarded fishhook, the dried blood from yesterday's catch. We stared silently at the tips of our rods, at the dragonflies that came and went. I lowered the tip of mine into the water, tentatively, pensively dislodging the fly, which darted two feet away, poised, darted two feet back, and came to rest again a little farther up the rod. There had been no years between the ducking of this dragonfly and the other one—the one that was part of memory. I looked at the boy, who was silently watching his fly, and it was my hands that held his rod, my eyes watching. I felt dizzy and didn't know which rod I was at the end of.

We caught two bass, hauling them in briskly as though they were mackerel, pulling them over the side of the boat in a businesslike manner without any landing net, and stunning them with a blow on the back of the head. When we got back for a swim before lunch, the lake was exactly where we had left it, the same number of inches from the dock, and there was only the merest suggestion of a breeze. This seemed an utterly enchanted sea, this lake you could leave to its own devices for a few hours and come back to, and find that it had not stirred, this constant and trustworthy body of water. In the shallows, the dark, water-soaked sticks and twigs, smooth and old, were undulating in clusters on the bottom against the clean ribbed sand, and the track of the mussel was plain. A school of minnows swam by, each minnow with its small individual shadow, doubling the attendance, so clear and sharp in the sunlight. Some of the other campers were in swimming, along the shore, one of them with a cake of soap, and the water felt thin and clear and unsubstantial. Over the years there had been this person with the cake of soap, this cultist, and here he was. There had been no years.

Up to the farmhouse to dinner through the teeming, dusty field, the road under our sneakers was only a two-track road. The middle track was missing, the one with the marks of the hooves and the splotches of dried, flaky manure. There had always been three tracks to choose from in choosing which track to walk in; now the choice was narrowed down to two. For a moment I missed terribly the middle alternative. But the way led past the tennis court, and something about the way it lay there in the sun reassured me; the tape had loosened along the backline, the alleys were green with plantains and other weeds, and the net (installed in June and removed in September) sagged in the dry noon, and the whole place steamed with midday heat and hunger and emptiness. There was a choice of pie for dessert, and one was blueberry and one was apple, and the waitresses were the same country girls, there having been no passage of time, only the illusion of it as in a dropped curtain—the waitresses were still fifteen; their hair had been washed, that was the only difference—they had been to the movies and seen the pretty girls with the clean hair.

Summertime, oh summertime, pattern of life indelible, the fadeproof lake, the woods unshatterable, the pasture with the sweetfern and the juniper forever and ever, summer without end; this was the background, and the life along the shore was the design, the cottages with their innocent and tranquil design, their tiny docks with the flagpole and the American flag floating against the white clouds in the blue sky, the little paths over the roots of the trees leading from camp to camp and the paths leading back to the outhouses and the can of lime for sprinkling, and at the souvenir counters at the store the miniature birch-bark canoes and the post cards that showed things looking a little better than they looked. This was the American family at play, escaping the city heat, wondering whether the newcomers in the camp at the head of the cove were "common" or "nice," wondering whether it was true that the people who drove up for Sunday dinner at the farmhouse were turned away because there wasn't enough chicken.

It seemed to me, as I kept remembering all this, that those times and those summers had been infinitely precious and worth saving. There had been jollity and peace and goodness. The arriving (at the beginning of August) had been so big a business in itself, at the railway station the farm wagon drawn up, the first smell of the pine-laden air, the first glimpse of the smiling farmer, and the great importance of the trunks and your father's enormous authority in such matters, and the feel of the wagon under you for the long ten-mile haul, and at the top of the last long hill catching the first view of the lake after eleven months of not seeing this cherished body of water. The shouts and cries of the other campers when they saw you, and the trunks to be unpacked, to give up their rich burden. (Arriving was less exciting nowadays, when you sneaked up in your car and parked it under a tree near the camp and took out the bags and in five minutes it was all over, no fuss, no loud wonderful fuss about trunks.)

Peace and goodness and jollity. The only thing that was wrong now, really, was the sound of the place, an unfamiliar nervous sound of the outboard motors. This was the note that jarred, the one thing that would sometimes break the illusion and set the years moving. In those other summertimes all motors were inboard; and when they were at a little distance, the noise they made was a sedative, an ingredient of summer sleep. They were one-cylinder and two-cylinder engines, and some were make-and-break and some were jump-spark, but they all made a sleepy sound across the lake. The one-lungers throbbed and fluttered, and the twin-cylinder ones purred and purred, and that was a quiet sound too. But now the campers all had outboards. In the daytime, in the hot mornings, these motors made a petulant, irritable sound; at night, in the still evening when the afterglow lit the water, they whined about one's ears like mosquitoes. My boy loved our rented outboard, and his great desire was to achieve singlehanded mastery over it, and authority, and he soon learned the trick of choking it a little (but not too much), and the adjustment of the needle valve. Watching him I would remember the things you could do with the old one-cylinder engine with the heavy flywheel, how you could have it eating out of your hand if you got really close to it spiritually. Motor boats in those days didn't have clutches, and you would make a landing by shutting off the motor at the proper time and coasting in with a dead rudder. But there was a way of reversing them, if you learned the trick, by cutting the switch and putting it on again exactly on the final dying revolution of the flywheel, so that it would kick back against compression and begin reversing. Approaching a dock in a strong following breeze, it was difficult to slow up sufficiently by the ordinary coasting method, and if a boy felt he had complete mastery over his motor, he was tempted to keep it running beyond its time and then reverse it a few feet from the dock. It took a cool nerve, because if you threw the switch a twentieth of a second too soon you would catch the flywheel when it still had speed enough to go up past center, and the boat would leap ahead, charging bull-fashion at the dock.

We had a good week at the camp. The bass were biting well and the sun shone endlessly, day after day. We would be tired at night and lie down in the accumulated heat of the little bedrooms after the long hot day and the breeze would stir almost imperceptibly outside and the smell of the swamp drift in through the rusty screens. Sleep would come easily and in the morning the red squirrel would be on the roof, tapping out his gay routine. I kept

10

remembering everything, lying in bed in the mornings—the small steamboat that had a long rounded stern like the lip of a Ubangi, and how quietly she ran on the moonlight sails, when the older boys played their mandolins and the girls sang and we ate doughnuts dipped in sugar, and how sweet the music was on the water in the shining night, and what it had felt like to think about girls then. After breakfast we would go up to the store and the things were in the same place—the minnows in a bottle, the plugs and spinners disarranged and pawed over by the youngsters from the boys' camp, the fig newtons and the Beeman's gum. Outside, the road was tarred and cars stood in front of the store. Inside, all was just as it had always been, except there was more Coca Cola and not so much Moxie and root beer and birch beer and sarsaparilla. We would walk out with a bottle of pop apiece and sometimes the pop would backfire up our noses and hurt. We explored the streams, quietly, where the turtles slid off the sunny logs and dug their way into the soft bottom; and we lay on the town wharf and fed worms to the tame bass. Everywhere we went I had trouble making out which was I, the one walking at my side, the one walking in my pants.

One afternoon while we were there at that lake a thunderstorm came up. It was like the revival of an old melodrama that I had seen long ago with childish awe. The second-act climax of the drama of the electrical disturbance over a lake in America had not changed in any important respect. This was the big scene, still the big scene. The whole thing was so familiar, the first feeling of oppression and heat and a general air around camp of not wanting to go very far away. In mid-afternoon (it was all the same) a curious darkening of the sky, and a lull in everything that had made life tick; and then the way the boats suddenly swung the other way at their moorings with the coming of a breeze out of the new quarter, and the premonitory rumble. Then the kettle drum, then the snare, then the bass drum and cymbals, then crackling light against the dark, and the gods grinning and licking their chops in the hills. Afterward the calm, the rain steadily rustling in the calm lake, the return of light and hope and spirits, and the campers running out in joy and relief to go swimming in the rain, their bright cries perpetuating the deathless joke about how they were getting simply drenched, and the children screaming with delight at the new sensation of bathing in the rain, and the joke about getting drenched linking the generations in a strong indestructible chain. And the comedian who waded in carrying an umbrella.

When the others went swimming my son said he was going in too. He pulled his dripping trunks from the line where they had hung all through the shower, and wrung them out. Languidly, and with no thought of going in, I watched him, his hard little body, skinny and bare, saw him wince slightly as he pulled up around his vitals the small, soggy, icy garment. As he buckled the swollen belt suddenly my groin felt the chill of death.

Questions of Subject and Theme

1. White says that he seemed to be living "a dual existence" as a father in the present and as a son in the remembered life of the past. Point to some

moments when that dual existence seems most natural and to some when it seems more difficult to maintain. What seems to explain the differences to him and to you?

2. What do you make of the final sentence of the essay? How is the earlier extended theme of annihilated time related to and resolved in the ending of the essay?

Questions of Method and Strategy

1. In what ways do White's physical descriptions of the lake and its surroundings suggest why he loves the place? Analyze an example or two in which emotion is created by style.

2. What makes the thunderstorm a good episode with which to end the essay? What earlier themes does the moment collect and connect?

DADDY

Sylvia Plath

Sylvia Plath (1932–1963) worked from childhood to become a poet and published her first poem in a newspaper when she was eight. In college she had poems published in national magazines and seemed destined for success. Unfortunately, though most people did not realize it, Plath fought a manic-depressive illness all her short life, which ended in suicide.

You do not do, you do not do   *1*
Any more, black shoe
In which I have lived like a foot
For thirty years, poor and white,
Barely daring to breath or Achoo.   *5*

Daddy, I have had to kill you.
You died before I had time—
Marble-heavy, a bag full of God,
Ghastly statue with one gray toe
Big as a Frisco seal   *10*

And a head in the freakish Atlantic
Where it pours bean green over blue
In the waters off beautiful Nauset.
I used to pray to recover you.
Ach, du.   *15*

In the German tongue, in the Polish town
Scraped flat by the roller
Of wars, wars, wars.
But the name of the town is common.
My Polack friend   *20*

Says there are a dozen or two.
So I never could tell where you
Put your foot, your root,
I never could talk to you.
The tongue stuck in my jaw.   *25*

It stuck in a barb wire snare.
Ich, ich, ich, ich,
I could hardly speak.
I thought every German was you.
And the language obscene   *30*

An engine, an engine
Chuffing me off like a Jew.
A Jew to Dachau, Auschwitz, Belsen.
I began to talk like a Jew.
I think I may well be a Jew.   *35*

The snows of the Tyrol, the clear beer of Vienna
Are not very pure or true.
With my gypsy ancestress and my weird luck
And my Taroc pack and my Taroc pack
I may be a bit of a Jew.   *40*

I have always been scared of *you,*
With your Luftwaffe, your gobbledygoo.
And your neat moustache
And your Aryan eye, bright blue.
Panzer-man, panzer-man, O You—   *45*

Not God but a swastika
So black no sky could squeak through.
Every woman adores a Fascist,
The boot in the face, the brute
Brute heart of a brute like you.   *50*

You stand at the blackboard, daddy,
In the picture I have of you,
A cleft in your chin instead of your foot
But no less a devil for that, no not
Any less the black man who   *55*

Bit my pretty red heart in two.
I was ten when they buried you.
At twenty I tried to die
And get back, back, back to you.
I thought even the bones would do.   *60*

But they pulled me out of the sack,
And they stuck me together with glue,
And then I knew what to do.
I made a model of you,
A man in black with a Meinkampf look   *65*

And a love of the rack and the screw.
And I said I do, I do.
So daddy, I'm finally through.
The black telephone's off at the root,
The voices just can't worm through.   *70*

If I've killed one man, I've killed two—
The vampire who said he was you
And drank my blood for a year,
Seven years, if you want to know.
Daddy, you can lie back now.   *75*

There's a stake in your fat black heart
And the villagers never liked you.
They are dancing and stamping on you.
They always *knew* it was you.
Daddy, daddy, you bastard, I'm through.   *80*

Questions of Subject and Theme

1. "How do I love thee? Let me count the ways"—so begins a famous sonnet. In how many ways and for what reasons does Plath announce her hatred for her father? Make a list.
2. In her second stanza Plath writes: "Daddy, I have had to kill you. / You died before I had time—." Does the rest of the poem explain this apparent paradox for you? If so, describe your reasoning. If not, describe the nature of your puzzlement.

Questions of Method and Strategy

1. Plath alludes to vampirism at the end of the poem, where she also repeats that she is "through." In what ways do the metaphoric implications of vampirism modify her apparent tone of triumph at the end?
2. Read aloud several times the famous lines 65–66: "A man in black with a Meinkampf look / And a love of the rack and the screw." Describe as best you can the tone of voice in which you think these lines are best recited and explain your decision. For example, do you hear a hissing, spitting contempt? Ironic exasperation and self-mockery? A cry of pain?

PHOTOGRAPH OF MY FATHER IN HIS TWENTY-SECOND YEAR

Raymond Carver

Raymond Carver (1939–1988) is better known as a writer of fiction than as a poet. Of his fictional method he once said: "It is possible to write a line of seemingly innocuous dialogue and have it send a chill along the reader's spine." Does he bring the same possibility to his poetry?

October. Here in this dank, unfamiliar kitchen   1
I study my father's embarrassed young man's face.
Sheepish grin, he holds in one hand a string
of spiny yellow perch, in the other
a bottle of Carlsberg beer.   5

In jeans and flannel shirt, he leans
against the front fender of a 1934 Ford.
He would like to pose brave and hearty for his posterity,
wear his old hat cocked over his ear.
All his life my father wanted to be bold.   10

But the eyes give him away, and the hands
that limply offer the string of dead perch
and the bottle of beer. Father, I love you,
yet how can I say thank you, I who can't hold my liquor either
and don't even know the places to fish.   15

Questions of Subject and Theme

1. Carver describes his father's face in the photograph as "embarrassed." Does Carver himself seem embarrassed within the poem? If you think so, say what he might be embarrassed about. Point to some examples. If you think not, describe his emotional attitude and explain your view with examples.
2. Carver says his father "wanted to be bold." Does Carver himself seem to you to want to be bold? Is he? Give evidence from the poem to explain your answers.

Questions of Method and Strategy

1. Does the setting described in the first line affect the rest of the poem? Would anything be lost if the poem began with line 2? Explain your answers.
2. At the end of the poem, do the apparent explanations for Carver's inability to "say thank you" make sense to you? Explain why or why not. Do other moments in the poem also suggest "explanations?" What is Carver's method and strategy of explanation?

MY PAPA'S WALTZ

Theodore Roethke

Theodore Roethke (1908–1963) was a poet who drew inspiration for many of the poems in his first volume of verse, *The Lost Son* (1948), from his memories of the greenhouse business operated by his father and grandfather. Roethke grew to be a large and powerfully built man, but he remains most famous for the small and helpless voice of "the lost son" heard in poems like this one.

The whiskey on your breath
Could make a small boy dizzy;
But I hung on like death:
Such waltzing was not easy.

We romped until the pans
Slid from the kitchen shelf;
My mother's countenance
Could not unfrown itself.

The hand that held my wrist
Was battered on one knuckle;
At every step you missed
My right ear scraped a buckle.

You beat time on my head
With a palm caked hard by dirt,
Then waltzed me off to bed
Still clinging to your shirt.

Questions of Subject and Theme

1. The speaker says "we romped," but for whom and in what sense is this "waltz" a romp? How do you think the father imagines what is happening? How the mother? How the son as a child? How the poet?
2. In your view does the poem have a form or a plot, or could one stanza be satisfactorily substituted in another's place while maintaining the effects of the poem as it is given here? Explain your answer.

Questions of Method and Strategy

1. Can whiskey breath literally intoxicate and "make a small boy dizzy?" What does make the boy dizzy? How are the literal and the figurative combined here?
2. The grammar of the poem implies a point of view on the past taken from

the present. Yet in what ways does Roethke create the point of view of the child undergoing the experience described in the poem?

———

Suggestions for Writing on the Juxtapositions

1. Each writer is concerned with both the past and the present. Building on your answers to question 4 at the beginning of this section, write an essay in which you analyze some of the ways each writer uses time in describing his or her relations with a father.
2. Write a poem or part of a prose memoir that expresses something of your own relations with your father. You may find it useful to focus on an event, a place, or a photograph to compose your thoughts and your writing.
3. Which writer moved your emotions most strongly? Write an essay that explains by analyzing examples what about the writing moved you.
4. Which writer did you find the least effective? Write an essay in which you explain your reservations by analyzing examples.

4 From Story to Film: "Paul's Case"

Willa Cather, "Paul's Case: A Study in Temperament"
Ron Cowan, screenplay excerpt from *Paul's Case*

How do different media treat a single subject? Willa Cather's classic short story is followed by an excerpt from a screenplay that attempts to dramatize the essence of Cather's psychological portrait while often changing what Cather wrote. Consider the following questions:

1. Paul's love for the theater is dramatized in both the short story and the script. Compare and contrast the ways in which that love is dramatized in each case. What does the story seem able to do best in this regard? What strengths does the film script display?

2. Paul speaks much more in the film script than he does in the story. Do you think that the scriptwriter, Ron Cowen, has rendered Paul's speech as you imagined it in reading the story? Use examples from each version to explain your answer.

3. The actor, Charlie, seems much more cynical in the script than in the story. What similar and what different uses does each writer seem to intend to make of his minor character?

4. "Flowers" is one theme from the story that the scriptwriter emphasizes in his treatment. Make a list of things that flowers seem to stand for to Paul. What do they stand for to the viewer and reader? For example, flowers are physically delicate and Paul is physically delicate. What other analogies suggest themselves to you?

PAUL'S CASE
A Study in Temperament

Willa Cather

Willa Cather (1873–1947) became famous for her fiction of pioneers in the American West. Yet her interest in "pioneering" was not limited by geography, as the following short story shows. The young protagonist of "Paul's Case" strives to be a spiritual pioneer in Pittsburgh, where he is willing to take the risks and pay the prices of other, more conventional adventurers.

It was Paul's afternoon to appear before the faculty of the Pittsburgh High School to account for his various misdemeanours. He had been suspended a week ago, and his father had called at the Principal's office and confessed his perplexity about his son. Paul entered the faculty room suave and smiling. His clothes were a trifle outgrown and the tan velvet on the collar of his open overcoat was frayed and worn; but for all that there was something of the dandy about him, and he wore an opal pin in his neatly knotted black four-in-hand, and a red carnation in his buttonhole. This latter adornment the faculty somehow felt was not properly significant of the contrite spirit befitting a boy under the ban of suspension.

Paul – doesn't fit in

Paul was tall for his age and very thin, with high, cramped shoulders and a narrow chest. His eyes were remarkable for a certain hysterical brilliancy and he continually used them in a conscious, theatrical sort of way, peculiarly offensive in a boy. The pupils were abnormally large, as though he were addicted to belladonna, but there was a glassy glitter about them which that drug does not produce.

When questioned by the Principal as to why he was there, Paul stated, politely enough, that he wanted to come back to school. This was a lie, but Paul was quite accustomed to lying; found it, indeed, indispensable for overcoming friction. His teachers were asked to state their respective charges against him, which they did with such a rancour and aggrievedness as evinced that this was not a usual case. Disorder and impertinence were among the offences named, yet each of his instructors felt that it was scarcely possible to put into words the real cause of the trouble, which lay in a sort of hysterically defiant manner of the boy's; in the contempt which they all knew he felt for them, and which he seemingly made not the least effort to conceal. Once, when he had been making a synopsis of a paragraph at the blackboard, his English teacher had stepped to his side and attempted to guide his hand. Paul had started back with a shudder and thrust his hands violently behind him. The astonished woman could scarcely have been more hurt and embarrassed had he struck at her. The insult was so involuntary and definitely personal as to be unforgettable. In one way and another, he had made all his teachers, men and women alike, conscious of the same feeling of physical aversion. In one class he habitually sat with his hand shading his eyes; in another he always looked out of the window during the recitation; in another he made a running commentary on the lecture, with humorous intention.

His teachers felt this afternoon that his whole attitude was symbolized by his shrug and his flippantly red carnation flower, and they fell upon him without mercy, his English teacher leading the pack. He stood through it smiling, his pale lips parted over his white teeth. (His lips were continually twitching, and he had a habit of raising his eyebrows that was contemptuous and irritating to the last degree.) Older boys than Paul had broken down and shed tears under that baptism of fire, but his set smile did not once desert him, and his only sign of discomfort was the nervous trembling of the fingers that toyed with the buttons of his overcoat, and an occasional jerking of the other hand that held his hat. Paul was always smiling, always glancing about him, seeming to feel that people might be watching him and trying to detect something. This conscious expression, since it was as far as possible from boyish mirthfulness, was usually attributed to insolence or "smartness."

As the inquisition proceeded, one of his instructors repeated an imper-   *5* tinent remark of the boy's, and the Principal asked him whether he thought that a courteous speech to have made a woman. Paul shrugged his shoulders slightly and his eyebrows twitched.

"I don't know," he replied. "I didn't mean to be polite or impolite, either. I guess it's a sort of way I have of saying things regardless."

The Principal, who was a sympathetic man, asked him whether he didn't think that a way it would be well to get rid of. Paul grinned and said he guessed so. When he was told that he could go, he bowed gracefully and went out. His bow was but a repetition of the scandalous red carnation.

His teachers were in despair, and his drawing master voiced the feeling of them all when he declared there was something about the boy which none of them understood. He added: "I don't really believe that smile of his comes altogether from insolence; there's something sort of haunted about it. The boy is not strong, for one thing. I happen to know that he was born in Colorado, only a few months before his mother died out there of a long illness. There is something wrong about the fellow."

The drawing master had come to realize that, in looking at Paul, one saw only his white teeth and the forced animation of his eyes. One warm afternoon the boy had gone to sleep at his drawing-board, and his master had noted with amazement what a white, blue-veined face it was; drawn and wrinkled like an old man's about the eyes, the lips twitching even in his sleep, and stiff with a nervous tension that drew them back from his teeth.

His teachers left the building dissatisfied and unhappy; humiliated to   *10* have felt so vindictive toward a mere boy, to have uttered this feeling in cutting terms, and to have set each other on, as it were, in the grewsome game of intemperate reproach. Some of them remembered having seen a miserable street cat set at bay by a ring of tormentors.

As for Paul, he ran down the hill whistling the Soldiers' Chorus from *Faust* looking wildly behind him now and then to see whether some of this teachers were not there to writhe under his light-heartedness. As it was now late in the afternoon and Paul was on duty that evening as usher at Carnegie Hall, he decided that he would not go home to supper. When he reached the concert hall the doors were not yet open and, as it was chilly outside, he decided to go up into the picture gallery—always deserted at this hour— where there were some of Raffelli's gay studies of Paris streets and an airy blue Venetian scene or two that always exhilarated him. He was delighted to find no one in the gallery but the old guard, who sat in one corner, a newspaper on his knee, a black patch over one eye and the other closed. Paul possessed himself of the place and walked confidently up and down, whistling under his breath. After a while he sat down before a blue Rico and lost himself. When he bethought him to look at his watch, it was after seven o'clock, and he rose with a start and ran downstairs, making a face at Augustus, peering out from the cast-room, and an evil gesture at the Venus of Milo as he passed her on the stairway.

When Paul reached the ushers' dressing-room half-a-dozen boys were there already, and he began excitedly to tumble into his uniform. It was one of the few that at all approached fitting, and Paul though it very becoming—though he knew that the tight, straight coat accentuated his narrow chest, about which he was exceedingly sensitive. He was always considerably excited while he dressed, twanging all over to the tuning of the strings and the preliminary flourishes of the horns in the music-room; but to-night he seemed quite beside himself, and he teased and plagued the boys until, telling him that he was crazy, they put him down on the floor and sat on him.

Somewhat calmed by his suppression, Paul dashed out to the front of the house to seat the early comers. He was a model usher; gracious and smiling he ran up and down the aisles; nothing was too much trouble for him; he carried messages and brought programmes as though it were his greatest pleasure in life, and all the people in his section thought him a charming boy, feeling that he remembered and admired them. As the house filled, he grew more and more vivacious and animated, and the colour came to his cheeks and lips. It was very much as though this were a great reception and Paul were the host. Just as the musicians came out to take their places, his English teacher arrived with checks for the seats which a prominent manufacturer had taken for the season. She betrayed some embarrassment when she handed Paul the tickets, and a *hauteur* which subsequently made her feel very foolish. Paul was startled for a moment, and had the feeling of wanting to put her out; what business had she here among all these fine people and gay colours? He looked her over and decided that she was not appropriately dressed and must be a fool to sit downstairs in such togs. The tickets had probably been sent her out of kindness, he reflected as he put down a seat for her, and she had about as much right to sit there as he had.

When the symphony began Paul sank into one of the rear seats with a long sigh of relief, and lost himself as he had done before the Rico. It was not that symphonies, as such, meant anything in particular to Paul, but the first sigh of the instruments seemed to free some hilarious and potent spirit within him; something that struggled there like the Genius in the bottle found by the Arab fisherman. He felt a sudden zest of life; the lights danced before his eyes and the concert hall blazed into unimaginable splendour. When the soprano soloist came on, Paul forgot even the nastiness of his teacher's being there and gave himself up to the peculiar stimulus such personages always had for him. The soloist chanced to be a German woman, by no means in her first youth, and the mother of many children; but she wore an elaborate gown and a tiara, and above all she had that indefinable air of achievement, that world-shine upon her, which, in Paul's eyes, made her a veritable queen of Romance.

After a concert was over Paul was always irritable and wretched until he got to sleep, and to-night he was even more than usually restless. He had the feeling of not being able to let down, of its being impossible to give up this delicious excitement which was the only thing that could be called living at all. During the last number he withdrew and, after hastily changing his clothes in the dressing-room, slipped out to the side door where the soprano's carriage stood. Here he began pacing rapidly up and down the walk, waiting to see her come out.

Over yonder the Schenley, in its vacant stretch, loomed big and square through the fine rain, the windows of its twelve stories glowing like those of a lighted cardboard house under a Christmas tree. All the actors and singers of the better class stayed there when they were in the city, and a number of the big manufacturers of the place lived there in the winter. Paul had often hung about the hotel, watching the people go in and out, longing to enter and leave school-masters and dull care behind him forever.

At last the singer came out, accompanied by the conductor, who helped her into her carriage and closed the door with a cordial *auf wiedersehen* which set Paul to wondering whether she were not an old sweetheart of his. Paul followed the carriage over to the hotel, walking so rapidly as not to be far from the entrance when the singer alighted and disappeared behind the swinging glass doors that were opened by a negro in a tall hat and a long coat. In the moment that the door was ajar it seemed to Paul that he, too, entered. He seemed to feel himself go after her up the steps, into the warm, lighted building, into an exotic, a tropical world of shiny, glistening surfaces and basking ease. He reflected up on the mysterious dishes that were brought into the dining-room, the green bottles in buckets of ice, as he had seen them in the supper party pictures of the *Sunday World* supplement. A quick gust of wind brought the rain down with sudden vehemence, and Paul was startled to find that he was still outside in the slush of the gravel driveway; that his boots were letting in the water and his scanty overcoat was clinging wet about him; that the lights in front of the concert hall were out, and that the rain was driving in sheets between him and the orange glow of the windows above him. There it was, what he wanted—tangibly

before him, like the fairy world of a Christmas pantomime, but mocking
spirits stood guard at the doors, and, as the rain beat in his face, Paul wondered whether he were destined always to shiver in the black night outside,
looking up at it.

He turned and walked reluctantly toward the car tracks. The end had to
come sometime; his father in his night-clothes at the top of the stairs, explanations that did not explain, hastily improvised fictions that were forever
tripping him up, his upstairs room and its horrible yellow wall-paper, the
creaking bureau with the greasy plush collar-box, and over his painted
wooden bed the pictures of George Washington and John Calvin, and the
framed motto, "Feed my Lambs," which had been worked in red worsted
by his mother.

Half an hour later, Paul alighted from his car and went slowly down one
of the side streets off the main thoroughfare. It was a highly respectable
street, where all the houses were exactly alike, and where business men of
moderate means begot and reared large families of children, all of whom
went to Sabbath-school and learned the shorter catechism, and were interested in arithmetic; all of whom were as exactly alike as their homes, and of
a piece with the monotony in which they lived. Paul never went up Cordelia Street without a shudder of loathing. His home was next to the house
of the Cumberland minister. He approached it to-night with the nerveless
sense of defeat, the hopeless feeling of sinking back forever into ugliness and
commonness that he had always had when he came home. The moment he
turned into Cordelia Street he felt the waters close above his head. After
each of these orgies of living, he experienced all the physical depression
which follows a debauch; the loathing of respectable beds, of common food,
of a house penetrated by kitchen odours; a shuddering repulsion for the
flavourless, colourless mass of every-day existence; a morbid desire for cool
things and soft lights and fresh flowers.

The nearer he approached the house, the more absolutely unequal Paul   20
felt to the sight of it all; his ugly sleeping chamber; the cold bathroom with
the grimy zinc tub, the cracked mirror, the dripping spiggots; his father, at
the top of the stairs, his hairy legs sticking out from his night-shirt, his feet
thrust into carpet slippers. He was so much later than usual that there would
certainly be inquiries and reproaches. Paul stopped short before the door.
He felt that he could not be accosted by his father to-night; that he could
not toss again on that miserable bed. He would not go in. He would tell his
father that he had no car fare, and it was raining so hard he had gone home
with one of the boys and stayed all night.

Meanwhile, he was wet and cold. He went around to the back of the
house and tried one of the basement windows, found it open, raised it cautiously, and scrambled down the cellar wall to the floor. There he stood,
holding his breath, terrified by the noise he had made, but the floor above
him was silent, and there was no creak on the stairs. He found a soap-box,
and carried it over to the soft ring of light that streamed from the furnace
door, and sat down. He was horribly afraid of rats, so he did not try to sleep,

all people
are the
same on the
street

but sat looking distrustfully at the dark, still terrified lest he might have awakened his father. In such reactions, after one of the experiences which made days and nights out of the dreary blanks of the calendar, when his senses were deadened, Paul's head was always singularly clear. Suppose his father had heard him getting in at the window and had come down and shot him for a burglar? Then, again, suppose his father had come down, pistol in hand, and he had cried out in time to save himself, and his father had been horrified to think how nearly he had killed him? Then, again, suppose a day should come when his father would remember that night, and wish there had been no warning cry to stay his hand? With this last supposition Paul entertained himself until daybreak.

The following Sunday was fine; the sodden November chill was broken by the last flash of autumnal summer. In the morning Paul had to go to church and Sabbath-school, as always. On seasonable Sunday afternoons the burghers of Cordelia Street always sat out on their front "stoops," and talked to their neighbours on the next stoop, or called to those across the street in neighbourly fashion. The men usually sat on gay cushions placed upon the steps that led down to the sidewalk, while the women, in their Sunday "waists," sat in rockers on the cramped porches, pretending to be greatly at their ease. The children played in the streets; there were so many of them that the place resembled the recreation grounds of a kindergarten. The men on the steps—all in their shirt sleeves, their vests unbuttoned—sat with their legs well apart, their stomachs comfortably protruding, and talked of the prices of things, or told anecdotes of the sagacity of their various chiefs and overlords. They occasionally looked over the multitude of squabbling children, listened affectionately to their high-pitched, nasal voices, smiling to see their own proclivities reproduced in their offspring, and interspersed their legends of the iron kings with remarks about their sons' progress at school, their grades in arithmetic, and the amounts they had saved in their toy banks.

On this last Sunday of November, Paul sat all the afternoon on the lowest step of his "stoop," staring into the street, while his sisters, in their rockers, were talking to the minister's daughters next door about how many shirt-waists they had made in the last week, and how many waffles some one had eaten at the last church supper. When the weather was warm, and his father was in a particularly jovial frame of mind, the girls made lemonade, which was always brought out in a red-glass pitcher, ornamented with forget-me-nots in blue enamel. This the girls thought very fine, and the neighbours always joked about the suspicious colour of the pitcher.

To-day Paul's father sat on the top step, talking to a young man who shifted a restless baby from knee to knee. He happened to be the young man model boy who was daily held up to Paul as a model, and after whom it was his father's dearest hope that he would pattern. This young man was of a ruddy complexion, with a compressed, red mouth, and faded, near-sighted eyes, over which he wore thick spectacles, with gold bows that curved about his ears. He was clerk to one of the magnates of a great steel corporation, and was looked upon in Cordelia Street as a young man with a future. There was a story that, some five years ago—he was now barely twenty-six—he had been a trifle dissipated but in order to curb his appetites and save the loss of time and strength that a sowing of wild oats might have entailed, he had taken his chief's advice, oft reiterated to his employees, and at twenty-one had married the first woman whom he could persuade to share his fortunes. She happened to be an angular school-mistress, much older than he, who also wore thick glasses, and who had now borne him four children, all near-sighted, like herself.

The young man was relating how his chief, now cruising in the Mediterranean, kept in touch with all the details of the business, arranging his office hours on his yacht just as though he were at home, and "knocking off work enough to keep two stenographers busy." His father told, in turn, the plan his corporation was considering, of putting in an electric railway plant at Cairo. Paul snapped his teeth; he had an awful apprehension that they might spoil it all before he got there. Yet he rather liked to hear these legends of the iron kings, that were told and retold on Sundays and holidays; these stories of palaces in Venice, yachts on the Mediterranean, and high play at Monte Carlo appealed to his fancy, and he was interested in the triumphs of these cash boys who had become famous, though he had no mind for the cash-boy stage.

After supper was over, and he had helped to dry the dishes, Paul nervously asked his father whether he could go to George's to get some help in his geometry, and still more nervously asked for car fare. This latter request he had to repeat, as his father, on principle, did not like to hear requests for money, whether much or little. He asked Paul whether he could not go to some boy who lived nearer, and told him that he ought not to leave his school work until Sunday; but he gave him the dime. He was not a poor man, but he had a worthy ambition to come up in the world. His only reason for allowing Paul to usher was, that he thought a boy ought to be earning a little.

Paul bounded upstairs, scrubbed the greasy odour of the dish-water from his hands with the ill-smelling soap he hated, and then shook over his fingers a few drops of violet water from the bottle he kept hidden in his drawer. He left the house with his geometry conspicuously under his arm, and the moment he got out of Cordelia Street and boarded a downtown car, he shook off the lethargy of two deadening days, and began to live again.

The leading juvenile of the permanent stock company which played at one of the downtown theatres was an acquaintance of Paul's, and the boy had been invited to drop in at the Sunday-night rehearsals whenever he could. For more than a year Paul had spent every available moment loitering about Charley Edwards's dressing-room. He had won a place among Edwards's following not only because the young actor, who could not afford to employ a dresser, often found him useful, but because he recognized in Paul something akin to what churchmen term "vocation."

25

*dad's
classifitions
. ambitions*

It was at the theatre and at Carnegie Hall that Paul really lived; the rest was but a sleep and a forgetting. This was Paul's fairy tale, and it had for him all the allurement of a secret love. The moment he inhaled the gassy, painty, dusty odour behind the scenes, he breathed like a prisoner set free, and felt within him the possibility of doing or saying splendid, brilliant, poetic things. The moment the cracked orchestra beat out the overture from *Martha,* or jerked at the serenade from *Rigoletto,* all stupid and ugly things slid from him, and his senses were deliciously, yet delicately fired.

Perhaps it was because, in Paul's world, the natural nearly always wore the guise of ugliness, that a certain element of artificiality seemed to him necessary in beauty. Perhaps it was because his experience of life elsewhere was so full of Sabbath-school picnics, petty economies, wholesome advice as to how to succeed in life, and the unescapable odours of cooking, that he found this existence so alluring, these smartly-clad men and women so attractive, that he was so moved by these starry apple orchards that bloomed perennially under the lime-light.

It would be difficult to put it strongly enough how convincingly the stage entrance of that theatre was for Paul the actual portal of Romance. Certainly none of the company ever suspected it, least of all Charley Edwards. It was very like the old stories that used to float about London of fabulously rich Jews, who had subterranean halls there, with palms, and fountains, and soft lamps and richly apparelled women who never saw the disenchanting light of London day. So, in the midst of that smoke-palled city, enamoured of figures and grimy toil, Paul had his secret temple, his wishing carpet, his bit of blue-and-white Mediterranean shore bathed in perpetual sunshine.

Several of Paul's teachers had a theory that his imagination had been perverted by garish fiction, but the truth was that he scarcely ever read at all. The books at home were not such as would either tempt or corrupt a youthful mind, and as for reading the novels that some of his friends urged upon him—well, he got what he wanted much more quickly from music; any sort of music, from an orchestra to a barrel organ. He needed only the spark, the indescribable thrill that made his imagination master of his senses, and he could make plots and pictures enough of his own. It was equally true that he was not stage struck—not, at any rate, in the usual acceptation of that expression. He had no desire to become an actor, any more than he had to become a musician. He felt no necessity to do any of these things; what he wanted was to see, to be in the atmosphere, float on the wave of it, to be carried out, blue league after blue league, away from everything.

After a night behind the scenes, Paul found the schoolroom more than ever repulsive; the bare floors and naked walls; the prosy men who never wore frock coats, or violets in their buttonholes; the women with their dull gowns, shrill voices, and pitiful seriousness about prepositions that govern the dative. He could not bear to have the other pupils think, for a moment, that he took these people seriously; he must convey to them that he considered it all trivial, and was there only by way of a jest, anyway. He had autographed pictures of all the members of the stock company which he showed his classmates, telling them the most incredible stories of his familiarity with these people, of his acquaintance with the soloists who came to Carnegie Hall, his suppers with them and the flowers he sent them. When these stories lost their effect, and his audience grew listless, he became desperate and would bid all the boys good-bye, announcing that he was going to travel for a while; going to Naples, to Venice, to Egypt. Then, next Monday, he would slip back, conscious and nervously smiling; his sister was ill, and he should have to defer his voyage until spring.

Matters went steadily worse with Paul at school. In the itch to let his instructors know how heartily he despised them and their homilies, and how thoroughly he was appreciated elsewhere, he mentioned once or twice that he had no time to fool with theorems; adding—with a twitch of the eyebrows and a touch of that nervous bravado which so perplexed them— that he was helping the people down at the stock company; they were old friends of his.

The upshot of the matter was that the Principal went to Paul's father,   *35* and Paul was taken out of school and put to work. The manager at Carnegie Hall was told to get another usher in his stead; the door-keeper at the theatre was warned not to admit him to the house; and Charley Edwards remorsefully promised the boy's father not to see him again.

The members of the stock company were vastly amused when some of Paul's stories reached them—especially the women. They were hardworking women, most of them supporting indigent husbands or brothers, and they laughed rather bitterly at having stirred the boy to such fervid and florid inventions. They agreed with the faculty and with his father that Paul's was a bad case.

The east-bound train was ploughing through a January snow-storm; the dull dawn was beginning to show grey when the engine whistled a mile out of Newark. Paul started up from the seat where he had lain curled in uneasy slumber, rubbed the breath-misted window glass with his hand, and peered out. The snow was whirling in curling eddies above the white bottom lands, and the drifts lay already deep in the fields and along the fences, while here and there the long dead grass and dried weed stalks protruded black above it. Lights shone from the scattered houses, and a gang of labourers who stood beside the track waved their lanterns.

Paul had slept very little, and he felt grimy and uncomfortable. He had made the all-night journey in a day coach, partly because he was ashamed, dressed as he was, to go into a Pullman, and partly because he was afraid of being seen there by some Pittsburgh business man, who might have noticed him in Denny & Carson's office. When the whistle awoke him, he clutched quickly at his breast pocket, glancing about him with an uncertain smile. But the little, clay-bespattered Italians were still sleeping, the slatternly women across the aisle were in open-mouthed oblivion, and even the crumby, crying babies were for the nonce stilled. Paul settled back to struggle with his impatience as best he could.

When he arrived at the Jersey City station, he hurried through his breakfast, manifestly ill at ease and keeping a sharp eye about him. After he reached the Twenty-third Street station, he consulted a cabman, and had himself driven to a men's furnishing establishment that was just opening for the day. He spent upward of two hours there, buying with endless reconsidering and great care. His new street suit he put on in the fitting-room; the frock coat and dress clothes he had bundled into the cab with his linen. Then he drove to a hatter's and a shoe house. His next errand was at Tiffany's, where he selected his silver and a new scarf-pin. He would not wait to have his silver marked, he said. Lastly, he stopped at a trunk shop on Broadway, and had his purchases packed into various travelling bags.

It was a little after one o'clock when he drove up to the Waldorf, and *40* after settling with the cabman, went into the office. He registered from Washington; said his mother and father had been abroad, and that he had come down to await the arrival of their steamer. He told his story plausibly and had no trouble, since he volunteered to pay for them in advance, in engaging his rooms; a sleeping-room, sitting-room and bath.

Not once, but a hundred times Paul had planned this entry into New York. He had gone over every detail of it with Charley Edwards, and in his scrap book at home there were pages of description about New York hotels, cut from the Sunday papers. When he was shown to his sitting-room on the eighth floor, he saw at a glance that everything was as it should be; there was but one detail in his mental picture that the place did not realize, so he rang for the bell boy and sent him down for flowers. He moved about nervously until the boy returned, putting away his new linen and fingering it delightedly as he did so. When the flowers came, he put them hastily into water, and then tumbled into a hot bath. Presently he came out of his white bathroom, resplendent in his new silk underwear, and playing with the tassels of his red robe. The snow was whirling so fiercely outside his windows that he could scarcely see across the street, but within the air was deliciously soft and fragrant. He put the violets and jonquils on the taboret beside the couch, and threw himself down with a long sigh, covering himself with a Roman blanket. He was thoroughly tired; he had been in such haste, he had stood up to such a strain, covered so much ground in the last twenty-four hours, that he wanted to think how it had all come about. Lulled by the sound of the wind, the warm air, and the cool fragrance of the flowers, he sank into deep, drowsy retrospection.

It had been wonderfully simple; when they had shut him out of the theatre and concert hall, when they had taken away his bone, the whole thing was virtually determined. The rest was a mere matter of opportunity. The only thing that at all surprised him was his own courage—for he realized well enough that he had always been tormented by fear, a sort of apprehensive dread that, of late years, as the meshes of the lies he had told closed about him, had been pulling the muscles of his body tighter and tighter.

Until now, he could not remember the time when he had not been dreading something. Even when he was a little boy, it was always there—behind him, or before, or on either side. There had always been the shadowed corner, the dark place into which he dared not look, but from which something seemed always to be watching him—and Paul had done things that were not pretty to watch, he knew.

But now he had a curious sense of relief, as though he had at last thrown down the gauntlet to the thing in the corner.

Yet it was but a day since he had been sulking in the traces; but yesterday afternoon that he had been sent to the bank with Denny & Carson's deposit, as usual—but this time he was instructed to leave the book to be balanced. There was above two thousand dollars in checks, and nearly a thousand in the bank notes which he had taken from the book and quietly transferred to his pocket. At the bank he had made out a new deposit slip. His nerves had been steady enough to permit of his returning to the office, where he had finished his work and asked for a full day's holiday to-morrow, Saturday, giving a perfectly reasonable pretext. The bank book, he knew, would not be returned before Monday or Tuesday, and his father would be out of town for the next week. From the time he slipped the bank notes into his pocket until he boarded the night train for New York, he had not known a moment's hesitation. It was not the first time Paul had steered through treacherous waters.

How astonishingly easy it had all been; here he was, the thing done; and this time there would be no awakening, no figure at the top of the stairs. He watched the snow flakes whirling by his window until he fell asleep.

When he awoke, it was three o'clock in the afternoon. He bounded up with a start; half of one of his precious days gone already! He spent more than an hour in dressing, watching every stage of his toilet carefully in the mirror. Everything was quite perfect; he was exactly the kind of boy he had always wanted to be.

When he went downstairs, Paul took a carriage and drove up Fifth Avenue toward the Park. The snow had somewhat abated; carriages and tradesmen's wagons were hurrying soundlessly to and fro in the winter twilight; boys in woollen mufflers were shovelling off the doorsteps; the avenue stages made fine spots of colour against the white street. Here and there on the corners were stands, with whole flower gardens blooming under glass cases, against the sides of which the snow flakes stuck and melted; violets, roses, carnations, lilies of the valley—somehow vastly more lovely and alluring that they blossomed thus unnaturally in the snow. The Park itself was a wonderful stage winterpiece.

When he returned, the pause of the twilight had ceased, and the tune of the streets had changed. The snow was falling faster, lights streamed from the hotels that reared their dozen stories fearlessly up into the storm, defying the raging Atlantic winds. A long, black stream of carriages poured down the avenue, intersected here and there by other streams, tending horizon-

(margin note: steal $ from work)

(margin note: 45)

(margin note: perfect)

tally. There were a score of cabs about the entrance of his hotel, and his driver had to wait. Boys in livery were running in and out of the awning stretched across the sidewalk, up and down the red velvet carpet laid from the door to the street. Above, about, within it all was the rumble and roar, the hurry and toss of thousands of human beings as hot for pleasure as himself, and on every side of him towered the glaring affirmation of the omnipotence of wealth.

The boy set his teeth and drew his shoulders together in a spasm of realization; the plot of all dramas, the text of all romances, the nerve-stuff of all sensations was whirling about him like the snow flakes. He burnt like a faggot in a tempest.

When Paul went down to dinner, the music of the orchestra came float-   *50* ing up the elevator shaft to greet him. His head whirled as he stepped into the thronged corridor, and he sank back into one of the chairs against the wall to get his breath. The lights, the chatter, the perfumes, the bewildering medley of colour—he had, for a moment, the feeling of not being able to stand it. But only for a moment; these were his own people, he told himself. He went slowly about the corridors, through the writing-rooms, smoking-rooms, reception-rooms, as though he were exploring the chambers of an enchanted palace, built and peopled for him alone.

When he reached the dining-room he sat down at a table near a window. The flowers, the white linen, the many-coloured wine glasses, the gay toilettes of the women, the low popping of corks, the undulating repetitions of the *Blue Danube* from the orchestra, all flooded Paul's dream with bewildering radiance. When the roseate tinge of his champagne was added— that cold, precious, bubbling stuff that creamed and foamed in his glass— Paul wondered that there were honest men in the world at all. This was what all the world was fighting for, he reflected; this was what all the struggle was about. He doubted the reality of his past. Had he ever known a place called Cordelia Street, a place where fagged-looking businessmen got on the early car; mere rivets in a machine they seemed to Paul,—sickening men, with combings of children's hair always hanging to their coats, and the smell of cooking in their clothes. Cordelia Street—Ah! that belonged to another time and country; had he not always been thus, had he not sat here night after night, from as far back as he could remember, looking pensively over just such shimmering textures, and slowly twirling the stem of a glass like this one between his thumb and middle finger? He rather thought he had.

He was not in the least abashed or lonely. He had no especial desire to meet or to know any of these people; all he demanded was the right to look on and conjecture, to watch the pageant. The mere stage properties were all he contended for. Nor was he lonely later in the evening, in his loge at the Metropolitan. He was now entirely rid of his nervous misgivings, of his forced aggressiveness, of the imperative desire to show himself different from his surroundings. He felt now that his surroundings explained him. Nobody questioned the purple; he had only to wear it passively. He had only to glance down at his attire to reassure himself that here it would be impossible for anyone to humiliate him.

He found it hard to leave his beautiful sitting-room to go to bed that night, and sat long watching the raging storm from his turret window. When he went to sleep it was with the lights turned on in his bedroom; partly because of his old timidity, and partly so that, if he should wake in the night, there would be no wretched moment of doubt, no horrible suspicion of yellow wall-paper, or of Washington and Calvin above his bed.

Sunday morning the city was practically snow-bound. Paul breakfasted late, and in the afternoon he fell in with a wild San Francisco boy, a freshman at Yale, who said he had run down for a "little flyer" over Sunday. The young man offered to show Paul the night side of the town, and the two boys went out together after dinner, not returning to the hotel until seven o'clock the next morning. They had started out in the confiding warmth of a champagne friendship, but their parting in the elevator was singularly cool. The freshman pulled himself together to make his train, and Paul went to bed. He awoke at two o'clock in the afternoon, very thirsty and dizzy, and rang for ice-water, coffee, and the Pittsburgh papers.

On the part of the hotel management, Paul excited **no suspicion**. There was this to be said for him, that he wore his spoils with dignity and in no way made himself conspicuous. Even under the glow of his wine he was never boisterous, though he found the stuff like a magician's wand for wonder-building. His chief greediness lay in his ears and eyes, and his excesses were not offensive ones. His dearest pleasures were the grey winter twilights in his sitting-room; his quiet enjoyment of his flowers, his clothes, his wide divan, his cigarette and his sense of power. He could not remember a time when he had felt so at peace with himself. The mere release from the necessity of petty lying, lying every day and every day, restored his self-respect. He had never lied for pleasure, even at school; but to be noticed and admired, to assert his difference from other Cordelia Street boys; and he felt a good deal more manly, more honest, even, now that he had no need for boastful pretensions, now that he could, as his actor friends used to say, "dress the part." It was characteristic that remorse did not occur to him. His golden days went by without a shadow, and he made each as perfect as he could.

On the eighth day after his arrival in New York, he found the whole affair exploited in the Pittsburgh papers, exploited with a wealth of detail which indicated that local news of a sensational nature was at a low ebb. The firm of Denny & Carson announced that the boy's father had refunded the full amount of the theft, and that they had no intention of prosecuting. The Cumberland minister had been interviewed, and expressed his hope of yet reclaiming the motherless lad, and his Sabbath-school teacher declared that she would spare no effort to that end. The rumour had reached Pittsburgh that the boy had been seen in a New York hotel, and his father had gone East to find him and bring him home.

55

Paul had just come in to dress for dinner; he sank into a chair, weak to the knees, and clasped his head in his hands. It was to be worse than jail, even; the tepid waters of Cordelia Street were to close over him finally and forever. The grey monotony stretched before him in hopeless, unrelieved years; Sabbath-school, Young People's Meeting, the yellow-papered room, the damp dish-towels; it all rushed back upon him with a sickening vividness. He had the old feeling that the orchestra had suddenly stopped, the sinking sensation that the play was over. The sweat broke out on his face, and he sprang to his feet, looked about him with his white, conscious smile, and winked at himself in the mirror. With something of the old childish belief in miracles with which he had so often gone to class, all his lessons unlearned, Paul dressed and dashed whistling down the corridor to the elevator.

He had no sooner entered the dining-room and caught the measure of the music than his remembrance was lightened by his old elastic power of claiming the moment, mounting with it, and finding it all sufficient. The glare and glitter about him, the mere scenic accessories had again, and for the last time, their old potency. He would show himself that he was game, he would finish the thing splendidly. He doubted, more than ever, the existence of Cordelia Street, and for the first time he drank his wine recklessly. Was he not, after all, one of those fortunate beings born to the purple, was he not still himself and in his own place? He drummed a nervous accompaniment to the Pagliacci music and looked about him, telling himself over and over that it had paid.

He reflected drowsily, to the swell of the music and the chill sweetness of his wine, that he might have done it more wisely. He might have caught an outbound steamer and been well out of their clutches before now. But the other side of the world had seemed too far away and too uncertain then; he could not have waited for it; his need had been too sharp. If he had to choose over again, he would do the same thing to-morrow. He looked affectionately about the dining-room, now gilded with a soft mist. Ah, it had paid indeed!

Paul was awakened next morning by a painful throbbing in his head and feet. He had thrown himself across the bed without undressing, and had slept with his shoes on. His limbs and hands were lead heavy, and his tongue and throat were parched and burnt. There came upon him one of those fateful attacks of clear-headedness that never occurred except when he was physically exhausted and his nerves hung loose. He lay still and closed his eyes and let the tide of things wash over him.

His father was in New York; "stopping at some joint or other," he told himself. The memory of successive summers on the front stoop fell upon him like a weight of black water. He had not a hundred dollars left; and he knew now, more than ever, that money was everything, the wall that stood between all he loathed and all he wanted. The thing was winding itself up; he had thought of that on his first glorious day in New York, and had even provided a way to snap the thread. It lay on his dressing-table now; he had got it out last night when he came blindly up from dinner, but the shiny metal hurt his eyes, and he disliked the looks of it.

He rose and moved about with a painful effort, succumbing now and again to attacks of nausea. It was the old depression exaggerated; all the world had become Cordelia Street. Yet somehow he was not afraid of anything, was absolutely calm; perhaps because he had looked into the dark corner at last and knew. It was bad enough, what he saw there, but somehow not so bad as his long fear of it had been. He saw everything clearly now. He had a feeling that he had made the best of it, that he had lived the sort of life he was meant to live, and for half an hour he sat staring at the revolver. But he told himself that was not the way, so he went downstairs and took a cab to the ferry.

When Paul arrived at Newark, he got off the train and took another cab, directing the driver to follow the Pennsylvania tracks out of the town. The snow lay heavy on the roadways and had drifted deep in the open fields. Only here and there the dead grass or dried weed stalks projected, singularly black, above it. Once well into the country, Paul dismissed the carriage and walked, floundering along the tracks, his mind a medley of irrelevant things. He seemed to hold in his brain an actual picture of everything he had seen that morning. He remembered every feature of both his drivers, of the toothless old woman from whom he had bought the red flowers in his coat, the agent from whom he had got his ticket, and all of his fellow-passengers on the ferry. His mind, unable to cope with vital matters near at hand, worked feverishly and deftly at sorting and grouping these images. They made for him a part of the ugliness of the world, of the ache in his head, and the bitter burning on his tongue. He stooped and put a handful of snow into his mouth as he walked, but that, too, seemed hot. When he reached a little hillside, where the tracks ran through a cut some twenty feet below him, he stopped and sat down.

The carnations in his coat were drooping with the cold, he noticed; their red glory all over. It occurred to him that all the flowers he had seen in the glass cases that first night must have gone the same way, long before this. It was only one splendid breath they had, in spite of their brave mockery at the winter outside the glass; and it was a losing game in the end, it seemed, this revolt against the homilies by which the world is run. Paul took one of the blossoms carefully from his coat and scooped a little hole in the snow, where he covered it up. Then he dozed a while, from his weak condition, seemingly insensible to the cold.

The sound of an approaching train awoke him, and he started to his feet, remembering only his resolution, and afraid lest he should be too late. He stood watching the approaching locomotive, his teeth chattering, his lips drawn away from them in a frightened smile; once or twice he glanced nervously sidewise, as though he were being watched. When the right moment came, he jumped. As he fell, the folly of his haste occurred to him with merciless clearness, the vastness of what he had left undone. There flashed

65

through his brain, clearer than ever before, the blue of Adriatic water, the *more dreams not filled, as he dies* yellow of Algerian sands.

He felt something strike his chest, and that his body was being thrown swiftly through the air, on and on, immeasurably far and fast, while his limbs were gently relaxed. Then, because the picture making mechanism was crushed, the disturbing visions flashed into black, and Paul dropped back into the (immense design of things.) *life to death, fade*

Questions of Subject and Theme

1. Cather's title, "Paul's Case: A Study in Temperament," is couched in a scientific (or mock-scientific, or would-be scientific) style. How would you describe Paul's "temperament?" Find examples from other stories, novels, or films to illustrate the kind of temperament you mean.

2. What about Cather's treatment seems "scientific?" What is *her* narrative "temperament?" Does she seem, for example, objective? Does she seem to invite us to view the character sympathetically? What if anything is gained for your sense of the story, and what if anything is lost by the *manner* of Cather's narration? Pick an example of her narration and analyze her apparent relations both to her character and to her audience.

Questions of Method and Strategy

1. Suppose the story had begun with Paul's arrival in New York. How would that method affect our sense of the New York experiences? Pick an example from the last part of the story and explain how the Pittsburgh part does or does not contribute to the effects created later.

2. At the end of the story Paul can't face the revolver, but resolutely throws himself in front of the train. Why do you suppose that method of suicide appeals more to him? What evidence does Cather provide earlier in the story to make its end artistically justified?

SCREENPLAY EXCERPT FROM PAUL'S CASE

Ron Cowen

Along with new dialogue, filmwriter Ron Cowen attempts to give visual equivalents of the emotions and thoughts evoked by Willa Cather's verbal structure. In the following excerpt from his script, the careful reader can note the many ways Cowen's vision of Paul complements the "detached" narrative treatment of the short story.

Set in 1905, the script opens with Paul, a Pittsburgh highschool student, 1
awaiting "trial" by a group of teachers to determine whether he should be readmitted to classes. Once reprimanded, he runs to the city concert hall where he works as a usher, soaks up the atmosphere of the foyer painting gallery, and is again reprimanded for inattention to duty, this time by the house manager. Once the concert begins, Paul thrills to the beauty of the soprano's voice, afterwards is warmed by the glamor of her presence. When Paul arrives home late, his widowed father reprimands him a third time, challenging him to do his best, since he has been readmitted to school. After Paul and his father walk home from church the next Sunday afternoon, the following scenes begin.

#26

Interior. Kitchen. Evening.

flower atop table (refers to flower later that he buys for hotel room)

Paul and his father sit in silence, eating supper. There is a flower in a little vase on the table between them—Paul's touch. Paul finally breaks the silence.

PAUL: Did you like the roast?

FATHER: Very tasty. [*Paul smiles.*] It must've been expensive.

PAUL: Not too. . . . I did what you told me, I complained to the butcher. I 5
said, "Twenty-nine a pound is highway robbery!" So he gave it to me for twenty-seven. I made your favorite dessert—rhubarb pie.

FATHER [*wiping his mouth*]: None for me tonight—no room for it.

He pushes his seat away from the table, takes out a pipe from his pocket, and lights it.

Paul rises and clears the table. He carries the dishes to the sink and begins washing them.

PAUL: George said if I came over, he'd help me with geometry. Could I have
a dime, for car fare?

His father puffs at his pipe to get it lit. He doesn't answer.   10

PAUL [*continuing*]: Could I . . . please?
FATHER: What's the point of your being an usher if you don't save your
money?
PAUL: I try to—
FATHER: Where's it all go?

Paul looks at the flowers on the table. He doesn't say anything.   15

FATHER [*continuing*]: I don't know why you can't study with someone who
lives in the neighborhood.
PAUL: I don't know anybody.
FATHER: You mean this boy, George, who lives on the other side of town, is
the only one who can help you?

Paul doesn't answer. His father begrudgingly digs into his pocket for a
dime. He lays it on the kitchen table.

FATHER: The next time I expect you to pay for it yourself, or else find some-   20
one around here to help you.

Paul looks at the dime waiting for him on the table. Finally he goes to
it and picks it up.

PAUL: Thank you—

Interior. Paul's Room. Night.

Paul stands at his dresser, splashing rose water on his hands. He hides the
bottle under the clothes in the top drawer. He leaves the room.

Interior. Stairs. Night.

Paul comes down the stairs, book in hand. He takes his coat from the
hook and puts it on. He calls to his father.

PAUL: Be back soon.   25
FATHER [VO]: Don't be late!

Paul opens the front door and leaves, closing it behind him.

#28-32

Interior. Stage of Theater. Night.

In bright lights and full costume, an acting company is performing Dumas's *La Dame Aux Camélias*.

MARGUERITE: Come along, little Saint-Gaudens! I want to dance!

Marguerite polkas with Saint-Gaudens. Armand plays the piano.   *30*

Exterior. Alley and Stage Door Behind Theater. Night.

Paul walks down the alley to the stage door. Propped up next to it is a signboard that reads: "The Pittsburgh Repertory Company presents *La Dame Aux Camélias* by Alexander Dumas."

Paul looks at the sign, then opens the stage door and enters.

Interior. Backstage. Night.

Paul closes the door quietly behind him. In the hallway, a backstage doorman sits by the callboard reading a newspaper. Paul nods to him.

The doorman looks up, nods at Paul, and goes back to reading.

Paul walks down the hallway to a door. He opens it.   *35*

Interior. Wings. Night.

Paul closes the door quietly behind him and steps into the darkened wings. He stops and breathes in the intoxicating backstage air. He walks softly to the edge of the wings for a view of the stage.

Interior. Stage. Night.

Paul's P.O.V.
Unreal stage

From Paul's POV: A very angled shot of the stage, brightly lit. Heavily made-up actors in full costume move about a French drawing room. The speech and mannerisms are highly exaggerated. Paul watches, transfixed.

Marguerite and Saint-Gaudens are dancing. She stops suddenly and coughs.

SAINT-GAUDENS: What is the matter?
MARGUERITE: Nothing—I lost my breath.   *40*
ARMAND [*stops playing the piano*]: I am afraid you are ill! [*He goes to her.*]

MARGUERITE: No, it's nothing. Don't stop.

PRUDENCE: Marguerite is ill!

MARGUERITE: But it is nothing, really. Please go into the other room, I'll be
   with you directly.

PRUDENCE [*to Saint-Gaudens*]: We had better leave her. She always wants to   45
   be alone when she feels like that.

MARGUERITE: Do go, I shall come presently.

Interior. Wings. Night.

Prudence and Saint-Gaudens exit past a starry-eyed Paul. Offstage,
the actors appear grotesque in their heavy makeup. Their costumes seem
shabby.

out of Paul's p.o.v. (we see him)

#36 offstage! gaudy

Close-up of Paul as he turns to watch them. They walk across the wings,
their backs to him. They vanish into the darkness, whispering to each other,
while we only hear the voices from the stage:

MARGUERITE [VO]: Take this flower. Bring it back to me.

ARMAND [VO]: When?   50

MARGUERITE [VO]: When it is faded—

Flower Fade

Interior. Wings. Night.

The camera follows the actor and actress from behind, acting once more
as Paul's eyes and ears. They climb a circular iron staircase to the second
floor dressing rooms. We hear their conversation. In voiceover, they speak
"dramatically," as Paul would expect them to do.

Paul's POV.

ACTOR [VO]: —magic in the air tonight! Did you feel it?

ACTRESS [VO]: As if Dumas himself had breathed every word into me!

ACTOR: I could tell by the way you spoke—your every gesture—   55

magic

Interior. Second Floor Hallway. Night.

The camera follows the actor and actress from behind as they walk down
the hallway to their dressing rooms. Their imagined conversation continues
in voiceover.

ACTOR [VO]: I felt as if the ghosts of the Comédie Française were on stage
   with us tonight! Molière! Corneille! Racine!

ACTRESS [VO]: The Divine Sarah!

ACTOR [VO]: Sarah herself!

Interior. Wings. Night.

Paul, looking off into the darkened wings, in the direction of the actor   *60*
and actress. A hand is placed on his shoulder. A voice.

CHARLIE [VO]: Hey!

Paul spins around.

Charlie Edwards stands there in front of him, in costume. He was playing the part of Armand. He removes his powdered wig. His makeup is dripping with perspiration.

CHARLIE: Didn't you hear me calling you?
PAUL: No, I—

Charlie takes him by the arm and pulls him along.   *65*

CHARLIE: Come on, I have to change for Act Two!

They vanish into the darkened wings.

Interior. Dressing Room. Night.

Charlie bursts into his dressing room with energy left over from the
stage. Paul follows, putting his geometry book down on the makeup table.

Charlie is out of his costume in a flash, handing pieces to Paul to
hang up.

CHARLIE: Did you see the first act?   *70*
PAUL: The last part—
CHARLIE: How was I?
PAUL [*simply*]: You were brilliant.
CHARLIE [*laughing*]: "Brilliant"?
PAUL [*feeling he's being made fun of*]: I thought so. . . .   *75*
CHARLIE [*convinced*]: That good? I suppose I *did* have a special feel for it
    tonight.
PAUL: I could tell.

Charlie hands Paul a piece of his costume to hang up.

CHARLIE: Here— Where are my pants?
PAUL: They're right here—   *80*

He hands Charlie his pants for the second act. Charlie puts them on.

PAUL [*continuing*]: It must be wonderful to say and do splendid things.

CHARLIE: It is, it is. That's what they call acting, m'boy! I bet you'd like to get out there on the boards yourself, wouldn't you?

PAUL: No, I—

CHARLIE: Come on, you can tell old Charlie! 85

PAUL: No, really—

CHARLIE: You don't have a great, secret desire to be an actor?

PAUL: I just want to . . .

CHARLIE: . . . What?

PAUL: Be. Here. In the atmosphere of it. Float on the wave of it, be carried 90 #32
off—

Charlie pulls on his wig.

CHARLIE: Such poetry!

PAUL: Where I live . . . all the houses are the same. All the people inside the #19
houses are the same . . . all they think about are their jobs, their suppers, sending their children to school and going to church on Sunday.

CHARLIE: A bit drab for you?

PAUL: I long for cool things . . . soft lights . . . fresh flowers. . . . 95

He picks up a flower bouquet that lies next to his geometry book.

CHARLIE: They're not real . . . they'd wilt under the lights. . . . Here, help me on with this—

Paul helps him on with his jacket. Charlie sits at his makeup table to touch up his face. Behind him, in the mirror, we see the actress who went #36
up the stairs earlier come into the dressing room. She wears a tattered bathrobe. Her hair is pinned up.

ACTRESS: Charlie, you got some lip rouge?

CHARLIE: Sure, love, come on in. 100

She comes into the room. She smiles at Paul. He blushes.

CHARLIE: That's Paul.

ACTRESS: Hello, Paul.

CHARLIE: He's a connoisseur of great art!

PAUL [*to actress*]: I've admired your performance greatly. 105

The actress curtsies to Paul.

CHARLIE: Here you go!

He tosses her the lip rouge.

ACTRESS: Thanks—you're a real gent.

She winks at Paul and walks out of the dressing room. 110

CHARLIE: You know, you should be in the big time with that act.
PAUL: I want to go to New York—some day.
CHARLIE: Don't we all! Don't we all!
PAUL: I have a scrapbook at home . . . with pictures of New York.

#4/

Charlie looks at Paul. His smile vanishes as he realizes how sad Paul   *115*
really is. He puts his hand on Paul's shoulder.

CHARLIE: I hope you get there, old man.

He smiles at Paul.

Questions of Subject and Theme

1. Money is the main theme of the conversation Paul has with his father. What are the main themes of the conversations he hears within the play and backstage? Compare the themes from Paul's point of view.
2. The play *La Dame Aux Camélias* dramatizes the pathos of a woman who longs to live but is dying of tuberculosis. The play does not appear in the short story, but what themes from that story do you imagine the scriptwriter wishes to dramatize in the filmed version by including the play?

Questions of Method and Strategy

1. The scenes selected here for the film contrast the drabness and banality of Paul's home life to the glamour he finds in the theater. Part of the atmosphere of his home is created verbally by the discussion of money. Point to some of the ways the atmosphere is dramatized visually and by silences in the film script.
2. The glamour of the theater both on stage and backstage seems to appeal strongly to Paul. Yet in what verbal and visual ways does the scriptwriter attempt to dramatize Paul's possibly naive attitude about the theater?

———

Suggestions for Writing on the Juxtapositions

1. Each version emphasizes Paul's loneliness. Write an essay in which you compare and contrast the ways Paul's essential loneliness is rendered in the two versions of his story.
2. Paul loves the theater and is himself very theatrical at times. Write an essay in which you show how the two versions of the story dramatize both Paul's theatricality and the strengths and weaknesses his theatricality shows in his life.
3. In your view, why does Paul kill himself? Does he feel, for example, that he has to "pay" for his crime? If so, does that imply that he has not really left behind the values and assumptions of his home as fully as he sometimes feels he has? What else might his suicide imply about him? What other possible motives do you feel operating? Write an essay in which you discuss the meaning that Paul's death gives to our sense of his life.

4. Pick a scene or part of a scene from the story with issues in some way different from those dramatized in the part of the script you have read. Now write your own script that renders your sense of the scene visually and verbally.

5 To Die by Law

Charles Dickens, "Among the Condemned"
George Orwell, "A Hanging"
H. L. Mencken, "Hangings I Have Known"
Norman Mailer, "Let's Do It"

Facing a man facing a death—this is the task four famous writers set themselves in the following accounts. As you read them, keep these questions in mind:

1. Only the first writer, Charles Dickens, attempts to give the prisoner's point of view directly. As you read, compare and contrast the differing ways the other writers attempt to convey such a point of view indirectly.

2. In the essays by Orwell and Mencken, what effects are created by the racial and ethnic vocabularies employed? Does either writer, for example, seem cautious in this regard? Defiant? Brutal? Make a few changes and compare the results with the original: *black* or *African-American* for *blackamoor* in Mencken's account, for example. How much does the sensitivity or insensitivity you imagine in each writer depend on such matters of diction? Does that sensitivity or insensitivity change your views of the essays? Of the essayists? Of the condemned?

3. In another account of his early assignments to cover hangings Mencken writes:

   I found the work light and instructive, and there was plenty of it to do, for a movement was afoot in my native Maryland at the time to "hang out," as the phrase went, the whole criminal population of the state, at all events in the higher brackets. The notion that murderers, rapists, and other such fiends in human form were simply unfortunates suffering from mental croups and catarrhs, and that the sensible way to deal with them was to send them to luxurious sanatoria, and there ply them with nourishing victuals, moral suasion and personality tests—that notion was still hidden in the womb of the future.

Does Mencken's irony here at the expense of modern criminology alter your sense of his account of the hanging when you read it? If you think so, say as clearly as you can how and why it does. If you think not, explain how your original sense is confirmed.

4. Compare Orwell's implied attitudes toward his sense of his official duty with those expressed in "Shooting an Elephant" in Juxtaposition 1 (p. 7).

5. Among Gary Gilmore's crimes was the cold-blooded killing of a gas station attendant who had given him the few dollars available. In the other cases we do not know the crimes of the men executed. Is the effect of this reticence the same in each case? What do you imagine as possible artistic and personal motives for the omission of such facts in each case? What evidence can you find to support your views?

AMONG THE CONDEMNED

Charles Dickens

The great nineteenth-century English novelist Charles Dickens (1812–1870) filled his novels with sympathetic portraits of the poor and downtrodden. A lifelong interest in crime and punishment pervades his work, and large audiences gathered to hear him read dramatic selections that were often passages of pathos. The essay below is taken from a nonfiction account, but it displays many of Dickens's novelistic techniques.

A few paces up the yard, and forming a continuation of the building, in which are the two rooms we have just quitted, lie the condemned cells. The entrance is by a narrow and obscure staircase leading to a dark passage, in which a charcoal stove casts a lurid tint over the objects in its immediate vicinity, and diffuses something like warmth around. From the left-hand side of this passage, the massive door of every cell on the story opens; and from it alone can they be approached. There are three of these passages, and three of these ranges of cells, one above the other; but in size, furniture and appearance, they are all precisely alike. Prior to the recorder's report being made, all the prisoners under sentence of death are removed from the day-room at five o'clock in the afternoon, and locked up in these cells, where they are allowed a candle until ten o'clock; and here they remain until seven next morning. When the warrant for a prisoner's execution arrives, he is removed to the cells and confined in one of them until he leaves it for the scaffold. He is at liberty to walk in the yard; but, both in his walks and in his cell, he is constantly attended by a turnkey, who never leaves him on any pretence.

We entered the first cell. It was a stone dungeon, eight feet long by six wide, with a bench at the upper end, under which were a common rug, a bible, and prayerbook. An iron candlestick was fixed into the wall at the side; and a small high window in the back admitted as much air and light as could struggle in between a double row of heavy, crossed iron bars. It contained no other furniture of any description.

Conceive the situation of a man, spending his last night on earth in this cell. Buoyed up with some vague and undefined hope of reprieve, he knew not why—indulging in some wild and visionary idea of escaping, he knew not how—hour after hour of the three preceding days allowed him for preparation, has fled with a speed which no man living would deem possible, for none but this dying man can know. He has wearied his friends with entreaties, exhausted the attendants with importunities, neglected in his feverish restlessness the timely warnings of his spiritual consoler; and, now that the illusion is at last dispelled, now that eternity is before him and guilt behind, now that his fears of death amount almost to madness, and an over-whelming sense of his helpless, hopeless state rushes upon him, he is lost and stupefied, and has neither thoughts to turn to, nor power to call upon, the Almighty Being, from whom alone he can seek mercy and forgiveness, and before whom his repentance can alone avail.

Hours have glided by, and still he sits upon the same stone bench with folded arms, heedless alike of the fast decreasing time before him, and the urgent entreaties of the good man at his side. The feeble light is wasting gradually, and the deathlike stillness of the street without, broken only by the rumbling of some passing vehicle which echoes mournfully through the empty yards, warns him that the night is waning fast away. The deep bell of St. Paul's strikes—one! He heard it; it has roused him. Seven hours left! He paces the narrow limits of his cell with rapid strides, cold drops of terror starting on his forehead, and every muscle of his frame quivering with agony. Seven hours! He suffers himself to be led to his seat, mechanically takes the bible which is placed in his hand, and tries to read and listen. No: his thoughts will wander. The book is torn and soiled by use—and like the book he read his lessons in, at school, just forty years ago! He has never bestowed a thought upon it, perhaps, since he left it as a child: and yet the place, the time, the room—nay, the very boys he played with, crowd as vividly before him as if they were scenes of yesterday; and some forgotten phrase, some childish word, rings in his ears like the echo of one uttered but a minute since. The voice of the clergyman recalls him to himself. He is reading from the sacred book its solemn promises of pardon for repentance, and its awful denunciation of obdurate men. He falls upon his knees and clasps his hands to pray. Hush! what sound was that? He starts upon his feet. It cannot be two yet. Hark! Two quarters have struck; the third—the fourth. It is! Six hours left! Tell him not of repentance! Six hours' repentance for eight times six years of guilt and sin! He buries his face in his hands, and throws himself on the bench.

Worn with watching and excitement, he sleeps, and the same unsettled state of mind pursues him in his dreams. An insupportable load is taken from his breast; he is walking with his wife in a pleasant field, with the bright sky above them, and a fresh and boundless prospect on every side—how differ-ent from the stone walls of Newgate! She is looking—not as she did when he saw her for the last time in that dreadful place, but as she used when he loved her—long, long ago, before misery and ill-treatment had altered her looks, and vice had changed his nature, and she is leaning upon his arm, and looking up into his face with tenderness and affection—and he does *not* strike her now, nor rudely shake her from him. And oh! how glad he is to tell her all he had forgotten in that last hurried interview, and to fall on his knees before her and fervently beseech her pardon for all the unkindness and cruelty that wasted her form and broke her heart! The scene suddenly changes. He is on his trial again: there are the judge and jury, and prosecu-tors, and witnesses, just as they were before. How full the Court is—with a sea of heads—with a gallows, too, and a scaffold—and how all those people stare at *him!* Verdict, 'Guilty.' No matter; he will escape.

The night is dark and cold, the gates have been left open, and in an instant he is in the street, flying from the scene of this imprisonment like the wind. The streets are cleared, the open fields are gained and the broad wide country lies before him. Onward he dashes in the midst of darkness, over hedge and ditch, through mud and pool, bounding from spot to spot with a speed and lightness, astonishing even to himself. At length he pauses; he must be safe from pursuit now; he will stretch himself on that bank and sleep till sunrise.

A period of unconsciousness succeeds. He wakes, cold and wretched. The dull grey light of morning is stealing into the cell, and falls upon the form of the attendant turnkey. Confused by his dreams, he starts from his uneasy bed in momentary uncertainty. It is but momentary. Every object in the narrow cell is too frightfully real to admit of doubt or mistake. He is the condemned felon again, guilty and despairing; and in two hours more will be dead.

Questions of Subject and Theme

1. Dickens's description begins with physical details before focusing on emotional and spiritual matters. But do the physical details themselves create emotional and spiritual effects for you? Explain your answer.
2. Dickens pays much attention to time and particularly to the speed of passing time here. What details of writing besides obvious individual words of time like *hours* does he employ? For example, what contribution is made by the short and choppy style that describes the end of the prisoner's trial?

Questions of Method and Strategy

1. How does Dickens create a sense of the condemned man's point of view even before the imagined dream sequence? Point to and analyze particular examples.
2. Dickens never mentions a specific crime. In what other ways of exclusion and inclusion does he work to evoke sympathy for the prisoner in his reader?

A HANGING

George Orwell

George Orwell was the pen name of Eric Arthur Blair (1903–1950), an Englishman perhaps most famous for his futuristic novel about totalitarianism, *1984.* Educated at the famous secondary school Eton, the young Orwell went on to serve with the Indian Imperial Police in Burma from 1922–1927. He became convinced of the basic evil of imperialism, though he never concealed his doubts about the abilities for self-rule among the people he helped to govern. "A Hanging" comes out of Orwell's Burmese experience as does the essay "Shooting an Elephant" in Juxtaposition 1 (p. 7).

It was in Burma, a sodden morning of the rains. A sickly light, like   *1* yellow tinfoil, was slanting over the high walls into the jail yard. We were waiting outside the condemned cells, a row of sheds fronted with double bars, like small animal cages. Each cell measured about ten feet by ten and was quite bare within except for a plank bed and a pot for drinking water. In some of them brown, silent men were squatting at the inner bars, with their blankets draped round them. These were the condemned men, due to be hanged within the next week or two.

One prisoner had been brought out of his cell. He was a Hindu, a puny wisp of a man, with a shaven head and vague liquid eyes. He had a thick, sprouting moustache, absurdly too big for his body, rather like the moustache of a comic man on the films. Six tall Indian warders were guarding him and getting him ready for the gallows. Two of them stood by with rifles and fixed bayonets, while the others handcuffed him, passed a chain through his handcuffs and fixed it to their belts, and lashed his arms tight to his sides. They crowded very close about him, with their hands always on him in a careful, caressing grip, as though all the while feeling him to make sure he was there. It was like men handling a fish which is still alive and may jump back into the water. But he stood quite unresisting, yielding his arms limply to the ropes, as though he hardly noticed what was happening.

Eight o'clock struck and a bugle call, desolately thin in the wet air, floated from the distant barracks. The superintendent of the jail, who was standing apart from the rest of us, moodily prodding the gravel with his stick, raised his head at the sound. He was an army doctor, with a grey toothbrush moustache and a gruff voice. "For God's sake hurry up, Francis," he said irritably. "The man ought to have been dead by this time. Aren't you ready yet?"

Francis, the head jailer, a fat Dravidian in a white drill suit and gold spectacles, waved his black hand. "Yes sir, yes sir," he bubbled. "All iss satisfactorily prepared. The hangman iss waiting. We shall proceed."

"Well, quick march, then. The prisoners can't get their breakfast till this   *5* job's over."

We set out for the gallows. Two warders marched on either side of the prisoner, with their rifles at the slope; two others marched close against him, gripping him by arm and shoulder, as though at once pushing and supporting him. The rest of us, magistrates and the like, followed behind. Suddenly, when we had gone ten yards, the procession stopped short without any order or warning. A dreadful thing had happened—a dog, come goodness knows whence, had appeared in the yard. It came bounding among us with a loud volley of barks, and leapt round us wagging its whole body, wild with glee at finding so many human beings together. It was a large woolly dog, half Airedale, half pariah. For a moment it pranced round us, and then, before anyone could stop it, it had made a dash for the prisoner, and jumping up tried to lick his face. Everyone stood aghast, too taken aback even to grab at the dog.

"Who let that bloody brute in here?" said the superintendent angrily. "Catch it, someone!"

A warder detached from the escort, charged clumsily after the dog, but it danced and gambolled just out of his reach, taking everything as part of the game. A young Eurasian jailer picked up a handful of gravel and tried to stone the dog away, but it dodged the stones and came after us again. Its yaps echoed from the jail walls. The prisoner, in the grasp of the two warders, looked on incuriously, as though this was another formality of the hanging. It was several minutes before someone managed to catch the dog. Then we put my handkerchief through its collar and moved off once more, with the dog still straining and whimpering.

It was about forty yards to the gallows. I watched the bare brown back of the prisoner marching in front of me. He walked clumsily with his bound arms, but quite steadily, with that bobbing gait of the Indian who never straightens his knees. At each step his muscles slid neatly into place, the lock of hair on his scalp danced up and down, his feet printed themselves on the wet gravel. And once, in spite of the men who gripped him by each shoulder, he stepped slightly aside to avoid a puddle on the path.

It is curious, but till that moment I had never realized what it means to *10* destroy a healthy, conscious man. When I saw the prisoner step aside to avoid the puddle I saw the mystery, the unspeakable wrongness, of cutting a life short when it is in full tide. This man was not dying, he was alive just as we are alive. All the organs of his body were working—bowels digesting food, skin renewing itself, nails growing, tissues forming—all toiling away in solemn foolery. His nails would still be growing when he stood on the drop, when he was falling through the air with a tenth-of-a-second to live. His eyes saw the yellow gravel and the grey walls, and his brain still remembered, foresaw, reasoned—reasoned even about puddles. He and we were a party of men walking together, seeing, hearing, feeling, understanding the same world; and in two minutes, with a sudden snap, one of us would be gone—one mind less, one world less.

The gallows stood in a small yard, separate from the main grounds of the prison, and overgrown with tall prickly weeds. It was a brick erection like three sides of a shed, with planking on top, and above that two beams and a crossbar with the rope dangling. The hangman, a grey-haired convict in the white uniform of the prison, was waiting beside his machine. He greeted us with a servile crouch as we entered. At a word from Francis the two warders, gripping the prisoner more closely than ever, half led half pushed him to the gallows and helped him clumsily up the ladder. Then the hangman climbed up and fixed the rope round the prisoner's neck.

We stood waiting, five yards away. The warders had formed in a rough circle round the gallows. And then, when the noose was fixed, the prisoner began crying out to his god. It was a high, reiterated cry of "Ram! Ram! Ram! Ram!" not urgent and fearful like a prayer or cry for help, but steady, rhythmical, almost like the tolling of a bell. The dog answered the sound with a whine. The hangman, still standing on the gallows, produced a small cotton bag like a flour bag and drew it down over the prisoner's face. But the sound, muffled by the cloth, still persisted, over and over again: "Ram! Ram! Ram! Ram! Ram!"

The hangman climbed down and stood ready, holding the lever. Minutes seemed to pass. The steady, muffled crying from the prisoner went on and on, "Ram! Ram! Ram!" never faltering for an instant. The superintendent, his head on his chest, was slowly poking the ground with his stick; perhaps he was counting the cries, allowing the prisoner a fixed number— fifty, perhaps, or a hundred. Everyone had changed colour. The Indians had gone grey like bad coffee, and one or two of the bayonets were wavering. We looked at the lashed, hooded man on the drop, and listened to his cries—each cry another second of life; the same thought was in all our minds: oh, kill him quickly, get it over, stop that abominable noise!

Suddenly the superintendent made up his mind. Throwing up his head he made a swift motion with this stick. "Chalo!" he shouted almost fiercely.

There was a clanking noise, and then dead silence. The prisoner had vanished, and the rope was twisting on itself. I let go of the dog, and it galloped immediately to the back of the gallows; but when it got there it stopped short, barked, and then retreated into a corner of the yard, where it stood among the weeds, looking timorously out at us. We went round the gallows to inspect the prisoner's body. He was dangling with his toes pointed straight downwards, very slowly revolving, as dead as a stone.

The superintendent reached out with his stick and poked the bare brown body; it oscillated slightly. "*He's* all right," said the superintendent. He backed out from under the gallows, and blew out a deep breath. The moody look had gone out of his face quite suddenly. He glanced at his wrist-watch. "Eight minutes past eight. Well, that's all for this morning, thank God."

The warders unfixed bayonets and marched away. The dog, sobered and conscious of having misbehaved itself, slipped after them. We walked out of the gallows yard, past the condemned cells with their waiting prisoners, into the big central yard of the prison. The convicts, under the command of warders armed with lathis, were already receiving their breakfast. They squatted in long rows, each man holding a tin pannikin, while two warders with buckets marched round ladling out rice; it seemed quite a homely, jolly scene, after the hanging. An enormous relief had come upon us now that the job was done. One felt an impulse to sing, to break into a run, to snigger. All at once everyone began chattering gaily.

The Eurasian boy walking beside me nodded towards the way we had come, with a knowing smile: "Do you know, sir, our friend (he meant the dead man) when he heard his appeal had been dismissed, he pissed on the floor of the cell. From fright. Kindly take one of my cigarettes, sir. Do you not admire my new silver case, sir? From the boxwallah, two rupees eight annas. Classy European style."

Several people laughed—at what, nobody seemed certain.

Francis was walking by the superintendent, talking garrulously: "Well, sir, all has passed off with the utmost satisfactoriness. It was all finished—flick! like that. It iss not always so—oah, no! I have known cases where the doctor wass obliged to go beneath the gallows and pull the prissoner's legs to ensure decease. Most disagreeable!"   20

"Wriggling about, eh? That's bad," said the superintendent.

"Ach, sir, it iss worse when they become refractory! One man, I recall, clung to the bars of hiss cage when we went to take him out. You will scarcely credit, sir, that it took six warders to dislodge him, three pulling at each leg. We reasoned with him. 'My dear fellow,' we said, 'think of all the pain and trouble you are causing to us!' But no, he would not listen! Ach, he wass very troublesome!"

I found that I was laughing quite loudly. Everyone was laughing. Even the superintendent grinned in a tolerant way. "You'd better all come out and have a drink," he said quite genially. "I've got a bottle of whisky in the car. We could do with it."

We went through the big double gates of the prison into the road. "Pulling at his legs!" exclaimed a Burmese magistrate suddenly, and burst into a loud chuckling. We all began laughing again. At that moment Francis' anecdote seemed extraordinarily funny. We all had a drink together, native and European alike, quite amicably. The dead man was a hundred yards away.

Questions of Subject and Theme

1. A word count makes it clear that Orwell gives more verbal attention to those who witness the hanging than he does to the man hanged. Make a list of the apparent particular emotions observed in others throughout the piece, and explain how each contributes to the general theme of horror.
2. Where in his account does Orwell separate his own emotional reactions from those of others, and where does he seem to share the same emotions? What sense of Orwell himself comes through for you out of the alternating senses of emotional separation and community?

Questions of Method and Strategy

1. Why does Orwell call the intrusion of the dog "dreadful?" How does he use the dog to create feelings in the reader? How is Orwell's use of the detail of the dog like his use of the detail of the puddle?
2. Do you distinguish the attitudes of Orwell the writer from those of Orwell the man who lived through the events described? If so, describe the difference that the distinction makes for the essay as a whole. If not, show how a unified sensibility makes itself apparent.

HANGINGS I HAVE KNOWN

H. L. Mencken

H. L. Mencken (1880–1956) was called "The Sage of Baltimore," and he made his home in that city all his life. As a critic of ideas, however, he exercised an enormous nationwide influence in the early third of this century. In his attacks on the assumptions of both the mass of ordinary citizens ("the booboisie") and intellectuals ("wizards" and "agents of the Uplift"), Mencken employed a frank and fearless style that made him widely admired and widely despised.

On July 28, 1899, when I was precisely eighteen years, ten months and sixteen days old, I saw my first hanging; more, it was a hanging of the very first chop, for no less than four poor blackamoors were stretched at once. When I was assigned to it as legman for one of the older reporters I naturally suffered certain unpleasant forebodings, but the performance itself did not shake me, though one of the condemned lost his black cap in going through the trap, and the contortions of his face made a dreadful spectacle. The affair was staged in the yard of the city jail, and there was a large gathering of journalists, some of them from other cities, for quadruple hangings, then as now, were fancy goods. I went through the big iron gate at 5 a.m., and found that at least a dozen colleagues had been on watch all night. Some of them had sustained themselves with drafts from a bottle, and were already wobbling. When, after hours of howling by relays of colored evangelists, the four candidates were taken out and hanged, two of these bibbers and six or eight other spectators fell in swoons, and had to be evacuated by the cops. The sheriff of Baltimore was required by law to spring the trap, and he had prepared himself for that office by resorting to a bottle of his own. When it was performed he was assisted out of the jail yard by his deputies, and departed at once for Atlantic City, where he dug in for a week of nightmare.

I saw a good many hangings after that, some in Baltimore and the rest in the counties of Maryland. The county sheriffs always took aboard so much liquor for the occasion that they were virtually helpless: they could, with some help, pull the trap, but they were quite unable to tie the knot, bind the candidate, or carry off the other offices of the occasion. These were commonly delegated to Joe Heine, a gloomy German who had been chief deputy sheriff in Baltimore for many years, and was such a master of all the technics of his post that no political upheaval could touch him. So far as I know, Joe never actually put a man to death in his life, for that was the duty of the sheriff, but he traveled the counties tying knots and making the condemned ready, and there was never a slip when he officiated. I missed the great day of his career, which fell in 1904 or thereabout, for I was becoming bored with hangings by that time, and when a nearby county sheriff invited

1

me to one as his private guest and well-wisher, I gave my ticket to my brother Charlie. This was Charlie's first experience and he saw a swell show indeed, for the candidate, a colored giant, fought Joe and the sheriff on the scaffold, knocked out the county cops who came to their aid, leaped down into the bellowing crowd, broke out of the jail yard, and took to an adjacent forest. It was an hour or more before he was run down and brought back. By that time all the fight had oozed out of him, and Joe and the sheriff turned him off with quiet elegance.

But a reporter chiefly remembers, not such routine themes of his art as hangings, fires and murders, which come along with dispiriting monotony, but the unprecedented novelties that occasionally inspire him, some of them gorgeous and others only odd. Perhaps the most interesting story I covered in my first six months had to do with the purloining of a cadaver from a medical college.

Questions of Subject and Theme

1. By the time he wrote his memoir Mencken was on record as against capital punishment. Can you see any evidence of that stance within his writing here? What seems to be the range of emotions experienced by the young Mencken? What seems to be the older man's attitude toward his younger self?

2. The essay comes from Mencken's experiences as a reporter. How does the theme of "news" as opposed to, say, "human suffering" organize the retelling? How do you imagine Mencken's tone in his news account differed from that of his writing here?

Questions of Method and Strategy

1. Mencken has often been called irreverent in his social attitudes. How is a sense of irreverence created by his style here? How, where, and to what effect, for example, does a theatrical vocabulary interact with an emotional one?

2. How and to what effect does Mencken's account of the behavior of the other witnesses and officials contribute to your sense of Mencken's own experience? What does drinking do for the others? What do they suppose it will do? How does Mencken's own sobriety contribute to our sense of his emotional life and character?

LET'S DO IT

Norman Mailer

Norman Mailer is a novelist who has explored the relations of fact
and fiction in what he calls in the subtitle to one of his books "*History
as the Novel, The Novel as History.*" In *The Executioner's Song* (1979)
Mailer combines techniques from both newspaper reporting and fiction to explore the life and death of Gary Gilmore, a man who fought
the legal system and his friends to ensure his own execution by a Utah
firing squad. The selection below begins as friends and family members
say their last words to Gilmore while he is strapped in the death chair.

Vern had gone first because he was the patriarch, then Bob Moody, but
Schiller had tried to be last. Stanger had thought, "You've got to be kidding,
you're even doing it now," and won the maneuvering. Larry went ahead.
When it came Stanger's turn, he couldn't think of anything to say. Just murmured, "Hang in there. Stick with it." Gary didn't look very tough. Wan,
in fact. His eye showed the effect of all those drugs wearing off. He was
trying to be brave, but just said, "Cool," like it wasn't that easy anymore to
get the words out, and they shook hands. Gary squeezed real hard, and Stanger put his arm around his shoulder, and Gary moved the hand that was
loose in the straps to touch Ron's arm. Stanger kept thinking that Gilmore's
hands were skinnier than you'd think they'd be. And they looked in each
other's eyes, kind of a final embrace.

As soon as Ron returned to his position behind the line, a prison official
came up to ask if he wanted cotton for his ears. Then Ron noticed that
everybody was taking cotton, so he stuffed some into his head, and watched
Sam Smith walk over to the back of the room where a red telephone was on
a chair. Then Sam Smith made a phone call, and walked back and came up
to Gary and started to read a declaration.

Schiller, trying to listen, decided it was some official document. Not the
sort, by the sound of it, that he would listen to normally but, through the
cotton he could hear Sam Smith going blah, blah, blah. All the while, Gary
was not looking at the Warden, but rather, leaning in his chair from side to
side in order to stare around the large body of Sam Smith, practically tipping
the chair over trying to see the faces behind the executioner's blind, catch a
glint of their expression.

Then the Warden said, "Do you have anything you'd like to say?" and
Gary looked up at the ceiling and hesitated, then said, "Let's do it." That
was it. The most pronounced amount of courage, Vern decided, he'd ever
seen, no quaver, no throatiness, right down the line. Gary had looked at
Vern as he spoke.

The way Stanger heard it, it came out like Gary wanted to say something good and dignified and clever, but couldn't think of anything pro-

found. The drugs had left him too dead. Rather than say nothing, he did his best to say it very clear, "Let's do it."

That was about what you'd expect of a man who'd been up for more than twenty-four hours and had taken everything and now was hung over, and coming down, and looking older than Ron had ever seen him. Ah, he was drained out. Ron could see deep lines in his face for the first time. Gilmore looked as white as the day the lawyers first met him after the suicide attempt.

Father Meersman walked up to give the last rites, and Noall Wootton braced himself and took a peep between the shoulders of some of the big men in front of him, and remembered Gary when he had come to the Board of Pardons Hearing, very confident that day, like he was holding all the cards, the ace and everything else you might need. Now, in Wootton's opinion, he didn't have it.

And Schiller, looking at the same man, thought he was resigned in his appearance, but with presence, and what you could call a certain authority.

Father Meersman finished giving Gary Gilmore the last rites. As they came forward with the hood, Gilmore said to him, "Dominus vobiscum." Father Meersman didn't know how to describe his emotion. Gary couldn't have said anything that brought back more of an automatic response. This was the greeting Father Meersman had given to the people again and again over the ten years and twenty and thirty since he had become a priest. "Dominus vobiscum," he would say at Mass and the response would come back, "Et cum spiritu tuo."

So now, when Gilmore said Dominus vobiscum, Father Meersman an-   10
swered like an altar boy, "Et cum spiritu tuo," and as the words came out of his mouth, Gary kind of grinned and said, "There'll always be a Meersman."

"He wants to say," said Father Meersman to himself, "that there will always be a priest present at a time like this."

Three or four men in red coats came up and put the hood on Gilmore's head. Nothing was said after that.

Absolutely nothing said. They put a waist strap on Gilmore, and a head strap, and Father Meersman began to think of how when they were first strapping him in the chair, Gilmore had wanted water and Father Meersman had given him water for the throat that was too dry. Then he had wanted another drink.

Now, the doctor was beside him, pinning a white circle on Gilmore's black shirt, and the doctor stepped back. Father Meersman traced the big sign of the cross, the last act he had to perform. Then, he, too, stepped over the line, and turned around, and looked back at the hooded figure in the chair. The phone began to ring.

Noall Wootton's first reaction was, God, it's just like in the movies, it   15
isn't going to happen. Schiller was taking notes on the checks he'd been careful to remove from the checkbook holder, and he noted that the hood came down loosely like a square carton over Gary's head. Not form fitting in any way. You could not have a sense of his features beneath the sack.

Stanger, listening to the phone, thought, "It is a final confirmation of some kind." Then Sam Smith hung up, and walked back to his place behind the line, and it happened to be next to Schiller. He handed Larry more cotton and they looked into each other's eyes. Then, Schiller didn't know if Sam Smith made a movement with his arm, or didn't, but he felt as if he saw something in the Warden's shoulder move, and Ron and Bob Moody and Cline Campbell heard a countdown begin, and Noall Wootton put his fingers in his ears on top of the cotton, and Gary's body looked calm to Campbell. Cline could not believe the calm he saw in that man. Gilmore was so strong in his desire to die right, that he didn't clench his fist as the count began.

Stanger said to himself, "I hope I don't fall down." He had his hand up to protect his head somehow. Right through the cotton, he heard the sound of heavy breathing and saw the barrels of the rifles projecting from the slits of the blind. He was shocked at how close those muzzles were to the victim. They sure didn't want to miss. Then it all got so quiet your attention was called to it. Right through the cotton, Ron heard these whispers, "One," and "Two," and they never got to say, "Three" before the guns went, "Bam. Bam. Bam." So loud it was terrifying. A muscle contracted from Ron's shoulder down to his lower back. Some entire school of muscles in a spasm.

Schiller heard three shots, expecting four. Gary's body did not jerk nor the chair move, and Schiller waited for the fourth shot and found out later that two must have come out simultaneously. Noall Wootton tried to look at Gary at that point, but couldn't see anything from the rear of the crowd and went out the door before anyone else, and straight to his car which was up by Minimum Security, got in it, drove out. There were reporters interviewing people and photographers, but he didn't stop. He didn't want to talk to anybody.

Questions of Subject and Theme

1. Courage is a theme that implicitly and explicitly pervades the passage, which is taken from a chapter called "The Turkey Shoot." Point to some moments where a sense of courage is conveyed and to some that seem to record a lack of courage.
2. The Latin words *Dominus vobiscum* and *et cum spiritu tuo* mean "the Lord be with you" and "and with your spirit." Finding words to say suitable to the occasion makes an important concern for people in the passage. Find some words that seem to you suitable to the dignity of death and some that do not. Explain the reasons for your choices.

Questions of Method and Strategy

1. In what ways does Mailer compare and contrast the behavior of Gary Gilmore with that of the people who surround him? What effects on his reader does Mailer create by the differences and similarities?

2. Some observers within the passage analyze Gilmore's last words "Let's do it." What else can you find to say about the style and content of these words and the impression they create for you of Gilmore?

Suggestions for Writing on the Juxtapositions

1. Like Orwell, Mencken had a "foreboding" and found his first hanging in part "dreadful." Unlike Orwell, Mencken claims not to have been "shaken." Do you find this contrast to be evidence of toughmindedness or coldheartedness on Mencken's part? Of human sympathy or sentimentality on Orwell's? Write an essay in which you compare and contrast your senses of their emotional lives as created by their writing.
2. Write an essay in which you describe with evidence how Orwell, Mencken, and Mailer use the theme of alcohol or drugs to create effects on their readers.
3. Write an essay in which you imagine a critique by any one of the writers on the writing of any other, Orwell on Mencken's essay, for example.
4. Write an essay comparing and contrasting the ways in which the various authors use techniques more usually associated with fiction in their non-fiction accounts.

6 Mothers

Alice Walker, "In Search of Our Mothers' Gardens"
David James Duncan, "Ma"
Maxine Hong Kingston, "Photographs of My Mother"
Jamaica Kincaid, "Girl"
Carolyn Kizer, from "The Blessing"

Whether through essay, fiction, or poetry, each writer in this section attempts to express his or her feelings about the meaning of motherhood and having a mother. As you read, consider the following questions:

1. All the writers in the section seem proud of something about their mothers. Discuss the ways in which at least two of the writers define their general ideas of motherhood through the pride they take in particular memories.

2. Waiving your approval or disapproval of the woman, which mother is brought most fully to life for you through language? Which least? Discuss the differences using examples.

3. The mothers here represent several different cultural backgrounds. Discuss the ways in which you come to understand the different mothers through the different cultures they inhabit.

4. Carolyn Kizer often uses paradox to express her feeling as a daughter toward her mother and as a mother toward her daughter. Discuss the ways in which the other writers use paradox to express some of the complexities of their relations with their mothers and their mothers' relations with themselves.

5. Fathers are explicitly or implicitly present in each selection. Discuss the ways in which the writers use these fathers to define something of what they feel about their mothers.

IN SEARCH OF OUR MOTHERS' GARDENS

Alice Walker

Alice Walker is the author of the novel *The Color Purple* and has written widely on the work of African-American writers, including Jean Toomer and Zora Neale Hurston, who were among her inspirations and models. Many of Walker's nonfiction writings are collected in *In Search of Our Mothers' Gardens,* which takes its title from the essay reprinted below.

I described her own nature and temperament. Told how they needed a larger life for their expression. . . . I pointed out that in lieu of proper channels, her emotions had overflowed into paths that dissipated them. I talked, beautifully I thought, about an art that would be born, an art that would open the way for women the likes of her. I asked her to hope, and build up an inner life against the coming of that day. . . . I sang, with a strange quiver in my voice, a promise song.

—JEAN TOOMER, "Avey," *Cane*
(The poet speaking to a prostitute who falls asleep while he's talking)

When the poet Jean Toomer walked through the South in the early twenties, he discovered a curious thing: black women whose spirituality was so intense, so deep, so *unconscious* that they were themselves unaware of the richness they held. They stumbled blindly through their lives: creatures so abused and mutilated in body, so dimmed and confused by pain, that they considered themselves unworthy even of hope. In the selfless abstractions their bodies became to the men who used them, they became more than "sexual objects," more even than mere women: they became "Saints." Instead of being perceived as whole persons, their bodies became shrines: what was thought to be their minds became temples suitable for worship. These crazy Saints stared out at the world, wildly, like lunatics—or quietly, like suicides; and the "God" that was in their gaze was as mute as a great stone.

Who were these Saints? These crazy, loony, pitiful women?

Some of them, without a doubt, were our mothers and grandmothers.

In the still heat of the post-Reconstruction South, this is how they seemed to Jean Toomer: exquisite butterflies trapped in an evil honey, toiling away their lives in an era, a century, that did not acknowledge them, except as "the *mule* of the world." They dreamed dreams that no one knew—not even themselves, in any coherent fashion—and saw visions no one could understand. They wandered or sat about the countryside crooning lullabies to ghosts, and drawing the mother of Christ in charcoal on courthouse walls.

They forced their minds to desert their bodies and their striving spirits   *5*
sought to rise, like frail whirlwinds from the hard red clay. And when those
frail whirlwinds fell, in scattered particles, upon the ground, no one mourned.
Instead, men lit candles to celebrate the emptiness that remained, as people
do who enter a beautiful but vacant space to resurrect a God.

Our mothers and grandmothers, some of them: moving to music not
yet written. And they waited.

They waited for a day when the unknown thing that was in them would
be made known; but guessed, somehow in their darkness, that on the day
of their revelation they would be long dead. Therefore to Toomer they
walked, and even ran, in slow motion. For they were going nowhere immediate, and the future was not yet within their grasp. And men took our
mothers and grandmothers, "but got no pleasure from it." So complex was
their passion and their calm.

To Toomer, they lay vacant and fallow as autumn fields, with harvest
time never in sight: and he saw them enter loveless marriages, without joy;
and become prostitutes, without resistance; and become mothers of children, without fulfillment.

For these grandmothers and mothers of ours were not Saints, but Artists; driven to a numb and bleeding madness by the springs of creativity in
them for which there was no release. They were Creators, who lived lives of
spiritual waste, because they were so rich in spirituality—which is the basis
of Art—that the strain of enduring their unused and unwanted talent drove
them insane. Throwing away this spirituality was their pathetic attempt to
lighten the soul to a weight their work-worn, sexually abused bodies
could bear.

What did it mean for a black woman to be an artist in our grandmoth-   *10*
ers' time? In our great-grandmothers' day? It is a question with an answer
cruel enough to stop the blood.

Did you have a genius of a great-great-grandmother who died under
some ignorant and depraved white overseer's lash? Or was she required to
bake biscuits for a lazy backwater tramp, when she cried out in her soul to
paint watercolors of sunsets, or the rain falling on the green and peaceful
pasturelands? Or was her body broken and forced to bear children (who
were more often than not sold away from her)—eight, ten, fifteen, twenty
children—when her one joy was the thought of modeling heroic figures of
rebellion, in stone or clay?

How was the creativity of the black woman kept alive, year after year
and century after century, when for most of the years black people have been
in America, it was a punishable crime for a black person to read or write?
And the freedom to paint, to sculpt, to expand the mind with action did not
exist. Consider, if you can bear to imagine it, what might have been the
result if singing, too, had been forbidden by law. Listen to the voices of
Bessie Smith, Billie Holiday, Nina Simone, Roberta Flack, and Aretha
Franklin, among others, and imagine those voices muzzled for life. Then

you may begin to comprehend the lives of our "crazy," "Sainted" mothers and grandmothers. The agony of the lives of women who might have been Poets, Novelists, Essayists, and Short-Story Writers (over a period of centuries), who died with their real gifts stifled within them.

And, if this were the end of the story, we would have cause to cry out in my paraphrase of Okot p'Bitek's great poem:

> O, my clanswomen
> Let us all cry together!
> Come,
> Let us mourn the death of our mother,
> The death of a Queen
> The ash that was produced
> By a great fire!
> O, this homestead is utterly dead
> Close the gates
> With *lacari* thorns,
> For our mother
> The creator of the Stool is lost!
> And all the young women
> Have perished in the wilderness!

But this is not the end of the story, for all the young women—our mothers and grandmothers, *ourselves*—have not perished in the wilderness. And if we ask ourselves why, and search for and find the answer, we will know beyond all efforts to erase it from our minds, just exactly who, and of what, we black American women are.

One example, perhaps the most pathetic, most misunderstood one, can provide a backdrop for our mothers' work: Phillis Wheatley, a slave in the 1700s.

Virginia Woolf, in her book *A Room of One's Own*, wrote that in order for a woman to write fiction she must have two things, certainly: a room of her own (with key and lock) and enough money to support herself.

What then are we to make of Phillis Wheatley, a slave, who owned not even herself? This sickly, frail black girl who required a servant of her own at times—her health was so precarious—and who, had she been white, would have been easily considered the intellectual superior of all the women and most of the men in the society of her day.

Virginia Woolf wrote further, speaking of course not of our Phillis, that "any woman born with a great gift in the sixteenth century [insert "eighteenth century," insert "black woman," insert "born or made a slave"] would certainly have gone crazed, shot herself, or ended her days in some lonely cottage outside the village, half witch, half wizard [insert "Saint"], feared and mocked at. For it needs little skill and psychology to be sure that a highly gifted girl who had tried to use her gift for poetry would have been so thwarted and hindered by contrary instincts [add "chains, guns, the lash, the ownership of one's body by someone else, submission to an alien religion"], that she must have lost her health and sanity to a certainty."

The key words, as they relate to Phillis, are "contrary instincts." For when we read the poetry of Phillis Wheatley—as when we read the novels of Nella Larsen or the oddly false-sounding autobiography of that freest of all black women writers, Zora Hurston—evidence of "contrary instincts" is everywhere. Her loyalties were completely divided, as was, without question, her mind.

But how could this be otherwise? Captured at seven, a slave of wealthy,   *20* doting whites who instilled in her the "savagery" of the Africa they "rescued" her from . . . one wonders if she was even able to remember her homeland as she had known it, or as it really was.

Yet, because she did try to use her gift for poetry in a world that made her a slave, she was "so thwarted and hindered by . . . contrary instincts, that she . . . lost her health. . . ." In the last years of her brief life, burdened not only with the need to express her gift but also with a penniless, friendless "freedom" and several small children for whom she was forced to do strenuous work to feed, she lost her health, certainly. Suffering from malnutrition and neglect and who knows what mental agonies, Phillis Wheatley died.

So torn by "contrary instincts" was black, kidnapped, enslaved Phillis that her description of the "Goddess"—as she poetically called the Liberty she did not have—is ironically, cruelly humorous. And, in fact, has held Phillis up to ridicule for more than a century. It is usually read prior to hanging Phillis's memory as that of a fool. She wrote:

> The Goddess comes, she moves divinely fair,
> Olive and laurel binds her *golden* hair.
> Wherever shines this native of the skies,
> Unnumber'd charms and recent graces rise. [My italics]

It is obvious that Phillis, the slave, combed the "Goddess's" hair every morning; prior, perhaps, to bringing in the milk, or fixing her mistress's lunch. She took her imagery from the one thing she saw elevated above all others.

With the benefit of hindsight we ask, "How could she?"

But at last, Phillis, we understand. No more snickering when your stiff,   *25* struggling, ambivalent lines are forced on us. We know now that you were not an idiot or a traitor; only a sickly little black girl, snatched from your home and country and made a slave; a woman who still struggled to sing the song that was your gift, although in a land of barbarians who praised you for your bewildered tongue. It is not so much what you sang, as that you kept alive, in so many of our ancestors, *the notion of song.*

Black women are called, in the folklore that so aptly identifies one's status in society, "the *mule* of the world," because we have been handed the burdens that everyone else—*everyone* else—refused to carry. We have also been called "Matriarchs," "Superwomen," and "Mean and Evil Bitches." Not to mention "Castraters" and "Sapphire's Mama." When we have pleaded for understanding, our character has been distorted; when we have asked for simple caring, we have been handed empty inspirational appellations, then stuck in the farthest corner. When we have asked for love, we have been given children. In short, even our plainer gifts, our labors of fidelity and love, have been knocked down our throats. To be an artist and a black woman, even today, lowers our status in many respects, rather than raises it: and yet, artists we will be.

Therefore we must fearlessly pull out of ourselves and look at and identify with our lives the living creativity some of our great-grandmothers were not allowed to know. I stress *some* of them because it is well known that the majority of our great-grandmothers, knew, even without "knowing" it, the reality of their spirituality, even if they didn't recognize it beyond what happened in the singing at church—and they never had any intention of giving it up.

How they did it—those millions of black women who were not Phillis Wheatley, or Lucy Terry or Frances Harper or Zora Hurston or Nella Larsen or Bessie Smith; or Elizabeth Catlett, or Katherine Dunham, either—brings me to the title of this essay, "In Search of Our Mothers' Gardens," which is a personal account that is yet shared, in its theme and its meaning, by all of us. I found, while thinking about the far-reaching world of the creative black woman, that often the truest answer to a question that really matters can be found very close.

In the late 1920s my mother ran away from home to marry my father. Marriage, if not running away, was expected of seventeen-year-old girls. By the time she was twenty, she had two children and was pregnant with a third. Five children later, I was born. And this is how I came to know my mother: she seemed a large, soft, loving-eyed woman who was rarely impatient in our home. Her quick, violent temper was on view only a few times a year, when she battled with the white landlord who had the misfortune to suggest to her that her children did not need to go to school.

She made all the clothes we wore, even my brothers' overalls. She made   *30* all the towels and sheets we used. She spent the summers canning vegetables and fruits. She spent the winter evenings making quilts enough to cover all our beds.

During the "working" day, she labored beside—not behind—my father in the fields. Her day began before sunup, and did not end until late at night. There was never a moment for her to sit down, undisturbed, to unravel her own private thoughts; never a time free from interruption—by work or the noisy inquiries of her many children. And yet, it is to my mother—and all our mothers who were not famous—that I went in search of the secret of what has fed that muzzled and often mutilated, but vibrant, creative spirit that the black woman has inherited, and that pops out in wild and unlikely places to this day.

But when, you will ask, did my overworked mother have time to know or care about feeding the creative spirit?

The answer is so simple that many of us have spent years discovering it. We have constantly looked high, when we should have looked high—and low.

For example: in the Smithsonian Institution in Washington, D.C., there hangs a quilt unlike any other in the world. In fanciful, inspired, and yet simple and identifiable figures, it portrays the story of the Crucifixion. It is considered rare, beyond price. Though it follows no known pattern of quilt-making, and though it is made of bits and pieces of worthless rags, it is obviously the work of a person of powerful imagination and deep spiritual feeling. Below this quilt I saw a note that says it was made by "an anonymous Black woman in Alabama, a hundred years ago."

If we could locate this "anonymous" black woman from Alabama, she   *35* would turn out to be one of our grandmothers—an artist who left her mark in the only materials she could afford, and in the only medium her position in society allowed her to use.

As Virginia Woolf wrote further, in *A Room of One's Own:*

> Yet genius of a sort must have existed among women as it must have existed among the working class. [Change this to "slaves" and "the wives and daughters of sharecroppers."] Now and again an Emily Brontë or a Robert Burns [change this to "a Zora Hurston or a Richard Wright"] blazes out and proves its presence. But certainly it never got itself on to paper. When, however, one reads of a witch being ducked, of a woman possessed by devils [or "Sainthood"], of a wise woman selling herbs [our root workers], or even a very remarkable man who had a mother, then I think we are on the track of a lost novelist, a suppressed poet, of some mute and inglorious Jane Austen. . . . Indeed, I would venture to guess that Anon, who wrote so many poems without signing them, was often a woman. . . .

And so our mothers and grandmothers have, more often than not anonymously, handed on the creative spark, the seed of the flower they themselves never hoped to see: or like a sealed letter they could not plainly read.

And so it is, certainly, with my own mother. Unlike "Ma" Rainey's songs, which retained their creator's name even while blasting forth from Bessie Smith's mouth, no song or poem will bear my mother's name. Yet so many of the stories that I write, that we all write, are my mother's stories. Only recently did I fully realize this: that through years of listening to my mother's stories of her life, I have absorbed not only the stories themselves, but something of the manner in which she spoke, something of the urgency that involves the knowledge that her stories—like her life—must be recorded. It is probably for this reason that so much of what I have written is about characters whose counterparts in real life are so much older than I am.

But the telling of these stories, which came from my mother's lips as naturally as breathing, was not the only way my mother showed herself as an artist. For stories, too, were subject to being distracted, to dying without conclusion. Dinners must be started, and cotton must be gathered before the big rains. The artist that was and is my mother showed itself to me only after many years. This is what I finally noticed:

Like Mem, a character in *The Third Life of Grange Copeland,* my mother   40
adorned with flowers whatever shabby house we were forced to live in. And not just your typical straggly country stand of zinnias, either. She planted ambitious gardens—and still does—with over fifty different varieties of plants that bloom profusely from early March until late November. Before she left home for the fields, she watered her flowers, chopped up the grass, and laid out new beds. When she returned from the fields she might divide clumps of bulbs, dig a cold pit, uproot and replant roses, or prune branches from her taller bushes or trees—until night came and it was too dark to see.

Whatever she planted grew as if by magic, and her fame as a grower of flowers spread over three counties. Because of her creativity with her flowers, even my memories of poverty are seen through a screen of blooms—sunflowers, petunias, roses, dahlias, forsythia, spirea, delphiniums, verbena . . . and on and on.

And I remember people coming to my mother's yard to be given cuttings from her flowers; I hear again the praise showered on her because whatever rocky soil she landed on, she turned into a garden. A garden so brilliant with colors, so original in its design, so magnificent with life and creativity, that to this day people drive by our house in Georgia—perfect strangers and imperfect strangers—and ask to stand or walk among my mother's art.

I notice that it is only when my mother is working in her flowers that she is radiant, almost to the point of being invisible—except as Creator: hand and eye. She is involved in work her soul must have. Ordering the universe in the image of her personal conception of Beauty.

Her face, as she prepares the Art that is her gift, is a legacy of respect she leaves to me, for all that illuminates and cherishes life. She has handed down respect for the possibilities—and the will to grasp them.

For her, so hindered and intruded upon in so many ways, being an artist   45
has still been a daily part of her life. This ability to hold on, even in very simple ways, is work black women have done for a very long time.

This poem is not enough, but it is something, for the woman who literally covered the holes in our walls with sunflowers:

> They were women then
> My mama's generation
> Husky of voice—Stout of
> Step
> With fists as well as
> Hands
> How they battered down
> Doors

And ironed
Starched white
Shirts
How they led
Armies
Headragged Generals
Across mined
Fields
Booby-trapped
Kitchens
To discover books
Desks
A place for us
How they knew what we
Must know
Without knowing a page
Of it
Themselves.

Guided by my heritage of a love of beauty and a respect for strength—in search of my mother's garden, I found my own.

And perhaps in Africa over two hundred years ago, there was just such a mother; perhaps she painted vivid and daring decorations in oranges and yellows and greens on the walls of her hut; perhaps she sang—in a voice like Roberta Flack's—*sweetly* over the compounds of her village; perhaps she wove the most stunning mats or told the most ingenious stories of all the village story-tellers. Perhaps she was herself a poet—though only her daughter's name is signed to the poems that we know.

Perhaps Phillis Wheatley's mother was also an artist.

Perhaps in more than Phillis Wheatley's biological life is her mother's signature made clear.   *50*

Questions of Subject and Theme

1. What answers does Walker find for her two basic questions: What did it mean for a black woman to be an artist in our grandmothers' day, and what does it mean to be an artist and a black woman today?
2. What are some of the many senses of "motherhood" that Walker explores in the essay? For example, how are Phillis Wheatley and her biological mother both "mothers" to her?

Questions of Method and Strategy

1. How does Walker invite her readers to revise stereotyped views of Phillis Wheatley? What are some of the methods and strategies she employs?
2. In what ways does Walker show how she has been inspired as an artist by women of the past?

MA

David James Duncan

David James Duncan wrote *The River Why* (1983) as a fictionalized autobiography of a boy who grew up so crazy about fishing that his mother knew he would never miss the TV fishing show, *Gaddabout Gaddis*. As the passage below suggests, that knowledge and the power it provided her are only two of the things that distinguished her from his father, whom the boy sneeringly calls "H2O."

I remember an adventure which shows a lot about the way Ma "got me brung up." Bill Bob wasn't born yet, but he had her stomach bulging. I was ten. It was December. And because Ma forced me to it I was engaged in the despicable business of selling Christmas cards door to door—her equivalent to teaching a coyote pup to forage for rodents. . . . I felt like a damned Witless. But if I sold 48 boxes I could get a little fiberglass canoe, so I dutifully beat the streets. I ended up selling twelve boxes, the last four of them to Ma. The reason Ma bought the last four was what happened on the last day of my sales career.

We lived in a posh Portland suburb, which was H2O's doing; for him, flyfishing was a business, and like most businesses it depended upon a city for its health. But though he picked the home-place, Ma ruled it, and as long as Ma lives, there will be a tinge of juniper, sage, dust and fresh blood in the air of the Orviston home. A few houses down and across the street from us was a space-age domicile, painted black, with lots of skylights and remote-control doors and gadgets, owned by a surgeon. The surgeon also owned a black speedboat, a black Oldsmobile and a black Doberman pinscher. This Doberman was a notorious mauler of children. It lived in the surgeon's backyard, which was surrounded by a cyclone fence, painted black. The creature was usually satisfied to roar and slaver at people passing on the street, but now and again it would get unusually excited by a solitary passing child, hop the five-foot fence as easily as a hurdler might a milkbox, perforate the unfortunate's arms, legs or face, hop back into its backyard, and wag its repulsive little circumsized tail at the surgeon when an irate parent came with a complaint and a medical bill. Of course these wounds were petty compared to the great slashes and slits the surgeon inflicted upon humanity daily, so he would calmly point to the five-foot fence, tell the parent how much it cost him and how unjumpable it was, refer to the great numbers of black Doberman pinschers roaming our suburbs, and send them home smiling and promising to come to him next time they needed a vital organ pruned or transplanted. Meanwhile the Doberman continued to ape its master with its own surgical methods, protected by the surgeon's suavity, the worthless fence, the timidity of suburbanites, and the fact that it had

1

done one thing right throughout its life: it had never crossed paths with Ma
Orviston's boy—
until the day I sold my last box of Christmas cards.

I was pedalling home fast, trying to make it in time to watch a "Gadabout Gaddis Show" about steelheading in British Columbia, and it wasn't
until I was right in front of the surgeon's black lair that I remembered why
I'd never bicycled down that side of the street before. . . . I peeked toward
the backyard: the Doberman hung high above the fence, its insane eyes riv-
etted to my ten-year-old flesh. When its feet struck earth it let out a Bas-
kerville howl that turned my brains to cottage cheese. Blind and sick with
panic, I set my crummy bike pedals shirring like an egg beater, hoping like
any terrified young coyote to make it home to the protection of my ferocious mother. I swerved into the street and wove between two cars, hoping
they'd mash my pursuer, but at the sight of me they slammed on their brakes
and the monster shot between them unscathed. I plowed straight into the
curb, caving in my front rim, but clung somehow to the lurching bike,
crossing our yard now and screaming "MAAA! MAAA!" Then the Doberman sprang, hit my shoulder and sent me sprawling like a gunned jackrabbit.
I curled instinctively into a ball, waiting for the beast to gut me, so drunk
with horror I thought I only imagined the explosion in my ears. But when
the attack never came I uncurled just enough to see what delayed it. The
Doberman lay quivering and jerking on the lawn a few feet away, its eyes
rolled back, its tongue lolling out and turning gray, a hole in its chest the
size of a cantaloupe. I squinted toward the house. There stood Ma, twelve-
gauge still smoking and the wildest green-eyed grin I'd ever see on her face.
She said,

"Got'm."

Anyone would have tended to agree. She sauntered over and warned,   *5*
"Plug yer ears." I plugged. She discharged the second barrel into the
dog's head.

I started to bawl, then threw up.

Ma stood me up, cleaned me off, hugged me, then—seeing my knees
were mush—slung me over her shoulder like a big bag of dog chow and
headed for the house. Jouncing along in the air I looked back at the scene
of the showdown: in the street the cars I'd slipped between had been joined
by a dozen others, and twenty or more wall-eyed Burbites stood gaping
across H2O's manicured lawn where the Doberman still twitched amid
spattered brain, four strewn boxes of gore-flecked Christmas cards twittered
jolly Xmases to the wind, and Ma strode easily away, a hundred pounds of
guns and sons on her shoulders and in her belly.

While I watched Gadabout catch Canadian steelhead Ma threw the
dead Doberman in her pickup, covered it with leaves, drove the landfill and
dumped it, picked up a bike rim at the repair shop, started for home, but
was interrupted by a brainstorm: she turned around, drove to the dogpound,
searched the kennels and came out with a ratlike mongrel of the Mexican
hairless/Chihuahua clan—eight inches tall, colored black. She took this

snivelling creature to the poodle parlour, had its tail circumsized and its ears clipped Doberman style. Then she deposited it in the surgeon's backyard.

When the black Oldsmobile hove into sight that night some neighbors who'd witnessed the afternoon's gunplay concealed themselves in upstairs windows overlooking the infamous backyard. According to their reports, the surgeon entered his house bearing two brown bags of groceries, turned on the kitchen light and began to put the groceries away; in one of the bags were two smaller bags, each containing a fifth of Bombay gin; in the other bag was an old newspaper wrapped around what proved to be an enormous bone covered with shreds of raw, bloody meat. The surgeon threw the bone onto the flood-lit back patio but didn't wait to see his dog snatch it, knowing he might be out munching children. The neighbors peered hard at this bone, hoping it came from the butcher's, not from the surgeon's place of employment.

After pouring himself a cocktail which he downed at two gulps, the surgeon poured himself a second which he downed at three gulps, followed closely by a third which he downed at four gulps. One of the neighbors computed that at this rate the surgeon would require seventeen gulps to down his sixteenth cocktail; we needn't argue with her mathematics, but must point out that one-seventeenth of a cocktail is scarcely a sip, let alone a gulp. Another neighbor conjectured that what the poor surgeon needed instead of a slough of cocktails was somebody to keep him company; this neighbor was a single woman in her late thirties who didn't yet realize that Ma had provided for this lack. 10

During his fourth cocktail the surgeon glanced at the patio to see what his black Doberman thought of the dubious bone. When he perceived the bone wandering across the shadowy lawn toward the shrubs—apparently of its own accord—he threw a suspicious look at the cocktail, took a careful sip, shook his head and stepped outside to investigate. Closer examination revealed the bone's deviant migration to be effected by a Doberman rat—a fantastic yet unmistakable little creature he had not known to exist. Full of wonder (and gin), he dropped to his hands and knees and began crawling toward it. The Doberman rat let him get within arm's length, then began to emit a soft, whirring sound something like a dentist's drill. This was its growl. This was also a signal. It meant that the rat had staked claim to the bone. It meant, "Back off, Jack." But being accustomed to his late Doberman's vastly more blatant signals, the surgeon extended a foolhardy finger, intending to validate the dear little thing's existence with a few gentle strokes. That finger promptly received four perforations that looked like this: • •
    • •

Hearing the surgeon cry out, the neighbors felt uniform fear for the little rat's safety—but the neighbors had forgotten two things: one was the four cocktails, the other was the surgeon's profession. Instead of growing angry he examine the wounds with expertise, awed by their perfect symmetry and the precision with which they'd been inflicted; his full-sized Doberman had certainly been incapable of any such performance. He finished his cocktail, sucked his finger, watched the Doberman rat chew, listened to it whir, and a lasting friendship was formed. He never inquired after the whereabouts of his child-mauler, and when he was forced by a malpractice scandal to change cities some years later, he took the Doberman rat with him.

Ma's account of how she happened to be in the yard with her shotgun at the very moment the Doberman attacked was quite simple: she reasoned that since Gadabout Gaddis's show had started I'd be hurrying, that in my hurry I might forget the Doberman, that hurrying children were its favorite prey, and that the world would be a better place without the Doberman; so she jumped up from the TV, grabbed the shotgun (it's always loaded), heard the tires and me shrieking as she rounded the house, took aim and squeezed the trigger. Given her martial skills, the rest was a foregone conclusion. Yet the fact that she could instantaneously assimilate and act upon these details implies a high degree of intelligence—an intelligence utterly belied by such deeds as her flunking out of high school, her inane piscatorial wrangling with H2O, and her inability to perceive that the wholesale slaughter of fish in the present must have some effect on the angling of the future. I think "native intelligence" is the best name for the type Ma possesses.

Questions of Subject and Theme

1. In a few words or short phrases, characterize the kind of woman the author thinks exemplified by his mother in the anecdote. What does his story also express about "the way Ma 'got me brung up'"?
2. In a few words or short phrases, characterize the kind of man the author thinks exemplified by the surgeon in the anecdote. How do the values and assumptions of the surgeon contrast with the values and assumptions by which the author was "brung up"?

Questions of Method and Strategy

1. In what ways do the "tinge of juniper, sage, dust and fresh blood" associated in the second paragraph with the author's home contrast with the description of the surgeon's home? In what other ways does the author invite us to imagine differences in lives by differences in associated physical details?
2. Toward the end of the second paragraph the Doberman is said to "ape" its owner. In what ways does the rest of the story confirm or contradict this remark?

PHOTOGRAPHS OF MY MOTHER

Maxine Hong Kingston

Maxine Hong Kingston won the National Book Critics' Circle award for nonfiction in 1976 for her autobiography *The Woman Warrior: Memoirs of a Childhood among Ghosts* from which the following excerpt is selected. Kingston's concern for her cultural heritage and the gains and losses in cultural identity associated with being a Chinese-American are partly represented in her description of mementos of the vanished times and places that defined her parents' lives.

Once in a long while, four times so far for me, my mother brings out *1* the metal tube that holds her medical diploma. On the tube are gold circles crossed with seven red lines each—"joy" ideographs in abstract. There are also little flowers that look like gears for a gold machine. According to the scraps of labels with Chinese and American addresses, stamps, and postmarks, the family airmailed the can from Hong Kong in 1950. It got crushed in the middle, and whoever tried to peel the labels off stopped because the red and gold paint came off too, leaving silver scratches that rust. Somebody tried to pry the end off before discovering that the tube pulls apart. When I open it, the smell of China flies out, a thousand-year-old bat flying heavy-headed out of the Chinese caverns where bats are as white as dust, a smell that comes from long ago, far back in the brain. Crates from Canton, Hong Kong, Singapore, and Taiwan have that smell too, only stronger because they are more recently come from the Chinese.

Inside the can are three scrolls, one inside another. The largest says that in the twenty-third year of the National Republic, the To Keung School of Midwifery, where she has had two years of instruction and Hospital Practice, awards its Diploma to my mother, who has shown through oral and written examination her Proficiency in Midwifery, Pediatrics, Gynecology, "Medecine," "Surgary," Therapeutics, Ophthalmology, Bacteriology, Dermatology, Nursing and Bandage. This document has eight stamps on it: one, the school's English and Chinese names embossed together in a circle; one, as the Chinese enumerate, a stork and a big baby in lavender ink; one, the school's Chinese seal; one, an orangish paper stamp pasted in the border design; one, the red seal of Dr. Wu Pak-liang, M.D., Lyon, Berlin, president and "Ex-assistant étranger à la clinique chirugicale et d'accouchement de l'université de Lyon"; one, the red seal of Dean Woo Yin-kam, M.D.; one, my mother's seal, her chop mark larger than the president's and the dean's; and one, the number 1279 on the back. Dean Woo's signature is followed by "(Hackett)." I read in a history book that Hackett Medical College for Women at Canton was founded in the nineteenth century by European women doctors.

The school seal has been pressed over a photograph of my mother at the age of thirty-seven. The diploma gives her age as twenty-seven. She looks younger than I do, her eyebrows are thicker, her lips fuller. Her naturally curly hair is parted on the left, one wavy wisp tendrilling off to the right. She wears a scholar's white gown, and she is not thinking about her appearance. She stares straight ahead as if she could see me and past me to her grandchildren and grandchildren's grandchildren. She has spacy eyes, as all people recently from Asia have. Her eyes do not focus on the camera. My mother is not smiling; Chinese do not smile for photographs. Their faces command relatives in foreign lands—"Send money"—and posterity forever—"Put food in front of this picture." My mother does not understand Chinese-American snapshots. "What are you laughing at?" she asks.

The second scroll is a long narrow photograph of the graduating class with the school officials seated in front. I picked out my mother immediately. Her face is exactly her own, though forty years younger. She is so familiar, I can only tell whether or not she is pretty or happy or smart by comparing her to the other women. For this formal group picture she straightened her hair with oil to make a chinlength bob like the others'. On the other women, strangers, I can recognize a curled lip, a sidelong glance, pinched shoulders. My mother is not soft; the girl with the small nose and dimpled underlip is soft. My mother is not humorous, not like the girl at the end who lifts her mocking chin to pose like Girl Graduate. My mother does not have smiling eyes; the old woman teacher (Dean Woo?) in front crinkles happily, and the one faculty member in the western suit smiles westernly. Most of the graduates are girls whose faces have not yet formed; my mother's face will not change anymore, except to age. She is intelligent, alert, pretty. I can't tell if she's happy.

The graduates seem to have been looking elsewhere when they pinned   5
the rose, zinnia, or chrysanthemum on their precise black dresses. One thin girl wears hers in the middle of her chest. A few have a flower over a left or right nipple. My mother put hers, a chrysanthemum, below her left breast. Chinese dresses at that time were dartless, cut as if women did not have breasts; these young doctors, unaccustomed to decorations, may have seen their chests as black expanses with no reference points for flowers. Perhaps they couldn't shorten that far gaze that lasts only a few years after a Chinese emigrates. In this picture too my mother's eyes are big with what they held—reaches of oceans beyond China, land beyond oceans. Most emigrants learn the barbarians' directness—how to gather themselves and stare rudely into talking faces as if trying to catch lies. In America my mother has eyes as strong as boulders, never once skittering off a face, but she has not learned to place decorations and phonograph needles, nor has she stopped seeing land on the other side of the oceans. Now her eyes include the relatives in China, as they once included my father smiling and smiling in his many western outfits, a different one for each photograph that he sent from America.

He and his friends took pictures of one another in bathing suits at

Coney Island beach, the salt wind from the Atlantic blowing their hair. He's the one in the middle with his arms about the necks of his buddies. They pose in the cockpit of a biplane, on a motorcycle, and on a lawn beside the "Keep Off the Grass" sign. They are always laughing. My father, white shirt sleeves rolled up, smiles in front of a wall of clean laundry. In the spring he wears a new straw hat, cocked at a Fred Astaire angle. He steps out, dancing down the stairs, one foot forward, one back, a hand in his pocket. He wrote to her about the American custom of stomping on straw hats come fall. "If you want to save your hat for next year," he said, "you have to put it away early, or else when you're riding the subway or walking along Fifth Avenue, any stranger can snatch it off your head and put his foot through it. That's the way they celebrate the change of seasons here." In the winter he wears a gray felt hat with his gray overcoat. He is sitting on a rock in Central Park. In one snapshot he is not smiling; someone took it when he was studying, blurred in the glare of the desk lamp.

There are no snapshots of my mother. In two small portraits, however, there is a black thumbprint on her forehead, as if someone had inked in bangs, as if someone had marked her.

"Mother, did bangs come into fashion after you had the picture taken?" One time she said yes. Another time when I asked, "Why do you have fingerprints on your forehead?" she said, "Your First Uncle did that." I disliked the unsureness in her voice.

The last scroll has columns of Chinese words. The only English is "Department of Health, Canton," imprinted on my mother's face, the same photograph as on the diploma. I keep looking to see whether she was afraid. Year after year my father did not come home or send for her. Their two children had been dead for ten years. If he did not return soon, there would be no more children. ("They were three and two years old, a boy and a girl. They could talk already.") My father did send money regularly, though, and she had nobody to spend it on but herself. She bought good clothes and shoes. Then she decided to use the money for becoming a doctor. She did not leave for Canton immediately after the children died. In China there was time to complete feelings. As my father had done, my mother left the village by ship. There was a sea bird painted on the ship to protect it against shipwreck and winds. She was in luck. The following ship was boarded by river pirates, who kidnapped every passenger, even old ladies. "Sixty dollars for an old lady" was what the bandits used to say. "I sailed alone," she says, "to the capital of the entire province." She took a brown leather suitcase and a seabag stuffed with two quilts.

Questions of Subject and Theme

1. What view of her mother's character and personality is expressed in Kingston's description of the diplomas in the second paragraph? In your opinion, does her description of the photograph in the following paragraph confirm and expand that view, or does it provide an alternative sense of her mother? Explain your answer with examples.

2. What does Kingston's father's photograph express about his life for Kingston? What contrasts between the lives of mother and father are implied?

Questions of Method and Strategy

1. Kingston discusses the diplomas before discussing the photograph of her mother and her mother's life before her father's life. Imagine differing orders that produce a different effect through structure, and explain what different experiences could be created for the reader.

2. Kingston speaks of the differences in how the eyes appear in photographs of Chinese in Asia and Chinese in America. With what "eyes," from what point of view, does Kingston describe her parents? Is her style analogous to the Chinese or Chinese-American pose, smiling, direct, "trying to catch lies," and so on? Explain your answer with examples.

GIRL

Jamaica Kincaid

Jamaica Kincaid was born and educated in St. Johns, Antigua, in the West Indies. An only child, she recalls that her family doted on her. Kincaid's brief unconventional stories focused on intense emotions are exemplified in "Girl," written in 1984.

Wash the white clothes on Monday and put them on the stone heap; wash the color clothes on Tuesday and put them on the clothesline to dry; don't walk barehead in the hot sun; cook pumpkin fritters in very hot sweet oil; soak your little cloths right after you take them off; when buying cotton to make yourself a nice blouse, be sure that it doesn't have gum on it, because that way it won't hold up well after a wash; soak salt fish overnight before you cook it; is it true that you sing benna in Sunday school?; always eat your food in such a way that it won't turn someone else's stomach; on Sundays try to walk like a lady and not like the slut you are so bent on becoming; don't sing benna in Sunday school; you mustn't speak to wharf-rat boys, not even to give directions; don't eat fruits on the street—flies will follow you; *but I don't sing benna on Sundays at all never in Sunday school;* this is how to sew on a button; this is how to make a button-hole for the button you have just sewed on; this is how to hem a dress when you see the hem coming down and so to prevent yourself from looking like the slut I know you are so bent on becoming; this is how you iron your father's khaki shirt so that it doesn't have a crease; this is how you iron your father's khaki pants so that they don't have a crease; this is how you grow okra—far from the house, because okra tree harbors red ants; when you are growing dasheen, make sure it gets plenty of water or else it makes your throat itch when you are eating it; this is how you sweep a corner; this is how you sweep a whole house; this is how you sweep a yard; this is how you smile to someone you don't like too much; this is how you smile to someone you don't like at all; this is how you smile to someone you like completely; this is how you set a table for tea; this is how you set a table for dinner; this is how you set a table for dinner with an important guest; this is how you set a table for lunch; this is how you set a table for breakfast; this is how to behave in the presence of men who don't know you very well, and this way they won't recognize immediately the slut I have warned you against becoming; be sure to wash every day, even if it is with your own spit; don't squat down to play marbles—you are not a boy, you know; don't pick people's flowers—you might catch something; don't throw stones at blackbirds, because it might not be a blackbird at all; this is how to make a bread pudding; this is how to make doukona; this is how to make pepper pot; this is how to make a good medicine for a cold; this is how to make a good medicine to throw away a child before it even becomes a child; this is how to catch a fish; this is how to throw back a fish you don't like, and that way something bad won't fall on you; this is how to bully a man; this is how a man bullies you; this is how to love a man, and if this doesn't work there are other ways, and if they don't work don't feel too bad about giving up; this is how to spit up in the air if you feel like it, and this is how to move quick so that it doesn't fall on you; this is how to make ends meet; always squeeze bread to make sure it's fresh; *but what if the baker won't let me feel the bread?;* you mean to say that after all you are really going to be the kind of woman who the baker won't let near the bread?

Questions of Subject and Theme

1. Elsewhere Kincaid recalls her family doting on her. In what sense might the voice of the mother in the story be said to dote on the girl spoken to? In what sense might other emotions be expressed? Explain your answers with examples.
2. From your sense of the story, how would you characterize what the mother means by (a) "the kind of woman who the baker won't let near the bread" and (b) the kind of woman he would?

Questions of Method and Strategy

1. In what ways are the pieces of advice related to one another? For example, two early directions have to do with "soaking," and "Sunday" connects a few others. How are some of the succeeding directions disjointed? In general, what effects on the reader do you think Kincaid creates by her methods of organization? For example, does she give you the impression of an overheard conversation on a given day?
2. The story ends with questions after so many imperative and declarative sentences. How else does the language that ends the story differ? How have earlier uses of language prepared the reader for the end?

FROM *THE BLESSING*

Carolyn Kizer

Carolyn Kizer began as a student of comparative literature specializing in Chinese and has published translations of poems from that language. She is the founder of *Poetry Northwest* and has published her own poetry in books that display her interests in free verse, more formal patterns, and combinations of the two.

I

Daughter-my-mother, *1*
you have observed my worst.
Holding me together at your expense
has made you burn cool.

So did I in childhood: *5*
nursed her old hurts and doubts,
myself made cool to shallowness.
She grew out as I grew in.
At mid-point our furies met.

My mother's dust has rested *10*
for fifteen years
in the front hall closet
because we couldn't bear to bury it.
Her dust-lined, dust-coated urn
squats among the size-eleven overshoes. *15*
My father, who never forgets
his overshoes,
has forgotten that.

Hysterical-tongued daughter
of a dead marriage, *20*
you shed hot tears in the bed
of that benign old woman
whose fierce joy you were:
tantrums in the closet
taking upon yourself the guilt *25*
the split parents never felt.

Child and old woman
soothing each other,
sharing the same face

in a span of seventy years
the same mother wit.   *30*

Questions of Subject and Theme

1. What is the meaning of Kizer's first line in the context of the poem as a whole? Who is she addressing in the line? When and how do you come to understand the line?
2. To what does *that* refer to at the end of line 18? Explain in your own words as fully as you can.

Questions of Method and Strategy

1. How would you describe the phrase "burn cool" at the end of line 4? Where does Kizer use the same or a similar technique elsewhere? How is this technique *like* the meaning of the poem?
2. The phrase "mother wit" at the end of the poem seems to have more than one meaning. What are its meanings for you? Who in the poem is said to possess the quality? Does Kizer's own voice possess it for you? Explain with examples why or why not.

Suggestions for Writing on the Juxtapositions

1. Walker implies that many women have been "mothers" to her. Do you think she would have included any of the other women described in this section, had she known them? Write an essay that explains your answer.
2. Like Robert Carver in the earlier section on fathers, Maxine Hong Kingston uses a photograph as a way of describing her parent and her attitudes toward that parent. Write an essay in which you compare and contrast the ways in which each writer analyzes photographic images.
3. Write a poem or a prose memoir that expresses something of your own relations with your mother. You may find it useful to focus on an event, a place, or a photograph to compose your thoughts and your writing.
4. Which writer moved your emotions most strongly? Write an essay in which you explain by analyzing examples what it is about the writing that moved you.
5. Motherhood is conventionally associated with ideas of tenderness. Write an essay in which you describe some of the ways the writers in the section confirm, qualify, or amplify this general expectation.

7 Fact and Fiction: Two Accounts of One Disaster

Stephen Crane, "News Account of the Disaster"
Stephen Crane, "The Open Boat"

While working as a reporter at the turn of the century, the novelist and short story writer Stephen Crane was shipwrecked. While the news account and the story that resulted differ in focus and technique, the sense of Crane as a writer is illuminated in each case. As you read, consider the following questions:

1. How is the sense of time passing, slowing down, and speeding up created by Crane's uses of language in each treatment of the disaster? Do you find any difference in the techniques of time that seems required by the genres of fiction or nonfiction? That seems better suited to either genre? Discuss these issues using particular examples.

2. Crane has comic moments in each of his treatments of the tragedy. Given the serious nature of the primary events in each case, do they seem out of place to you or in poor taste? Attack or defend Crane's use of comedy.

3. Great courage and willpower are shown in each account. How are courage and human will shown to be valuable in the news report? How does Crane indicate their praiseworthy nature? How much do courage and human will matter in the short story? Discuss particular examples from both versions.

4. What if anything about Crane's writing varies between the modes of fiction and nonfiction? Can you find examples of narrative performance in one version that could not be used in the other? Why do you imagine each piece focuses on a different aspect of the disaster? In other words, is there anything about the writing as writing that identifies it for you as fiction or nonfiction? Discuss the issues involved using particular examples.

NEWS ACCOUNT OF THE DISASTER

Stephen Crane

Stephen Crane had never seen a battle before he wrote, in 1895, *The Red Badge of Courage,* a novel about the Civil War, but the enormous success of that book led him to a career as a war correspondent. By 1897 the Cuban revolt against Spain enlisted the American sympathy that was to culminate in the Spanish-American War a few years later. Sympathizers called "filibusters" first smuggled and then openly sent arms to the insurgents. Stephen Crane went as a reporter to cover one such voyage. He wrote about the ensuing shipwreck twice, once in a newspaper account and once in a short story. The differences and similarities of focus and technique illuminate the limits and possibilities of both fiction and nonfiction.

JACKSONVILLE, FLA., Jan. 6.—It was the afternoon of New Year's. The   *1*
Commodore lay at her dock in Jacksonville and negro stevedores processioned steadily toward her with box after box of ammunition and bundle after bundle of rifles. Her hatch, like the mouth of a monster, engulfed them. It might have been the feeding time of some legendary creature of the sea. It was in broad daylight and the crowd of gleeful Cubans on the pier did not forbear to sing the strange patriotic ballads of their island.

Everything was perfectly open. The Commodore was cleared with a cargo of arms and munition for Cuba. There was none of that extreme modesty about the proceeding which had marked previous departures of the famous tug. She loaded up as placidly as if she were going to carry oranges to New York, instead of Remingtons to Cuba. Down the river, furthermore, the revenue cutter Boutwell, the old isosceles triangle that protects United States interests in the St. John's, lay at anchor, with no sign of excitement aboard her.

Exchanging Farewells

On the decks of the Commodore there were exchanges of farewells in two languages. Many of the men who were to sail upon her had many intimates in the old Southern town, and we who had left our friends in the remote North received our first touch of melancholy on witnessing these strenuous and earnest goodbys.

It seems, however, that there was more difficulty at the custom house. The officers of the ship and the Cuban leaders were detained there until a mournful twilight settled upon the St. John's, and through a heavy fog the lights of Jacksonville blinked dimly. Then at last the Commodore swung clear of the dock, amid a tumult of goodbys. As she turned her bow toward the distant sea the Cubans ashore cheered and cheered. In response the Commodore gave three long blasts of her whistle, which even to this time *sad* impressed me with their sadness. Somehow, they sounded as wails.

Then at last we began to feel like filibusters. I don't suppose that the *5* most stolid brain could contrive to believe that there is not a mere trifle of danger in filibustering, and so as we watched the lights of Jacksonville swing past us and heard the regular thump, thump, thump of the engines we did considerable reflecting.

But I am sure that there were no hifalutin emotions visible upon any of the faces which fronted the speeding shore. In fact, from cook's boy to cap- *satisfied* tain, we were all enveloped in a gentle satisfaction and cheerfulness. But less than two miles from Jacksonville, this atrocious fog caused the pilot to ram *aground in* the bow of the Commodore hard upon the mud and in this ignominious *fog* position we were compelled to stay until daybreak.

Help from the Boutwell

It was to all of us more than a physical calamity. We were now no longer filibusters. We were men on a ship stuck in the mud. A certain mental som- ersault was made once more necessary.

But word had been sent to Jacksonville to the captain of the revenue cutter Boutwell, and Captain Kilgore turned out promptly and generously fired up his old triangle, and came at full speed to our assistance. She dragged *ship pulled* us out of the mud, and again we headed for the mouth of the river. The *out* revenue cutter pounded along a half mile astern of us, to make sure that we did not take on board at some place along the river men for the Cuban army.

This was the early morning of New Year's Day, and the fine golden southern sunlight fell full upon the river. It flashed over the ancient Bout- well, until her white sides gleamed like pearl, and her rigging was spun into little threads of gold.

Cheers greeted the old Commodore from passing ship and from the *10* shore. It was a cheerful, almost merry, beginning to our voyage. At Mayport, however, we changed our river pilot for a man who could take her to open *open sea* sea, and again the Commodore was beached. The Boutwell was fussing around us in her venerable way, and, upon seeing our predicament, she came again to assist us, but this time, with engines reversed, the Commodore dragged herself away from the grip of the sand and again headed for the open sea.

The captain of the revenue cutter grew curious. He hailed the Com- modore: "Are you fellows going to sea to-day?"

Captain Murphy of the Commodore called back: "Yes, sir."

And then as the whistle of the Commodore saluted him, Captain Kil- gore doffed his cap and said: "Well, gentlemen, I hope you have a pleasant cruise," and this was our last word from shore.

When the Commodore came to enormous rollers that flee over the bar a certain light-heartedness departed from the ship's company.

Sleep Impossible

As darkness came upon the waters, the Commodore was a broad, flam-   *15*
ing path of blue and silver phosphorescence, and as her stout bow lunged at
the great black waves she threw flashing, roaring cascades to either side. And
all that was to be heard was the rhythmical and mighty pounding of the
engines. Being an inexperienced filibuster, the writer had undergone considerable mental excitement since the starting of the ship, and in consequence he had not yet been to sleep and so I went to the first mate's bunk
to indulge myself in all the physical delights of holding one's-self in bed.
Every time the ship lurched I expected to be fired through a bulkhead, and
it was neither amusing nor instructive to see in the dim light a certain ac-
cursed valise aiming itself at the top of my stomach with every lurch of the
vessel.

The Cook Is Hopeful

The cook was asleep on a bench in the galley. He is of a portly and noble
exterior, and by means of a checker board he had himself wedged on this
bench in such a manner the motion of the ship would be unable to dislodge
him. He woke as I entered the galley and delivered himself of some dolorous
sentiments: "God," he said in the course of his observations, "I don't feel
right about this ship, somehow. It strikes me that something is going to
happen to us. I don't know what it is, but the old ship is going to get it in
the neck, I think."
    "Well, how about the men on board of her?" said I. "Are any of us
going to get out, prophet?"
    "Yes," said the cook. "Sometimes I have these damned feelings come
over me, and they are always right, and it seems to me, somehow, that you
and I will both get out and meet again somewhere, down at Coney Island,
perhaps, or some place like that."

One Man Has Enough

Finding it impossible to sleep, I went back to the pilot house. An old
seaman, Tom Smith, from Charleston, was then at the wheel. In the darkness I could not see Tom's face, except at those times when he leaned forward to scan the compass and the dim light from the box came upon his
weatherbeaten features.
    "Well, Tom," said I, "how do you like filibustering?"   *20*
    He said "I think I am about through with it. I've been in a number of
these expeditions and the pay is good, but I think if I ever get back safe this
time I will cut it."
    I sat down in the corner of the pilot house and almost went to sleep. In
the meantime the captain came on duty and he was standing near me when
the chief engineer rushed up the stairs and cried hurriedly to the captain that

there was something wrong in the engine room. He and the captain de-   *trouble*
parted swiftly.

I was drowsing there in my corner when the captain returned, and, going to the door of the little room directly back of the pilot house, he cried to the Cuban leader:

"Say, can't you get those fellows to work. I can't talk their language and I can't get them started. Come on and get them going."

Helps in the Fireroom

The Cuban leader turned to me and said: "Go help in the fireroom.   *25*
They are going to bail with buckets."

The engine room, by the way, represented a scene at this time taken   *bailing out*
from the middle kitchen of hades. In the first place, it was insufferably   *ship*
warm, and the lights burned faintly in a way to cause mystic and grewsome   *boiler room=*
shadows. There was a quantity of soapish sea water swirling and sweeping   *hell*
and swishing among machinery that roared and banged and clattered and
steamed, and, in the second place, it was a devil of a ways down below.

Here I first came to know a certain young oiler named Billy Higgins. He was sloshing around this inferno filling buckets with water and passing them to a chain of men that extended up the ship's side. Afterward we got orders to change our point of attack on water and to operate through a little door on the windward side of the ship that led into the engine room.

No Panic on Board

During this time there was much talk of pumps out of order and many other statements of a mechanical kind, which I did not altogether compre- hend but understood to mean that there was a general and sudden ruin in the engine room.

There was no particular agitation at this time, and even later there was   *no*
never a panic on board the Commodore. The party of men who worked   *panic*
with Higgins and me at this time were all Cubans, and we were under the direction of the Cuban leaders. Presently we were ordered again to the afterhold, and there was some hesitation about going into the abomin- able fireroom again, but Higgins dashed down the companion way with a bucket.

Lowering Boats

The heat and hard work in the fireroom affected me and I was obliged   *30*
to come on deck again. Going forward, I heard as I went talk of lowering   *possible*
the boats. Near the corner of the galley the mate was talking with a man.   *doom*
    overheard
"Why don't you send up a rocket?" said this unknown man. And the mate replied: "What the hell do we want to send up a rocket for? The ship is all right."

Returning with a little rubber and cloth overcoat, I saw the first boat about to be lowered. A certain man was the first person in this first boat, and they were handing him in a valise about as large as a hotel. I had not entirely recovered from astonishment and pleasure in witnessing this noble deed when I saw another valise go to him.

Human Hog Appears

This valise was not perhaps so large as a hotel, but it was a big valise anyhow. Afterward there went to him something which looked to me like an overcoat.

Seeing the chief engineer leaning out of his little window, I remarked to him:

"What do you think of that blank, blank, blank?"   35

"Oh, he's a bird," said the old chief.

It was now that was heard the order to get away the lifeboat, which was stowed on top of the deckhouse. The deckhouse was a mighty slippery place, and with each roll of the ship, the men were thought themselves likely to take headers into the deadly black sea.

Higgins was on top of the deckhouse, and, with the first mate and two colored stokers, we wrestled with that boat, which, I am willing to swear, weighed as much as a Broadway cable car. She might have been spiked to the deck. We could have pushed a little brick schoolhouse along a corduroy road as easily as we could have moved this boat. But the first mate got a tackle to her from a leeward davit, and on the deck below the captain corralled enough men to make an impression upon the boat.

We were ordered to cease hauling then, and in this lull the cook of the ship came to me and said: "What are you going to do?"

I told him of my plans, and he said: 40

"Well, my God, that's what I am going to do."

Now the whistle of the Commodore had been turned loose, and if there ever was a voice of despair and death, it was in the voice of this whistle. It had gained a new tone. It was as if its throat was already choked by the water, and this cry on the sea at night, with a wind blowing the spray over the ship, and the waves roaring over the bow, and swirling white along the decks, was to each of us probably a song of man's end.

It was now that the first mate showed a sign of losing his grip. To us who were trying in all stages of competence and experience to launch the lifeboat he raged in all terms of fiery satire and hammerlike abuse. But the boat moved at last and swung down toward the water.

Afterward, when I went aft, I saw the captain standing, with his arm in a sling, holding on to a stay with his one good hand and directing the launching of the boat. He gave me a five-gallon jug of water to hold, and asked me what I was going to do. I told him what I thought was about the proper thing, and he told me then that the cook had the same idea, and ordered me to go forward and be ready to launch the ten-foot dingy.

In the Ten-Foot Dingy

I remember well that he turned then to swear at a colored stoker who   45
was prowling around, done up in life preservers until he looked like a feather
bed. I went forward with my five-gallon jug of water, and when the captain
came we launched the dingy, and they put me over the side to fend her off
from the ship with an oar.

They handed me down the water jug, and then the cook came into the
boat, and we sat there in the darkness, wondering why, by all our hopes of
future happiness, the captain was so long in coming over to the side and
ordering us away from the doomed ship.

The captain was waiting for the other boat to go. Finally he hailed in
the darkness: "Are you all right, Mr. Graines?"

The first mate answered: "All right, sir."

"Shove off, then," cried the captain.

The captain was just about to swing over the rail when a dark form came   50
forward and a voice said: "Captain, I go with you."

The captain answered: "Yes, Billy; get in."

Higgins Last to Leave Ship

It was Billy Higgins, the oiler. Billy dropped into the boat and a moment
later the captain followed, bringing with him an end of about forty yards of
lead line. The other end was attached to the rail of the ship.

As we swung back to leeward the captain said: "Boys, we will stay right
near the ship till she goes down."

This cheerful information, of course, filled us all with glee. The line
kept us headed properly into the wind, and as we rode over the monstrous
waves we saw upon each rise the swaying lights of the dying Commodore.

When came the gray shade of dawn, the form of the Commodore grew   55
slowly clear to us as our little ten-foot boat rose over each swell. She was
floating with such an air of buoyancy that we laughed when we had time,
and said "What a gag it would be on those other fellows if she didn't sink
at all."

But later we saw men aboard of her, and later still they began to hail us.

I had forgot to mention that previously we had loosened the end of the
lead line and dropped much further to leeward. The men on board were a
mystery to us, of course, as we had seen all the boats leave the ship. We
rowed back to the ship, but did not approach too near, because we were
four men in a ten-foot boat, and we knew that the touch of a hand on our
gunwale would assuredly swamp us.

The first mate cried out from the ship that the third boat had foundered
alongside. He cried that they had made rafts, and wished us to tow them.

The captain said, "All right."

Their rafts were floating astern. "Jump in!" cried the captain, but there   60
was a singular and most harrowing hesitation. There were five white men

and two negroes. This scene in the gray light of morning impressed one as would a view into some place where ghosts move slowly. These seven men on the stern of the sinking Commodore were silent. Save the words of the mate to the captain there was no talk. Here was death, but here also was a most singular and indefinable kind of fortitude.

Four men, I remember, clambered over the railing and stood there watching the cold, steely sheen of the sweeping waves.

"Jump," cried the captain again.

The old chief engineer first obeyed the order. He landed on the outside raft and the captain told him how to grip the raft and he obeyed as promptly and as docilely as a scholar in riding school.

The Mate's Mad Plunge

A stoker followed him, and then the first mate threw his hands over his head and plunged into the sea. He had no life belt and for my part, even when he did this horrible thing, I somehow felt that I could see in the expression of his hands, and in the very toss of his head, as he leaped thus to death, that it was rage, rage, rage unspeakable that was in his heart at the time.

And then I saw Tom Smith, the man who was going to quit filibustering after this expedition, jump to a raft and turn his face toward us. On board the Commodore three men strode, still in silence and with their faces turned toward us. One man had his arms folded and was leaning against the deck-house. His feet were crossed, so that the toe of his left foot pointed downward. There they stood gazing at us, and neither from the deck nor from the rafts was a voice raised. Still was there this silence.

Tried to Tow the Rafts

The colored stoker on the first raft threw us a line and we began to tow. Of course, we perfectly understood the absolute impossibility of any such thing; our dingy was within six inches of the water's edge, there was an enormous sea running, and I knew that under the circumstances a tugboat would have no light task in moving these rafts.

But we tried it, and would have continued to try it indefinitely, but that something critical came to pass. I was at an oar and so faced the rafts. The cook controlled the line. Suddenly the boat began to go backward and then we saw this negro on the first raft pulling on the line hand over hand and drawing us to him.

He had turned into a demon. He was wild—wild as a tiger. He was crouched on this raft and ready to spring. Every muscle of him seemed to be turned into an elastic spring. His eyes were almost white. His face was the face of a lost man reaching upward, and we knew that the weight of his hand on our gunwale doomed us.

The cook let go of the line. We rowed around to see if we could not get a line from the chief engineer, and all this time, mind you, there were no shrieks, no groans, but silence, silence and silence, and then the Commodore sank.

[margin note: silence as sunk]

She lurched to windward, then swung afar back, righted and dove into the sea, and the rafts were suddenly swallowed by this frightful maw of the ocean. And then by the men on the ten-foot dingy were words said that were still not words—something far beyond words.

[margin note: 70]

[margin note: rafts sink]

The lighthouse of Mosquito Inlet stuck up above the horizon like the point of a pin. We turned our dingy toward the shore.

The history of life in an open boat for thirty hours would no doubt be instructive for the young, but none is to be told here and now. For my part I would prefer to tell the story at once, because from it would shine the splendid manhood of Captain Edward Murphy and of William Higgins, the oiler, but let it suffice at this time to say that when we were swamped in the surf and making the best of our way toward the shore the captain gave orders amid the wildness of the breakers as clearly as if he had been on the quarter deck of a battleship.

[margin note: 1-story tells this]

[margin note: manliness]

John Kitchell of Daytona came running down the beach, and as he ran the air was filled with clothes. If he had pulled a single lever and undressed, even as the fire horses harness, he could not seem to me to have stripped with more speed. He dashed into the water and dragged the cook. Then he went after the captain, but the captain sent him to me, and then it was that he saw Billy Higgins lying with his forehead on sand that was clear of the water, and he was dead.

[margin note: dinghy men rescued]

[margin note: but Billy dies]

Questions of Subject and Theme

1. What about the account seems most frightening to you? What about the events make it most frightening for those involved? What about the writing makes the story most frightening for you?
2. How do you respond to Crane's sentence in the fourth paragraph from the end? What do you imagine as "words that were still not words—something far beyond words"? Do you think Crane failed as a correspondent by not trying further to describe how the men felt in words? Discuss the issue.

Questions of Method and Strategy

1. When he wrote the beginning of his account, Crane of course knew how the voyage would end. Do you detect any trace of that knowledge in the writing of the early part of the account itself? Describe the strengths and weaknesses of Crane's use of a point of view that changes in time by pointing to particular examples.
2. Crane records a great variety of behaviors in the face of disaster. Pick two examples where he individuates people by focusing on a particular aspect of "body language." Compare and contrast the effects created for the reader.

THE OPEN BOAT

Stephen Crane

I

None of them knew the colour of the sky. Their eyes glanced level, and *1*
were fastened upon the waves that swept toward them. These waves were of
the hue of slate, save for the tops, which were of foaming white, and all of
the men knew the colours of the sea. The horizon narrowed and widened,
and dipped and rose, and at all times its edge was jagged with waves that
seemed thrust up in points like rocks.

Many a man ought to have a bathtub larger than the boat which here
rode upon the sea. These waves were most wrongfully and barbarously
abrupt and tall, and each froth-top was a problem in small-boat navigation.

The cook squatted in the bottom, and looked with both eyes at the six
inches of gunwale which separated him from the ocean. His sleeves were
rolled over his fat forearms, and the two flaps of his unbuttoned vest dangled
as he bent to bail out the boat. Often he said, "Gawd! that was a narrow
clip." As he remarked it he invariably gazed eastward over the broken sea.

The oiler, steering with one of the two oars in the boat, sometimes
raised himself suddenly to keep clear of water that swirled in over the stern.
It was a thin little oar, and it seemed often ready to snap.

The correspondent, pulling at the other oar, watched the waves and *5*
wondered why he was there.

The injured captain, lying in the bow, was at this time buried in that
profound dejection and indifference which comes, temporarily at least, to
even the bravest and most enduring when, willy-nilly, the firm fails, the
army loses, the ship goes down. The mind of the master of a vessel is rooted
deep in the timbers of her, though he command for a day or a decade; and
this captain had on him the stern impression of a scene in the greys of dawn
of seven turned faces, and later a stump of a topmast with a white ball on it,
that slashed to and fro at the waves, went low and lower, and down. Thereafter there was something strange in his voice. Although steady, it was deep
with mourning, and of a quality beyond oration or tears.

"Keep 'er a little more south, Billie," said he.

"A little more south, sir," said the oiler in the stern.

A seat in his boat was not unlike a seat upon a bucking broncho, and by
the same token a broncho is not much smaller. The craft pranced and reared
and plunged like an animal. As each wave came, and she rose for it, she
seemed like a horse making at a fence outrageously high. The manner of
her scramble over these walls of water is a mystic thing, and, moreover, at
the top of them were ordinarily these problems in white water, the foam
racing down from the summit of each wave requiring a new leap, and a leap

from the air. Then, after scornfully bumping a crest, she would slide and race and splash down a long incline, and arrive bobbing and nodding in front of the next menace.

A singular disadvantage of the sea lies in the fact that after successfully surmounting one wave you discover that there is another behind it just as important and just as nervously anxious to do something effective in the way of swamping boats. In a ten-foot dinghy one can get an idea of the resources of the sea in the line of waves that is not probable to the average experience which is never at sea in a dinghy. As each slaty wall of water approached, it shut all else from the view of the men in the boat, and it was not difficult to imagine that this particular wave was the final outburst of the ocean, the last effort of the grim water. There was a terrible grace in the move of the waves, and they came in silence, save for the snarling of the crests.

In the wan light the faces of the men must have been grey. Their eyes must have glinted in strange ways as they gazed steadily astern. Viewed from a balcony, the whole thing would doubtless have been weirdly picturesque. But the men in the boat had no time to see it, and if they had had leisure, there were other things to occupy their minds. The sun swung steadily up the sky, and they knew it was broad day because the colour of the sea changed from slate to emerald green streaked with amber lights, and the foam was like tumbling snow. The process of the breaking day was unknown to them. They were aware only of this effect upon the colour of the waves that rolled toward them.

In disjointed sentences the cook and the correspondent argued as to the difference between a life-saving station and a house of refuge. The cook had said: "There's a house of refuge just north of the Mosquito Inlet Light, and as soon as they see us they'll come off in their boat and pick us up."

"As soon as who see us?" said the correspondent.

"The crew," said the cook.

"Houses of refuge don't have crews," said the correspondent. "As I understand them, they are only places where clothes and grub are stored for the benefit of shipwrecked people. They don't carry crews."

"Oh, yes, they do," said the cook.

"No, they don't," said the correspondent.

"Well, we're not there yet, anyhow," said the oiler, in the stern.

"Well," said the cook, "perhaps it's not a house of refuge that I'm thinking of as being near Mosquito Inlet Light; perhaps it's a life-saving station."

"We're not there yet," said the oiler in the stern.

II

As the boat bounced from the top of each wave the wind tore through the hair of the hatless men, and as the craft plopped her stern down again the spray slashed past them. The crest of each of these waves was a hill, from the top of which the men surveyed for a moment a broad tumultuous expanse, shining and wind-riven. It was probably splendid, it was probably glorious, this play of the free sea, wild with lights of emerald and white and amber.

"Bully good thing it's an on-shore wind," said the cook. "If not, where would we be? Wouldn't have a show."

"That's right," said the correspondent.

The busy oiler nodded his assent.

Then the captain, in the bow, chuckled in a way that expressed humour, contempt, tragedy, all in one. "Do you think we've got much of a show now, boys?" said he.

Whereupon the three were silent, save for a trifle of hemming and hawing. To express any particular optimism at this time they felt to be childish and stupid, but they all doubtless possessed this sense of the situation in their minds. A young man thinks doggedly at such times. On the other hand, the ethics of their condition was decidedly against any open suggestion of hopelessness. So they were silent.

"Oh, well," said the captain, soothing his children, "we'll get ashore all right."

But there was that in his tone which made them think; so the oiler quoth, "Yes! if this wind holds."

The cook was bailing. "Yes! if we don't catch hell in the surf."

Canton-flannel gulls flew near and far. Sometimes they sat down on the sea, near patches of brown seaweed that rolled over the waves with a movement like carpets on a line in a gale. The birds sat comfortably in groups, and they were envied by some in the dinghy, for the wrath of the sea was no more to them than it was to a covey of prairie chickens a thousand miles inland. Often they came very close and stared at the men with black bead-like eyes. At these times they were uncanny and sinister in their unblinking scrutiny, and the men hooted angrily at them, telling them to be gone. One came, and evidently decided to alight on the top of the captain's head. The bird flew parallel to the boat and did not circle, but made short sidelong jumps in the air in chicken-fashion. His black eyes were wistfully fixed upon the captain's head. "Ugly brute," said the oiler to the bird. "You look as if you were made with a jackknife." The cook and the correspondent swore darkly at the creature. The captain naturally wished to knock it away with the end of the heavy painter, but he did not dare do it, because anything resembling an emphatic gesture would have capsized this freighted boat; and so, with his open hand, the captain gently and carefully waved the gull away. After it had been discouraged from the pursuit the captain breathed easier on account of his hair, and others breathed easier because the bird struck their minds at this time as being somehow gruesome and ominous.

In the meantime the oiler and the correspondent rowed. And also they rowed. They sat together in the same seat, and each rowed an oar. Then the oiler took both oars; then the correspondent took both oars; then the oiler; then the correspondent. They rowed and they rowed. The very ticklish part of the business was when the time came for the reclining one in the stern to

25

30

Marginal annotations (handwritten):
Foolish optimism but not too say hopeless
birds
fragile afloat

take his turn at the oars. By the very last star of truth, it is easier to steal eggs from under a hen than it was to change seats in the dinghy. First the man in the stern slid his hand along the thwart and moved with care, as if he were of Sevres. Then the man in the rowing-seat slid his hand along the other thwart. It was all done with the most extraordinary care. As the two sidled past each other, the whole party kept watchful eyes on the coming wave, and the captain cried: "Look out, now! Steady, there!"

The brown mats of seaweed that appeared from time to time were like islands, bits of earth. They were travelling, apparently, neither one way nor the other. They were, to all intents, stationary. They informed the men in the boat that it was making progress slowly toward the land.

The captain, rearing cautiously in the bow after the dinghy soared on a great swell, said that he had seen the lighthouse at Mosquito Inlet. Presently the cook remarked that he had seen it. The correspondent was at the oars then, and for some reason he too wished to look at the lighthouse; but his back was toward the far shore, and the waves were important, and for some time he could not seize an opportunity to turn his head. But at last there came a wave more gentle than the others, and when at the crest of it he swiftly scoured the western horizon.

"See it?" said the captain.

"No," said the correspondent, slowly; "I didn't see anything."

"Look again," said the captain. He pointed. "It's exactly in that direction."

At the top of another wave the correspondent did as he was bid, and this time his eyes chanced on a small, still thing on the edge of the swaying horizon. It was precisely like the point of a pin. It took an anxious eye to find a lighthouse so tiny.

"Think we'll make it, Captain?"

"If this wind holds and the boat don't swamp, we can't do much else," said the captain.

The little boat, lifted by each towering sea and splashed viciously by the crests, made progress that in the absence of seaweed was not apparent to those in her. She seemed just a wee thing wallowing, miraculously top up, at the mercy of five oceans. Occasionally a great spread of water, like white flames, swarmed into her.

"Bail her, cook," said the captain, serenely.

"All right, Captain," said the cheerful cook.

III

It would be difficult to describe the subtle brotherhood of men that was here established on the seas. No one said that it was so. No one mentioned it. But it dwelt in the boat, and each man felt it warm him. They were a captain, an oiler, a cook, and a correspondent, and they were friends— friends in a more curiously iron-bound degree than may be common. The hurt captain, lying against the water-jar in the bow, spoke always in a low voice and calmly; but he could never command a more ready and swiftly obedient crew than the motley three of the dinghy. It was more than a mere recognition of what was best for the common safety. There was surely in it a quality that was personal and heart-felt. And after this devotion to the commander of the boat, there was this comradeship, that the correspondent, for instance, who had been taught to be cynical of men, knew even at the time was the best experience of his life. But no one said that it was so. No one mentioned it.

"I wish we had a sail," remarked the captain. "We might try my over-coat on the end of an oar, and give you two boys a chance to rest." So the cook and the correspondent held the mast and spread wide the overcoat; the oiler steered; and the little boat made good way with her new rig. Some-times the oiler had to scull sharply to keep a sea from breaking into the boat, but otherwise sailing was a success.

Meanwhile the lighthouse had been growing slowly larger. It had now almost assumed colour, and appeared like a little grey shadow on the sky. The man at the oars could not be prevented from turning his head rather often to try for a glimpse of this little grey shadow.

At last, from the top of each wave, the men in the tossing boat could see land. Even as the lighthouse was an upright shadow on the sky, this land seemed but a long black shadow on the sea. It certainly was thinner than paper. "We must be about opposite New Smyrna," said the cook, who had coasted this shore often in schooners. "Captain, by the way, I believe they abandoned that life-saving station there about a year ago."

"Did they?" said the captain.

The wind slowly died away. The cook and the correspondent were not now obliged to slave in order to hold high the oar. But the waves continued their old impetuous swooping at the dinghy, and the little craft, no longer under way, struggled woundily over them. The oiler or the correspondent took the oars again.

Shipwrecks are apropos of nothing. If men could only train for them and have them occur when the men had reached pink condition, there would be less drowning at sea. Of the four in the dinghy none had slept any time worth mentioning for two days and two nights previous to embarking in the dinghy, and in the excitement of clambering about the deck of a foundering ship they had also forgotten to eat heartily.

For these reasons, and for others, neither the oiler nor the correspon-dent was fond of rowing at this time. The correspondent wondered ingenu-ously how in the name of all that was sane could there be people who thought it amusing to row a boat. It was not an amusement; it was a dia-bolical punishment, and even a genius of mental aberrations could never conclude that it was anything but a horror to the muscles and a crime against the back. He mentioned to the boat in general how the amusement of row-ing struck him, and the weary-faced oiler smiled in full sympathy. Previ-ously to the foundering, by the way, the oiler had worked a double watch in the engine-room of the ship.

"Take her easy, now, boys," said the captain. "Don't spend yourselves. If we have to run a surf you'll need all your strength, because we'll sure have to swim for it. Take your time."

50

will have to swim when close

Slowly the land arose from the sea. From a black line it became a line of black and a line of white—trees and sand. Finally the captain said that he could make out a house on the shore. "That's the house of refuge, sure," said the cook. "They'll see us before long, and come out after us."

The distant lighthouse reared high. "The keeper ought to be able to make us out now, if he's looking through a glass," said the captain. "He'll notify the life-saving people."

"None of those other boats could have got ashore to give word of this wreck," said the oiler, in a low voice, "else the life-boat would be out hunting us."

Slowly and beautifully the land loomed out of the sea. The wind came again. It had veered from the north-east to the south-east. Finally a new sound struck the ears of the men in the boat. It was the low thunder of the surf on the shore. "We'll never be able to make the lighthouse now," said the captain. "Swing her head a little more north, Billie."

"A little more north, sir," said the oiler.

55

Whereupon the little boat turned her nose once more down the wind, and all but the oarsman watched the shore grow. Under the influence of this expansion doubt and direful apprehension were leaving the minds of the men. The management of the boat was still most absorbing, but it could not prevent a quiet cheerfulness. In an hour, perhaps, they would be ashore.

safety "assured"

Their backbones had become thoroughly used to balancing in the boat, and they now rode this wild colt of a dinghy like circus men. The correspondent thought that he had been drenched to the skin, but happening to feel in the top pocket of his coat, he found therein eight cigars. Four of them were soaked with sea-water; four were perfectly scatheless. After a search, somebody produced three dry matches; and thereupon the four waifs rode impudently in their little boat and, with an assurance of an impending rescue shining in their eyes, puffed at the big cigars, and judged well and ill of all men. Everybody took a drink of water.

cigars

IV

"Cook," remarked the captain, "there don't seem to be any signs of life about your house of refuge."

"No," replied the cook. "Funny they don't see us!"

no one to save them

A broad stretch of lowly coast lay before the eyes of the men. It was of low dunes topped with dark vegetation. The roar of the surf was plain, and sometimes they could see the white lip of a wave as it spun up the beach. A tiny house was blocked out black upon the sky. Southward, the slim lighthouse lifted its little grey length.

60

Tide, wind, and waves were swinging the dinghy northward. "Funny they don't see us," said the men.

The surf's roar was here dulled, but its tone was nevertheless thunderous and mighty. As the boat swam over the great rollers the men sat listening to this roar. "We'll swamp sure," said everybody.

It is fair to say here that there was not a life-saving station within twenty miles in either direction; but the men did not know this fact, and in consequence they made dark and opprobrious remarks concerning the eyesight of the nation's life-savers. Four scowling men sat in the dinghy and surpassed records in the invention of epithets.

"Funny they don't see us."

The light-heartedness of a former time had completely faded. To their 65 sharpened minds it was easy to conjure pictures of all kinds of incompetency and blindness and, indeed, cowardice. There was the shore of the populous land, and it was bitter and bitter to them that from it came no sign.

"Well," said the captain, ultimately, "I suppose we'll have to make a try for ourselves. If we stay out here too long, we'll none of us have strength left to swim after the boat swamps."

And so the oiler, who was at the oars, turned the boat straight for the shore. There was a sudden tightening of muscles. There was some thinking.

"If we don't all get ashore," said the captain—"if we don't all get ashore, I suppose you fellows know where to send news of my finish?"

They then briefly exchanged some addresses and admonitions. As for the reflections of the men, there was a great deal of rage in them. Perchance they might be formulated thus: "If I am going to be drowned—if I am going to be drowned—if I am going to be drowned, why, in the name of the seven mad gods who rule the sea, was I allowed to come thus far and contemplate sand and trees? Was I brought here merely to have my nose dragged away as I was about to nibble the sacred cheese of life? It is preposterous. If this old ninny-woman, Fate, cannot do better than this, she should be deprived of the management of men's fortunes. She is an old hen who knows not her intention. If she has decided to drown me, why did she not do it in the beginning and save me all this trouble? The whole affair is absurd.—But no; she cannot mean to drown me. She dare not drown me. She cannot drown me. Not after all this work." Afterward the man might have had an impulse to shake his fist at the clouds. "Just you drown me, now, and then hear what I call you!"

The billows that came at this time were more formidable. They seemed 70 always just about to break and roll over the little boat in a turmoil of foam. There was a preparatory and long growl in the speech of them. No mind unused to the sea would have concluded that the dinghy could ascend these sheer heights in time. The shore was still afar. The oiler was a wily surfman. "Boys," he said swiftly, "she won't live three minutes more, and we're too far out to swim. Shall I take her to sea again, Captain?"

"Yes; go ahead!" said the captain.

This oiler, by a series of quick miracles and fast and steady oarsmanship, turned the boat in the middle of the surf and took her safely to sea again.

There was a considerable silence as the boat bumped over the furrowed sea to deeper water. Then somebody in gloom spoke: "Well, anyhow, they must have seen us from the shore by now."

The gulls went in slanting flight up the wind toward the grey, desolate east. A squall, marked by dingy clouds and clouds brick-red like smoke from a burning building, appeared from the south-east.

"What do you think of those life-saving people? Ain't they peaches?"

"Funny they haven't see us." 75

"Maybe they think we're out here for sport! Maybe they think we're fishin'. Maybe they think we're damned fools."

bitterness over no rescue

It was a long afternoon. A changed tide tried to force them southward, but wind and wave said northward. Far ahead, where coast-line, sea, and sky formed their mighty angle, there were little dots which seemed to indicate a city on the shore.

"St. Augustine?" — *city of God*

The captain shook his head. "Too near Mosquito Inlet." 80

And the oiler rowed, and then the correspondent rowed; then the oiler rowed. It was a weary business. The human back can become the seat of more aches and pains than are registered in books for the composite anatomy of a regiment. It is a limited area, but it can become the theatre of innumerable muscular conflicts, tangles, wrenches, knots, and other comforts.

"Did you ever like to row, Billie!" asked the correspondent.

"No," said the oiler; "hang it!"

When one exchanged the rowing-seat for a place in the bottom of the boat, he suffered a bodily depression that caused him to be careless of everything save an obligation to wiggle one finger. There was cold sea-water swashing to and fro in the boat, and he lay in it. His head, pillowed on a thwart, was within an inch of the swirl of a wave-crest, and sometimes a particularly obstreperous sea came inboard and drenched him once more. But these matters did not annoy him. It is almost certain that if the boat had capsized he would have tumbled comfortably out upon the ocean as if he felt sure that it was a great soft mattress.

"Look! There's a man on the shore!" 85

"Where?"

"There! See 'im? See 'im?"

"Yes, sure! He's walking along."

"Now he's stopped. Look! He's facing us!"

"He's waving at us!" 90

"So he is! By thunder!"

"Ah, now we're all right! Now we're all right! There'll be a boat out here for us in half an hour."

man sees them

"He's going on. He's running. He's going up to that house there."

The remote beach seemed lower than the sea, and it required a searching glance to discern the little black figure. The captain saw a floating stick, and they rowed to it. A bath towel was by some weird chance in the boat, and, tying this on the stick, the captain waved it. The oarsman did not dare turn his head, so he was obliged to ask questions.

"What's he doing now?"   95

"He's standing still again. He's looking, I think.—There he goes again—toward the house.—Now he's stopped again."

"Is he waving at us?"

"No, not now; he was, though."

"Look! There comes another man!"

"He's running."   100

"Look at him go, would you!"

"Why, he's on a bicycle. Now he's met the other man. They're both waving at us. Look!"

"There comes something up the beach."

"What the devil is that thing?"   105

"Why, it looks like a boat."

"Why, certainly, it's a boat."

"No; it's on wheels."

"Yes, so it is. Well, that must be the life-boat. They drag them along shore on a wagon."

"That's the life-boat, sure."   110

"No, by God, it's—it's an omnibus."

"I tell you it's a life-boat."

"It is not! It's an omnibus. I can see it plain. See? One of these big hotel omnibuses."

"By thunder, you're right. It's an omnibus, sure as fate. What do you suppose they are doing with an omnibus? Maybe they are going around collecting the life-crew, hey?"

"That's it, likely. Look! There's a fellow waving a little black flag. He's standing on the steps of the omnibus. There come those other two fellows. Now they're all talking together. Look at the fellow with the flag. Maybe he ain't waving it!"

"That ain't a flag, is it? That's his coat. Why, certainly, that's his coat."   115

"So it is; it's his coat. He's taken it off and is waving it around his head. But would you look at him swing it!"

"Oh, say, there isn't any life-saving station there. That's just a winter-resort hotel omnibus that has brought over some of the boarders to see us drown."

"What's that idiot with the coat mean? What's he signalling, anyhow?"

"It looks as if he were trying to tell us to go north. There must be a life-saving station up there."

"No; he thinks we're fishing. Just giving us a merry hand. See? Ah,   120 there, Willie!"

"Well, I wish I could make something out of those signals. What do you suppose he means?"

"He don't mean anything; he's just playing."

"Well, if he'd just signal us to try the surf again, or to go to sea and wait, or go north, or go south, or go to hell, there would be some reason in it. But look at him! He just stands there and keeps his coat revolving like a wheel. The ass!"

"There come more people."   125

"Now there's quite a mob. Look! Isn't that a boat?"

"Where? Oh, I see where you mean. No, that's no boat."

"That fellow is still waving his coat."

"He must think we like to see him do that. Why don't he quit it? It don't mean anything."

"I don't know. I think he is trying to make us go north. It must be that there's a life-saving station there somewhere."

"Say, he ain't tired yet. Look at 'im wave!"   130

"Wonder how long he can keep that up. He's been revolving his coat ever since he caught sight of us. He's an idiot. Why aren't they getting men to bring a boat out? A fishing-boat—one of those big yawls—could come out here all right. Why don't he do something?"

"Oh, it's all right now."

"They'll have a boat out here for us in less than no time, now that they've seen us."

A faint yellow tone came into the sky over the low land. The shadows on the sea slowly deepened. The wind bore coldness with it, and the men began to shiver.

"Holy smoke!" said one, allowing his voice to express his impious   135 mood, "if we keep on monkeying out here! If we've got to flounder out here all night!"

"Oh, we'll never have to stay here all night! Don't you worry. They've seen us now, and it won't be long before they'll come chasing out after us."

The shore grew dusky. The man waving a coat blended gradually into this gloom, and it swallowed in the same manner the omnibus and the group of people. The spray, when it dashed uproariously over the side, made the voyagers shrink and swear like men who were being branded.

"I'd like to catch the chump who waved the coat. I feel like socking him one, just for luck."

"Why? What did he do?"

"Oh, nothing, but then he seemed so damned cheerful."   140

In the meantime the oiler rowed, and then the correspondent rowed, and the oiler rowed. Grey-faced and bowed forward, they mechanically, turn by turn, plied the leaden oars. The form of the lighthouse had vanished from the southern horizon, but finally a pale star appeared, just lifting from the sea. The streaked saffron in the west passed before the all-merging darkness, and the sea to the east was black. The land had vanished, and was expressed only by the low and drear thunder of the surf.

"If I am going to be drowned—if I am going to be drowned—if I am going to be drowned, why, in the name of the seven mad gods who rule the sea, was I allowed to come thus far and contemplate sand and trees? Was I brought here merely to have my nose dragged away as I was about to nibble the sacred cheese of life?"

The patient captain, drooped over the water-jar, was sometimes obliged to speak to the oarsman.

"Keep her head up! Keep her head up!"

"Keep her head up, sir." The voices were weary and low.   *145*

This was surely a quiet evening. All save the oarsman lay heavily and listlessly in the boat's bottom. As for him, his eyes were just capable of noting the tall black waves that swept forward in a most sinister silence, save for an occasional subdued growl of a crest.

The cook's head was on a thwart, and he looked without interest at the water under his nose. He was deep in other scenes. Finally he spoke. "Billie," he murmured, dreamfully, "what kind of pie do you like best?"

V

"Pie!" said the oiler and the correspondent, agitatedly. "Don't talk about those things, blast you!"

"Well," said the cook, "I was just thinking about ham sandwiches and—"

A night on the sea in an open boat is a long night. As darkness settled   *150* finally, the shine of the light, lifting from the sea in the south, changed to full gold. On the northern horizon a new light appeared, a small bluish gleam on the edge of the waters. These two lights were the furniture of the world. Otherwise there was nothing but waves.

lights

Two men huddled in the stern, and distances were so magnificent in the dinghy that the rower was enabled to keep his feet partly warm by thrusting them under his companions. Their legs indeed extended far under the rowing-seat until they touched the feet of the captain forward. Sometimes, despite the efforts of the tired oarsman, a wave came piling into the boat, an icy wave of the night, and the chilling water soaked them anew. They would twist their bodies for a moment and groan, and sleep the dead sleep once more, while the water in the boat gurgled about them as the craft rocked.

The plan of the oiler and the correspondent was for one to row until he lost the ability, and then arouse the other from his sea-water couch in the bottom of the boat.

The oiler plied the oars until his head drooped forward and the overpowering sleep blinded him; and he rowed yet afterward. Then he touched a man in the bottom of the boat, and called his name. "Will you spell me for a little while?" he said, meekly.

"Sure, Billie," said the correspondent, awaking and dragging himself to a sitting position. They exchanged places carefully, and the oiler, cuddling down in the sea-water at the cook's side, seemed to go to sleep instantly.

The particular violence of the sea had ceased. The waves came without   *155* snarling. The obligation of the man at the oars was to keep the boat headed so that the tilt of the rollers would not capsize her, and to preserve her from filling when the crests rushed past. The black wave were silent and hard to be seen in the darkness. Often one was almost upon the boat before the oarsman was aware.

In a low voice the correspondent addressed the captain. He was not sure that the captain was awake, although this iron man seemed to be always awake. "Captain, shall I keep her making for that light north, sir?"

The same steady voice answered him. "Yes. Keep it about two points off the port bow."

The cook had tied a life-belt around himself in order to get even the warmth which this clumsy cork contrivance could donate, and he seemed almost stove-like when a rower, whose teeth invariably chattered wildly as soon as he ceased his labour, dropped down to sleep.

The correspondent, as he rowed, looked down at the two men sleeping underfoot. The cook's arm was around the oiler's shoulders, and, with their fragmentary clothing and haggard faces, they were the babes of the sea—a grotesque rendering of the old babes in the wood.

Later he must have grown stupid at his work, for suddenly there was a growling of water, and a crest came with a roar and a swash into the boat, and it was a wonder that it did not set the cook afloat in his life-belt. The cook continued to sleep, but the oiler sat up, blinking his eyes and shaking with the new cold.

"Oh, I'm awful sorry, Billie," said the correspondent, contritely.

"That's all right, old boy," said the oiler, and lay down again and was asleep.

Presently it seemed that even the captain dozed, and the correspondent thought that he was the one man afloat on all the oceans. The wind had a voice as it came over the waves, and it was sadder than the end.

There was a long, loud swishing astern of the boat, and a gleaming trail of phosphorescence, like blue flame, was furrowed on the black waters. It might have been made by a monstrous knife.

Then there came a stillness, while the correspondent breathed with open mouth and looked at the sea.

Suddenly there was another swish and another long flash of bluish light, and this time it was alongside the boat, and might almost been reached with an oar. The correspondent saw an enormous fin speed like a shadow through the water, hurling the crystalline spray and leaving the long glowing trail.

The correspondent looked over his shoulder at the captain. His face was hidden, and he seemed to be asleep. He looked at the babes of the sea. They certainly were asleep. So, being bereft of sympathy, he leaned a little way to one side and swore softly into the sea.

But the thing did not then leave the vicinity of the boat. Ahead or astern, on one side or the other, at intervals long or short, fled the long sparkling streak, and there was to be heard the *whirroo* of the dark fin. The speed and power of the thing was greatly to be admired. It cut the water like a gigantic and keen projectile.

The presence of this biding thing did not affect the man with the same horror that it would if he had been a picnicker. He simply looked at the sea dully and swore in an undertone.

Nevertheless, it is true that he did not wish to be alone with the thing. He wished one of his companions to awake by chance and keep him company with it. But the captain hung motionless over the water-jar, and the oiler and the cook in the bottom of the boat were plunged in slumber.

VI

fate
refrain

"If I am going to be drowned—if I am going to be drowned—if I am going to be drowned, why, in the name of the seven mad gods who rule the sea, was I allowed to come thus far and contemplate sand and trees?"

During this dismal night, it may be remarked that a man would conclude that it was really the intention of the seven mad gods to drown him,

injust &
unnatural
to die now

despite the abominable injustice of it. For it was certainly an abominable injustice to drown a man who had worked so hard, so hard. The man felt it would be a crime most unnatural. Other people had drowned at sea since galleys swarmed with painted sails, but still—

When it occurs to a man that nature does not regard him as important,

nature:
man is not
of import

and that she feels she would not maim the universe by disposing of him, he at first wishes to throw bricks at the temple, and he hates deeply the fact that there are no bricks and no temples. Any visible expression of nature would surely be pelleted with his jeers.

Then, if there be no tangible thing to hoot, he feels, perhaps, the desire to confront a personification and indulge in pleas, bowed to one knee, and with hands supplicant, saying, "Yes, but I love myself."

A high cold star on a winter's night is the word he feels that she says to him. Thereafter he knows the pathos of his situation.

175

The men in the dinghy had not discussed these matters, but each had, no doubt, reflected upon them in silence and according to his mind. There was seldom any expression upon their faces save the general one of complete weariness. Speech was devoted to the business of the boat.

To chime the notes of his emotion, a verse mysteriously entered the correspondent's head. He had even forgotten that he had forgotten this verse, but it suddenly was in mind.

> *A soldier of the Legion lay dying in Algiers;*
> *There was lack of woman's nursing, there was dearth of woman's tears;*
> *But a comrade stood beside him, and he took that comrade's hand,*
> *And he said, "I never more shall see my own, my native land."*

not to see
land

In his childhood the correspondent had been made acquainted with the fact that a soldier of the Legion lay dying in Algiers, but he had never re-

death—not
of import

garded the fact as important. Myriads of his school-fellows had informed him of the soldier's plight, but the dinning had naturally ended by making him perfectly indifferent. He had never considered it his affair that a soldier of the Legion lay dying in Algiers, nor had it appeared to him as a matter for sorrow. It was less to him than the breaking of a pencil's point.

Now, however, it quaintly came to him as a human, living thing. It was no longer merely a picture of a few throes in the breast of a poet, meanwhile drinking tea and warming his feet at the grate; it was an actuality—stern, mournful, and fine.

The correspondent plainly saw the soldier. He lay on the sand with his   *180*
feet out straight and still. While his pale left hand was upon his chest in an
attempt to thwart the going of his life, the blood came between his fingers.
In the far Algerian distance, a city of low square forms was set against a sky
that was faint with the last sunset hues. The correspondent, plying the oars
and dreaming of the slow and slower movements of the lips of the soldier,
was moved by a profound and perfectly impersonal comprehension. He was   *feels now for*
sorry for the soldier of the Legion who lay dying in Algiers.   *soldier*

The thing which had followed the boat and waited had evidently grown   *shark gone*
bored at the delay. There was no longer to be heard the slash of the cutwater,
and there was no longer the flame of the long trail. The light in the north
still glimmered, but it was apparently no nearer to the boat. Sometimes the
boom of the surf rang in the correspondent's ears, and he turned the craft
seaward then and rowed harder. Southward, some one had evidently built a
watch-fire on the beach. It was too low and too far to be seen, but it made
a shimmering, roseate reflection upon the bluff in back of it, and this could
be discerned from the boat. The wind came stronger, and sometimes a wave
suddenly raged out like a mountain cat, and there was to be seen the sheen
and sparkle of a broken crest.

The captain, in the bow, moved on his water-jar and sat erect. "Pretty
long night," he observed to the correspondent. He looked at the shore.
"Those life-saving people take their time."

"Did you see that shark playing around?"

"Yes, I saw him. He was a big fellow, all right."

"Wish I had known you were awake."   *185*

Later the correspondent spoke into the bottom of the boat. "Billie!"
There was a slow and gradual disentanglement. "Billie, will you spell me?"

"Sure," said the oiler.

As soon as the correspondent touched the cold, comfortable sea-water
in the bottom of the boat and had huddled close to the cook's life-belt he
was deep in sleep, despite the fact that he teeth played all the popular airs.
This sleep was so good to him that it was but a moment before he heard a
voice call his name in a tone that demonstrated the last stages of exhaustion.
"Will you spell me?"   *soldier's p.o.v.*

"Sure, Billie."

The light in the north had mysteriously vanished, but the correspondent   *190*
took his course from the wide-awake captain.

Later in the night they took the boat farther out to sea, and the captain
directed the cook to take one oar at the stern and keep the boat facing the
seas. He was to call out if he should hear the thunder of the surf. This plan
enabled the oiler and the correspondent to get respite together. "We'll give
those boys a chance to get into shape again," said the captain. They curled
down and, after a few preliminary chatterings and trembles, slept once more
the dead sleep. Neither knew they had bequeathed to the cook the company
of another shark, or perhaps the same shark.

As the boat caroused on the waves, spray occasionally bumped over the side and gave them a fresh soaking, but this had no power to break their repose. The ominous slash of the wind and the water affected them as it would have affected mummies.

"Boys," said the cook, with the notes of every reluctance in his voice, "she's drifted in pretty close. I guess one of you had better take her to sea again." The correspondent, aroused, heard the crash of the toppled crests.

As he was rowing, the captain gave him some whisky-and-water, and this steadied the chills out of him. "If I ever get ashore and anybody shows me even a photograph of an oar—"

At last there was a short conversation.   195

"Billie!—Billie, will you spell me?"

"Sure," said the oiler.

VII

When the correspondent again opened his eyes, the sea and the sky were each of the grey hue of the dawning. Later, carmine and gold was painted upon the waters. The morning appeared finally, in its splendour, with a sky of pure blue, and the sunlight flamed on the tips of the waves.

On the distant dunes were set many little black cottages, and a tall white windmill reared above them. No man, nor dog, nor bicycle appeared on the beach. The cottages might have formed a deserted village.

The voyagers scanned the shore. A conference was held in the boat.   200 "Well," said the captain, "if no help is coming, we might better try a run through the surf right away. If we stay out here much longer we will be too weak to do anything for ourselves at all." The others silently acquiesced in this reasoning. The boat was headed for the beach. The correspondent wondered if none ever ascended the tall wind-tower, and if then they never looked seaward. This tower was a giant, standing with its back to the plight of the ants. It represented in a degree, to the correspondent, the serenity of nature amid the struggles of the individual—nature in the wind, and nature in the vision of men. She did not seem cruel to him then, nor beneficent, nor treacherous, nor wise. But she was indifferent, flatly indifferent. It is, perhaps, plausible that a man in this situation, impressed with the unconcern of the universe, should see the innumerable flaws of his life, and have them taste wickedly in his mind, and wish for another chance. A distinction between right and wrong seems absurdly clear to him, then, in this new ignorance of the grave-edge, and he understands that if he were given another opportunity he would mend his conduct and his words, and be better and brighter during an introduction or at a tea.

"Now, boys," said the captain, "she is going to swamp sure. All we can do is to work her in as far as possible, and then when she swamps, pile out and scramble for the beach. Keep cool now, and don't jump until she swamps sure."

The oiler took the oars. Over his shoulders he scanned the surf. "Captain," he said, "I think I'd better bring her about and keep her head-on to the seas and back her in."

"All right, Billie," said the captain. "Back her in." The oiler swung the boat then, and, seated in the stern, the cook and the correspondent were obliged to look over their shoulders to contemplate the lonely and indifferent shore.

The monstrous inshore rollers heaved the boat high until the men were again enabled to see the white sheets of water scudding up the slanted beach. "We won't get in very close," said the captain. Each time a man could wrest his attention from the rollers, he turned his glance toward the shore, and in the expression of the eyes during this contemplation there was a singular quality. The correspondent, observing the others, knew that they were not afraid, but the full meaning of their glances was shrouded.

As for himself, he was too tired to grapple fundamentally with the fact. *205* He tried to coerce his mind into thinking of it, but the mind was dominated at this time by the muscles, and the muscles said they did not care. It merely occurred to him that if he should drown it would be a shame.

There were no hurried words, no pallor, no plain agitation. The men simply looked at the shore. "Now, remember to get well clear of the boat when you jump," said the captain.

Seaward the crest of a roller suddenly fell with a thunderous crash, and the long white comber came roaring down upon the boat. "Steady now," said the captain. The men were silent. They turned their eyes from the shore to the comber and waited. The boat slid up the incline, leaped at the furious top, bounced over it, and swung down the long back of the wave. Some water had been shipped, and the cook bailed it out.

But the next crest crashed also. The tumbling, boiling flood of white water caught the boat and whirled it almost perpendicular. Water swarmed in from all sides. The correspondent had his hands on the gunwale at this time, and when the water entered at that place he swiftly withdrew his fingers, as if he objected to wetting them.

The little boat, drunken with this weight of water, reeled and snuggled *210* deeper into the sea.

"Bail her out, cook! Bail her out!" said the captain.

"All right, Captain," said the cook.

"Now, boys, the next one will do for us sure," said the oiler. "Mind to jump clear of the boat."

The third wave moved forward, huge, furious, implacable. It fairly swallowed the dinghy, and almost simultaneously the men tumbled into the sea. A piece of life-belt had laid in the bottom of the boat, and as the correspondent went overboard he held this to his chest with his left hand.

The January water was icy, and he reflected immediately that it was *215* colder than he had expected to find it off the coast of Florida. This appeared to his dazed mind as a fact important enough to be noted at the time. The coldness of the water was sad; it was tragic. This fact was somehow mixed and confused with his opinion of his own situation, so that it seemed almost a proper reason for tears. The water was cold.

When he came to the surface he was conscious of little but the noisy water. Afterward he saw his companions in the sea. The oiler was ahead in the race. He was swimming strongly and rapidly. Off to the correspondent's left, the cook's great white and corked back bulged out of the water; and in the rear the captain was hanging with his one good hand to the keel of the overturned dinghy.

There is a certain immovable quality to a shore, and the correspondent wondered at it amid the confusion of the sea.

It seemed also very attractive; but the correspondent knew that it was a long journey, and he paddled leisurely. The piece of life-preserver lay under him, and sometimes he whirled down the incline of a wave as if he were on a hand-sled.

But finally he arrived at a place in the sea where travel was beset with difficulty. He did not pause swimming to inquire what manner of current had caught him, but there his progress ceased. The shore was set before him like a bit of scenery on a stage, and he looked at it and understood with his eyes each detail of it.

As the cook passed, much farther to the left, the captain was calling to   220
him, "Turn over on your back, cook! Turn over on your back and use the oar."

"All right, sir." The cook turned on his back, and, paddling with an oar, went ahead as if he were a canoe.

Presently the boat also passed to the left of the correspondent, with the captain clinging with one hand to the keel. He would have appeared like a man raising himself to look over a board fence if it were not for the extraordinary gymnastics of the boat. The correspondent marvelled that the captain could still hold to it.

They passed on nearer to shore—the oiler, the cook, the captain—and following them went the water-jar, bouncing gaily over the seas.

The correspondent remained in the grip of this strange new enemy—a current. The shore, with its white slope of sand and its green bluff topped with little silent cottages, was spread like a picture before him. It was very near to him then, but he was impressed as one who, in a gallery, looks at a scene from Brittany or Holland.

He thought: "I am going to drown? Can it be possible? Can it be pos-   225
sible? Can it be possible?" Perhaps an individual must consider his own death to be the final phenomenon of nature.

But later a wave perhaps whirled him out of this small deadly current, for he found suddenly that he could again make progress toward the shore. Later still he was aware that the captain, clinging with one hand to the keel of the dinghy, had his face turned away from the shore and toward him, and was calling his name. "Come to the boat! Come to the boat!"

In his struggle to reach the captain and the boat, he reflected that when one gets properly wearied drowning must really be a comfortable arrangement—a cessation of hostilities accompanied by a large degree of relief; and he was glad of it, for the main thing in his mind for some moments had been horror of the temporary agony. He did not wish to be hurt. *relief of drowning*

Presently he saw a man running along the shore. He was undressing with most remarkable speed. Coat, trousers, shirt, everything flew magically off him.

"Come to the boat!" called the captain.

"All right, Captain." As the correspondent paddled, he saw the captain let himself down to bottom and leave the boat. Then the correspondent performed his one little marvel of the voyage. A large wave caught him and flung him with ease and supreme speed completely over the boat and far beyond it. It struck him even then as an event in gymnastics and a true miracle of the sea. An overturned boat in the surf is not a plaything to a swimming man. *230*

The correspondent arrived in water that reached only to his waist, but his condition did not enable him to stand for more than a moment. Each wave knocked him into a heap, and the undertow pulled at him.

Then he saw the man who had been running and undressing, and undressing and running, come bounding into the water. He dragged ashore the cook, and then waded toward the captain; but the captain waved him away and sent him to the correspondent. He was naked—naked as a tree in winter; but a halo was about his head, and he shone like a saint. He gave a strong pull, and a long drag, and a bully heave at the correspondent's hand. The correspondent, schooled in the minor formulae, said, "Thanks, old man." But suddenly the man cried, "What's that?" He pointed a swift finger. The correspondent said, "Go." *angel/st naked rescue man*

In the shallows, face downward, lay the oiler. His forehead touched sand that was periodically, between each wave, clear of the sea. *oiler dead*

The correspondent did not know all that transpired afterward. When he achieved safe ground he fell, striking the sand with each particular part of his body. It was as if he had dropped from a roof, but the thud was grateful to him.

It seemed that instantly the beach was populated with men with blankets, clothes, and flasks, and women with coffee-pots and all the remedies sacred to their minds. The welcome of the land to the men from the sea was warm and generous; but a still and dripping shape was carried slowly up the beach, and the land's welcome for it could only be the different and sinister hospitality of the grave. *235* *land: warm, generous or land: sinister*

When it came night, the white waves paced to and fro in the moonlight, and the wind brought the sound of the great sea's voice to the men on the shore, and they felt that they could then be interpreters. *interpret sea*

Questions of Subject and Theme

1. Crane sent the Captain a copy of his story to see whether it sounded right from the Captain's point of view. "You've got it, Steve," was the reply. "That is just how it happened and how it felt." Pick a moment when you think that you too know how it felt; then try to describe as clearly as you can what that feeling is.
2. Crane became known as a writer of the kind of fiction called "naturalism." What does Nature come to mean within the story for the narrator? Describe the characteristics of the Nature presented here.

Questions of Method and Strategy

1. "None of them knew the color of the sky." What do you think of this as a way of beginning the story? What effects does it achieve that an alternative opening might not have done? Imagine at least one such alternative and compare and contrast your beginning to Crane's.
2. Crane uses several kinds of repetition in the story: The invocation of "the seven mad gods who rule the sea" is repeated, for example. Pick an example of Crane's use of repetition as a technique, and describe as fully as you can what it contributes to the story both locally and generally.

Suggestions for Writing on the Juxtapositions

1. Pick a dangerous moment in your own life—an accident or near accident or an operation, for example. Describe it first in a factual manner, as if you were writing a news account and then treat the same subject using any of the resources of fiction that seem appropriate. In a final paragraph or so, describe what differences the genres of fiction and nonfiction have or have not made in your writing.
2. A few paragraphs from the beginning of section II of "The Open Boat" an ethical dilemma presents itself and results in silence. There are also many silences in the face of ethical dilemmas in the nonfiction account. Pick one such moment and write an essay in which you compare and contrast the effects and meanings dramatized by silence in the account to the effects and meanings dramatized by the silences in "The Open Boat."
3. At the beginning of section III of "The Open Boat" the narrator says "It would be difficult to describe the subtle brotherhood of men that was here established on the seas." Difficult as it may have been, do you think that Crane succeeds in dramatizing the condition? Would "subtle brotherhood" describe any moment where human relations are dramatized in the nonfiction account? Write an essay in which you compare and contrast the senses of human relations Crane achieves in each version of his experience.

4. Pick what to you is the single most moving moment in each version. Write an essay in which you describe as clearly as you can both what in the content moved you in each case and how Crane's writing techniques helped him achieve his effects. It may be helpful to write a paraphrase of each moment.

8 An Ancient Story Told and Retold

King James Bible, "Ruth and Naomi"
Thomas Hood, "Ruth"
lucille clifton, "naomi watches as ruth sleeps"

Stories from the Bible have continued to stimulate the imaginations of poets for thousands of years. In reading the story of Ruth and Naomi and the poems that it inspired, keep in mind the following questions:

1. The poet lucille clifton takes for granted the sexual attraction of Ruth for Boaz, whereas Thomas Hood's poem dramatizes that attraction. In your view, does the Book of Ruth contain this theme among others? If you think so, show how it is explicitly or implicitly expressed. If you think not, describe the qualities that in your view lead Boaz to marry Ruth in the source story.

2. Fertility, both agricultural and human, seems an important concern of both the Bible story and Hood's poem. How are the two fertilities connected in each version? Pick some particular uses of language in each version and discuss the ways in which the two kinds of fertility seem to be related.

3. In lucille clifton's poem, Naomi does not seem to relish the idea of Ruth's "becoming" her. How is this idea of the two women being essentially identical or of sharing the same identity treated in the Bible story? For example Naomi becomes a stranger in the land of the Moabites and Ruth becomes a stranger in Israel. What other aspects of identity figure in the Bible story and how might they create a context for clifton's interpretation of Naomi's feelings toward Ruth?

4. In each version Ruth seems to affect the people in her life with mysterious force in spite of an apparent passivity. Which of the forces is most mysterious to you? Which least? Explain the sources of your reactions by pointing to particular examples.

THE BOOK OF RUTH

The "King James" or "Authorized" version of the Bible (a new translation was authorized by King James I of England and published in 1611) has exerted an enormous influence on religion in the English-speaking nations and on English literature as well. In Ruth and Naomi's story the vigor and dignity of the prose of the High Renaissance found content worthy of its power.

Chapter 1

1. Now it came to pass in the days when the judges ruled, that there was a famine in the land. And a certain man of Beth-lehem-judah went to sojourn in the country of Mō′ăb, he, and his wife, and his two sons.

2. And the name of the man *was* Ē-lĭm′ē-lĕch, and the name of his wife Nā′ō-mī, and the name of his two sons Măh′lŏn and Chĭl′ĭ-ŏn, Ĕph′răth-ītes of Beth-lehem-judah. And they came into the country of Mō′ăb, and continued there.

3. And Ē-lĭm′ē-lĕch Nā′ō-mī's husband died; and she was left, and her two sons.

4. And they took them wives of the women of Mō′ăb; the name of the one *was* Ôr′păh, and the name of the other Ruth: and they dwelt there about ten years.

5. And Măh′lŏn and Chĭl′ĭ-ŏn died also both of them; and the woman was left of her two sons and her husband.

6. ¶ Then she arose with her daughters-in-law, that she might return from the country of Mō′ăb: for she had heard in the country of Mō′ăb how that the LORD had visited his people in giving them bread.

7. Wherefore she went forth out of the place where she was, and her two daughters-in-law with her; and they went on the way to return unto the land of Judah.

8. And Nā′ō-mī said unto her two daughters-in-law, Go, return each to her mother's house: the LORD deal kindly with you, as ye have dealt with the dead, and with me.

9. The LORD grant you that ye may find rest, each *of you* in the house of her husband. Then she kissed them; and they lifted up their voice, and wept.

10. And they said unto her, Surely we will return with thee unto they people.

11. And Nā′ō-mī said, Turn again, my daughters: why will ye go with me? *are* there yet *any more* sons in my womb, that they may be your husbands?

12. Turn again, my daughters, go *your way;* for I am too old to have a husband. If I should say, I have hope, *if* I should have a husband also to-night, and should also bear sons;

13. Would ye tarry for them till they were grown? would ye stay for them from having husbands? nay, my daughters; for it grieveth me much for your sakes that the hand of the LORD is gone out against me.

14. And they lifted up their voice, and wept again: and Ôr'päh kissed her mother-in-law; but Ruth clave unto her.

15. And she said, Behold, thy sister-in-law is gone back unto her people, and unto her gods: return thou after thy sister-in-law.

16. And Ruth said, Entreat me not to leave thee, *or* to return from following after thee: for whither thou goest, I will go; and where thou lodgest, I will lodge: thy people *shall be* my people, and thy God my God:

17. Where thou diest, will I die, and there will I be buried: the LORD do so to me, and more also, *if aught* but death part thee and me.

18. When she saw that she was steadfastly minded to go with her, then she left speaking unto her.

19. ¶ So they two went until they came to Beth-lehem. And it came to pass, when they were come to Beth-lehem, that all the city was moved about them, and they said, *Is* this Nā'ō-mī?

20. And she said unto them, Call me not Nā'ō-mī, call me Mā'rà: for the Almighty hath dealt very bitterly with me.

21. I went out full, and the LORD hath brought me home again empty: why *then* call ye me Nā'ō-mī, seeing the LORD hath testified against me, and the Almighty hath afflicted me?

22. So Nā'ō-mī returned, and Ruth the Mō'ăb-īt'ĕss, her daughter-in-law, with her, which returned out of the country of Mō'ăb: and they came to Beth-lehem in the beginning of barley harvest.

Chapter 2

1. And Nā'ō-mī had a kinsman of her husband's, a mighty man of wealth, of the family of Ē-lĭm'ē-lĕch; and his name *was* Boaz.

gleaning fields

2. And Ruth the Mō'ăb-īt'ĕss said unto Nā'ō-mī, Let me now go to the field, and glean ears of corn after *him* in whose sight I shall find grace. And she said unto her, Go, my daughter.

3. And she went, and came, and gleaned in the field after the reapers: and her hap was to light on a part of the field *belonging* unto Boaz, who *was* of the kindred of Ē-lĭm'ē-lĕch.

4. ¶ And, behold, Boaz came from Beth-lehem, and said unto the reapers, The LORD *be* with you. And they answered him, The LORD bless thee.

5. Then said Boaz unto his servant that was set over the reapers, Whose damsel *is* this?

6. And the servant that was set over the reapers answered and said, It *is* the Mō'ăb-īt'ĭsh damsel that came back with Nā'ō-mī out of the country of Mō'ăb:

7. And she said, I pray you, let me glean and gather after the reapers among the sheaves: so she came, and hath continued even from the morning until now, that she tarried a little in the house.

8. Then said Boaz unto Ruth, Hearest thou not, my daughter? Go not to glean in another field, neither go from hence, but abide here fast by my maidens:

9. Let thine eyes be on the field that they do reap, and go thou after them: have I not charged the young men that they shall not touch thee? and when thou art athirst, go unto the vessels, and drink of *that* which the young men have drawn.

10. Then she fell on her face, and bowed herself to the ground, and said unto him, Why have I found grace in thine eyes, that thou shouldest take knowledge of me, seeing I *am* a stranger?

11. And Boaz answered and said unto her, It hath fully been showed me, all that thou hast done unto thy mother-in-law since the death of thine husband; and *how* thou hast left thy father and thy mother, and the land of thy nativity, and art come unto a people which thou knewest not heretofore.

12. The LORD recompense thy work, and a full reward be given thee of the LORD God of Ĭṣ'rā-ĕl, under whose wings thou art come to trust.

13. Then she said, Let me find favor in thy sight, my lord; for that thou hast comforted me, and for that thou hast spoken friendly unto thine handmaid, though I be not like unto one of thine handmaidens.

14. And Boaz said unto her, At meal-time come thou hither, and eat of the bread, and dip thy morsel in the vinegar. And she sat beside the reapers: and he reached her parched *corn,* and she did eat, and was sufficed, and left.

15. And when she was risen up to glean, Boaz commanded his young men, saying, Let her glean even among the sheaves, and reproach her not:

16. And let fall also *some* of the handfuls of purpose for her, and leave *them,* that she may glean *them,* and rebuke her not.

17. So she gleaned in the field until even, and beat out that she had gleaned: and it was about an ē'phàh of barley.

18. ¶ And she took *it* up, and went into the city; and her mother-in-law saw what she had gleaned: and she brought forth, and gave to her that she had reserved after she was sufficed.

19. And her mother-in-law said unto her, Where hast thou gleaned to-day? and where wroughtest thou? blessed be he that did take knowledge of thee. And she showed her mother-in-law with whom she had wrought, and said, The man's name with whom I wrought today *is* Bōaz.

20. And Nā'ō-mī said unto her daughter-in-law, Blessed *be* he of the LORD, who hath not left off his kindness to the living and to the dead. And Nā'ō-mī said unto her, The man *is* near of kin unto us, one of our next kinsmen.

21. And Ruth the Mō'ăb-īt-ĕss said, He said unto me also, Thou shalt keep fast by my young men, until they have ended all my harvest.

22. And Nā'ō-mī said unto Ruth her daughter-in-law, *It is* good, my daughter, that thou go out with his maidens, that they meet thee not in any other field.

23. So she kept fast by the maidens of Boaz to glean unto the end of barley harvest and of wheat harvest; and dwelt with her mother-in-law.

Chapter 3

1. Then Nā'ō-mī her mother-in-law said unto her, My daughter, shall I not seek rest for thee, that it may be well with thee?

2. And now *is* not Boaz of our kindred, with whose maidens thou wast? Behold, he winnoweth barley to-night in the threshingfloor.

3. Wash thyself therefore, and anoint thee, and put the raiment upon thee, and get thee down to the floor: *but* make not thyself known unto the man, until he shall have done eating and drinking.

4. And it shall be, when he lieth down, that thou shalt mark the place where he shall lie, and thou shalt go in, and uncover his feet, and lay thee down; and he will tell thee what thou shalt do.

5. And she said unto her, All that thou sayest unto me I will do.

6. ¶ And she went down unto the floor, and did according to all that her mother-in-law bade her.

7. And when Boaz had eaten and drunk, and his heart was merry, he went to lie down at the end of the heap of corn: and she came softly, and uncovered his feet, and laid her down.

8. ¶ And it came to pass at midnight, that the man was afraid, and turned himself: and, behold, a woman lay at his feet.

9. And he said, Who *art* thou? And she answered, I *am* Ruth thine handmaid: spread therefore thy skirt over thine handmaid; for thou *art* a near kinsman.

10. And he said, Blessed *be* thou of the LORD, my daughter: *for* thou hast showed more kindness in the latter end than at the beginning, inasmuch as thou followedst not young men, whether poor or rich.

11. And now, my daughter, fear not; I will do to thee all that thou requirest: for all the city of my people doth know that thou *art* a virtuous woman.

12. And now it is true that I *am thy* near kinsman; howbeit there is a kinsman nearer than I.

13. Tarry this night, and it shall be in the morning, *that* if he will perform unto thee the part of a kinsman, well; let him do the kinsman's part: but if he will not do the part of a kinsman to thee, then will I do the part of a kinsman to thee, *as* the LORD liveth: lie down until the morning.

14. ¶ And she lay at his feet until the morning; and she rose up before one could know another. And he said, Let it not be known that a woman came into the floor.

15. Also he said, Bring the veil that *thou hast* upon thee, and hold it. And when she held it, he measured six *measures* of barley, and laid *it* on her: and she went into the city.

16. And when she came to her mother-in-law, she said, Who *art* thou, my daughter? And she told her all that the man had done to her.

17. And she said, These six *measures* of barley gave he me; for he said to me, Go not empty unto thy mother-in-law.

18. Then said she, Sit still, my daughter, until thou know how the mat-

ter will fall: for the man will not be in rest, until he have finished the thing this day.

Chapter 4

arranging marriage

1. Then went Boaz up to the gate, and sat him down there: and, behold, the kinsman of whom Boaz spake came by; unto whom he said, Ho, such a one! turn aside, sit down here. And he turned aside, and sat down.

2. And he took ten men of the elders of the city, and said, Sit ye down here. And they sat down.

3. And he said unto the kinsman, Nā'ō-mī, that is come again out of the country of Mō'ăb, selleth a parcel of land, which *was* our brother Ē-lĭm'ē-lĕєh's:

4. And I thought to advertise thee, saying, But *it* before the inhabitants, and before the elders of my people. If thou wilt redeem *it,* redeem *it:* but if thou wilt not redeem *it, then* tell me, that I may know: for *there is* none to redeem *it* besides thee; and I *am* after thee. And he said, I will redeem *it.*

5. Then said Boaz, What day thou buyest the field of the hand of Nā'ō-mī, thou must buy *it* also of Ruth the Mō'ăb-īt'ĕss, the wife of the dead, to raise up the name of the dead upon his inheritance.

6. ¶ And the kinsman said, I cannot redeem *it* for myself, lest I mar mine own inheritance: redeem thou my right to thyself; for I cannot redeem *it.*

7. Now this *was the manner* in former time in Ĭṣ'rā-ĕl concerning redeeming and concerning changing, for to confirm all things; a man plucked off his shoe, and gave *it* to his neighbor: and this *was* a testimony in Ĭṣ'rā-ĕl.

8. Therefore the kinsman said unto Boaz, Buy *it* for thee. So he drew off his shoe.

9. ¶ And Boaz said unto the elders, and *unto* all the people, Ye *are* witnesses this day, that I have bought all that *was* Ē-lĭm'ē-lĕєh's, and all that *was* Єhĭl'ĭ-ŏn's and Mäh'lŏn's, of the hand of Nā'ō-mī.

10. Moreover Ruth the Mō'ăb-īt'ĕss, the wife of Mäh'lŏn, have I purchased to be my wife, to raise up the name of the dead upon his inheritance, that the name of the dead be not cut off from among his brethren, and from the gate of his place: ye *are* witnesses this day.

11. And all the people that *were* in the gate, and the elders, said, *We are* witnesses. The Lord make the woman that is come into thine house like Rachel and like Lē'ăh, which two did build the house of Ĭṣ'rā-ĕl: and do thou worthily in Ĕph'rȧ-täh, and be famous in Beth-lehem:

12. And let thy house be like the house of Phä'rēz, whom Tā'mȧr bare unto Judah, of the seed which the Lord shall give thee of this young woman.

13. ¶ So Boaz took Ruth, and she was his wife: and when he went in unto her, the Lord gave her conception, and she bare a son.

14. And the women said unto Nā'ō-mī, Blessed *be* the Lord, which hath not left thee this day without a kinsman, that his name may be famous in Ĭṣ'rā-ĕl.

15. And he shall be unto thee a restorer of *thy* life, and a nourisher of thine old age: for thy daughter-in-law, which loveth thee, which is better to thee than seven sons, hath borne him.

16. And Nā'ō-mī took the child, and laid it in her bosom, and became nurse unto it.

17. And the women her neighbors gave it a name, saying, There is a son born to Nā'ō-mī; and they called his name Ō'bĕd: he *is* the father of Jesse, the father of David.

18. ¶ Now these *are* the generations of Phā'rēz: Phā'rēz begat Hĕz'rŏn,

19. And Hĕz'rŏn begat Răm, and Răm begat Ȧm-mĭn'ȧ-dăb,

20. And Ȧm-mĭn'ȧ-dăb begat Näh'shŏn, and Näh'shŏn began Săl'mŏn,

21. And Săl'mŏn begat Boaz, and Boaz begat Ō'bĕd,

22. And Ō'bĕd begat Jesse, and Jesse begat David.

Questions of Subject and Theme

1. The story of Ruth has intrigued readers for many reasons for many years. In the two poems that follow the selection from the King James Bible—one from the nineteenth century and one from the twentieth—the thoughts of Boaz and Naomi are imagined. What about the story as given in the Book of Ruth do you suppose stimulated this need for imagination? What makes the story intriguing and mysterious? Find two examples of narrative insufficiency, moments where you feel the need for more explanation, and explain in your own words what it is about those moments that make them intriguing or mysterious.

2. At the end of the story the women tell Naomi that Ruth is better to her than seven sons. What meaning of "better" and hence of "good" does the story dramatize? In other words, what qualities does Ruth display that lead the women to make this appraisal of her?

Questions of Method and Strategy

1. "Gleaning" in agriculture is the act of searching for whatever grain remains after most of the stalks have been cut and gathered by reapers. In what ways does "gleaning"—or the idea of finding lost or overlooked value—operate in the story as an agricultural metaphor for the story's human themes?

2. The narrative proceeds at a leisurely pace, and the modern reader used to faster food for thought may find the story needlessly drawn out. But try editing it. Try to cut out passages to reduce the story to half its length without losing its point. Then describe in a paragraph the principles behind your deletions and in another paragraph defend or attack your claim to retaining the essential points of the story.

RUTH

Thomas Hood

Thomas Hood (1799–1845), today considered only a minor Romantic poet, was strongly influenced by his contemporary, the more famous John Keats. Like Keats, Hood attempts to dramatize the glory of human psychology in its largest sense, and here he imagines Boaz's point of view, which remains largely unexpressed in the bible version.

She stood breast high amid the corn,   *stands out*   *like sun*   1
Clasped by the golden light of morn,
Like the sweetheart of the sun,
Who many a glowing kiss had won.

On her cheek an autumn flush,   5
Deeply ripened;—such a blush   *like autumn flowers*
In the midst of brown was born,
Like red poppies grown in corn.

Round her eyes her tresses fell,
Which were blackest none could tell,   10
But long lashes veiled a light,
That had else been all too bright.

And her hat, with shady brim,
Made her tressy forehead dim;—
Thus she stood amid the stooks,   *her looks praise God or she praises God*   15
Praising God with sweetest looks:—

Sure, I said, heaven did not mean,
Where I reap thou shouldst but glean;
Lay thy sheaf adown and come,
Share my harvest and my home.   20

Questions of Subject and Theme

1. *Corn* in British usage is any food grain and *stooks* (line 15) means the same thing as *stalks*. Thus, Boaz returns to his initial image of Ruth immersed in the fertility of nature just before he speaks to her. In what ways might Boaz see her as like her surroundings?

2. In Hood's poem Boaz tells us his thoughts in the first four stanzas and what he says to Ruth in the final stanza. What differences if any do you see between the nature of his thoughts and the nature of what he says? What if any similarities do you see among them?

Questions of Method and Strategy

1. In the first sixteen lines Boaz describes how Ruth appeared to him. How would you describe the movement of his attention within that description? How and in what ways do your eyes follow in imagination his eyes?

2. In line 16 do you understand "sweetest looks" to refer to "glances" or to "general appearance" or both? Explain your answer. John Keats, a poet Hood admired, wrote that "a thing of beauty is a joy forever." Can you understand how, just as beauty can be joy, sweetest looks can be praise? Explain.

NAOMI WATCHES AS RUTH SLEEPS

lucille clifton

The African-American poet lucille clifton finds in the story of Ruth a different focus from Thomas Hood. Her vision gives the enigmatic figure of Naomi the central role in the story and suggests a new aspect of her suffering.

she clings to me   *1*
like a shadow
when all that i wish
is to sit alone   *alone desire*
longing for my husband,   *5*
my sons.
she has promised
to follow me,
to become me
if i allow it.   *10*
i am leading her
to boaz country.
he will find her beautiful   *get rid of Ruth*
and place her among
his concubines.   *15*
jehovah willing
i can grieve in peace.

 Questions of Subject and Theme

1. It is often surprising to first-time readers that Ruth (as imagined by lucille clifton) seems a burden to Naomi. Drawing on your knowledge of the full story, explain the senses in which Ruth's claims to loyalty might justifiably seem oppressive to her mother-in-law.
2. Naomi's tone of voice is never affectionate, but does it change to your ear in the second half of the poem? If you think so, say from what to what. If you think not, characterize her consistent tone of voice as clearly as you can.

 Questions of Method and Strategy

1. In what sense or senses is it that Naomi "watches?" Does it mean only that she looks at Ruth? Look up the word in a good dictionary and explain the full flavor of the word clifton chooses for her title.
2. Exactly in the middle of the poem is the line "to become me." What seems to be the effect of this line on what Naomi subsequently says?

Given the poem as a whole, does the line seem to you to make an effective turning point? Explain how and why it does or does not.

———

Suggestions for Writing on the Juxtapositions

1. Pick an episode from the Book of Ruth and rewrite it in contemporary English. Then use particular examples of language from both versions to write an essay on what has been gained and what lost in your "translation." For example, in "Whither thou goest I will go" compared with "Wherever you go I will go," what sense of intimacy and tenderness has been lost through the loss to modern English of the second person singular pronoun *thou?*

2. Considering all the versions presented in the section, which character has been most interestingly realized for you? Write an essay in which you explain how any or all of the writers have contributed to your sense of a memorable character.

3. Human bonding through blood ties and ties of marriage are themes present in each version. Write an essay in which you compare and contrast the ways those themes are dramatized by the authors presented here.

4. How many forms of love are dramatized in the different versions of Ruth's story? Write an essay in which you use examples from all three versions to describe the varieties of love expressed and the various reactions to those forms of love.

9 *Immigrants: Horror and Hope*

Charles Ball, "Slave Ship"

Mary Gordon, "More Than Just a Shrine: Paying
  Homage to the Ghosts of Ellis Island"

Vo Thi Tam, "A Boat Person's Story"

In modern times the territory of the United States has become populated in many ways, some of them horrible. Consider the following questions as you read accounts of three of those ways:

1. Human cruelty appears in all three accounts. What do the various cruelties have in common? What do their descriptions have in common? What if anything distinguishes the accounts in these regards?

2. Do the differences of race and sex among the authors seem to you to affect the ways in which they view their own stories? Explain your answer with examples.

3. The second writer, Mary Gordon, finds "national definition" a process "somewhat tiresome but always self-absorbing." Whatever the general truth of this proposition, do you find it fits her own account? Does it fit any of the others?

4. Having read all the accounts, re-read Mary Gordon's essay. Does the context of the section as a whole change your reactions to her writing? Explain.

SLAVE SHIP

Charles Ball

Charles Ball tells his own story too well to need any other introduction. His narrative was one of many oral accounts collected and published by abolitionists in their campaign to end slavery in the United States before the Civil War.

At the time we came into this ship, she was full of black people, who   *1* were all confined in a dark and low place, in irons. The women were in irons as well as the men.

About twenty persons were seized in our village at the time I was; and amongst these were three children so young that they were not able to walk or to eat any hard substance. The mothers of these children had brought them all the way with them and had them in their arms when we were taken on board this ship.

When they put us in irons to be sent to our place of confinement in the ship, the men who fastened the irons on these mothers took the children out of their hands and threw them over the side of the ship into the water. When this was done, two of the women leaped overboard after the children—the third was already confined by a chain to another woman and could not get into the water, but in struggling to disengage herself, she broke her arm and died a few days after of a fever. One of the two women who were in the river was carried down by the weight of her irons before she could be rescued; but the other was taken up by some men in a boat and brought on board. This woman threw herself overboard one night when we were at sea.

The weather was very hot whilst we lay in the river and many of us died every day; but the number brought on board greatly exceeded those who died, and at the end of two weeks, the place in which we were confined was so full that no one could lie down; and we were obliged to sit all the time, for the room was not high enough for us to stand. When our prison could hold no more, the ship sailed down the river; and on the night of the second day after she sailed, I heard the roaring of the ocean as it dashed against her sides.

After we had been at sea some days, the irons were removed from the   *5* women and they were permitted to go upon deck; but whenever the wind blew high, they were driven down amongst us.

We had nothing to eat but yams, which were thrown amongst us at random—and of those we had scarcely enough to support life. More than one third of us died on the passage and when we arrived in Charleston, I was not able to stand. It was more than a week after I left the ship before I could straighten my limbs. I was bought by a trader with several others, brought up the country and sold to my present master. I have been here five years.

Questions of Subject and Theme

1. Make a list of the physical and emotional sufferings Ball records. Does he so distinguish among his sufferings? Give examples to support your answer.
2. Does Ball distinguish his own suffering from the suffering he observes? If you think so, show where and how he makes the distinction. If you think not, show where and how he treats them similarly.

Questions of Method and Strategy

1. Ball's account was originally given orally. How would you describe Ball's tone of voice throughout his story? How does his tone of voice contribute to the overall horror of the effect?
2. Time seems to accelerate toward the end of the narrative. What effects does this more rapid passage of time create for the reader?

MORE THAN JUST A SHRINE
Paying Homage to the Ghosts of Ellis Island

Mary Gordon

As her essay makes clear, Mary Gordon is a descendent of many immigrants who define her "Americanness" for her. A novelist who has dramatized themes stemming from her Roman Catholic youth, Gordon here explores another part of her heritage, symbolized for her by the facilities at Ellis Island, which were the first experience of the United States for so many European immigrants.

I once sat in a hotel in Bloomsbury trying to have breakfast alone. A *1* Russian with a habit of compulsively licking his lips asked if he could join me. I was afraid to say no; I thought it might be bad for détente. He explained to me that he was a linguist, and that he always liked to talk to Americans to see if he could make any connection between their speech and their ethnic background. When I told him about my mixed ancestry—my mother is Irish and Italian, my father a Lithuanian Jew—he began jumping up and down in his seat, rubbing his hands together, and licking his lips even more frantically.

"Ah," he said, "so you are really somebody who comes from what is called the boiling pot of America." Yes, I told him, yes I was, but I quickly rose to leave. I thought it would be too hard to explain to him the relation of the boiling potters to the main course, and I wanted to get to the British Museum. I told him that the only thing I could think of that united people whose backgrounds, histories, and points of view were utterly diverse was that their people had landed at a place called Ellis Island.

I didn't tell him that Ellis Island was the only American landmark I'd ever visited. How could I describe to him the estrangement I'd always felt from the kind of traveler who visits shrines to America's past greatness, those rebuilt forts with muskets behind glass and sabers mounted on the walls and gift shops selling maple sugar candy in the shape of Indian headdresses, those reconstructed villages with tables set for fifty and the Paul Revere silver gleaming? All that Americana—Plymouth Rock, Gettysburg, Mount Vernon, Valley Forge—it all inhabits for me a zone of blurred abstraction with far less hold on my imagination than the Bastille or Hampton Court. I suppose I've always known that my uninterest in it contains a large component of the willed: I am American, and those places purport to be my history. But they are not mine.

Ellis Island is, though; it's the one place I can be sure my people are connected to. And so I made a journey there to find my history, like any Rotarian traveling in his Winnebago to Antietam to find his. I had become part of that humbling democracy of people looking in some site for a past that has grown unreal. The monument I traveled to was not, however, a tribute to some old glory. The minute I set foot upon the island I could feel all that it stood for: insecurity, obedience, anxiety, dehumanization, the terrified and careful deference of the displaced. I hadn't traveled to the Battery and boarded a ferry across from the Statue of Liberty to raise flags or breathe a richer, more triumphant air. I wanted to do homage to the ghosts.

I felt them everywhere, from the moment I disembarked and saw the building with its high-minded brick, its hopeful little lawn, its ornamental cornices. The place was derelict when I arrived; it had not functioned for more than thirty years—almost as long as the time it had operated at full capacity as a major immigration center. I was surprised to learn what a small part of history Ellis Island had occupied. The main building was constructed in 1892, then rebuilt between 1898 and 1900 after a fire. Most of the immigrants who arrived during the latter half of the nineteenth century, mainly northern and western Europeans, landed not at Ellis Island but on the western tip of the Battery at Castle Garden, which had opened a receiving center for immigrants in 1855.

By the 1880s the facilities at Castle Garden had grown scandalously inadequate. Officials looked for an island on which to build a new immigration center because they thought that on an island immigrants could be more easily protected from swindlers and quickly transported to railroad terminals in New Jersey. Bedloe's Island was considered, but New Yorkers were aghast at the idea of a "Babel" ruining their beautiful new treasure, "Liberty Enlightening the World." The statue's sculptor, Frédéric Auguste Bartholdi, reacted to the prospect of immigrants landing near his masterpiece in horror; he called it a "monstrous plan." So much for Emma Lazarus.

Ellis Island was finally chosen because the citizens of New Jersey petitioned the federal government to remove from the island an old naval powder magazine that they thought dangerously close to the Jersey shore. The explosives were removed; no one wanted the island for anything. It was the perfect place to build an immigration center.

I thought about the island's history as I walked into the building and made my way to the room that was the center in my imagination of the Ellis Island experience: the Great Hall. It had been made real for me in the stark, accusing photographs of Louis Hine and others who took those pictures to make a point. It was in the Great Hall that everyone had waited—waiting, always, the great vocation of the dispossessed. The room was empty, except for me and a handful of other visitors and the park ranger who showed us around. I felt myself grow insignificant in that room, with its huge semicircular windows, its air, even in dereliction, of solid and official probity.

I walked in the deathlike expansiveness of the room's disuse and tried to think of what it might have been like, filled and swarming. More than sixteen million immigrants came through that room: approximately 250,000 were rejected. Not really a large proportion, but the implications for the rejected were dreadful. For some, there was nothing to go back to, or there was certain death; for others, who left as adventurers, to return would be to adopt in local memory the fool's role, and the failure's. No wonder that the island's history includes reports of three thousand suicides.

Sometimes immigrants could pass through Ellis Island in mere hours, though for some the process took days. The particulars of the experience in the Great Hall were often influenced by the political events and attitudes on the mainland. In the 1890s and the first years of the new century, when cheap labor was needed, the newly built receiving center took in its immigrants with comparatively little question. But as the century progressed, the economy worsened, eugenics became both scientifically respectable and popular, and World War I made American xenophobia seem rooted in fact.   *10*

Immigration acts were passed; newcomers had to prove, besides moral correctness and financial solvency, their ability to read. Quota laws came into effect, limiting the number of immigrants from southern and eastern Europe to less than 14 percent of the total quota. Intelligence tests were biased against all non-English-speaking persons and medical examinations became increasingly strict, until the machinery of immigration nearly collapsed under its own weight. The Second Quota Law of 1924 provided that all immigrants be inspected and issued visas at American consular offices in Europe, rendering the center almost obsolete.

On the day of my visit, my mind fastened upon the medical inspections, which had always seemed to me most emblematic of the ignominy and terror the immigrants endured. The medical inspectors, sometimes dressed in uniforms like soldiers, were particularly obsessed with a disease of the eyes called trachoma, which they checked for by flipping back the immigrants' top eyelids with a hook used for buttoning gloves—a method that sometimes resulted in the transmission of the disease to healthy people. Mothers feared that if their children cried too much, their red eyes would be mistaken for a symptom of the disease and the whole family would be sent home. Those immigrants suspected of some physical disability had initials chalked on their coats. I remembered the photographs I'd seen of people standing, dumbstruck and innocent as cattle, with their manifest numbers hung around their necks and initials marked in chalk upon their coats: "E" for eye trouble, "K" for hernia, "L" for lameness, "X" for mental defects, "H" for heart disease.

I thought of my grandparents as I stood in the room; my seventeen-year-old grandmother, coming alone from Ireland in 1896, vouched for by a stranger who had found her a place as a domestic servant to some Irish who had done well. I tried to imagine the assault it all must have been for her; I've been to her hometown, a collection of farms with a main street—smaller than the athletic field of my local public school. She must have watched the New York skyline as the first- and second-class passengers were whisked off the gangplank with the most cursory of inspections while she was made to board a ferry to the new immigration center.

What could she have made of it—this buff-painted wooden structure with its towers and its blue slate roof, a place *Harper's Weekly* described as "a latter-day watering place hotel"? It would have been the first time she'd have heard people speaking something other than English. She would have mingled with people carrying baskets on their heads and eating foods unlike any she had ever seen—dark-eyed people, like the Sicilian she would marry ten years later, who came over with his family, responsible even then for his mother and sister. I don't know what they thought, my grandparents, for they were not expansive people, nor romantic; they didn't like to think of what they called "the hard times," and their trip across the ocean was the single adventurous act of lives devoted after landing to security, respectability, and fitting in.

What is the potency of Ellis Island for someone like me—an American, *15* obviously, but one who has always felt that the country really belonged to the early settlers, that, as J. F. Powers wrote in "Morte D'Urban," it had been "handed down to them by the Pilgrims, George Washington and others, and that they were taking a risk in letting you live in it." I have never been the victim of overt discrimination; nothing I have wanted has been denied me because of the accidents of blood. But I suppose it is part of being an American to be engaged in a somewhat tiresome but always self-absorbing process of national definition. And in this process, I have found in traveling to Ellis Island an important piece of evidence that could remind me I was right to feel my differentness. Something had happened to my people on that island, a result of the eternal wrongheadedness of American protectionism and the predictabilities of simple greed. I came to the island, too, so I could tell the ghosts that I was one of them, and that I honored them—their stoicism, and their innocence, the fear that turned them inward, and their pride. I wanted to tell them that I liked them better than the Americans who made them pass through the Great Hall and stole their names and chalked their weaknesses in public on their clothing. And to tell the ghosts what I have always thought: that American history was a very classy party that was not much fun until they arrived, brought the good food, turned up the music, and taught everyone to dance.

Questions of Subject and Theme

1. List some of the points about Ellis Island as a symbol of America that Gordon makes in her essay. Which points does she seem to feel most strongly about? Describe the emotions.
2. Gordon says she feels an estrangement from other kinds of Americans and other kinds of tourists. Are these estrangements related in your view? Explain your answer with examples.

Questions of Method and Strategy

1. What does Gordon's opening anecdote do for her essay and its reader? Might the essay have begun with the fourth paragraph just as well? Explain your view.
2. In her last paragraph Gordon tries to define her complex feelings about herself as an American. In what ways does she attempt to show that the issue is a complex one for her?

A BOAT PERSON'S STORY

Vo Thi Tam

> The author was one of the many "boat people" who escaped from Vietnam after North Vietnam won the war. Shortly after the following narrative ends, she discovered that her husband had been captured on the day of their planned escape and sent again to a "reeducation" camp.

My husband was a former officer in the South Vietnamese air force. After the fall of that government in 1975, he and all the other officers were sent to a concentration camp for reeducation. When they let him out of the camp, they forced all of us to go to one of the "new economic zones," that are really just jungle. There was no organization, there was no housing, no utilities, no doctor, nothing. They gave us tools and a little food, and that was it. We just had to dig up the land and cultivate it. And the land was very bad.

It was impossible for us to live there, so we got together with some other families and bought a big fishing boat, about thirty-five feet long.

Altogether, there were thirty-seven of us that were to leave—seven men, eight women, and the rest children. I was five months pregnant.

After we bought the boat we had to hide it, and this is how: We just anchored it in a harbor in the Mekong Delta. It's very crowded there and very many people make their living aboard the boats by going fishing, you know. So we had to make ourselves like them. We took turns living and sleeping on the boat. We would maneuver the boat around the harbor, as if we were fishing or selling stuff, you know, so the Communist authorities could not suspect anything.

Besides the big boat, we had to buy a smaller boat in order to carry supplies to it. We had to buy gasoline and other stuff on the black market— everywhere there is a black market—and carry these supplies, little by little, on the little boat to the big boat. To do this we sold jewelry and radios and other things that we had left from the old days.

On the day we left we took the big boat out very early in the morning— all the women and children were in that boat and some of the men. My husband and the one other man remained in the small boat, and they were to rendezvous with us outside the harbor. Because if the harbor officials see too many people aboard, they might think there was something suspicious. I think they were suspicious anyway. As we went out, they stopped us and made us pay them ten taels of gold—that's a Vietnamese unit, a little heavier than an ounce. That was nearly all we had.

Anyway, the big boat passed through the harbor and went ahead to the rendezvous point where we were to meet my husband and the other man in the small boat. But there was no one there. We waited for two hours, but we did not see any sign of them. After a while we could see a Vietnamese navy boat approaching, and there was a discussion on board our boat and the end of it was the people on our boat decided to leave without my husband and the other man. [*Long pause.*]

When we reached the high seas, we discovered, unfortunately, that the water container was leaking and only a little bit of the water was left. So we had to ration the water from then on. We had brought some rice and other food that we could cook, but it was so wavy that we could not cook anything at all. So all we had was raw rice and a few lemons and very little water. After seven days we ran out of water, so all we had to drink was the sea water, plus lemon juice.

Everyone was very sick and, at one point, my mother and my little boy, four years old, were in agony, about to die. And the other people on the boat said that if they were agonizing like that, it would be better to throw them overboard so as to save them pain.

During this time we had seen several boats on the sea and had waved to   *10* them to help us, but they never stopped. But that morning, while we were discussing throwing my mother and son overboard, we could see another ship coming and we were very happy, thinking maybe it was people coming to save us. When the two boats were close together, the people came on board from there—it happened to be a Thai boat—and they said all of us had to go on the bigger boat. They made us all go there and then they began to search us—cutting off our blouses, our bras, looking everywhere. One woman, she had some rings she hid in her bra, and they undressed her and took out everything. My mother had a statue of our Lady, a very precious one, you know, that she had had all her life—she begged them just to leave the statue to her. But they didn't want to. They slapped her and grabbed the statue away.

Finally they pried up the planks of our boat, trying to see if there was any gold or jewelry hidden there. And when they had taken everything, they put us back on our boat and pushed us away.

They had taken all our maps and compasses, so we didn't even know which way to go. And because they had pried up the planks of our boat to look for jewelry, the water started getting in. We were very weak by then. But we had no pump, so we had to use empty cans to bail the water out, over and over again.

That same day we were boarded again by two other boats, and these, too, were pirates. They came aboard with hammers and knives and everything. But we could only beg them for mercy and try to explain by sign language that we'd been robbed before and we had nothing left. So those boats let us go and pointed the way to Malaysia for us.

That night at about 9:00 p.m. we arrived on the shore, and we were so happy finally to land somewhere that we knelt down on the beach and prayed, you know, to thank God.

While we were kneeling there, some people came out of the woods and   *15* began to throw rocks at us. They took a doctor who was with us and they beat him up and broke his glasses, so that from that time on he couldn't see anything at all. And they tied him up, his hands behind him like this [demonstrates], and they beat up the rest of the men, too. They searched us for anything precious that they could find, but there was nothing left except our few clothes and our documents. They took these and scattered them all over the beach.

Then five of the Malaysian men grabbed the doctor's wife, a young woman with three little children, and they took her back into the woods and raped her—all five of them. Later, they sent her back, completely naked, to the beach.

After this, the Malaysians forced us back into the boat and tried to push us out to sea. But the tide was out and the boat was so heavy with all of us on board that it just sank in the sand. So they left us for the night. . . .

In the morning, the Malaysian military police came to look over the area, and they dispersed the crowd and protected us from them. They let us pick up our clothes and our papers from the beach and took us in a big truck to some kind of a warehouse in a small town not far away. They gave us water, some bread, and some fish, and then they carried us out to Bidong Island. . . .

Perhaps in the beginning it was all right there, maybe for ten thousand people or so, but when we arrived there were already fifteen to seventeen thousand crowded onto thirty acres. There was no housing, no facilities, nothing. It was already full near the beach, so we had to go up the mountain and chop down trees to make room for ourselves and make some sort of a temporary shelter. There was an old well, but the water was very shallow. It was so scarce that all the refugees had to wait in a long line, day and night, to get our turn of the water. We would have a little can, like a small Coke can at the end of a long string, and fill that up. To fill about a gallon, it would take an hour, so we each had to just wait, taking our turn to get our Coke can of water. Sometimes one, two, or three in the morning we would get our water. I was pregnant, and my boys were only four and six, and my old mother with me was not well, but we all had to wait in line to get our water. That was just for cooking and drinking of course. We had to do our washing in the sea.

The Malaysian authorities did what they could, but they left most of the   20 administration of the camp to the refugees themselves, and most of us were sick. There were, of course, no sanitary installations, and many people had diarrhea. It was very hard to stop sickness under those conditions. My little boys were sick and my mother could hardly walk. And since there was no man in our family, we had no one to chop the wood for our cooking, and it was very hard for us just to survive. When the monsoons came, the floor of our shelter was all mud. We had one blanket and a board to lie on, and that was all. The water would come down the mountain through our shelter, so we all got wet.

After four months in the camp it was time for my baby to be born. Fortunately, we had many doctors among us, because many of them had tried to escape from Vietnam, so we had medical care but no equipment. There was no bed there, no hospital, no nothing, just a wooden plank to lie down on and let the baby be born, that was all. Each mother had to supply a portion of boiling water for the doctor to use and bring it with her to the medical hut when it was time. It was a very difficult delivery. The baby came legs first. But, fortunately, there were no complications. After the delivery I had to get up and go back to my shelter to make room for the next woman.

When we left Vietnam we were hoping to come to the United States, because my sister and her husband were here already. They came in 1975 when the United States evacuated so many people. We had to wait in the camp a month and a half to be interviewed, and then very much longer for the papers to be processed. Altogether we were in the camp seven months.

All this time I didn't know what had happened to my husband, although I hoped that he had been able to escape some other way and was, perhaps, in another camp, and that when I came to the United States I would find him.

We flew out here by way of Tokyo and arrived the first week in July. It was like waking up after a bad nightmare. Like coming out of hell into paradise. . . .

Questions of Subject and Theme

1. Make a list of the physical and emotional sufferings Tam records. Does she so distinguish among her sufferings? Give examples to support your answer.
2. Does Tam distinguish her own sufferings from those she observes? If you think so, show where and how she does so. If you think not, show where and how she treats the two similarly.

Questions of Method and Strategy

1. The author gives few details about her tormentors, referring to them as "the officials," or "the people," or simply as "they." What effect does this have on the emotional impact of her narrative?
2. Tam's account was originally given orally in an interview. Does she ever seem to vary in her tone of voice? What emotional impact does this variety or lack of variety create on the reader?

Suggestions for Writing on the Juxtapositions

1. Which account did you find most personally moving? Write an essay that explains the sources of your emotions.

2. Write a letter as if from one of the authors to any one of the others. Let the letter express what you imagine the writer's feelings might be on reading the other author's account.
3. Mary Gordon seems to have little use for immigration quotas. Write an essay that expresses your own views on the issue, being sure to take into account her views, whether to affirm or refute them.
4. Has reading this section affected your own self-definition as an American? Write an essay that explains why or why not.

Analysis and Explanation

10   *Twentieth-Century Homelessness*

Jack London, "Among the London Poor"
Scott Shuger, "Who Are the Homeless?"

At the beginning of the century, the novelist Jack London wandered among the poor and talked with them; near the end of the century Scott Shuger did the same. As you compare their accounts, consider the following questions:

1. What aspect of the suffering he observes seems most to horrify London? What aspect most horrifies Shuger? Compare and contrast the emotional attitudes of the two writers toward their common subject.

2. Among the people Shuger encounters, which ones are most like London's Carter and Carpenter? Which least? Discuss the similarities and differences.

3. Given these two representative accounts of homelessness, how much about the issue seems to you to have changed in the course of the century? How much has remained the same? Discuss your position with examples.

4. A folksy poet has said, "It takes a heap o' livin' / To make a house a home." Using examples from your reading of these essays and from your own experience, discuss the differences between "houselessness" and "homelessness."

AMONG THE LONDON POOR

Jack London

American novelist and social critic Jack London (1876–1916) was himself born in poverty in San Francisco and quit school to support himself at the age of fourteen. Nearly all of London's writing derives from firsthand experiences, like the following essay from his collection *The People of the Abyss* (1903).

The Carter, with his clean-cut face, chin beard, and shaved upper lip, I should have taken in the United States for anything from a master workman to a well-to-do farmer. The Carpenter—well, I should have taken him for a carpenter. He looked it, lean and wiry, with shrewd, observant eyes, and hands that had grown twisted to the handles of tools through forty-seven years' work at the trade. The chief difficulty with these men was that they were old, and that their children, instead of growing up to take care of them, had died. Their years had told on them, and they had been forced out of the whirl of industry by the younger and stronger competitors who had taken their places.

These two men, turned away from the casual ward of the Whitechapel Workhouse, were bound with me for Poplar Workhouse. Not much of a show, they thought, but to chance it was all that remained to us. It was Poplar, or the streets and night. Both men were anxious for a bed, for they were "about gone," as they phrased it. The Carter, fifty-eight years of age, had spent the last three nights without shelter or sleep, while the Carpenter, sixty-five years of age, had been out five nights.

But, O dear, soft people, full of meat and blood, with white beds and airy rooms waiting for you each night, how can I make you know what it is to suffer as you would suffer if you spent a weary night on London's streets? Believe me, you would think a thousand centuries had come and gone before the east paled into dawn; you would shiver till you were ready to cry aloud with the pain of each aching muscle; and you would marvel that you could endure so much and live. Should you rest upon a bench, and your tired eyes close, depend upon it the policeman would rouse you and gruffly order you to "move on." You may rest upon the bench, and benches are few and far between; but if rest means sleep, on you must go, dragging your tired body through the endless streets. Should you, in desperate slyness, seek some forlorn alley or dark passageway and lie down, the omnipresent policeman will rout you out just the same. It is his business to rout you out. It is a law of the powers that be that you shall be routed out.

But when the dawn came, the nightmare over, you would hie you home to refresh yourself, and until you died you would tell the story of your adventure to groups of admiring friends. It would grow into a mighty story. Your little eight-hour night would become an Odyssey and you a Homer.

Not so with these homeless ones who walked to Poplar Workhouse   5 with me. And there are thirty-five thousand of them, men and women, in London Town this night. Please don't remember it as you go to bed; if you are as soft as you ought to be you may not rest so well as usual. But for old men of sixty, seventy, and eighty, ill-fed, with neither meat nor blood, to greet the dawn unrefreshed, and to stagger through the day in mad search for crusts, with relentless night rushing down upon them again, and to do this five nights and days—O dear, soft people, full of meat and blood, how can you ever understand?

I walked up Mile End Road between the Carter and the Carpenter. Mile End Road is a wide thoroughfare, cutting the heart of East London, and there were tens of thousands of people abroad on it. I tell you this so that you may fully appreciate what I shall describe in the next paragraph. As I say, we walked along, and when they grew bitter and cursed the land, I cursed with them, cursed as an American waif would curse, stranded in a strange and terrible land. And, as I tried to lead them to believe, and succeeded in making them believe, they took me for a "seafaring man," who had spent his money in riotous living, lost his clothes (no unusual occurrence with seafaring men ashore), and was temporarily broke while looking for a ship. This accounted for my ignorance of English ways in general and casual wards in particular, and my curiosity concerning the same.

The Carter was hard put to keep the pace at which we walked (he told me that he had eaten nothing that day), but the Carpenter, lean and hungry, his gray and ragged overcoat flapping mournfully in the breeze, swung on in a long and tireless stride which reminded me strongly of the plains coyote. Both kept their eyes upon the pavement as they walked and talked, and every now and then one or the other would stoop and pick something up, never missing the stride the while. I thought it was cigar and cigarette stumps they were collecting, and for some time took no notice. Then I did notice.

From the slimy, spittle-drenched side-walk, they were picking up bits of orange peel, apple skin, and grape stems, and they were eating them. The pits of green gage plums they cracked between their teeth for the kernels inside. They picked up stray crumbs of bread the size of peas, apple cores so black and dirty one would not take them to be apple cores, and these things these two men took into their mouths, and chewed them, and swallowed them; and this, between six and seven o'clock in the evening of August 20, year of our Lord 1902, in the heart of the greatest, wealthiest, and most powerful empire the world has ever seen.

These two men talked. They were not fools. They were merely old. And, quite naturally, a-reek with pavement offal, they talked of bloody revolution. They talked as anarchists, fanatics, and madmen would talk. And who shall blame them? In spite of my three good meals that day, and the snug bed I could occupy if I wished, and my social philosophy, and my evolutionary belief in the slow development and metamorphosis of things—in spite of all this, I say, I felt impelled to talk rot with them or hold my tongue. Poor fools! Not of their sort are revolutions bred. And when they are dead and dust, which will be shortly, other fools will talk bloody revolution as they gather offal from the spittle-drenched side-walk along Mile End Road to Poplar Workhouse.

Being a foreigner, and a young man, the Carter and the Carpenter explained things to me and advised me. Their advice, by the way, was brief and to the point; it was to get out of the country. "As fast as God'll let me," I assured them; "I'll hit only the high places, till you won't be able to see my trail for smoke." They felt the force of my figures rather than understood them, and they nodded their heads approvingly.

"Actually make a man a criminal against 'is will," said the Carpenter. "'Ere I am, old, younger men takin' my place, my clothes gettin' shabbier an' shabbier, an' makin' it 'arder every day to get a job. I go to the casual ward for a bed. Must be there by two or three in the afternoon or I won't get in. You saw what happened today. What chance does that give me to look for work? S'pose I do get into the casual ward? Keep me in all day tomorrow, let me out mornin' o' next day. What then? The law sez I can't get in another casual ward that night less'n ten miles distant. Have to hurry an' walk to be there in time that day. What chance does that give me to look for a job? S'pose I don't walk. S'pose I look for a job? In no time there's night come, an' no bed. No sleep all night, nothin' to eat, what shape am I in the mornin' to look for work? Got to make up my sleep in the park somehow" (the vision of Christ's Church, Spitalfield, was strong on me) "an' get something to eat. An' there I am! Old, down, an' no chance to get up."

"Used to be a toll-gate 'ere," said the Carter, "Many's the time I've paid my toll 'ere in my cartin' days."

"I've 'ad three 'a'penny rolls in two days," the Carpenter announced, after a long pause in the conversation.

"Two of them I ate yesterday, an' the third to-day," he concluded, after another long pause.

"I ain't 'ad anything today," said the Carter. "An' I'm fagged out. My legs is hurtin' me somethin' fearful."

"The roll you get in the 'spike' is that 'ard you can't eat it nicely with less than a pint of water," said the Carpenter, for my benefit. And, on asking him what the "spike" was, he answered, "The casual ward. It's a cant word, you know."

But what surprised me was that he should have the word "cant" in his vocabulary that I found was no mean one before we parted.

I asked him what I may expect in the way of treatment, if we succeeded in getting into the Poplar Workhouse, and between them I was supplied with much information. Having taken a cold bath on entering, I would be given for supper six ounces of bread and "three parts of skilly." "Three

parts" means three-quarters of a pint, and "skilly" is a fluid concoction of
three quarts of oatmeal stirred into three buckets and a half of hot water.

"Milk and sugar, I suppose, and a silver spoon?" I queried.

"No fear. Salt's what you'll get, an' I've seen some places where you'd   *20*
not get any spoon. 'Old 'er up an' let 'er run down, that's 'ow they do it."

"You do get good skilly at 'Ackney," said the Carter.

"Oh, wonderful skilly, that," praised the Carpenter, and each looked
eloquently at the other.

"Flour an' water at St. George's in the East," said the Carter.

The Carpenter nodded. He has tried them all.

"Then what?" I demanded.   *25*

And I was informed that I was sent directly to bed. "Call you at half
after five in the mornin', an' you get up an' take a 'sluice'—if there's
any soap. Then breakfast, same as supper, three parts o' skilly an' a six-
ounce loaf."

"'Tisn't always six ounces," corrected the Carter.

"'Tisn't, no; an' often that sour you can 'ardly eat it. When first I started
I couldn't eat the skilly nor the bread, but now I can eat my own an' another
man's portion."

"I could eat three other men's portions," said the Carter. "I 'aven't 'ad a
bit this blessed day."

"Then what?"   *30*

"Then you've got to do your task, pick four pounds of oakum, or clean
an' scrub, or break ten to eleven hundredweight o' stones. I don't 'ave to
break stones; I'm past sixty, you see. They'll make you do it, though. You're
young an' strong."

"What I don't like," grumbled the Carter, "is to be locked up in a cell
to pick oakum. It's too much like prison."

"But suppose after you've had your night's sleep, you refuse to pick
oakum, or break stones, or do any work at all?" I asked.

"No fear you'll refuse the second time; they'll run you in," answered
the Carpenter. "Wouldn't advise you to try it on, my lad."

"Then comes dinner," he went on. "Eight ounces of bread, one and a   *35*
'arf ounces of cheese, an' cold water. Then you finish your task and 'ave
supper, same as before, three parts o' skilly an' six ounces of bread. Then to
bed, six o'clock, an' next mornin' you're turned loose, provided you've finished your task."

We had long since left Mile End Road, and after traversing a gloomy
maze of narrow, winding streets, we came to Poplar Workhouse. On a low
stone wall we spread our handkerchiefs, and each in his handkerchief put all
his worldly possessions with the exception of the "bit o' baccy" down his
sock. And then, as the last light was fading from the drab-colored sky, the
wind blowing cheerless and cold, we stood, with our pitiful little bundles in
our hands, a forlorn group at the workhouse door.

Three working girls came along, and one looked pityingly at me; as she passed I followed her with my eyes, and she still looked pityingly back at me. The old men she did not notice, Dear Christ, she pitied me, young and vigorous and strong, but she had no pity for the two old men who stood by my side! She was a young woman, and I was a young man, and what vague sex promptings impelled her to pity me put her sentiment on the lowest plane. Pity for old men is an altruistic feeling, and besides, the workhouse door is the accustomed place for old men. So she showed no pity for them, only for me, who deserved it least or not at all. Not in honor do gray hairs go down to the grave in London Town.

On one side the door was a bell handle, on the other side a press button.

"Ring the bell," said the Carter to me.

And just as I ordinarily would at anybody's door, I pulled out the handle   40
and rang a peal.

"Oh! Oh!" they cried in one terrified voice. "Not so 'ard!"

I let go, and they looked reproachfully at me, as though I had imperilled their chance for a bed and three parts of skilly. Nobody came. Luckily, it was the wrong bell, and I felt better.

"Press the button," I said to the Carpenter.

"No, no, wait a bit," the Carter hurriedly interposed.

From all of which I drew the conclusion that a poorhouse porter, who   45
commonly draws a yearly salary of from thirty to forty dollars, is a very finicky and important personage, and cannot be treated too fastidiously by—paupers.

So we waited, ten times a decent interval, when the Carter stealthily advanced a timid forefinger to the button, and gave it the faintest possible push. I have looked at waiting men where life and death was the issue; but anxious suspense showed less plainly on their faces than it showed on the faces of these two men as they waited for the coming of the porter.

He came. He barely looked at us. "Full up," he said, and shut the door.

"Another night of it," groaned the Carpenter. In the dim light the Carter looked wan and gray.

Indiscriminate charity is vicious, say the professional philanthropists. Well, I resolved to be vicious.

"Come on; get your knife out and come here," I said to the Carter,   50
drawing him into a dark alley.

He glared at me in a frightened manner, and tried to draw back. Possibly he took me for a latter-day Jack-the-Ripper, with a penchant for elderly male paupers. Or he may have thought I was inveigling him into the commission of some desperate crime. Anyway, he was frightened.

It will be remembered, at the outset, that I sewed a pound inside my stoker's singlet under the arm-pit. This was my emergency fund, and I was now called upon to use it for the first time.

Not until I had gone through the acts of a contortionist, and shown the round coin sewed in, did I succeed in getting the Carter's help. Even then his hand was trembling so that I was afraid he would cut me instead of the stitches, and I was forced to take the knife away and do it myself. Out rolled the gold piece, a fortune in their hungry eyes; and away we stampeded for the nearest coffee-house.

Of course, I had to explain to them that I was merely an investigator, a social student, seeking to find out how the other half lived. And at once they shut up like clams. I was not of their kind; my speech had changed, the tones of my voice were different, in short, I was a superior, and they were superbly class conscious.

"What will you have?" I asked, as the waiter came for the order.   55

"Two slices an' a cup of tea," meekly said the Carter.

"Two slices an' a cup of tea," meekly said the Carpenter.

Stop a moment, and consider the situation. Here were two men, invited by me into the coffee-house. They had seen my gold piece, and they could understand that I was no pauper. One had eaten a ha'penny roll that day, the other had eaten nothing. And they called for "two slices an' a cup of tea!" Each man had given a tu'penny order. "Two slices," by the way, means two slices of bread and butter.

That was the same degraded humility that had characterized their attitude toward the poorhouse porter. But I wouldn't have it. Step by step I increased their orders—eggs, rashers of bacon, more eggs, more bacon, more tea, more slices, and so forth—they denying wistfully all the while that they cared for anything more, and devouring it ravenously as fast as it arrived.

"First cup o' tea I've 'ad in a fortnight," said the Carter.   60

"Wonderful tea, that," said the Carpenter.

They each drank two pints of it, and I assure you that it was slops. It resembled tea less than lager beer resembles champagne. Nay, it was "water-bewitched," and did not resemble tea at all.

It was curious, after the first shock, to notice the effect the food had on them. At first they were melancholy, and talked of the divers times they had contemplated suicide. The Carter, not a week before, had stood on the bridge and looked at the water, and pondered the question. Water, the Carpenter insisted with heat, was a bad route. He, for one, he knew, would struggle. A bullet was "'andier," but how under the sun was he to get hold of a revolver? That was the rub.

They grew more cheerful as the hot "tea" soaked in, and talked more about themselves. The Carter had buried his wife and children, with the exception of one son, who grew to manhood and helped him in his little business. Then the thing happened. The son, a man of thirty-one, died of the smallpox. No sooner was this over than the father came down with fever and went to the hospital for three months. Then he was done for. He came out weak, debilitated, no strong young son to stand by him, his little business gone glimmering, and not a farthing. The thing had happened, and the game was up. No chance for an old man to start again. Friends all poor and unable to help. He tried for work when they were putting up stands for the first coronation parade. "An' I got fair sick of the answer: 'No! no! no!' It rang in my ears at night when I tried to sleep, always the same, 'No! no!

no!'" Only the past week he had answered an advertisement in Hackney, and on giving his age was told, "Oh, too old, too old by far."

The Carpenter had been born in the army, where his father had served twenty-two years. Likewise, his two brothers had gone into the army; one, troop sergeant-major of the Seventh Hussars, dying in India after the Mutiny; the other, after nine years under Roberts in the East, had been lost in Egypt. The Carpenter had not gone into the army, so here he was, still on the planet.

"But 'ere, give me your 'and," he said, ripping open his ragged shirt. "I'm fit for the anatomist, that's all. I'm wastin' away, sir, actually wastin' away for want of food. Feel my ribs an' you'll see."

I put my hand under his shirt and felt. The skin was stretched like parchment over the bones, and the sensation produced was for all the world like running one's hand over a washboard.

"Seven years o' bliss I 'ad," he said. "A good missus and three bonnie lassies. But they all died. Scarlet fever took the girls inside a fortnight."

"After this, sir," said the Carter, indicating the spread, and desiring to turn the conversation into more cheerful channels; "after this, I wouldn't be able to eat a workhouse breakfast in the morning."

"Nor I," agreed the Carpenter, and they fell to discussing stomach delights and the fine dishes their respective wives had cooked in the old days.

"I've gone three days and never broke my fast," said the Carter.

"And I, five," his companion added, turning gloomy with the memory of it. "Five days once, with nothing on my stomach but a bit of orange peel, an' outraged nature wouldn't stand it, sir, an' I near died. Sometimes, walkin' the streets at night, I've been that desperate I've made up my mind to win the horse or lose the saddle. You know what I mean sir—to commit some big robbery. But when mornin' come, there was I, too weak from 'unger an' cold to 'arm a mouse."

As their poor vitals warmed to the food, they began to expand and wax boastful, and to talk politics. I can only say that they talked politics as well as the average middle-class man, and a great deal better than some of the middle-class men I have heard. What surprised me was the hold they had on the world, its geography and peoples, and on recent and contemporaneous history. As I say, they were not fools, these two men. They were merely old, and their children had undutifully failed to grow up and give them a place by the fire.

One last incident, as I bade them good-by on the corner, happy with a couple of shillings in their pockets and the certain prospect of a bed for the night. Lighting a cigarette, I was about to throw away the burning match when the Carter reached for it. I proffered him the box, but he said, "Never mind, won't waste it, sir." And while he lighted the cigarette I had given him, the Carpenter hurried with the filling of his pipe in order to have a go at the same match.

"It's wrong to waste," said he.

65

70

75

"Yes," I said, but I was thinking of the washboard ribs over which I had run my hand.

Questions of Subject and Theme

1. Suffering and politics are two of the essay's themes. Describe London's attitude toward each and explain how the themes are related and distinguished.
2. London waited a long time before he revealed his money. Why do you imagine he waited so long? He says his act of charity changed the attitude of the men toward him. Why did it do so, in your opinion? Did it change London's attitude toward the men? Explain why you do or do not think so.

Questions of Method and Strategy

1. London never names the two homeless men, referring to them by their former occupations alone. What theme in the essay does this technique emphasize?
2. London repeats that the men were not foolish, just old. What theme in the essay does this repetition emphasize?

WHO ARE THE HOMELESS?

Scott Shuger

> In the 1990s investigative reporter Scott Shuger made a pilgrimage through the lives of the homeless similar to Jack London's at the beginning of the century. How much has changed, and how much remains the same?

For anyone living in a city, the dilemma unfolds dozens of times a day: There he is, between me and my immediate goal—The Man With The Styrofoam Cup, asking me a simple question: "Spare some change?" That question lights off others of my own that go unspoken: "What does this guy do with the money?" "How much does he make a day?" "Doesn't begging like this make him feel awful?" "Why doesn't it make him feel awful enough to stop and get a job?" "How did he get in this fix?" "Is he really in a fix, or is he taking me for a sucker?" "Why should I give to this guy rather than the other beggars on the block?" "Or do they think I can give to them all?"

"Spare some change?" comes up because I am in a limited way accessible to The Man With The Styrofoam Cup. My questions come up because he is in a radical way inaccessible to me. To most of us, the homeless are a visible mystery. Perhaps some of the most hardened among us would prefer them to be invisible. But the rest of us would prefer them to be less of a mystery. We want to help, yes, but we want our efforts to go where they will make a difference. For that to happen, we have to know what we're up against.

Hype for the Holidays

Although there have been some harder-edged stories on the homeless, the main message the media delivers about them is that despite their predicament, they're just like us. In a news special, Tom Brokaw stated that the homeless are "people you know." Robert Hayes, director of the National Coalition for the Homeless, told *The New York Times* that when he is contacted by television news programs or congressional committees looking at homelessness, "they always want white, middle-class people to interview." A recent study that examined the national print and broadcast coverage given the homeless between November 1986 and February 1989 discovered that a quarter of the homeless people featured in stories were children. That was equal to the number of those identified as unemployed and three times the number identified as substance abusers. Only 4 percent of the stories attributed the plight of the homeless to their personal problems.

A recent publication of the Better Business Bureau reported, "Many of those living in shelters or on the street are no different from those with a place to live. . . . Being on the street is often something out of their control."

In a *New York Times* op-ed piece, Rep. Charles Schumer wrote that "the slightest misstep or misfortune—a temporary layoff, a large medical bill, a divorce—could send [a low-income] family onto the streets. Indeed that's exactly what's been happening." The concrete examples of the homeless Schumer cited are a working mother of eight whose eldest is an honor student, and a 63-year-old woman forced to retire from her job as a waitress because of arthritis. In another *Times* op-ed piece entitled "The Homeless: Victims of Prejudice," two Ivy League law students said that the homeless people they met during a summer of intern work included a Broadway playwright, a highly decorated World War II veteran, and an ex-professional basketball player. Not to mention "pregnant women who lost the race to stay one step ahead of the housing marshal, students trying to study in noisy shelters, and average families working diligently to save enough money for an apartment."

Jonathan Kozol, in his book on homeless families, *Rachel and Her Children,* features: a couple who, after their house burns down, lose their five children to foster homes and are reduced to panhandling; a 35-year-old woman, a college graduate who worked for many years before medical complications wiped out her savings, forced her to lose her home, ended her marriage, made her give up her kids, and left her sleeping on the beach; and a teacher, who when the heater in her building failed, was "in a matter of weeks . . . reduced from working woman and householder to a client of the welfare system." To the question "Why are they without homes?" Kozol responds, "Unreflective answers might retreat to explanations with which readers are familiar: 'family breakdown,' 'drugs,' 'culture of poverty,' 'teen pregnancies,' 'the underclass,' etc. While these are precipitating factors for some people, they are not the cause of homelessness. *The cause of homelessness is lack of housing.*" (Italics in the original.)

Last December, the Salvation Army came out with a special TV commercial to boost its Christmas campaign for the homeless in New York City: *On the sidewalk in front of a wrought-iron fence, framed by a shopping bag on one side and a suitcase on the other, there's a mother and her child together in a sleeping bag, their white skins reflecting the street lights. As a man carrying a briefcase walks by, the child sits up; you can see her long blonde hair now. The mother kisses the girl and pulls her back down, hugging and patting her as they drift back to sleep.* "Home for the Holidays," the ad's caption says.

Honor students and playwrights, college graduates sleeping on the beach, mothers and daughters sleeping in the park—this is what I can read about or see on TV. But this is not what I see in Washington. Where in all this is the Man With The Styrofoam Cup?

Although real homeless people are all around me every day, I've been vulnerable to the more idealized representations of the press because my approach to street people has been typical of the white middle class: Usually, I stare straight ahead and walk on by, my head full of those skeptical questions. Sometimes, something—an excess of change, a particularly good day, or just a weariness of skepticism—would make me stop and give some money. But no matter what, there was one thing I would never, ever, do: Talk to these people. Recently, however, I decided to break that nervous middle class habit. I resolved to talk to the homeless, to ask them some of the questions I had been keeping to myself in all the years of walking right by.

Nights of Wine and Poses

I first put my new approach into effect one night last winter. On the stretch of Connecticut Avenue just above Dupont Circle, it was cold and rainy, and the panhandlers were huddled in bunches near the entrances of the restaurants on the block. With most of the dinner crowd already gone, the best pickings were over for the day. That left only pedestrians like me.

Two men come up to me, styrofoam cups in hand: "Spare some change?" Both men are unsteady on their feet and hard to understand, with 100-proof breath. I make a donation and learn that the tall black man is named Mike and the short one is K.C. I ask them how long they've been on the streets, and they tell me six months. They've both had jobs in construction. Mike says he used to work as a bartender until he lost his job because of his drinking. When I ask where they stay at night, Mike says that the owner of an art gallery across the street lets them sleep in the lobby of the building. Mike says they get to bathe every two days at a shelter in Alexandria.

"What do you do with the money you get?" I ask. Mike gives me a thumb–to–the–lip bottle motion. Then he shrugs his shoulders in embarrassment. "I got to go to a program. An in–patient program so I cain't get out so I cain't mess up. I got to clean my act up."

Mike is very polite, calling me "sir" frequently and saying "excuse me" to every passerby. K.C. is a little closer to the edge of his personal envelope tonight. When a couple turns into the restaurant behind us, he snaps at them, "If you don't eat all your food, bring a doggy bag for us."

Some surveys say that an inordinate number of the District's homeless are veterans. So I ask, "Were either of you guys in the service?" "I was on the Ho Chi Minh Trail," replies Mike. "I was over there in Korea," says K.C. "Quit telling the man lies," scolds Mike. I ask K.C. where and when. "I'm trying to 'member man. I'm shell-blocked," he says. "I ain't no dummy. Now hold it. All I know is I was in the 101 Screaming Eagles Fort Campbell Kentucky. Basic Training Fort Dix. But where I was, I can't re-member. I got shell-blocked. I've been shot up and all that shit, but I'm still alive."

Before I can pursue this, a completely drunk or stoned black woman comes over. She's in her late twenties, I'd guess. Her head is covered by a tight bandana and her eyes are only slits. Without saying anything, she greets Mike with a French kiss that lasts about ten seconds. Then she spends at least that long sticking her tongue in his ear. Even so, she's hanging on to Mike as much for navigation as for affection. "Sandra, this is him," Mike says, pointing towards me.

10

"I'm Chocolate," says Sandra. "That's Memphis and that's um, Black."   *15*
Mike shrugs his shoulders in embarrassment again. Just then, a younger guy,
more drugged than drunk, charges toward us. This guy is really revved up
on something. He starts shouting at me from 25 feet away. He's in his late
teens, early twenties, with a fighter's build and a bull neck. "That's my girl-
fren'—what you all doing to her?" He pushes the other three behind him
and gets in my face. "Who do you see on this corner first? What's wrong?
You gonna help us out?"

As I start to leave, Mike offers his hand. His handshake is solid. I bet the
rest of him was too, several thousand drinks ago. "Give me your address,"
demands Sandra. "Can I go home with you tonight?" It was somewhere
between pitiful and sexual. "I don't want no shelter. I want to go to your
house. I want to sleep in a bed, a real righteous bed."

A block away I cross paths with two guys standing out of the rain under
the overhang of a closed lunch stand. Both in their twenties, one white, the
other black. It quickly becomes apparent that all they have in common is
this dry spot of sidewalk. The white guy, who tells me his name is Wayne,
asks me for some change, telling me he got laid off from a construction job.
The black guy, without introducing himself, quickly tries to take over.
"Hey, I'm in a situation too. I'm a starving artist, and nobody's giving me
nothing. I don't have a job. But I'm a millionaire, I know that inside. That
my art is worth money, OK? But I know I'm gonna make it. All I got to do
is go to New York. I've been trying for four years to get back there. I just
need enough money to go to New York. The only thing I need is like
150 bucks."

I ask him if he ever tries finding work in the want ads. "Everybody
keeps saying that, man! The paper is to get you to buy it or look at it.
They're still making money off you! Hey, see all these stores out here? Every
one of them got a loan to get what they've got. Well, I need a loan. If I
had a loan for about $10,000, I'd be a multimillionaire, man, because my
art is fuckin' baaad. That's the only way I'm gonna make it—if I get a
fuckin' loan."

Wayne hasn't said a word during this rap. But when the starving artist,
now pretty agitated, nervously walks to the corner to search out better possibilities than me, Wayne rolls his eyes and says to me out of the corner of
his mouth, "It don't take nobody no four years to get back to New York,
I'm sorry." Wayne is not wildly drunk, but now that I'm standing close to
him I can tell he's pretty numbed up. Wayne is one of the truly unsheltered
homeless. In good weather he sleeps in the park just opposite the Q street
Metro exit. In bad weather he sleeps under the portico of an attorney's office
or in a nearby building that's under construction. He has shoulder-length
light-blond hair coming down from under his ball cap, a moustache, and
the beginnings of a beard. About four years ago, he came to this area from
Texas with his family. Then his mother died and his father started a house-
painting company in Virginia. Wayne used to work there. I ask him why he
quit. This was, after all, the decision that finally put him on the street. I
figure there had to be a pretty dramatic reason. All Wayne comes up with is

this: "I just couldn't deal with it, too many Spanish workers—they can't speak English because most of them are illegal immigrants—and being the boss's son."

The artist comes back. "Can you give me a buck or 50 cents, man, so I can get on the subway?" he asks me. As I give him two quarters, I notice that he's wearing a Burberry scarf. After he leaves, Wayne says, "I don't like him. He's a con artist. I'm watching right now to see if he gets on the subway." He doesn't.

Wayne turns his attention back to me. "I used to be in trouble all the time until I got my head cleared. Put it this way," he chuckles, "I got a few tatoos from prison." Wayne says his conviction for knifing a guy in a Texas bar fight is a problem when he's looking for work. "That's why I go for jobs that are under the table."

Hope for Some Homeless

In my travels around Washington, I rarely see homeless women on the street. But there are places outdoors where they congregate. One such spot is a steep stretch of Belmont Street in the northwest quadrant of the city. Walking north on 14th Street and turning onto Belmont any evening at around 5:30, you will gradually become aware of a pilgrimage—first just a few shadows moving through the uneven light, but eventually a line of them making the daily trek up to the top of the hill. Most of the shadows are families, virtually all black, living in temporary housing for the homeless. There are very few men, either by themselves or attached to a family group. I fall in step with the shadow families, curious to see what could have this drawing power.

At the top of the hill is the one-time Pitts Hotel, a ramshackle building now operated as a shelter for homeless families. Parked out front under the archway is a gleaming yellow Rolls Royce, District license plate 347. A man standing next to it tells me that it belongs to the building's owner, Cornelius Pitts. [For more on Pitts, see "How the Homeless Bought a Rolls for Cornelius Pitts," Marianne Szegedy-Maszak, July/August 1987.] The people file by it without taking much notice. The building has room for only 50 or so families, but every day the District's Department of Human Services deposits four additional busloads of shelter residents—mostly families—at the foot of the hill so that they can get a cooked meal.

Watching the women come and go on Belmont, you can't avoid the feeling that they are fighting some powerful obstacles in addition to the lack of a permanent place to live. Many seem tired and cranky, snapping at their children and cuffing them for transgressions that are hard to see in this light. "I'm not here because I'm all drugged up," says a plump woman with four kids in tow, hurrying down the hill to make the last bus. "I work as a nurse's assistant at D.C. General, and the truth is"—her voice lowers—"I had to leave where I was living because my friend was beating on me."

Despite these dark overtones, the longer I watch and listen, the more I become aware of the many hopeful signs on Belmont Street. As a group, these women seem fairly straight. Straight enough for Tom Brokaw. They stand in stark contrast to street hustlers like K.C. or the artist. Although the meals and the pick-up buses run on such a tight schedule that most of the women are in too much of a hurry to talk to me, those who do tell me that they are working, leaving their kids with babysitters during the day. A gregarious teenage mother of an 11-month-old tells me her biggest complaint: these daily crosstown voyages for food have left her baby with a persistent cold. A soft-spoken woman with three kids tells me that she has just gotten herself on a list downtown for housing placement; she hopes that in a few more weeks the city will be able to locate a place for her. Most of the women are dressed neatly, and some of the kids are in adorable get-ups: Bows in hair and party shoes for the girls, superhero jackets and team ball-caps for the boys. Obviously, many of these people are using their meager means for the right things; given more sustenance, most of them would only do more of the same. Yes, for the Belmont families, it seems that housing *would* be a big part of the answer.

Heartbreak Hotel

At Mt. Carmel House, a homeless women's shelter in Washington's Chinatown, you can meet the people the Belmont Street women are trying not to become. Ann, for instance—a sad-eyed 41-year-old black woman who has come to this women's shelter straight from a stint at the detox unit at D.C. General. Ann discovered she couldn't handle alcohol after many years of what she calls "trial and error." Before booze derailed her life, she was a data clerk at the Veterans' Administration. But now she's lost her job, and her 18-year-old daughter lives with Ann's mother.

Or there's Marsha, a black woman in her twenties whose five years on cocaine and one year of living on the streets have somehow left her eyeballs and her teeth the same yellow color. This time last year, she was pawning anything she could get her hands on and working as a prostitute to raise drug money. A high-school dropout who was sexually abused by her father, Marsha has a daughter by a man she used to live with; she no longer has any contact with him and the authorities have taken the child away. Last November, Marsha got shot in the head by "some crackhead going around in the streets shooting for the hell of it. I should have gone to the doctor right away," she says. "But I wouldn't go to the doctor until I'd done all my cocaine first."

Celeste Valente, who's been a social worker at Mt. Carmel House for eight years, says that the shelter's 40-odd resident population now includes more younger women than it used to. There's been a decrease in the mentally ill clientele (now 30 percent of the population, down from 80 percent a few years ago) and an increase in drug addicts (almost all those in the shelter who are not mentally ill are substance abusers). Valente guesses that "more than 80 percent of the women who come here have been raped or were the victims of incest."

Another woman living at Mt. Carmel is Virginia, who's spent the last year in shelters—four in all. She's white, in her forties, with "done" hair, pink lipstick, and rouged cheeks. Her handbag says "Maui" on it. She could easily pass for a suburbanite down here doing volunteer work. In fact, she now volunteers a couple of nights a week at a nearby dinner program. "When I was working," Virginia remembers, "I gave about $1,500 of my United Way funds to the House of Ruth [another women's shelter in Washington]. And when I became homeless, that's the first place I went." Virginia's father was career Army. She was born in Austria. She has a literature degree from Georgetown. "I had the life," she says.

Here it seems I've come across a person worthy of Jonathan Kozol, the 30 Salvation Army, and all the other "it could happen to anyone" theorists. But there's a difference they might not like. Virginia's an alcoholic. And she spent a long time in what she describes as a "sick" relationship with a sexually abusive man. After she was laid off from her job managing an engineering office, she stayed in her apartment, watched TV, and drank for eight months. "I drank copious amounts of beer," she tells me, "three six-packs to a case a day."

Karmic Crossed Wires

During the eighties, Lafayette Park, just across Pennsylvania Avenue from the White House, became a campground for homeless squatters. Indeed, some people have lived there for most of the decade, conducting what they call a "peace vigil." The vigil is often on the itinerary of school classes visiting from out of town. The peace squatters have positioned themselves along the south edge of the park, where their placards about Hiroshima and nuclear freeze face the president's front door. Sixties-like, they give themselves new names like "Sunrise." One vigiler I talk to, who's lived here for three years, used to work as an art restorer before joining the scene he describes as a "karmic crossfire." He doesn't want to live anywhere else. He supports himself by performing three nights a week in a "folk rock" band. The rest of the time he's out in the park, sometimes sleeping in his jury-rigged plastic shelter, sometimes cooking up a stew, or greeting pedestrians with lines like, "Peace, brother. Thanks for smiling"—whether the guy is smiling or not.

But some of the homeless in Lafayette Park are conducting more private vigils. Take the man on the park bench, hands on knees, open bottle of beer at his feet, just staring intensely at the White House. With the green of his poncho and the way his eyes are bulging, he looks like a frog on a lily pad. "I'm here to talk to George," he tells me. When he sees my fatigue pants, he goes to Red Alert, "Are you Marine Corps, FBI, Secret Service? Are you wearing a tape recorder?" I reassure him. He's so close to jumping out of his skin that I worry about what would happen if he were to notice the two men in uniform on the White House roof. "Yeah, George is a good man," the guy on the bench says, continuing to stare straight ahead. "I don't have nothing against him. He's a naval aviator and all that. When he went out to San Francisco after that earthquake, I talked to him." I asked the man if he flew out there to do that. "Nope," he says, never taking his eyes off his quarry, "talked to him by Telstar."

The Telstar man has plenty of company in Washington. Near my office for instance, there is the tall, helmeted man who keeps a guardpost at the corner of Q and Connecticut. When you get close to him, you can see that he's wearing a flannel West German army uniform. He's sort of handsome and he has that straight-from-the-diaphragm voice and ramrod posture so valued in drill instructors. His long reddish brown hair runs in a thin, tight braid down his back. Tucked in his helmet and pointing straight up are three toothbrushes, looking like periscopes.

When I ask him his name, he replies, "General. U.S. General. None of that Noriega thing for me." I notice that he's wearing a Top Gun squadron patch; he tells me where he got it: "The Surgeon General distributed it to the field artillery and ballistics command and the dominions of trade. Top Gun. Miramar California. I took the training out there about eight weeks ago. It was about the failure to inform people at the White House. And to maintain gun standards, computer standards, or surgical standards."

When I ask General what he's doing at this corner, he tells me, "This is   35
the field marshal air combat warning post here for the businesses and the banks. This post is the way that the military has become involved about the levering of the topmost business developments." What's he watching out for? The answer comes back instantly: "The Turks." As to how long he'll be in this assignment, General guesses about 40 years. "It should improve sometime in the nineties as far as the Motorola business is concerned. Eventually I will tend towards Walkman business. How the General maintains his districting or vector businesses is highly dependent upon Walkman skills."

General does not know he's homeless. When I ask him where he goes at night and in bad weather, he tells me that he confers with the president. He readily distinguishes himself from panhandlers, whom he dismisses as "people who have no ownership interests or no mortgage or paper interests." However, in a way, he does have his own version of "Spare some change?" As I'm leaving, he says to me, "You should bring me a banknote so that the interests you represent can be represented here."

The Grate Society

Under an overpass in Foggy Bottom just east of the Potomac and just north of the exclusive Watergate apartment complex are some steam grates that have long served as a thermal oasis for the homeless. The night I walk by is chilly, so the grates are pretty full. When I approach, several of the men there ask me for change. The hot air rushing out of this hole in the ground produces a loud hum you have to shout over. The steam itself provides a two-part sensation: first your face gets hit by a pleasant rush of warmth, then your nose gets hit by the stench of stale booze. Booze that's soaked through clothes, that's soaked through skin, that's soaked through lives.

There are nine or ten men at the grate this night. It's an interracial group. Some are huddled at the edges, some just racked out across it. The two men who asked me for money talk to me a lot, but some of the others never even look in my direction.

One man tells me he's been out here for two years, another says eight. The liveliest talker is a young black guy named Tony. In his midtwenties, he's handsome and, in an alcoholic sort of way, articulate. Tony points to a woman coming our way. "Here comes my girlfriend. That's way I'm out here, because of her." A black woman weaves towards us. She's really drunk. She plops down sullenly at the edge of the grate, no use for anybody. "I met her in July when I came out the Navy," Tony says, unaccountably thrilled to see her.

Tony says he's not really homeless because he can stay with his aunt at   *40* 14th and Euclid. But it's real late and he's still out here drinking.

Tony says he was in the Navy for eight years. "Aviation. Backseater in F-14s. I was a second lieutenant. I worked in the Indian Ocean on the *Nimitz*. Just got out in July. I'm going back. I'm in the reserves." There's a pause. "I was supposed to been back—I'm not going to lie to you. I'm AWOL. When I came out of high school and went to the Navy, I started out as an NCO—a noncommissioned officer. I was an NCO all the way. I went to school in Annapolis. When I go back, they may drop me down to like E-4. After I get out of the brig. I see Navy cars go by here every day. They're MPs, man, I know they lookin' for me.

"I want to re-up for maybe four more years. And then come back and get me a job at one of these airports as an aviator or air traffic controller. But it's gonna be a while for me now because last Saturday night, some girl stabbed me in my chest. And all I got is one lung now." As he's telling me this, Tony's unbuttoning his shirt. He shows me a Band-Aid just under his clavicle. It's not a very elaborate dressing, and I don't see any signs of actual injury. "I just got out of the hospital. And today two guys tried to jump on me." Tony shows me his punching hand. The knuckles on it are very swollen. "So it's gonna be a while—maybe another two months— until I go back."

Tony says the Navy sent him here on shore leave to bury his grand-mother. "That's when I met Karen," he tells me, nodding toward the poor woman who just joined us. "Took a liking to her. And she turned my head around." He says Karen used to drive trucks in the Army, that she was in Vietnam. He says she's 38. She looks 58. Tony reaches between his knees into the red plastic milk crate he's sitting on and pulls out a white plastic flask. Gin, he tells me. A pint a day. Pointing at the others, he explains, "They drink that hard stuff."

Tony's story was fascinating, but it wasn't true. You can't start out in the service as an NCO, and "second lieutenant" is not a rank in the Navy.

The old man at my feet, whom Tony introduces as Jimmy, "the grand-   *45* daddy of the grates," mumbles at me. In the slurred words of a lifelong drunk he tells me that he's worked as a tow-truck driver at an Amoco station for 18 years. But, he says, "See those," pointing at some of Georgetown's poshest apartments, "I don't make enough money to rent no apartment for

$250 a month. So I say here." Jimmy's incredibly dirty. He never looks up at me. His attention is riveted on a little pack of picture cards he keeps riffling through. They're not baseball cards, although they're that size. Because they're predominantly pink, I assume they're pornographic. When Jimmy hands me one, I see they're not. They're pictures of food. The card in my hand is "Shrimp with Greens."

The closest thing to an American monument to homelessness is the shelter run by the Community for Creative Non-Violence (CCNV) in the former Federal City College building at the intersection of 2nd and D in downtown Washington. This is the building that the federal government agreed to lease to homeless advocate Mitch Snyder in 1984 after Snyder led a 51-day fast. Housing 1,400 homeless—1,265 men and 135 women—it's the largest shelter in the country, perhaps in the world. CCNV's literature calls it "a national model."

Since its inception, the CCNV shelter has received over $13 million in combined federal and D.C. appropriations, and another $500,000 in corporate donations. I wanted to get an idea of what that money is buying. To do that, I decided to take my idea of talking to the homeless one step further by going to the shelter and asking for help.

Shelter Skelter

I showed up at CCNV late on a Saturday afternoon in January, dressed in my worst clothes and having not washed or shaved for days. In front of the building, Saturday night is already well underway. Thirty or so men are standing on the porch and along the sidewalk, talking loudly and taking regular pulls from the brown paper bags they all seem to have. One of the louder guys is a gapped-toothed man in a purple parka. He's shouting out at anybody walking by and going through a loud review of the lunch he had at some soup kitchen: "Uhhhh-uhhhh, barbecue chicken! I'm telling you, they got *down*. . . ."

When they're not drinking and cursing, the men spend a lot of time spitting. The sidewalk is phlegm-spotted. It's hard to find a dry spot on the steps to sit on. Almost as soon as I do, I attract the attention of a disastrously drunk man who until then had been working full-time trying to keep from impacting the sidewalk. He's lurching about furiously, like a man on the deck of a storm-blown ship. He finally makes it over next to me. Even sitting down, he's weaving. He mumbles something to me I can't make out. The second time, I catch it: "Do you have five cents?" When I say I don't, he repeats the question. Then he mumbles something else, "What's in the bag?" For authenticity, I have a paper bag with me. The drunk grabs my arm and tries to pull me towards him. "What's in the bag?" "Nothing for you," I tell him, moving away. This catches Purple Parka's attention. From his perch, he looks down at me and barks. "Talk to the man like that and I'll bust yo' ass on the sidewalk."

When a woman comes to the front of the building with some stuff to   *50* donate, Purple Parka comes down and swarms all over her, putting his arm around her and trying to take her through a door where she doesn't want to go. "Be sociable," another man tells him. "You not on the staff." Parka snaps back, "I ain't yo' nigger." When a girl with a pretty hairstyle walks by, he shouts at her, "I want your hair!" She replies, "You gonna buy me some more?"

I move down to the wooden benches near one corner of the building. From here, I can see something that I couldn't before. Behind a van across the street, two guys are fighting. They must be pretty drunk; the pace doesn't let up a bit even when one guy slams the other's head into the van.

There's a constant stream of men coming in and out of the building. A beer can in a paper sack is practically part of the uniform. A few weeks before tonight, *Newsweek* ran a picture of the area where I'm sitting now. In the shot, the CCNV building and grounds looked spic-and-span. The three guys now on the bench to my right, sharing a joint, weren't there. And neither were the two women and one guy on the sidewalk right in front of me, passing a reefer between them. A young black guy dressed in the immaculate fashion of followers of Muslim leader Louis Farrakhan—black suit, bow tie, highly polished shoes—comes over to the trio. I expect him to tell them to put the joint out. But instead he takes off his Walkman and lends it to one of the women. She closes her eyes and sways to the music, continuing to take her tokes. A guy yells down to the group from the balcony, "You know she be horny when she smokes that shit!"

So far, out of the hundred or so people I've seen at CCNV, I'm the only white. That's why I notice when three white guys come out of the building. They're walking down the ramp when a tall man with one of those Eraserhead hairdos that's high and flat on top and shaved bald all around the sides suddenly comes up in their faces and edges them towards the wall. He says something to them and then they sheepishly continue on their way. Eraserhead has now joined Purple Parka out front as one of CCNV's unofficial greeters. He's got a pocket square tucked into his sports jacket, and is wearing a fancy-looking watch and four rings.

I go inside to find out what prospects there are for getting put up for the night. I'm told that the shelter is full until Tuesday, but that a van will eventually come to take me to one of the city's emergency shelters. I decide to wait in the lobby. Over the next couple of hours there I see a lot.

Residents continue to stream in and out of the building. (There is no sign-in or sign-out. The building is open most of the time. Between midnight and 4 a.m. the front door is opened for five minutes every half hour.) About a third of the people I see are carrying Walkman sets. At least half are carrying beer or liquor. The stuff's usually in a paper bag, but several people, Eraserhead among them, are carrying beer in plastic cups. Later, a CCNV spokesman named Lawrence Lyles tells me that CCNV policy is that "we allow people to have beer and hard stuff, but not illegal drugs. As long as they maintain themselves. This is the residents' house. If you were home, you'd drink a little beer, wouldn't you?" But more than a few of the residents are not maintaining themselves. Drunks—weaving, falling-down drunks—are a common sight in the lobby. Some of them get up the steps only because they are carried up. Only once does a staff member ask anybody what he's carrying in. And when the resident laughs off the question, the staff member doesn't pursue it. What I see supports what an experienced city social worker tells me later: "There are drugs in CCNV. The place is out of control."

Conversation here tends to be animated, often hostile. "If all you needed to live was a teaspoon of water," one man snaps at another, "I wouldn't give it to you." Another man explains in a loud voice why he wants a stiletto. "Because if I miss you one way, I'll cut you coming back." "Look," says one laughing guy to his friend, pointing to a bearded, wasted white man whose eyes are set on infinite, "Charlie Manson is on parole."

A handsome man with longish gray-black hair comes down to get his mail. He's carrying two books, the first I've seen here. He's neatly dressed in a completely coordinated Army camouflage uniform. In this scene, he looks as solid as a rock. He's walking towards me as he finishes his letter. "They say they will give me money if I go to a psychiatrist," he tells me, his face lit up now by a scary smile. "But I will stay here instead!"

Even in this chaos, there are some touches fit for a public service announcement. An older black man asks a feeble-looking white man about how he's mending since he got hit by a car. He listens patiently as the man shows him his injuries and explains what medical appointments he has set up in the days ahead. A lady gives a man in a wheelchair a spin he clearly enjoys.

At about 8 p.m., one of the staff members very politely informs the few of us who've been waiting for transportation that there will be no van run tonight. He quickly goes on to tell us that there's room at one of the city's newest emergency shelters. And it's within walking distance, over at the Department of Employment Services just around the corner.

On my way there, I fall in with two other guys, Tom and James, headed for the same place. They are both refreshingly clean-cut and substance-free. We all shake hands and quickly hit it off. The DES shelter is actually in the employees' parking garage underneath the building. It's well heated, and the nice lady volunteer who checks us in issues us like-new Army cots and a tuna sandwich apiece. There are about 50 people already on cots when we arrive—the place is full. The three of us help each other set up our cots. Tom takes a shower and brings some cups and water back from the bathroom to make up some Kool-Aid he's brought with him. He shares it with James and me and gives us each a cookie, too. The shelter atmosphere is pretty much like that of a barracks; there's plenty of "smokin' and jokin'" but the drunks are mostly down for the count. The roving armed guard probably helps.

The three of us talk among ourselves. Tom's a white guy with a bushy moustache. He just got out of jail—during a routine traffic stop the day before, he got arrested on an old warrant for driving without a license. He made bail, but he's from Virginia, and without a license or car (it got impounded), and low on money, he has no way to get back. And he has no

60

place to stay here. His court date is next month, and he figures he will get some jail because, as he puts it, "this isn't the first time."

James is black and works in the kitchen at the Marriott in Crystal City. He's wearing an Army jacket, from his days as a parachute rigger in the Airborne. This is his first day on the streets. He had been living with his girlfriend, but they had a fight. James works on the side as a party DJ. At one of these parties, a girl gave him her phone number to give to a friend of his, but James's girlfriend discovered it in his jacket and went nuts, throwing James out of the house and all of his stuff down the stairs. I ask James if there isn't a family member he can stay with until this boils over. "I tried staying with my mother," he answers, "but she had too many restrictions—she won't give me a key, she won't let me in past 11 at night, and there's no TV downstairs. I'm a party animal."

Lying back on my cot, I spend a long time staring at the garage ceiling, trying to figure out James's logic. Why would somebody clean and employed choose this—and tomorrow night maybe something much worse—over coming in at 11 to a house with only one TV? Would "people you know" do that?

Conspicuous Dysfunction

The Depression taught most Americans that there are plenty of ways to become poor that aren't one's fault. By now this is a lesson well-learned. Perhaps too well-learned. Americans tend to believe that homelessness is exclusively a social problem, a system failure. This idea goes hand-in-hand with the traditional liberal notion that the solution to the problem is simply the provision of housing and jobs. While there is something to this, it's not *the* solution—as I found out for myself there's too much else going on with the homeless.

Allowing for the possibility of some overlap, here's how I would roughly   65
classify the homeless people I met: At least three-quarters were (current or recovering) substance abusers, three-quarters were unattached men, and about a third seemed to some degree mentally ill. But there is another important factor I observed in about half of the homeless people I talked to—one that takes a little explaining. I call it the "X-factor" because I'm not having much luck figuring it out.★

Ronald Reagan once came in for a lot of well-deserved criticism for saying that anybody who is homeless is so only because he chooses to be. That's a ridiculous notion. Sleeping in the park in the winter, being chronically sick and disoriented—nobody chooses *that*. But just the same, people like the New York artist, Wayne from Texas, and James are carrying some-

---

★It's interesting to compare my description of the homeless population based on my own experience with what you can find in print elsewhere. Most respected policy studies and surveys are now saying that about a third of the homeless are mentally ill, a third are substance abusers, and a third are "other." That is, they find less substance abuse than I did, about the same amount of mental illness, and tend to leave the rest of the population an undifferentiated mystery while I think some of that remainder is in the grip of X-factor thinking.

thing around in their heads that's separating them from opportunities and propelling them towards ruin. The artist has his incoherent put-down of the classifieds, Wayne has his equally confused contempt for the work at his father's business, and James has his odd standards about acceptable living conditions. Here are some other examples of the X-factor I came across in talking to the homeless:

- One of the beggars I frequently see is a 24-year-old black guy who goes by the street name "Quickness." He can usually be found around Dupont Circle either zoned out or trying to be. He tells me that he originally came to Washington to sell PCP, but he got caught and spent three years in jail. He's been on the streets for the seven months since he got out. When I ask him what he wants out of life, he tells me "money." His parents are back in Florida, and they know he's up here, but he won't go back to them and he won't even tell them he's homeless. Quickness prefers staying in the streets to that.

- A fiftyish man whom I often see late at night begging near my office, an articulate man who appears sane and drug- and alcohol-free, tells me that he served in submarines in the Navy and then worked at the Nuclear Regulatory Commission. He says that he lost his job at the NRC because of differences with this bosses. Later, he landed a job stuffing envelopes for a political organization, but he quit because he didn't agree with the material he was mailing and went back to the streets, where he makes about $2 an hour (it turns out that's the typical figure for a Washington beggar).

- A young woman I met who splits her begging between Dupont Circle and Georgetown tells me that she recently failed the Civil Service exam. I ask her if she has tried to get into a job training program. "I feel that I don't have the time for that. I just want something right now. Something I can just walk into and get right then and there."

All of these people fail the Bill Shade test. Bill is the only single male homeless person I met who I am convinced is actively trying every day to become unhomeless. Bill was working in construction when he got burned out of his apartment. Most of what Bill collects from begging he turns over to the woman who takes care of his daughter. Once I was talking to Bill when I noticed the Help Wanted sign behind his head. He read my mind: "I already went in there, but they want a girl to work behind the counter." So instead he sweeps the sidewalk in front of the shop. He works odd jobs whenever he can. He cleans up around the bank where he sleeps. He puts quarters in expired parking meters to save people he doesn't know from paying the $15 ticket. He's hoping to get the funds together to move back to Baltimore with his daughter. If reading this story makes you feel like helping a single homeless person directly, call me or write me about Bill Shade.

I'm finding it hard to articulate the troublesome mental baggage that hampers the New York artist or Quickness say, but not Bill Shade. It's not, contra the Reagan camp, mere laziness—these people work much harder every day than most just to keep from freezing to death. It's something more like a twisted sense of pride—a sense of personal specialness tweaked so ridiculously high that anything—even sleeping outside and begging for food—is viewed as better than forms of compromise that you and I would readily accept, like fitting in at work, getting a job out of the newspaper, or coming home at 11. For all I can tell, some of this odd thinking is the extreme rationalization so common in alcoholics and substance abusers, and some is a sign of a treatable organic thought disorder, like mild schizophrenia. But I'm also convinced that some of the homeless I met who evinced the X-factor were neither mentally ill nor addicts. What do we make of them?

If you've raised children in the seventies and eighties, then you know how the emphasis on rampant instant gratification and conspicuous consumption of such television fare as "Dallas," "Lifestyles of the Rich & Famous," and "L.A. Law" can distort your children's desires and expectations. Sometimes being "tough"—emphasizing setting goals and working hard to achieve them, etc.—brings kids around on this. But many parents have experienced the bewilderment that comes when that doesn't work. How do we reach Johnny? How do we bring him down to earth so that he can make a good life for himself? Parents can use up a decade or more wrestling with such questions, often without arriving at an answer. Well, maybe the bewilderment I feel in the face of the foregoing examples is similar, with a similar cause. But about two or three times more extreme. It seems that some of the homeless have just soaked up way too much of our culture's obsession with "too much, too soon."

There can be all the low-cost housing in the world, and an untreated paranoid won't set foot in it, and an untreated schizophrenic might burn it down. (Dr. E. Fuller Torrey, a psychiatrist who is an expert on the homeless mentally ill, told me that he has encountered both outcomes.) And a drug addict will spend the rent money on crack. So homelessness is in large measure a mental health problem and a drug problem that defies the conventional liberal answers of housing and jobs. But notice this about the X-factor homeless: They aren't likely to be people for whom jobs and housing alone would be the answer, either. Once a man decides to eat only caviar, he will turn down bread as fervently as an ordinary man turns down poison. If low cost housing were made available to the New York artist (and for all I know, it already has been), but there was no $10,000 loan, how would he pay the rent? If he were offered a nonglamorous job to make the rent, would he take it?

There certainly seem to be homeless people who are nearly like you and me, save for some intervening bad breaks. Many of the women on Belmont Street appear to fit that bill, as does Bill Shade. So for people like these, fixing the bad break—making jobs and housing available—*is* what's called for. But media depictions to the contrary, there are more homeless people—the untreated mentally ill, the addicted, and those with the X-factor—*who are not like us.* As a result, if they are ever to realize secure and steady lives, they will require different kinds of help.

70

Traditional liberals don't want to admit such differences—and that's wrong—because they want us to help all the homeless—that's right. Neoconservatives admit the differences (right) because they don't want to help them all (wrong). The correct position is to admit the differences among the homeless while strenuously working to help them all. If conservatives need to care more, liberals need to *see* more. It's a cruel joke to pretend that an untreated mentally ill person is better off in the streets than he would be if he were compelled somehow to take medication, or to pretend that Quickness would hold down a job with the same tenacity as Bill Shade. To make real progress in the fight against homelessness, we must first be honest about who the homeless are.

Questions of Subject and Theme

1. Which of the people he encounters does Shuger seem to have most sympathy for? Which least? Explain what seems to make the difference for him.
2. At the end of the essay Shuger finds fault with both the "conservative" and "liberal" views of homelessness. Explain his own views and their relation to those he opposes.

Questions of Method and Strategy

1. Many of the titles of Shuger's sections make puns or ironic comments. What attitude toward his content does Shuger create through this technique? What attitude does it invite in his reader? How are these attitudes related to the complex and unconventional position on the issue that Shuger stakes out for himself at the end of the essay?
2. Which of the people Shuger encounters is most vividly evoked for you? Discuss the ways in which Shuger uses techniques of writing to individuate the figure you choose.

Suggestions for Writing on the Juxtapositions

1. Write an essay in which you analyze, compare, and contrast the methods by which the two writers work to elicit the sympathies of their audiences while making their own sympathies clear.
2. In spite of their sympathies, both writers insist on their differences from the people they describe. Write an essay in which you compare and contrast the techniques each writer uses to describe people different from himself.
3. Think of an episode in your own life in which you have found yourself in the company of people less fortunate than yourself. Write an essay about the event with the idea of considering what charity means to you.
4. Do you agree with Shuger's analysis of the problem at the end of his essay? Write an essay in which you defend or criticize his conclusions while making your own position on the issue plain.

11 Imagining the End of the World

Robert Frost, "Fire and Ice"
Sir Frederick Hoyle, "The Next Ice Age"
Carl Sagan, "The Warming of the World"

Two scientists and a poet consider the meaning of the end of the world through fire or ice. Examine the processes of their imaginations while asking yourself the following questions:

1. This section provides examples of both scientific and poetic sensibilities. Use these selections to compare and contrast the two methods of apprehending life. For example, what does *life* mean for each sensibility? What about *apprehending?* How does scientific discourse use personal concepts and how does poetic discourse use scientific ones?

2. Compare and contrast the methods of Sagan and Hoyle with regard to their uses of evidence and manner of reasoning. On what assumptions does each writer base his predictions? Do they implicitly answer the arguments and objections raised by opposing views of the future of the earth?

3. The strengths of science are said to come from its goal of detached, impersonal, objective observation of facts. Does each writer seem to you to strive for this goal? Explain your answers with examples.

4. Time is a concept that is notoriously difficult to understand and discuss. A past when neither writers nor readers were alive, a future in which neither writers nor readers will be alive—describe as best you can the difficulties that such issues present for the imagination and how you think Hoyle and Sagan attempt to meet those difficulties.

FIRE AND ICE

Robert Frost

Robert Frost (1875–1963) became in his own lifetime the best known and most widely admired of American poets. He became such a national institution that he was invited to read a poem at the inauguration of President John F. Kennedy. Much of his popularity was no doubt due to the apparent simplicity of his verse, but his ironic habits expand and deepen his poems. In "Desert Places," for example, he sees the life-emptiness of a snowscape and connects it to the universe and the courage needed to face its facts:

> They cannot scare me with their empty spaces
> Between stars—on stars where no human race is.
> I have it in me so much nearer home
> To scare myself with my own desert places.

Frost makes something like the same attempt to connect the non-human with the human in the following poem.

Some say the world will end in fire,   1
Some say in ice.
From what I've tasted of desire
I hold with those who favor fire.
But if it had to perish twice,   5
I think I know enough of hate
To say that for destruction ice
Is also great
And would suffice.

 ### Questions of Subject and Theme

1. In what ways does Frost's voice in the poem seem to you to be serious and in what ways playful? Could the world, as defined by Hoyle and Sagan, really "perish twice?" What other senses of the words *world* and *destruction* do people use in personal rather than geological discourses? Would any of these senses make an alternative reading of the poem more serious?
2. Frost said that for most people *thinking* means "voting" on issues they have had no part in defining. How would you define the kind of thinking that seems expressed in this poem?

 ### Questions of Method and Strategy

1. Does the title of the poem seem well chosen? What other titles might fit in some way? "The End of the Earth," for example, or "Desire and

Hate?" Defend or criticize Frost's choice of the title in its relation to the poem.

2. Do the short lines make any difference in the effect of their meaning? Before discussing the issue, try reading the poem aloud while paying attention to the lines as units of sound and sense.

THE NEXT ICE AGE

Sir Frederick Hoyle

Sir Frederick Hoyle was educated at Cambridge University in England and later became the first director of Cambridge's Institute of Theoretical Astronomy. He has had a long and varied career, both as a scientist and as a popularizer of scientific ideas and discoveries. He has produced many books, including some science fiction.

More than three-quarters of all the ice in the world is in the southern polar continent of Antarctica, a conveniently distant place. Most of the rest of the world's ice lies in Greenland, also a remote place. So we are accustomed to thinking of the heavily populated lands of the Earth as being ice-free, except for the minute smears of the stuff we encounter in winter.

The Stone Age people who executed the magnificent cave paintings to be seen in southwest France and Spain did not enjoy such a pleasant situation. Twenty thousand years ago an ice sheet comparable to the one now in Greenland lay across Scandinavia. It had extensions reaching into Russia, Germany, and Britain. Another ice sheet of polar dimensions lay across the heartland of Canada, and its extensions reached beyond Chicago.

Nor was the grim situation of 20,000 years ago confined to the northern temperate latitudes. That ice age extended fingers even into the tropics. Substantial glaciers appeared on high tropical mountains such as those in Hawaii.

In the luxury of our present ice-free state we are apt to think that the ice age is over. But all the evidence is that the piling of vast quantities of ice onto the northern temperate latitudes (a belt of land running from the U.S.S.R. through Western Europe to Canada and the U.S.) has scarcely begun. To understand the overwhelming threat the future has in store for mankind, let us go back several tens of millions of years.

It is well known that the continents of the Earth are not in fixed positions; they drift about slowly in characteristic periods of 50 to 100 million years. And 40 million years ago the continent of Antarctica moved toward the South Pole. This caused the first glaciers there, and about 20 million years ago Antarctica was substantially ice covered.

A sinister process then set in, with its origin in the remarkable inability of the direct rays of the sun to melt either snow or ice. Most sunshine is reflected by snow, while it penetrates ice so deeply and diffusely that it has little melting effect at its surface. The sun does nothing directly to Antarctic ice, which would accumulate indefinitely from repeated snowfalls if icebergs did not break away into the sea at the outer edges of the ice sheet.

By about 20 million years ago a balance between the gain of new ice and the loss of old ice had been set up. The icebergs chilled the surrounding salty water. If this cooled water had remained at the ocean surface no harm would have been done. Despite its inability to melt ice and snow, sunlight is highly effective at warming the surface layers of the ocean, and would soon have resupplied the heat lost to the icebergs. This did not happen, however, because the dense, cool water sank from the surface to the ocean depths and the deep basins began to fill with water that was literally ice-cold.

This process eventually changed the warm world ocean of 50 million years ago into today's overwhelmingly ice-cold world ocean—with a thin skin of warmer water at its surface. Only this thin warm skin protects us from the next ice age.

As the chilling of the deep ocean occurred slowly and inexorably the Earth's climate worsened. By about 10 million years ago glaciers had appeared in Alaska. The first major intrusion of ice onto the lands of the northern temperate belt occurred about two million years ago. From time to time the ice would melt and for a while the land would be ice-free. Then the ice would come, again and again.

The ice-age periods became progressively longer than the intervening, interglacials. In the past million years the situation has worsened, until the average interglacial period has now shrunk to no more than 10,000 years. Since this is just the length of time since the present warm interglacial period began, our ration of ice-free conditions is over. The next ice age is already due.

A sequence of ice ages continues for as long as the continent in question resides at the pole in question. Our present sequence of ice ages will therefore continue for as long as the continent of Antarctica remains at the South Pole, which will probably be for several more tens of millions of years. The conclusion is that the present sequence of ice ages has scarcely begun. There are hundreds of ice ages still to come.

Why should there be an alternating sequence of ice ages and interglacials? At present snow lies during the winter over most of the northern temperate region. Instead of accumulating year by year into continental ice sheets, it melts each spring and summer. This is the essence of the interglacial condition. We are ice-free now, not because of a lack of snowfall but because of the spring thaw.

Melting comes from warmth in the air. Unlike the sun's direct rays, the longer-wave heat radiation generated by warm air is absorbed in snow or ice, which therefore melts almost immediately, thin surface layer after thin surface layer. The process is highly efficient and, given a sufficient supply of warm air, a whole winter's snow melts in a few days. Thus winter snow stays until warm air comes, and almost in a flash it is gone.

Where does the warm air get its heat? Mostly from the surface layer of warm ocean water that overlies the mass of ice-cold deeper water. Remove the surface layer of warm ocean water and there would then be no warm air. The snows of winter would not melt, ice sheets would begin to build, and the next ice age would have arrived.

The important surface layer of warm ocean water stores about ten times   15
more heat than is required by the air and the land each year, a ten-to-one margin of safety. That is enough to have prevented the next ice age for 10,000 years, but not sufficient to withstand every kind of accident. The finest particles of ash thrown into the air by the recent eruption of the Mount St. Helens volcano will take about ten years to settle down to ground level. Fine particles of any electrically insulating material reflect sunlight back into space and so reduce the amount available to heat the ocean surface. The Mount St. Helens volcanic eruption was not remotely big enough to have produced such a reflecting layer around the Earth.

In 1815 Mount Tambora in the Dutch East Indies produced an explosion that threw a sufficient quantity of fine ash into the high atmosphere to have a noticeable effect on the Northern Hemisphere summer of 1816. It was a summer of agricultural disaster in New England, the coldest on record at places as widely separated as New Haven and Geneva.

As an astronomer, I prefer to consider the possibility of a similar but much more violent effect triggered from outside the Earth: the impact of a giant meteorite. There is no question that giant meteorites, half a mile long or more, must hit the Earth from time to time, and such collisions must throw a vast quantity of debris into the atmosphere.

The most notable meteoritic event of modern times occurred in July, 1908. Miss K. Stephens wrote to *The Times* from Godmanchester about a strange light she had seen in the midnight sky, commenting that "it would be interesting if anyone could explain the cause." It was not until 1927 that even the point of impact of the meteorite was discovered, by an expedition that penetrated to the Tunguska River region in Siberia. An enormous area of devastation was found, almost twice that caused by Mount St. Helens, showing that a comparatively minor meteoritic collision can be far more destructive than the explosion of a volcano.

Once in every 5,000 to 10,000 years a meteoritic collision occurs which projects sufficient fine dust into the high atmosphere to make the Earth into a temporarily reflective planet. The resulting cutoff of sunlight robs the surface waters of the terrestrial ocean of their protective store of heat, and the air that blows over the land from the sea is then no longer warm enough to melt the snows of winter.

How long will the snow accumulate? Within two or three decades at   20
most, all the fine dust will have settled to the Earth's surface under gravity and sunlight will no longer be reflected back into space. Warm summer air will blow again over the land, and within only a further year or two the accumulated snows will be melted into lakes, streams, and rivers. Admittedly, there would have been a number of very bad years, enough to throw

human society into a crisis beside which the multitudinous troubles which now dog our daily lives would seem like pinpricks. But after half a century things would be back to normal—seemingly.

This apparent loophole in what had seemed an inexorable line of reasoning troubled me for a long time until the day I chanced on a description of the following simple experiment: If air that has not been thoroughly dried, that contains a number of very small water drops, is cooled progressively in a chamber, the droplets do not solidify into ice crystals as their temperature falls below the normal freezing point, but remain as a supercooled liquid down to a remarkably low temperature, close to −40°C, when at last the liquid water goes into ice.

If a beam of light passes through the chamber, and if one looks at it from a direction at right angles to the beam, the chamber appears dark so long as the droplets stay liquid. Their transition to ice is signaled by a sudden radiance from the interior of the chamber. This means that whereas liquid droplets transmit light beams, ice crystals scatter them.

Even in the driest desert regions of the Earth there is always more than sufficient water in the air, if it is condensed from vapor into fine crystals of ice, to produce an almost perfectly reflective blanket. Does this happen anywhere? It does, particularly in the polar regions. The ice crystals are known to polar explorers as "diamond dust," a name that illustrates their brilliant reflective properties. Diamond dust is responsible for a bewildering range of optical effects—halos, mock suns, arcs, coronas, and iridescent clouds.

Why does diamond dust not form everywhere? Because except in the polar regions, water droplets in the atmosphere are kept above the critical temperature, near −40°C, at which they would be transformed into ice. What prevents the temperature of water droplets from falling to −40°C throughout much of the high atmosphere is heat from the oceans. Reduce the heat supplied by the oceans to the air by about 25 per cent and diamond dust would form, not just in the polar regions but over much of the Earth.

But this is exactly what would happen in the situation I have described: *25*
fine particles thrown up into the high atmosphere, either by an enormous volcano or by the collision of a giant meteorite, would cool the surface of the ocean and the ability of the ocean to supply heat to the air would be significantly reduced. Diamond dust would create an additional particle blanket around the Earth that would stay long after the first particles had fallen to ground level under gravity, and the diamond dust would then take over the job of reflecting sunlight, and so keep the ocean cool indefinitely.

Clearly, there are two distinct self-maintaining cycles of the world climate. If the surface layer of the ocean is warm, as it is at present, enough heat passes from the ocean to the air to prevent diamond dust forming, except in polar regions. Sunlight comes through to the ocean and keeps the surface warm. This is the first cycle.

The second goes exactly the opposite way. If the surface of the ocean is cool, insufficient heat goes into the air to prevent diamond dust forming.

Significantly more sunlight is then reflected back into space and the surface of the ocean remains cool.

Both the first and second cycles are logically consistent. If the Earth happens to be in either of them it tends to stay in that cycle, unless a catastrophic incident causes a sudden jump from the one cycle to the other. Indeed, the two cycles are exactly those I have described as interglacials and ice ages, and the interlaced sequence of ice ages and the interglacials arises because of such catastrophic events as collisions of the Earth with giant meteorites or explosions of volcanoes.

Ice ages have exceedingly abrupt terminations. Something about the end of the last ice age took the mammoths by surprise. Along with the mastodon and woolly rhinoceros, they became extinct. Complete mammoths with surprisingly little degeneration have been recovered from present-day ice in Siberia. Either they died of hypothermia caused by freezing rain, or they blundered into bogs and pools of exceedingly cold water formed from melting permafrost.

When one considers the effect on mammoths of sudden heat from a brassy sky caused by the absorbent particles thrown up by an iron meteorite, all the evidence falls into place. The frozen ground would soften and the mammoths would flounder. Frozen pools and lakes would partially melt. In the conditions of poor visibility, the mammoths and other animals would be likely to blunder to their deaths in the icy bogs. *30*

The progression of catastrophic events controls the sequence of ice ages and interglacial periods. The grim aspect of this is that because of the suddenness of the catastrophic events, switches back and forth between interglacial cycles and ice-age cycles occur swiftly, in timespans of a few decades at most.

One may derive some consolation from the possibility that the switch to the next ice age may still be several thousand years into the future. On the other hand, the switch could have occurred in 1908, if the giant meteorite whose light was seen by Miss K. Stephens had happened to be larger. The switch could occur tomorrow, and if it were to do so there is no human being, young or old, who would escape its appalling consequences.

Questions of Subject and Theme

1. What two causes would trigger a cooling of the earth sufficient to bring on a new ice age? Which does Hoyle "prefer" and why?
2. What does Hoyle see as the "two distinct self-maintaining cycles of world climate?" How do they operate? Why are they self-maintaining? How might one cease and the other begin?

Questions of Method and Strategy

1. How does Hoyle convey in the beginning of his essay the sense of remoteness associated with an ice age? How are time and space both used?

211 FREDERICK HOYLE/THE NEXT ICE AGE   211

2. What effect does Hoyle create by calling the normal expectations of our contemporary climate a "luxury" in his fourth paragraph? How do the metaphor's implications illuminate Hoyle's later arguments and conclusions?

THE WARMING OF THE WORLD

Carl Sagan

Carl Sagan received both his undergraduate and graduate degrees from the University of Chicago and has since taught astronomy at major universities. He has extended the reach of his teaching as the writer of popular books on scientific subjects and as the originator and host of the television series *Cosmos.*

When humans first evolved—in the savannahs of East Africa a few million years ago—our numbers were few and our powers feeble. We knew almost nothing about controlling our environment—even clothing had yet to be invented. We were creatures of the climate, utterly dependent upon it.

A few degrees hotter or colder on average, and our ancestors were in trouble. The toll taken much later by the ice ages, in which average land temperatures dropped some 8°C (centigrade, or Celsius), must have been horrific. And yet, it is exactly such climatic change that pushed our ancestors to develop tools and technology, science and civilization. Certainly, skills in hunting, skinning, tanning, building shelters and refurbishing caves must owe much to the terrors of the deep ice age.

Today, we live in a balmy epoch, 10,000 years after the last major glaciation. In this climatic spring, our species has flourished; we now cover the entire planet and are altering the very appearance of our world. Lately— within the last century or so—humans have acquired, in more ways than one, the ability to make major changes in that climate upon which we are so dependent. The Nuclear Winter findings are one dramatic indication that we can change the climate—in this case, in the spasm of nuclear war. But I wish here to describe a different kind of climatic danger, this one slower, more subtle and arising from intentions that are wholly benign.

It is warm down here on Earth because the Sun shines. If the Sun were somehow turned off, the Earth would rapidly cool. The oceans would freeze, eventually the atmosphere itself would condense out and our planet would be covered everywhere by snowbanks of solid oxygen and nitrogen 10 meters (about 30 feet) high. Only the tiny trickle of heat from the Earth's interior and the faint starlight would save our world from a temperature of absolute zero.

We know how bright the Sun is; we know how far from it we are; and we know what fraction of the sunlight reaching the Earth is reflected back to space (about 30 percent). So we can calculate—with a simple mathematical equation—what the average temperature of the Earth should be. But when we do the calculation, we find that the Earth's temperature should be about 20°C below the freezing point of water, in stark contradiction to our everyday experience. What have we done wrong?

As in many such cases in science, what we've done wrong is to forget something—in this case, the atmosphere. Every object in the universe radiates some kind of light to space; the colder the object, the longer the wavelength of radiation it emits. The Earth—much colder than the Sun—radiates to space mainly in the infrared part of the spectrum, not the visible. Were the Sun turned off, the Earth would soon be indetectable in ordinary visible light, though it would be brilliantly illuminated in infrared light.

When sunlight strikes the Earth, part is reflected back into the sky; much of the rest is absorbed by the ground and heats it—the darker the ground, the greater the heating. The ground radiates back upward in the infrared. Thus, for an airless Earth, the temperature would be set solely by a balance between the incoming sunlight absorbed by the surface and the infrared radiation that the surface emits back to space.

When you put air on a planet, the situation changes. The Earth's atmosphere is, generally, still transparent to visible light. That's why we can see each other when we talk, glimpse distant mountains and view the stars.

But in the infrared, all that is different. While the oxygen and nitrogen in the air are transparent in both the infrared and the visible, minor constituents such as water vapor (H_2O) and carbon dioxide (CO_2) tend to be much more opaque in the infrared. It would be useless for us to have eyes that could see at a wavelength, say, of 15 microns in the infrared, because the air is murky black there.

Accordingly, if you add air to a world, you heat it: The surface now has   10
difficulty when it tries to radiate back to space in the infrared. The atmosphere tends to absorb the infrared radiation, keeping heat near the surface and providing an infrared blanket for the world. There is very little CO_2 in the Earth's atmosphere—only 0.03 percent. But that small amount is enough to make the Earth's atmosphere opaque in important regions of the infrared spectrum. CO_2 and H_2O are the reason the global temperature is not well below freezing. We owe our comfort—indeed, our very existence—to the fact that these gases are present and are much more transparent in the visible than in the infrared. Our lives depend on a delicate balance of invisible gases. Too much blanket, or too little, and we're in trouble.

This property of many gases to absorb strongly in the infrared but not in the visible, and thereby to heat their surroundings, is called the "greenhouse effect." A florist's greenhouse keeps its planty inhabitants warm. The phrase "greenhouse effect" is widely used and has an instructive ring to it, reminding us that we live in a planetary-scale greenhouse and recalling the admonition about living in glass houses and throwing stones. But, in fact, florists' greenhouses do not keep warm by the greenhouse effect; they work mainly by inhibiting the movement of air inside, another matter altogether.

We need look only as far as the nearest planet to see an example of an atmospheric greenhouse effect gone wild. Venus has in its atmosphere an enormous quantity of carbon dioxide (roughly as much as is buried as carbonates in all the rocks of the Earth's crust). There is an atmosphere of CO_2 on Venus 90 times thicker than the atmosphere of the Earth and containing some 200,000 times more CO_2 than in our air. With water vapor and other minor atmospheric constituents, this is enough to make a greenhouse effect that keeps the surface of Venus around 470°C (900°F)—enough to melt tin or lead.

When humans burn wood or "fossil fuels" (coal, oil, natural gas, etc.), they put carbon dioxide into the air. One carbon atom (C) combines with a molecule of oxygen (O_2) to produce CO_2. The development of agriculture, the conversion of dense forest to comparatively sparsely vegetated farms, has moved carbon atoms from plants on the ground to carbon dioxide in the air. About half of this new CO_2 is removed by plants or by the layering down of carbonates in the oceans. On human time-scales, these changes are irreversible: Once the CO_2 is in the atmosphere, human technology is helpless to remove it. So the overall amount of CO_2 in the air has been growing—at least since the industrial revolution. If no other factors operate, and if enough CO_2 is put into the atmosphere, eventually the average surface temperature will increase perceptibly.

There are other greenhouse gases that are increasingly abundant in the Earth's atmosphere—halocarbons, such as the freon used in refrigerator cooling systems; or nitrous oxide (N_2O), produced by automobile exhausts and nitrogenous fertilizers; or methane (CH_4), produced partly in the intestines of cows and other ruminants.

But let's for the moment concentrate on carbon dioxide: How long, at the present rates of burning wood and fossil fuels, before the global climate becomes significantly warmer? And what would the consequences be?

It is relatively simple to calculate the immediate warming from a given increase in the CO_2 abundance, and all competent calculations seem to be in good agreement. More difficult to estimate are (1) the rate at which carbon dioxide will continue to be put into the atmosphere (it depends on population growth rates, economic styles, alternative energy sources and the like) and (2) feedbacks—ways in which a slight warming might produce other, more drastic, effects.

The recent increase in atmospheric CO_2 is well documented. Over the last century, this CO_2 buildup should have resulted in a few tenths of a degree of global warming, and there is some evidence that such a warming has occurred.

The National Academy of Sciences estimates that the present atmospheric abundance of CO_2 is likely to double by the year 2065, although experts at the academy predict a one-in-20 chance that it will double before 2035—when an infant born today becomes 50 years old. Such a doubling would warm the air near the surface of the Earth by 2°C or 3°C—maybe by as much as 4°C. These are average temperature values; there would naturally be considerable local variation. High latitudes would be warmed much more, although a baked Alaska will be some time coming.

There would be precipitation changes. The annual discharge of rivers would be altered. Some scientists believe that central North America—including much of the area that is now the breadbasket of the world—would be parched in summer if the global temperature increases by a few degrees. There would be some mitigating effects; for example, where plant growth is not otherwise limited, more CO_2 should aid photosynthesis and make more luxuriant growth (of weeds as well as crops). If the present CO_2 injection into the atmosphere continued over a few centuries, the warming would be greater than from all other causes over the last 100,000 years.

As the climate warms, glacial ice melts. Over the last 100 years, the level 20 of the world's oceans has risen by 15 centimeters (6 inches). A global warming of 3°C or 4°C over the next century is likely to bring a further rise in the average sea level of about 70 centimeters (28 inches). An increase of this magnitude could produce major damage to ports all over the world and induce fundamental changes in the patterns of land development. A serious speculation is that greenhouse temperature increases of 3°C or 4°C could, in addition, trigger the disintegration of the West Antarctic Ice Sheet, with huge quantities of polar ice falling into the ocean. This would raise sea level by some 6 meters (20 feet) over a period of centuries, with the eventual inundation of all coastal cities on the planet.

There are many other possibilities that are poorly understood, including the release of other greenhouse gases (for example, methane from peat bogs) accelerated by the warming climate. The circulation of the oceans might be an important aspect of the problem. The scientific community is attempting to make an environmental-impact statement for the entire planet on the consequences of continued burning of fossil fuels. Despite the uncertainties, a kind of consensus is in: Over the next century or more, with projected rates of burning of coal, oil and gas, there is trouble ahead.

The problem is difficult for at least three different reasons:

(1) We do not yet fully understand how severe the greenhouse consequences will be.

(2) Although the effects are not yet strikingly noticeable in everyday life, to deal with the problem, the present generation might have to make sacrifices for the next.

(3) The problem cannot be solved except on an international scale: The 25 atmosphere is ignorant of national boundaries. South African carbon dioxide warms Taiwan, and Soviet coal-burning practices affect productivity in America. The largest coal resources in the world are found in the Soviet Union, the United States and China, in that order. What incentives are there for a nation such as China, with vast coal reserves and a commitment to rapid economic development, to hold back on the burning of fossil fuels because the result might, decades later, be a parched American sunbelt or still more ghastly starvation in sub-Saharan Africa? Would countries that might benefit from a warmer climate be as vigorous in restraining the burning of fossil fuels as nations likely to suffer greatly?

Fortunately, we have a little time. A great deal can be done in decades. Some argue that government subsidies lower the price of fossil fuels, inviting waste; more efficient usage, besides its economic advantage, could greatly ameliorate the CO_2 greenhouse problem. Parts of the solution might involve alternative energy sources, where appropriate: solar power, for example, or safer nuclear fission reactors, which, whatever their other dangers, produce no greenhouse gases of importance. Conceivably, the long-awaited advent of commercial nuclear fusion power might happen before the middle of the next century.

However, any technological solution to the looming greenhouse problem must be worldwide. It would not be sufficient for the United States or the Soviet Union, say, to develop safe and commercially feasible fusion power plants: That technology would have to be diffused worldwide, on terms of cost and reliability that would be more attractive to developing. nations than a reliance on fossil fuel reserves or imports. A serious, very high-level look at patterns of U.S. and world energy development in light of the greenhouse problem seems overdue.

During the last few million years, human technology, spurred in part by climatic change, has made our species a force to be reckoned with on a planetary scale. We now find, to our astonishment, that we pose a danger to ourselves. The present world order is, unfortunately, not designed to deal with global-scale dangers. Nations tend to be concerned about themselves, not about the planet; they tend to have short-term rather than long-term objectives. In problems such as the increasing greenhouse effect, one nation or region might benefit while another suffers. In other global environmental issues, such as nuclear war, all nations lose. The problems are connected: Constructive international efforts to understand and resolve one will benefit the others.

Further study and better public understanding are needed, of course. But what is essential is a global consciousness—a view that transcends our exclusive identification with the generational and political groupings into which, by accident, we have been born. The solution to these problems requires a perspective that embraces the planet and the future. We are all in this greenhouse together.

Questions of Subject and Theme

1. Why, according to Sagan, do only a few degrees in temperature make such a big difference for human life? What does he mean when he says in paragraph 3 that we live in a "balmy" epoch?
2. What would be the temperature of the earth if there were no atmosphere? What would heat the earth and what would cool it? How does the atmosphere make the temperatures we in fact experience?

Questions of Method and Strategy

1. Why is the term *greenhouse effect* not exactly correct? What, if anything, would be gained by dropping the term from the essay? What, if anything, is gained by keeping it?

2. In paragraph 4 Sagan imagines "snowbanks" of oxygen and nitrogen. What is so striking about his image, and what does it convey for his argument?

———

Suggestions for Writing on the Juxtapositions

1. Which of the scientists seems to you most convincing in his prediction? Write an essay in which you defend your choice through analysis and examples, being sure to take into account the views of the other scientist, if only to refute them.
2. Sagan and Hoyle cannot both be right about the future. Waiving the issue of who you find most convincing, write an essay in which you analyze examples from each essay to show how and why they create such a sense of conviction in both writer and audience.
3. Frost uses fire and ice as metaphors for human emotions. Write an essay in which you analyze examples of the uses made of metaphor by the two scientists in their writing.
4. It might be said that scientists generally write about an impersonal world impersonally. Write an essay in which you describe how Robert Frost writes about a personal world personally.

12 Thought for Food

M. F. K. Fisher, "The Indigestible:
   The Language of Food"
William Safire, "A Bottle of Ketchup"

Both food and language satisfy basic human needs, but seldom are the two subjects examined together. As you read these two analyses by prominent writers, consider the following questions:

1. Both writers use a grammatical vocabulary for their analyses. How and where do they differ in their purposes for using such a vocabulary, and how and where do they seem to operate similarly?

2. William Safire suggests that some words like *shirtings* are employed to imply more "class" and some like *vehicle operator* are used to avoid that implication. Where and how does M. F. K. Fisher raise similar issues about linguistic ambitions to change the implications of facts?

3. Fisher sticks to the dual topic of food and language while Safire seems to wander afield by the force of associations. What other differences, and what similarities, do you mark in the sensibilities of the two writers? Explain with examples.

4. Fisher writes partly out of the conviction that appetite is natural and that something unnatural is being done to it by some uses of language. Does Safire convey a sense of a firm belief in the importance of distinguishing the natural from the unnatural?

THE INDIGESTIBLE
The Language of Food

M. F. K. Fisher

> Mary Frances Kennedy Fisher grew up as the daughter of an
> editor and went on to become a writer on her two consuming
> interests—food and writing. As her title suggests, she does not take
> her gastronomical subjects piously but is incensed by the perversion of
> those subjects by the language of advertising.

Hunger is, to describe it most simply, an urgent need for food. It is a   *1*
craving, a desire. It is, I would guess, much older than man as we now think
of him, and probably synonymous with the beginnings of sex. It is strange
that we feel that anything as intrinsic as this must continually be wooed and
excited, as if it were an unwilling and capricious part of us. If someone is
not hungry, it indicates that his body does not, for a time and a reason, want
to be fed. The logical thing, then, is to let him rest. He will either die, which
he may have been meant to do, or he will once more feel the craving, the
desire, the urgency to *eat*. He will have to do that before he can satisfy most
of his other needs. Then he will revive again, which apparently he was
meant to do.

It is hard to understand why this instinct to eat must be importuned,
since it is so strong in all relatively healthy bodies. But in our present Western world, we face a literal bombardment of cajolery from all the media to
eat this or that. It is as if we had been born without appetite, and must be
led gently into an introduction to oral satisfaction and its increasingly dubious results, the way nubile maidens in past centuries were prepared for
marriage proposals and then their legitimate defloration.

The language that is developing, in this game of making us *want* to eat,
is far from subtle. To begin with, we must be made to feel that we really find
the whole atavistic process difficult, or embarrassing or boring. We must be
coaxed and cajoled to crave one advertised product rather than another, one
taste, on presentation of something that we might have chosen anyway if
let alone.

The truth is that we are born hungry and in our own ways will die so.
But modern food advertising assumes that we are by nature bewildered and
listless. As a matter of fact, we come into the world howling for Mother's
Milk. We leave it, given a reasonable length of time, satisfied with much the
same bland if lusty precursor of "pap and pabulum," tempered perhaps with
a brush of wine on our lips to ease the parting of body and spirit. And in
between, today, now, we are assaulted with the most insulting distortion of
our sensory linguistics that I can imagine. We are treated like innocents and

idiots by the advertisers, here in America and in Western Europe. (These are the only two regions I know, even slightly, but I feel sure that this same attack on our innate common sense is going on in the Orient, in India, in Brazil. . . .)

We are told, on radio and television and in widely distributed publica-   5
tions, not only how but what to eat, and when, and where. The pictures are colorful. The prose, often written by famous people, is deliberately persua-sive, if often supercilious in a way that makes us out as clumsy louts, gastro-nomical oafs badly in need of guidance toward the satisfaction of appetites we are unaware of. And by now, with this constant attack on innate desires, an attack that can be either overt or subliminal, we apparently feel fogged-out, bombed, bewildered about whether we really crave some peanut butter on crackers as a post-amour snack, or want to sleep forever. And first, before varied forms of physical dalliance, should we share with our partner a French aperitif that keeps telling us to, or should we lead up to our accomplishments by sipping a tiny glass of Sicilian love potion?

The language for this liquid aphro-cut is familiar to most of us, thanks to lush ads in all the media. It becomes even stronger as we go into solid foods. Sexually the ads are aimed at two main groups—the Doers and the Dones. Either the reader/viewer/listener is out to woo a lover, or has married and acquired at least two children and needs help to keep the machismo-level high. Either way, one person is supposed to feed another so as to get the partner into bed and then, if possible, to pay domestic maintenance—that is, foot the bills.

One full-page color ad, for instance, shows six shots of repellently mingled vegetables, and claims boldly that these combinations "will do al-most anything to get a husband's attentions." They will "catch his passing fancy . . . on the first vegetables he might even notice." In short, the ad goes on with skilled persuasion, "they're vegetables your husband can't ignore." This almost promises that he may not ignore the cook either, a heartening if vaguely lewd thought if the pictures in the ad are any intimation of his tastes.

It is plain that if a man must be kept satisfied at table, so must his progeny, and advertisers know how to woo mothers as well as plain sexual companions. Most of their nutritional bids imply somewhat unruly family life, that only food can ease: "No more fights over who gets what," one ad proposes, as it suggests buying not one but three different types of frozen but "crisp hot fried chicken at a price that take-out can't beat": thighs and drumsticks, breast portions and wings, all coated with the same oven-crunchy-golden skin, and fresh from freezer to stove in minutes. In the last quarter of this family ad there is a garishly bright new proposal, the "no-fire, sure-fire, barbecue-sauced" chicken. Personal experience frowns on this daring departure from the national "finger-lickin'" syndrome: with children who fight over who gets what, it would be very messy.

It is easy to continue such ever-loving family-style meals, as suggested by current advertising, all in deceptively alluring color in almost any home-oriented magazine one finds. How about enjoying a "good family western," whatever that may be, by serving a mixture of "redy-rice" and leftover chicken topped with a blenderized sauce of ripe avocado? This is called "love food from California," and it will make us "taste how the West was won." The avocado, the ad goes on, will "open new frontiers of wholesome family enjoyment." And of course the pre-spiced-already-seasoned "instant" rice, combined with cooked chicken, will look yummy packed into the hollowed fruit shells and covered with nutlike green stuff. All this will help greatly to keep the kids from hitting each other about who gets what.

The way to a man's heart is through his stomach, we have been assured   10
for a couple of centuries, and for much longer than that good wives as well as noted courtesans have given their time and thought to keeping the male belly full (and the male liver equally if innocently enlarged). By now this precarious mixture of sex and gastronomy has come out of the pantry, so to speak, and ordinary cookbook shelves show *Cuisine d'amour* and *Venus in the Kitchen* alongside Mrs. Rombauer and Julia Child.

In order to become a classic, which I consider the last two to be, any creation, from a potato soufflé to a marble bust or a skyscraper, must be honest, and that is why most cooks, as well as their methods, are never known. It is also why dishonesty in the kitchen is driving us so fast and successfully to the world of convenience foods and franchised eateries.

If we look at a few of the so-called cookbooks now providing a kind of armchair gastronomy (to read while we wait for the wife and kids to get ready to pile in the car for supper at the nearest drive-in), we understand without either amazement or active nausea some such "homemade" treat as I was brought lately by a generous neighbor. The recipe she proudly passed along to me, as if it were her great-grandmother's secret way to many a heart, was from a best-selling new cookbook, and it included a large package of sweet chocolate bits, a box of "Butter Fudge" chocolate cake mix, a package of instant vanilla pudding, and a cup of imitation mayonnaise. It was to be served with synthetic whipped cream sprayed from an aerosol can. It was called *Old-Fashion Fudge Torte*.

This distortion of values, this insidious numbing of what we once knew without question as either True or False, can be blamed, in part anyway, on the language we hear and read every day and night about the satisfying of such a basic need as hunger. Advertising, especially in magazines and books devoted to such animal satisfaction, twists us deftly into acceptance of the new lingo of gastronomical seduction.

A good example: an impossibly juicy-looking pork chop lies like a Matisse odalisque in an open microwave oven, cooked until "fall-from-the-bone-tender." This is a new word. It still says that the meat is so overcooked that it will fall off its bone (a dubious virtue!), but it is supposed to beguile the reader into thinking that he or she (1) speaks a special streamlined language, and (2) deserves to buy an oven to match, and (3) appreciates all such finer things in life. It takes *know-how,* the ad assures us subliminally, to understand all that "fall-from-the-bone-tender" really means!

This strange need to turn plain descriptive English into hyphenated hy-   *15* perbole can be found even in the best gastronomical reviews and articles as well as magazine copy. How about "fresh-from-the-oven apple cobbler," as described by one of the more reputable food writers of today? What would be wrong, especially for someone who actually knows syntax and grammar, in saying "apple cobbler, fresh from the oven"? A contemporary answer is that the multiple adjective is more . . . uh . . . contemporary. This implies that it should reach the conditioned brain cells of today's reader in a more understandable, coherent way—or does it?

The vocabulary of our kitchen comes from every part of the planet, sooner or later, because as we live, so we speak. After the Norman Conquest in 1066, England learned countless French nouns and verbs that are now part of both British and American cooking language: *appetite, dinner, salmon, sausage, lemon, fig, almond,* and so on. We all say *roast, fry, boil,* and we make *sauces* and put them in *bowls* or on *plates.* And the German kitchen, the Aztecan: they too gave us words like *cookie* and *chocolate.* We say *borscht* easily (Russian before it was Yiddish). From slavetime Africa there is the word *gumbo,* for okra, and in *benne* biscuits there is the black man's sesame. Some people say that *alcohol* came from the nonalcoholic Arabs.

But what about the new culinary language of the media, the kind we now hear and view and read? What can "freezer-fresh" mean? *Fresh* used to imply new, pure, lively. Now it means, at best, that when a food was pack- aged, it would qualify as ready to be eaten: "oven-fresh" cookies a year on the shelf, "farm-fresh" eggs laid last spring, "corn-on-the-cob fresh" dehy- drated vegetable soup-mix. . . .

Personal feelings and opinions and prejudices (sometimes called skun- ners) have a lot to do with our reactions to gastronomical words, and other kinds. I know a man who finally divorced his wife because, even by indirec- tion, he could not cure her of "calling up." She called up people, and to her it meant that she used the telephone—that is, she was not calling across a garden or over a fence, but was calling up when she could not *see* her friends. Calling and calling up are entirely different, she and a lot of interested ama- teur semanticists told her husband. He refused to admit this. "Why not simply *telephone* them? To telephone you don't say telephone *up,*" he would say. Her phrase continued to set his inner teeth, the ones rooted directly in his spiritual law, on such an edge that he finally fled. She called up to tell me.

This domestic calamity made me aware, over many years but never with such anguish, how *up* can dangle in our language. And experience has shown me that if a word starts dangling, it is an easy mark for the careless users and the overt rapists of syntax and meaning who write copy for mass- media outlets connected, for instance, with hunger, and its current quasi- satisfactions. Sometimes the grammatical approach is fairly conventional and old-fashioned, and the *up* is tacked onto a verb in a fairly comprehen- sible way. "Perk up your dinner," one magazine headline begs us, with vaguely disgusting suggestions about how to do it. "Brighten up a burger," a full-page lesson in salad-making with an instant powder tells us. (This ad sneaks in another call on home unity with its "unusually delicious . . . bright . . . tasty" offering: "Sit back and listen to the cheers," it says. "Your family will give them to this tasty-zesty easy-to-make salad!")

Of course *up* gets into the adjectives as well as the verbs: *souped up chicken*   20 and *souped up dip* are modish in advertising for canned pudding-like concoctions that fall in their original shapes from tin to saucepan or mixing bowl, to be blended with liquids to make fairly edible "soups," or to serve in prefab sauces as handy vehicles for clams or peanuts or whatever is added to the can-shaped glob to tantalize drinkers to want one more Bloody Mary. They dip up the mixture on specially stiffened packaged "chips" made of imitation tortillas or even imitation reconditioned potatoes, guaranteed not to crumble, shatter, or otherwise mess up the landscape. . . .

Verbs are more fun than adjectives, in this game of upmanship. And one of the best/worst of them is creeping into our vocabularies in a thoroughly unsubtle way. It is *to gourmet up*. By now the word *gourmet* has been so distorted, and so overloaded, that to people who know its real meaning it is meaningless. They have never misused it and they refuse to now. To them a gourmet is a person, and perforce the word is a noun. Probably it turned irrevocably into an adjective with descriptive terms like *gourmet-style* and *gourmet-type*. I am not sure. But it has come to mean fancy rather than fastidious. It means expensive, or exotic, or pseudoelegant and classy and pricey. It rarely describes enjoyment. It describes a style, at best, and at worst a cheap imitation of once-stylish and always costly affectation.

There is gourmet food. There are gourmet restaurants, or gourmet-style eating places. There are packaged frozen cubes of comestibles called gourmet that cost three times as much as plain fast foods because, the cunningly succulent mouth-watering ads propose, their sauces are made by world-famous chefs, whose magical blends of spices and herbs have been touched off by a personalized fillip of rare old Madeira. In other words, at triple the price, they are worth it because they have been gourmeted up. Not long ago I heard a young woman in a supermarket say to a friend who looked almost as gaunt and harried as she, "Oh god . . . why am I here? You ask! Harry calls to say his sales manager is coming to dinner, and I've got to gourmet up the pot roast!"

I slow my trundle down the pushcart aisle.

"I could slice some olives into it, maybe? Pitted. Or maybe dump in a can of mushrooms. Sliced. It's got to be more expensive."

The friend says, "A cup of wine? Red. Or sour cream . . . a kind of   25 Stroganoff . . . ?"

I worm my way past them, feeling vaguely worried. I long to tell them something—perhaps not to worry.

There are, of course, even more personal language shocks than the one that drove a man to leave his dear girl because she had to call people up. Each of us has his own, actively or dimly connected with hunger (which only an adamant Freudian could call his!). It becomes a real embarrassment, for example, when a friend or a responsible critic of cookbooks or restaurants uses words like *yummy,* or *scrumptious.* There is no dignity in such infantile evasions of plain words like *good*—or even *delicious* or *excellent.*

My own word aversion is longstanding, and several decades from the first time I heard it I still pull back, like the flanges of a freshly opened oyster. It is the verb *to drool,* when applied to written prose, and especially to anything I myself have written. Very nice people have told me, for a long time now, that some things they have read of mine, in books or magazines, have made them drool. I know they mean to compliment me. They are saying that my use of words makes them oversalivate, like hapless dogs waiting for a bell to say "Meat!" to them. It has made them more alive than they were, more active. They are grateful to me, perhaps, for being reminded that they are still functioning, still aware of some of their hungers.

I too should be grateful, and even humble, that I have reminded people   *30* of what fun it is, vicariously or not, to eat/live. Instead I am revolted. I see a slavering slobbering maw. It dribbles helplessly, in a Pavlovian response. It *drools.* And drooling, not over a meaty bone or a warm bowl of slops, is what some people have done over my printed words. This has long worried me. I feel grateful but repelled. They are nice people, and I like them and I like dogs, but dogs *must* drool when they are excited by the prospect of the satisfaction of alerted tastebuds, and two-legged people do not need to, and in general I know that my reaction to the fact that some people slobber like conditioned animals is a personal skunner, and that I should accept it as such instead of meeting it like a stiff-upper-lipped Anglo-Saxon (and conditioned!) nanny.

I continue, however, to be regretfully disgusted by the word *drool* in connection with all writing about food, including my own. And a few fans loyal enough to resist being hurt by this statement may possibly call me up.

It is too easy to be malicious, but certainly the self-styled food experts of our current media sometimes seem overtly silly enough to be fair game. For anyone with half an ear for the English-American language we write and speak, it is almost impossible not to chuckle over the unending flow of insults to our syntax and grammar, not to mention our several levels of intelligence.

How are we supposed to react to descriptive phrases like "crisply crunchy, to snap in your mouth"? We know this was written, and for pay, by one or another of the country's best gastronomical hacks. We should not titter. He is a good fellow. Why then does he permit himself to say that some corn on the cob is so tender that "it dribbles milk down your chin"? He seems, whether or not he means well, to lose a little of the innate dignity that we want from our gourmet-judges. He is like a comedian who with one extra grimace becomes coarse instead of funny, or like an otherwise sensitive reader who says that certain writing makes him drool.

Not all our food critics, of course, are as aware of language as the well-known culinary experts who sign magazine articles and syndicated columns. And for one of them, there are a hundred struggling copywriters who care less about mouth-watering prose than about filling ad space with folksy propaganda for "kwik" puddings and suchlike. They say shamelessly, to keep their jobs, that Mom has just told them how to make instant homemade gravy taste "like I could never make before!" "*Believe* me," they beg, "those other gravies just aren't the same! This has a real homemade flavor and a rich brown color. Just add it to your pot drippings." And so on.

Often these unsung kitchen psalmists turn, with probable desperation, to puns and other word games. They write, for instance, that frozen batter-fried fish are so delicious that "one crunch and you're hooked!" Oh, hohoho ha ha. And these same miserable slaves produce millions of words, if they are fortunate enough to find and keep their jobs, about things like synthetic dough that is "pre-formed" into "old-fashioned shapes that taste cooky-fresh and crunchy" in just fifteen minutes from freezer to oven to the kiddies' eager paws and maws. 35

When the hacks have proved that they can sling such culinary lingo, they are promoted to a special division that deals even more directly with oral satisfaction. They write full-page ads in juicy color, about cocktail nibbles with "a fried-chicken taste that's lip-lickin' good." This, not too indirectly, is aimed to appeal to hungry readers familiar with a franchised fried chicken that is of course known worldwide as finger-lickin good, and even packaged Kitty Krums that are whisker-lickin good. (It is interesting and reassuring, although we must drop a few *g*'s to understand it, that modern gastronomy still encourages us to indulge in public tongueplay.)

Prose by the copywriters usually stays coy, but is somewhat more serious about pet foods than humanoid provender. Perhaps it is assumed that most people who buy kibbles do not bother to read the printed information on all four sides of their sacks, but simply pour the formula into bowls on the floor and hope for the best. Or perhaps animal-food companies recognize that some of their slaves are incurably dedicated to correct word usage. Often the script on a bag of dry pet food is better written than most paperback novels. Possibly some renegade English instructor has been allowed to explain "Why Your Cat Will Enjoy This." He is permitted tiny professorial jokes, now and then: "As Nutritious As It Is Delicious," one caption says, and another section is called "Some Reading on Feeding," and then the prose goes all out, almost euphorically, with "Some Raving on Saving." The lost academician does have to toss in a few words like *munchy* to keep his job, but in general there is an enjoyably relaxed air about the unread prose on pet-food packages, as opposed to the stressful cuteness of most fashionable critics of our dining habits.

Of course the important thing is to stay abreast of the lingo, it seems. Stylist restaurants go through their phases, with beef Wellington and chocolate mousse high in favor one year and strictly for Oskahoola, Tennessee, the next. We need private dining-out guides as well as smart monthly magazines to tell us what we are eating tonight, as well as what we are paying for it.

A lot of our most modish edibles are dictated by their scarcity, as always in the long history of gastronomy. In 1978, for instance, it became *de rigueur* in California to serve caviar in some guise, usually with baked or boiled potatoes, because shipments from Iran grew almost as limited as they had long been from Russia. (Chilled caviar, regal fare, was paired with the quaintly plebeian potato many years ago, in Switzerland I think, but by 1978 its extravagant whimsy had reached Hollywood and the upper West Coast by way of New York, so that desperate hostesses were buying and even trying to "homemake" caviar from the Sacramento River sturgeons. Results: usually lamentable, but well meant.)

All this shifting of gustatory snobbism should probably have more influ- *40* ence on our language than it does. Writers for both elegant magazines and "in" guides use much the same word-appeal as do the copywriters for popular brands of convenience foods. They may not say "lip-smackin" or "de-lish," but they manage to imply what their words will make readers do. They use their own posh patter, which like the humbler variety seldom bears any kind of scrutiny, whether for original meaning or plain syntax.

How about "unbelievably succulent luscious scallops which boast a nectar-of-the-sea freshness"? Or "a *beurre blanc,* that ethereally light, grand-motherly sauce"? Or "an onion soup, baked *naturellement,* melting its knee-deep crust of cheese and croutons"? Dressings are "teasingly-tart," not teasing or tart or even teasingly tart. They have "breathtakingly visual appeal," instead of looking yummy, and some of them, perhaps fortunately, are "almost too beautiful to describe," "framed in a picture-perfect garnish of utter perfection and exquisiteness," "a pinnacle of gastronomical delight." (Any of these experiences can be found, credit card on the ready, in the bistros-of-the-moment.)

It is somewhat hard to keep one's balance, caught between the three stools of folksy lure, stylist gushing, and a dictionary of word usage. How does one *parse,* as my grandfather would say, a complete sentence like "The very pinkness it was, of mini-slices"? Or "A richly eggy and spiritous Za-baglione, edged in its serving dish with tiny dots of grenadine"? These are not sentences, at least to my grandfather and to me, and I think *spirituous* is a better word in this setting, and I wonder whether the dots of grenadine were wee drops of the sweet syrup made from pomegranates or the glowing seeds of the fruit itself, and how and why anyone would preserve them for a chic restaurant. And were those pink mini-slices from a lamb, a calf? Then there are always verbs to ponder on, in such seductive reports on what and where to dine. One soup "packs chunks" of something or other, to prove its masculine heartiness in a stylish lunchtime brasserie. "Don't forget to special-order!" Is this a verb, a split infinitive, an attempt of the reporter to sound down-to-earth?

Plainly it is as easy to carp, criticize, even dismiss such unworthy verbiage as it is to quibble and shudder about what the other media dictate, that we may subsist. And we continue to carp, criticize, dismiss—and to *eat,* not always as we are told to, and not always well, either! But we were born *hungry.*

Questions of Subject and Theme

1. According to Fisher, some foods and the language that describes them are becoming "indigestible." Point out some examples and explain what she means in each case.
2. What assumptions does Fisher find offensive in the people who want to present her with recipes? How are those assumptions like the assumptions of the language of advertising?

Questions of Method and Strategy

1. Fisher uses many quotation marks in her essay to call attention to particular words and phrases. Find some examples and explain what attitude she creates by this technique.
2. Fisher defines several words within her essay. List them and their definitions. What does this stylistic habit express about her, and how does it support her main point?

A BOTTLE OF KETCHUP

William Safire

William Safire began his career in public relations and went on to become a speech writer for President Nixon. Since that time he has filled two roles: political columnist and weekly commentator on language for the *New York Times*.

I picked up a bottle of Del Monte ketchup (they spell it *catsup,* but most others spell the Chinese-derived word *ketchup*) and read the label: "Made from red ripe tomatoes, natural sweeteners, distilled vinegar, salt and natural flavorings." Three thoughts:

Why does the label read *flavorings* instead of *flavors?* The gerund form is in most dictionaries, of course—"an essence or extract added to a food to give it a certain taste"—but that is also one of the meanings of the base word, *flavor.* So who needs *flavorings?*

Randall Rothenberg, senior editor of the New Jersey Monthly, has been crusading against what he calls "the nominative gerund," a label he says describes "the addition of *-ing* to a noun, to create another noun that seems to have more class." He sends this example, or exampling: "*Shirtings* by Kilgour, French and Stanbury."

A quick check with James McCawley, professor of linguistics at the University of Chicago and author of "Thirty Million Theories of Grammar," straightens Mr. Rothenberg out on his label: "not *nominative* (which is a case, contrasting with *accusative, genitive,* etc.), but rather *denominal,* the standard word meaning 'derived from a noun.'"

O.K., Jim—what's with the trend toward denominal gerunds?

"*Shirting* is a perfectly respectable word that is listed by most dictionaries—'fabric, such as broadcloth, suitable for making shirts.' I suspect it is more common in England than in the U.S.A. It is very common in India, where I spent last summer (virtually all the instances I have seen of the word have been in signs on Indian tailor shops)."

I would not like to get in a scrap with Professor McCawley, who is capable of taking on Noam Chomsky barehanded, and I accept *shirting* as a good, short name for a certain kind of fabric. (When Margaret Fuller said, "I accept the universe," Thomas Carlyle replied, "By God! She'd better.") But I have a hunch *shirting* was used by the copywriter to evoke an elegant English image, and the word the ad should have used is *shirt.* That is the finished product, after the shirting has been tailored into a form that can be sent to the laundry for mangling and burning.

This straining for effect, says editor Rothenberg, "is one of the most obvious abuses—sorry, abusings—of the English language." Although most linguistic types would tell him to keep his shirting on, he has put his finger on a usage that has a distinctly la-di-da flavoring.

"*Red ripe tomatoes . . .*" reads the label on the bottle.

The comma is under attack. This most flexible of punctuation marks,   *10*
rivaled only by the period in frequency of use, was invented to separate
words or thoughts within a sentence that could not stand as sentences by
themselves. (If you want to separate a dependent clause from the main part
of the sentence, use a comma. Sometimes you have two connected thoughts
that can stand by themselves; in that case, use a semicolon.)

We are into a run of deliberate runnings-on. The most obvious function
of a comma (from the Latin "to cut off") is to separate items in a list: *Kilgour,
French and Stanbury.* The use of a comma after the word *French* is optional.
(I've been consulting too many grammar texts; change that last sentence to
read, "You can use a comma after *French* if you like.") The purpose of the
comma in that case is to say, "I mean that guy, and that guy, and that guy."
Without a comma, *Kilgour French* could be one tailor.

"Where have all the commas gone?" writes Gilbert Cranberg, former
editorial writer of the Des Moines Register. "Dow Jones, Merrill Lynch,
Doyle Dane Bernbach. Commas are free. Why don't they use them?"

Charles Dow and Edward Jones were individual men. Their firm was
founded in 1882 as "Dow, Jones & Company." About 1950, the comma
disappeared. "The comma was dropped from *Dow, Jones,*" says Lloyd Wendt,
who wrote "The Wall Street Journal: The Story of Dow Jones and the Nation's Business Newspaper," "because it was felt that it detracted from the
name and was unnecessary. *Dow Jones* has a one-name quality. . . ."

That response is strictly from Hog, Wash & Company. The truth, I
suspect, is that the admen were disposed to dehumanize poor old Dow and
Jones. (They went even further at Sears, Roebuck—they obliterated the
memory of Alvah Roebuck, relegating his memory to the name for "Western wear.") The comma took up time, space, money. *Dow Jones* is snappier
and more modern-looking than the old, plodding, accurate *Dow, Jones.*

Can you imagine how Charles Dow feels about being remembered in   *15*
history as the first name of Edward Jones? That's what comes from playing
the averages.

William Bernbach, one of the founders of Doyle Dane Bernbach, who
died recently, used to answer the comma question with a quip: "We didn't
want anything, not even punctuation, to come between us."

Over at Merrill Lynch & Company Inc., holding company for the bro-
kerage firm of Merrill Lynch, Pierce, Fenner and Smith, there is this explanation of why there is no comma between *Merrill* and *Lynch:* "In 1916 or
1917, on an early stationery order," says spokesman Henry Hecht, "a
printer dropped the comma. Mr. Merrill and Mr. Lynch decided to keep
the paper anyway. This is a true story. Then after the paper ran out, the
comma was reinstated and kept until the company incorporated in 1938.
Then it was 'Merrill Lynch' without the comma; why it was dropped, we
don't know."

Thirty years ago, I interviewed Charles Merrill for The New York Herald Tribune, and wondered why there was no comma between *Merrill* and

Lynch, when there were commas between those names and the rest of the "thundering herd," as the long list of names came to be called. "Merrill Lynch was my company," he replied, "and then we added the other guys."

Thus, there is often sinister purpose in the kamikaze comma-killing. Advertising men profess to see style in the absence of punctuation. Others see error and see red. In examining the label about "red ripe tomatoes," with nary a pause between the adjectives, I am reminded of the character of Archy, the cockroach created by Don Marquis, who could not use the shift key for capitals and punctuation on his boss's typewriter. He wrote: "soon ripe soon rotten" (no period, of course).

"Made from red ripe tomatoes, natural sweeteners . . ."   20

What is a "natural" sweetener? We all know what unnatural sweeteners are—saccharin and aspartame and those chemicals that are usually identified as "artificial" sweeteners.

I have a sneaking suspicion that a "natural" sweetener is that stuff that nobody with a tire around his midsection wants to know about in a list of ingredients. This department, however, is not afraid to confront the word:

Fructose. That's a natural sweetener. "*Natural sweeteners,*" says Mark Gutsche, a Del Monte spokesman, "is not table sugar or sucrose. It is a corn sweetener, which is high in fructose. Fructose, unlike sucrose, is not processed and refined; it is the natural form of sugar found in fruits and vegetables; it is natural."

Among the Lexicographic Irregulars, there is a special group that calls itself the Sweet-Talk Patrol. Just as the Squad Squad specializes in redundancies, these correspondents deal with euphemisms (like "natural sweeteners" for the unfamiliar and suspicious-sounding "fructose"). Ed Cowan, my *Times* colleague, has noted the change in White House telephone listings over the years from *chauffeur* to *driver* and most recently to *vehicle operator.* Nobody wants to let on that the White House staff is transported in cars, much less limousines.

Similarly, Paul Hampden of Ridgefield, Conn., has noted a radio com-   25 mercial for a laundry product that uses *delicate* as a noun: "add a little to the water for your *delicates.*" Not long ago, these stockings, brassieres and diaphanous panties were called *unmentionables;* before that, *undergarments,* and before that, the horrifying or ludicrous *underwear.* (Students of dialect will recall that *delicate thins* is the name of a type of pancake; it's nice to know we have a product that can rinse off the maple syrup.)

All this heavy analysis from the label on one bottle of ketchup. It's a good thing my family won't let me read the newspaper at the table.

Questions of Subject and Theme

1. Is Safire's essay mainly about a bottle of ketchup? Discuss the advantages and disadvantages of his title and its effectiveness or lack of effectiveness.
2. How does Safire's method of writing about grammar differ from the ways you were taught grammar? Explain with examples.

Questions of Method and Strategy

1. What characteristics does Safire seem to imagine as defining his audience? Point to some moments when the author seems to take for granted particular values and assumptions on the part of his readers.
2. Is the section on commas representative of Safire's general method? Explain your answer with examples.

———

Suggestions for Writing on the Juxtapositions

1. Both writers in the section object to pretentious language applied to food. Find an example of pretentious language in an advertisement or label of a different sort and use some of Fisher's and Safire's techniques to write a satirical analysis of your example.
2. Cookbooks and diet books take up a great deal of space in commercial bookstores and publishers' lists. Find an example of the language used to promote "slimming," and write an essay that analyzes the ways in which that language tries to influence its reader.
3. Fisher says that appetite is natural and should be described naturally. Choose one of your favorite foods, and try to write in praise of it using language that you think Fisher would approve. In a final paragraph explain how your use of language meets her standards.
4. Sex is another natural appetite that presents problems for language. Find an example of language used about sex that in some way does not do proper justice to its subject. Write an essay that explores your objections through analysis and exemplification.

13 Mickey Mouse: An American Myth

Walt Disney, "The Story of Mickey Mouse"

Stephen Jay Gould, "A Biological Homage to Mickey Mouse"

John Updike, "The Mystery of Mickey Mouse"

George Vlahogiannis, "Weird World of Disney"

Recognizable almost worldwide, Mickey Mouse has come to be a cultural icon. But what does the icon stand for? Consider these questions while examining the following analyses:

1. Which writer seems most to agree with Walt Disney's assessment of the spirit and meaning of Mickey Mouse? Which least? Discuss the issues with examples.

2. Compare and contrast the ways in which Disney the businessman and Disney the artist are discussed by the other authors in the section.

3. John Updike says "it's all in the ears" to explain what he sees as the essence of Mickey. What specific aspects of the icon do the other writers focus on as crucially symptomatic of the Mickey Mouse phenomenon?

4. Updike and Gould grew up when Mickey Mouse was relatively new and liked him. Vlahogiannis, a much younger man, grew up with Mickey's long-established fame and dislikes him. Do you find the issue of affection a generational matter? Discuss your sense of the issue with examples.

THE STORY OF MICKEY MOUSE

Walt Disney

In his lifetime, Walt Disney was one of the most famous American artists, and his most famous creation, Mickey Mouse, was known throughout the world. In his dual role as fantasist and businessman, his creation of Disneyland made a revolution in recreation and travel. The following essay was originally delivered on University of the Air in 1948.

Mickey Mouse to me is the symbol of independence. He was a means to an end. He popped out of my mind onto a drawing pad twenty years ago on a train ride from Manhattan to Hollywood at a time when the business fortunes of my brother Roy and myself were at lowest ebb and disaster seemed right around the corner. Born of necessity the little fellow literally freed us of immediate worry. He provided the means for expanding our organization to its present dimensions and for extending the medium of cartoon animation toward new entertainment levels. Mickey enabled me to go ahead and do the things I had in mind and the things I foresaw as a natural trend of film fantasy. He spelled production liberation for us. His first actual screen appearance was at the old Colony Theater in New York in *Steamboat Willie* with its sound effects and cautious speech. His current appearance is in our new musical fantasy feature in Technicolor, combining living and animated action, *Fun and Fancy Free*. In between he has appeared in more pictures that any flesh and blood star. He was the first cartoon character to express personality and to be constantly kept in character. I thought of him from the first as a distinct individual, not just a cartoon type or symbol going through a comedy routine. I kept him away from stock symbols and situations. We exposed him in close-ups. Instead of speeding the cartoons, as was then the fashion, we were not afraid to slow down the tempo and let Mickey emote. We allowed audiences to get acquainted with him. To recognize him as a personage, motivated by character instead of situations.

Quite consciously I had been preparing Mickey and his screen pals for the advent of sound. I'd made quite a few silent pictures prior to *Steamboat Willie*. It may seem a curious thing that even in those early films with their explanatory balloons, I had thought of them in terms of sound and speech and dreamed of the day when the voice would be synchronized with the silent action. But I felt sure it was coming. Our tempo and rhythm and general animation technique were already being adjusted so that sound could fit in readily when it came. As early as 1923, I was doing song films. I seldom thought out our silent product without some musical complement. I used to talk to the organist in the theater on arrangements before a film

1

was shown. I even had a gadget which insured a crude kind of synchroni-
zation between the organ music and the picture action. In 1925 I had an
animated cat in one of our silents direct the orchestra in the pit from the
screen. While this was all preliminary to sound and film it was preparatory
background and equipment for that first Mickey Mouse talkie and the subsequent swift evolvement of sound.

Of course, sound had a very considerable effect on our treatment of
Mickey Mouse. It gave his character a new dimension. It rounded him into
complete life-likeness. And it carried us into a new phase of his development. Mickey had reached the state where we had to be very careful about
what we permitted him to do. He'd become a hero in the eyes of his audiences, especially the youngsters. Mickey could do no wrong. I could never
attribute any meanness or callous traits to him. We kept him loveable although ludicrous in his blundering heroics. And that's the way he's remained
despite any outside influences. He's grown into a consistent, predictable
character to whom we could assign only the kind of role and antics which
were correct for his reputation. Naturally, I am pleased with his continued
popularity here and abroad; with the esteem he has won as an entertainment
name among youngsters and grownups; with the honors he's brought our
studio; with the high compliment bestowed when his name was the pass-
word for the invasion of France and with his selection for insignia by scores
of fighting units during the war years. These are tributes beyond all words
of appreciation.

In a business way, as I've indicated, Mickey meant almost incalculable
things to my brother Roy, and to me, as we went through our ups and
downs towards founding our present organization with its Burbank Studio,
its extensive personnel, and its continuous picture schedules. At this turning
point in our career, already referred to, I needed just such a fresh cartoon
personality to sell a projected series of short subjects. . . . I felt I had to rely
on a sustained character appeal rather than on the merit of each separate
issue. Mickey fitted the need exactly. He brought in the money which saved
the day. He paved the way for a more elaborate screen venture. He enabled
us to explore our medium and to evolve the technical advances which were
to appear in our first feature length animation fantasy, *Snow White and the
Seven Dwarfs*, and successively in other features like *Bambi*, *Dumbo*, *Pinocchio*,
Fantasia, *The Three Caballeros*, *Saludos Amigos*, *Make Mine Music*, *Song of the
South* and so up to our latest and current production, *Fun and Fancy Free*. In
his immediate and continuously successful appeal to all kinds of audiences,
Mickey first subsidized our first Silly Symphony Series. From there he sustained other ventures, plugging along as our bread and butter hero. He was
a studio prodigy and pet and we treated him accordingly. In due time we
gave Mickey that contrasting, temperamental sidekick, Donald Duck. Then
Pluto the naive, credulous hound came along. We used to play these three
together in the same picture. Later, we divided them into separate vehicles.
Mickey, Donald and Pluto. These meant fewer pictures for each. And, of

course, Mickey appeared less often. But you'll see him again . . . in "Mickey and the Beanstalk," an escapade from *Fun and Fancy Free*. Prior to this his top performance was in *Fantasia* as the Sorcerer's Apprentice.

In the early days, I did the voice of most of our characters. It wasn't   5
financially feasible to hire people for such assignments. In *Steamboat Willie,* in addition to speaking for Mickey, I also supplied a few sound effects for Minnie, his girl friend, and for the parrot. For Mickey's first picture, I had planned to go all out on sound. And those plans came very near spelling a major disaster for us. To launch our picture impressively, I had hired a full New York orchestra with a famous director to do the recording. The musicians were to cost $10 an hour. I thought fifteen men would be enough but the director insisted on having thirty men. Because I was awed by him I was finally persuaded to take the thirty. The upshot was that I had to borrow on my automobile and Roy and I had to mortgage our homes as well to cover the cost of the first synchronization of *Steamboat Willie*. And when it was finished the picture wouldn't synchronize with the sound. And we had to do it all over after the orchestra leader had reluctantly consented to follow the mechanics that we had prepared at the studio. What I wanted most of all I didn't get. A bull fiddle for the base. The recording room was so small that the orchestra could hardly be jammed into it. The bull fiddle blasted so loud it ruined the other sound and depth blowing out all of the recording lamps. A sad thing, I thought at the time, to launch our Mickey without benefit of bull fiddle in so precarious a world of new possibilities and increased competition. But he survived and thrived and set the pace in his entertainment field. The cost of his first vehicles ranged from . . . a bare $1,200 for *Steamboat Willie* to seven figures for *Fun and Fancy Free* in which he shared prominence with Donald, Goofy, Jiminy Cricket and several new cartoon creations, and with Edgar Bergen and his pals, Charlie McCarthy, Mortimor Snerd and also Dinah Shore and our own little starlet, Luana Patten.

I often find myself surprised at what has been said about our redoubtable little Mickey who was never really a mouse nor yet wholly a man, although always recognizably human, I hope. The psychoanalysts have probed him. Wise men of critical inclination have pondered him. Columnists have kidded him. Admirers have saluted him in extravagant terms. The League of Nations gave him a special medal as a symbol of international good will. Hitler was infuriated by him. And thunderingly forbade his people to wear the then popular Mickey Mouse lapel button in place of the swastika. The little fellow's grin was too infectious for Nazism. But all we ever intended for him and expected of him was that he should continue to make people everywhere chuckle with him and at him. We didn't burden him with any social symbolism. We made him no mouthpiece for frustrations or harsh satire. Mickey was simply a little personality assigned to the purposes of laughter. And it is certainly gratifying that the public which first welcomed him two decades ago, as well their children, have not permitted us, even if we had wished to do so, to change him in any manner or degree, other than a few minor revisions of his physical appearance. In a sense, he was never young. In the same sense, he never grows old in our eyes. All we can do is give him things to overcome in his own, rather stubborn way, in his cartoon universe. There is much nostalgia for me in these reflections. The life and ventures of Mickey Mouse have been closely bound up with my own personal and professional life. It is understandable that I should have sentimental attachment for the little personage who played so big a part in the course of Disney productions and has been so happily accepted as an amusing friend wherever films are shown around the world. He still speaks for me and I still speak for him. *Disney's alter ego*

 ### Questions of Subject and Theme

1. Disney begins by speaking of Mickey Mouse as a "symbol of independence." What is the full range of meanings for "independence" given by his essay as a whole?
2. Disney speaks at one point of Mickey as "lovable and ludicrous" and at another of his being "young and old." What other paradoxes seem to define Disney's ideas of his creature's identity both for the public and for himself?

 ### Questions of Method and Strategy

1. In what ways does Disney manage the transitions between his discussions of business and artistic matters? Point to some examples and explain how they work.
2. Disney speaks of Mickey's personality, but what kind of personality does Disney's style create for himself? His sentences are generally declarative and relatively short. What else do you notice about his style? What do the things you notice do to create your sense of the man who writes?

A BIOLOGICAL HOMAGE
TO MICKEY MOUSE

Stephen Jay Gould

Stephen Jay Gould is a paleontologist at Harvard and the author of many popular books on science. His ability to bring scientific analysis to bear on popular culture has resulted, for example, in an analysis of the historical relations of decrease in the size of Hershey Bars to their increase in price. In the following essay he applies evolutionary theory to the evolution of a cartoon.

Age often turns fire to placidity. Lytton Strachey, in his incisive portrait of Florence Nightingale, writes of her declining years:

> Destiny, having waited very patiently, played a queer trick on Miss Nightingale. The benevolence and public spirit of that long life had only been equalled by its acerbity. Her virtue had dwelt in hardness. . . . And now the sarcastic years brought the proud woman her punishment. She was not to die as she had lived. The sting was to be taken out of her; she was to be made soft; she was to be reduced to compliance and complacency.

I was therefore not surprised—although the analogy may strike some people as sacrilegious—to discover that the creature who gave his name as a synonym for insipidity had a gutsier youth. Mickey Mouse turned a respectable fifty last year. To mark the occasion, many theaters replayed his debut performance in *Steamboat Willie* (1928). The original Mickey was a rambunctious, even slightly sadistic fellow. In a remarkable sequence, exploiting the exciting new development of sound, Mickey and Minnie pummel, squeeze, and twist the animals on board to produce a rousing chorus of "Turkey in the Straw." They honk a duck with a tight embrace, crank a goat's tail, tweak a pig's nipples, bang a cow's teeth as a stand-in xylophone, and play bagpipe on her udder.

Christopher Finch, in his semiofficial pictorial history of Disney's work, comments: "The Mickey Mouse who hit the movie houses in the late twenties was not quite the well-behaved character most of us are familiar with today. He was mischievous, to say the least, and even displayed a streak of cruelty." But Mickey soon cleaned up his act, leaving to gossip and speculation only his unresolved relationship with Minnie and the status of Morty and Ferdie. Finch continues: "Mickey . . . had become virtually a national symbol, and as such he was expected to behave properly at all times. If he occasionally stepped out of line, any number of letters would arrive at the Studio from citizens and organizations who felt that the nation's moral well-being was in their hands. . . . Eventually he would be pressured into the role of straight man."

As Mickey's personality softened, his appearance changed. Many Disney fans are aware of this transformation through time, but few (I suspect) have recognized the coordinating theme behind all the alterations—in fact, I am not sure that the Disney artists themselves explicitly realized what they were doing, since the changes appeared in such a halting and piecemeal fashion. In short, the blander and inoffensive Mickey became progressively more juvenile in appearance. (Since Mickey's chronological age never altered—like most cartoon characters he stands impervious to the ravages of time—this change in appearance at a constant age is a true evolutionary transformation. Progressive juvenilization as an evolutionary phenomenon is called neoteny. More on this later.)

[margin note: personality & appearance soften]

[margin note: progressively younger looking]

The characteristic changes of form during human growth have inspired a substantial biological literature. Since the head-end of an embryo differentiates first and grows more rapidly in utero than the foot-end (an anteroposterior gradient, in technical language), a newborn child possesses a relatively large head attached to a medium-sized body with diminutive legs and feet. This gradient is reversed through growth as legs and feet overtake the front end. Heads continue to grow but so much more slowly than the rest of the body that relative head size decreases.

[margin note: 5]

[margin note: head to body proportion in babies vs. adults]

In addition, a suite of changes pervades the head itself during human growth. The brain grows very slowly after age three, and the bulbous cranium of a young child gives way to the more slanted, lower-browed configuration of adulthood. The eyes scarcely grow at all and relative eye size declines precipitously. But the jaw gets bigger and bigger. Children, compared with adults, have larger heads and eyes, smaller jaws, a more prominent, bulging cranium, and smaller, pudgier legs and feet. Adult heads are altogether more apish, I'm sorry to say.

[margin note: head shape kids vs. adults]

Mickey, however, has traveled this ontogenetic pathway in reverse during his fifty years among us. He has assumed an ever more childlike appearance as the ratty character of *Steamboat Willie* became the cute and inoffensive host to a magic kingdom. By 1940, the former tweaker of pig's nipples gets a kick in the ass for insubordination (as the *Sorcerer's Apprentice* in *Fantasia*). By 1953, his last cartoon, he has gone fishing and cannot even subdue a squirting clam.

[margin note: Mickey grew in reverse]

The Disney artists transformed Mickey in clever silence, often using suggestive devices that mimic nature's own changes by different routes. To give him the shorter and pudgier legs of youth, they lowered his pants line and covered his spindly legs with a baggy outfit. (His arms and legs also thickened substantially—and acquired joints for a floppier appearance.) His head grew relatively larger and its features more youthful. The length of Mickey's snout has not altered, but decreasing protrusion is more subtly suggested by a pronounced thickening. Mickey's eye has grown in two modes: first, by a major, discontinuous evolutionary shift as the entire eye of

Mickey's evolution during 50 years (left to right). As Mickey became increasingly well behaved over the years, his appearance became more youthful. Measurements of three stages in

ancestral Mickey became the pupil of his descendants, and second, by
gradual increase thereafter.

Mickey's improvement in cranial bulging followed an interesting path
since his evolution has always been constrained by the unaltered convention
of representing his head as a circle with appended ears and an oblong snout.
The circle's form could not be altered to provide a bulging cranium directly.
Instead, Mickey's ears moved back, increasing the distance between nose
and ears, and giving him a rounded, rather than a sloping, forehead.

To give these observations the cachet of quantitative science, I applied   *10*
my best pair of dial calipers to three stages of the official phylogeny—the
thin-nosed, ears-forward figure of the early 1930s (stage 1), the latter-day
Jack of Mickey and the Beanstalk (1947, stage 2), and the modern mouse
(stage 3). I measured three signs of Mickey's creeping juvenility: increasing
eye size (maximum height) as a percentage of head length (base of the nose
to top of rear ear); increasing head length as a percentage of body length;
and increasing cranial vault size measured by rearward displacement of the
front ear (base of the nose to top of front ear as a percentage of base of
the nose to top of rear ear).

All three percentages increased steadily—eye size from 27 to 42 percent
of head length; head length from 42.7 to 48.1 percent of body length; and
nose to front ear from 71.7 to a whopping 95.6 percent of nose to rear ear.
For comparison, I measured Mickey's young "nephew" Morty Mouse. In
each case, Mickey has clearly been evolving toward youthful stages of his
stock, although he still has a way to go for head length.

You may, indeed, now ask what an at least marginally respectable scientist has been doing with a mouse like that. In part, fiddling around and
having fun, of course. (I still prefer *Pinocchio* to *Citizen Kane*.) But I do
have a serious point—two, in fact—to make. We must first ask why Disney
chose to change his most famous character so gradually and persistently in

his development revealed a larger relative head size, larger eyes, and an enlarged cranium—
all traits of juvenility. © The Walt Disney Company

the same direction? National symbols are not altered capriciously and market researchers (for the doll industry in particular) have spent a good deal of
time and practical effort learning what features appeal to people as cute and
friendly. Biologists also have spent a great deal of time studying a similar
subject in a wide range of animals.

In one of his most famous articles, Konrad Lorenz argues that humans
use the characteristic differences in form between babies and adults as important behavioral cues. He believes that features of juvenility trigger "innate releasing mechanisms" for affection and nurturing in adult humans.
When we see a living creature with babyish features, we feel an automatic
surge of disarming tenderness. The adaptive value of this response can
scarcely be questioned, for we must nurture our babies. Lorenz, by the way,
lists among his releasers the very features of babyhood that Disney affixed
progressively to Mickey: "a relatively large head, predominance of the brain
capsule, large and low-lying eyes, bulging cheek region, short and thick ex-
tremities, a springy elastic consistency, and clumsy movements." (I propose
to leave aside for this article the contentious issue of whether or not our
affectionate response to babyish features is truly innate and inherited directly
from ancestral primates—as Lorenz argues—or whether it is simply learned
from our immediate experience with babies and grafted upon an evolutionary predisposition for attaching ties of affection to certain learned signals.
My argument works equally well in either case for I only claim that babyish
features tend to elicit strong feelings of affection in adult humans, whether
the biological basis be direct programming or the capacity to learn and
fix upon signals. I also treat as collateral to my point the major thesis of
Lorenz's article—that we respond not to the totality or *Gestalt,* but to a set
of specific features acting as releasers. This argument is important to Lorenz
because he wants to argue for revolutionary identity in modes of behavior
between other vertebrates and humans, and we know that many birds, for

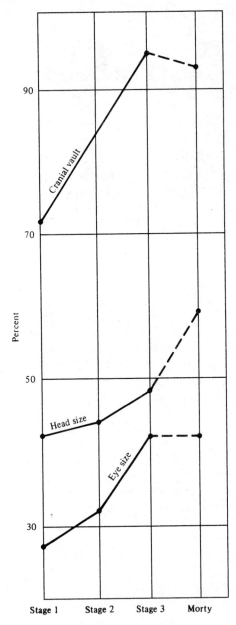

At an early stage in his evolution, Mickey had a smaller head, cranial vault, and eyes. He evolved toward the characteristics of his young nephew Morty (connected to Mickey by a dotted line).

example, often respond to abstract features rather than *Gestalten*. Lorenz's article published in 1950, bears the title *Ganzheit und Teil in der tierischen und menschlichen Gemeinschaft*—"Entirety and part in animal and human society." Disney's piecemeal change of Mickey's appearance does make sense in this context—he operated in sequential fashion upon Lorenz's primary releasers.)

Lorenz emphasizes the power that juvenile features hold over us, and the abstract quality of their influence, by pointing out that we judge other animals by the same criteria—although the judgment may be utterly inappropriate in an evolutionary context. We are, in short, fooled by an evolved response to our own babies, and we transfer our reaction to the same set of features in other animals. *affection for baby animal features*

Many animals, for reasons having nothing to do with the inspiration of affection in humans, possess some features also shared by human babies but not by human adults—large eyes and a bulging forehead with retreating chin, in particular. We are drawn to them, we cultivate them as pets, we stop and admire them in the wild—while we reject their small-eyed, long-snouted relatives who might make more affectionate companions or objects of admiration. Lorenz points out that the German names of many animals with features mimicking human babies end in the diminutive suffix *chen*, even though the animals are often larger than close relatives without such *15*

Humans feel affection for animals with juvenile features: large eyes, bulging craniums, retreating chins (left column). Small-eyed, long-snouted animals (right column) do not elicit the same response. From *Studies in Animal and Human Behavior*, Vol. II, by Konrad Lorenz, 1971. Methuen & Co. Ltd.

features—*Rotkehlchen* (robin), *Eichhornchen* (squirrel), and *Kaninchen* (rabbit), for example.

In a fascinating section, Lorenz then enlarges upon our capacity for biologically inappropriate response to other animals, or even to inanimate objects that mimic human features. "The most amazing objects can acquire remarkable, highly specific emotional values of 'experiential attachment' of human properties. . . . Steeply rising, somewhat overhanging cliff faces or dark stormclouds piling up have the same, immediate display value as a human being who is standing at full height and leaning slightly forwards"—that is, threatening.

We cannot help regarding a camel as aloof and unfriendly because it mimics, quite unwittingly and for other reasons, the "gesture of haughty rejection" common to so many human cultures. In this gesture, we raise our heads, placing our nose above our eyes. We then half-close our eyes and blow out through our nose—the "harumph" of the stereotyped upperclass Englishman or his well-trained servant. "All this," Lorenz argues quite cogently, "symbolizes resistance against all sensory modalities emanating from the disdained counterpart." But the poor camel cannot help carrying its nose above its elongate eyes, with mouth drawn down. As Lorenz reminds us, if you wish to know whether a camel will eat out of your hand or spit, look at its ears, not the rest of its face.

In his important book *Expression of the Emotions in Man and Animals,* published in 1872, Charles Darwin traced the evolutionary basis of many common gestures to originally adaptive actions in animals later internalized as symbols in humans. Thus, he argued for evolutionary continuity of emotion, not only of form. We snarl and raise our upper lip in fierce anger—to expose our nonexistent fighting canine tooth. Our gesture of disgust repeats the facial actions associated with the highly adaptive act of vomiting in necessary circumstances. Darwin concluded, much to the distress of many Victorian contemporaries: "With mankind some expressions, such as the bristling of the hair under the influence of extreme terror, or the uncovering of the teeth under that of furious rage, can hardly be understood, except on the belief that man once existed in a much lower and animal-like condition."

In any case, the abstract features of human childhood elicit powerful emotional responses in us, even when they occur in other animals. I submit that Mickey Mouse's evolutionary road down the course of his own growth in reverse reflects the unconscious discovery of this biological principle by Disney and his artists. In fact, the emotional status of most Disney characters rests on the same set of distinctions. To this extent, the magic kingdom trades on a biological illusion—our ability to abstract and our propensity to transfer inappropriately to other animals the fitting responses we make to changing form in the growth of our own bodies.

Donald Duck also adopts more juvenile features through time. His elongated beak recedes and his eyes enlarge; he converges on Huey, Louie, and Dewey as surely as Mickey approaches Morty. But Donald, having in-

20

herited the mantle of Mickey's original misbehavior, remains more adult in form with his projecting beak and more sloping forehead.

Mouse villains or sharpies, contrasted with Mickey, are always more adult in appearance, although they often share Mickey's chronological age. In 1936, for example, Disney made a short entitled *Mickey's Rival*. Mortimer, a dandy in a yellow sports car, intrudes upon Mickey and Minnie's quiet country picnic. The thoroughly disreputable Mortimer has a head only 29 percent of body length, to Mickey's 45, and a snout 80 percent of head length, compared with Mickey's 49. (Nonetheless, and was it ever different, Minnie transfers her affection until an obliging bull from a neighboring field dispatches Mickey's rival.) Consider also the exaggerated adult features of other Disney characters—the swaggering bully Peg-leg Pete or the simple, if lovable, dolt Goofy.

[margin note: villains — "more adult]

As a second, serious biological comment on Mickey's odyssey in form, I note that his path to eternal youth repeats, in epitome, our own evolutionary story. For humans are neotenic. We have evolved by retaining to adulthood the originally juvenile features of our ancestors. Our australopithecine forebears, like Mickey in *Steamboat Willie,* had projecting jaws and low vaulted craniums.

Our embryonic skulls scarcely differ from those of chimpanzees. And

Dandified, disreputable Mortimer (here stealing Minnie's affections) has strikingly more adult features than Mickey. His head is smaller in proportion to body length; his nose is a full 80 percent of head length. © The Walt Disney Company

Cartoon villains are not the only Disney characters with exaggerated adult features. Goofy, like Mortimer, has a small head relative to body length and a prominent snout. © The Walt Disney Company

we follow the same path of changing form through growth: relative decrease of the cranial vault since brains grow so much more slowly than bodies after birth, and continuous relative increase of the jaw. But while chimps accentuate these changes, producing an adult strikingly different in form from a baby, we proceed much more slowly down the same path and never get nearly so far. Thus, as adults, we retain juvenile features. To be sure, we change enough to produce a notable difference between baby and adult, but our alteration is far smaller than that experienced by chimps and other primates.

A marked slowdown of development rates has triggered our neoteny. Primates are slow developers among mammals, but we have accentuated the trend to a degree matched by no other mammal. We have very long periods of gestation, markedly extended childhoods, and the longest life span of any mammal. The morphological features of eternal youth have served us well. Our enlarged brain is, at least in part, a result of extending rapid prenatal growth rates to later ages. (In all mammals, the brain grows rapidly in utero but often very little after birth. We have extended this fetal phase into postnatal life.)

But the changes in timing themselves have been just as important. We   *25*
are preeminently learning animals, and our extended childhood permits the
transference of culture by education. Many animals display flexibility and
play in childhood but follow rigidly programmed patterns as adults. Lorenz
writes, in the same article cited above: "The characteristic which is so vital
for the human peculiarity of the true man—that of always remaining in a
state of development—is quite certainly a gift which we owe to the neoten-
ous nature of mankind."

In short, we, like Mickey, never grow up although we, alas, do grow
old. Best wishes to you, Mickey, for your next half-century. May we stay as
young as you, but grow a bit wiser.

(handwritten margin note: like Mickey, humans don't grow up—just old)

Questions of Subject and Theme

1. In his essay Walt Disney said that he had made only minor changes in the
   appearance of Mickey. What, according to Gould, is the result of those
   changes?
2. According to Gould, how does Mickey's evolutionary history epitomize
   human evolutionary history?

Questions of Method and Strategy

1. What are some of the ways in which Gould tries to make technical, scientific terms less threatening to the general reader? Point to some examples and explain Gould's strategies.
2. Does Gould maintain a consistent attitude toward Mickey throughout
   his essay? If you think so, describe the view he takes in a sentence or two,
   pointing to some examples. If you think not, describe the view and show
   how different examples confirm its inconsistency.

THE MYSTERY OF MICKEY MOUSE

John Updike

John Updike is one of the country's most distinguished authors having won almost all the nation's critical awards. He has published dozens of novels and collections of essays, as well as books of reviews and poetry. The following piece was selected for inclusion in *The Best American Essays 1992*.

It's all in the ears. When Mickey Mouse was born, in 1927, the world   1
of early cartoon animation was filled with two-legged zoomorphic human-
oids, whose strange half-black faces were distinguished one from another
chiefly by the ears. Felix the Cat had pointed triangular ears and Oswald the
Rabbit—Walt Disney's first successful cartoon creation, which he abandoned when his New York distributor, Charles Mintz, attempted to swindle
him—had long floppy ears, with a few notches in the end to suggest fur.
Disney's Oswald films, and the Alice animations that preceded them, had
mice in them, with linear limbs, wiry tails, and ears that are oblong, not yet
round. On the way back to California from New York by train, having left
Oswald enmeshed for good in the machinations of Mr. Mintz, Walt and his
wife Lillian invented another character based—the genesis legend claims—
on the tame field mice that used to wander into Disney's old studio in Kansas
City. His first thought was to call the mouse Mortimer; Lillian proposed
instead the less pretentious name Mickey. Somewhere between Chicago
and Los Angeles, the young couple concocted the plot of Mickey's first
cartoon short, *Plane Crazy,* costarring Minnie and capitalizing on 1927's
Lindbergh craze. The next short produced by Disney's fledgling studio—
which included, besides himself and Lillian, his brother Roy and his old
Kansas City associate Ub Iwerks—was *Gallopin' Gaucho,* and introduced a
fat and wicked cat who did not yet wear the prosthesis that would give him
his name of Pegleg Pete. The third short, *Steamboat Willie,* incorporated that
brand-new novelty a sound track, and was released first, in 1928. Mickey
Mouse entered history, as the most persistent and pervasive figment of
American popular culture in this century.

His ears are two solid black circles, no matter the angle at which he
holds his head. Three-dimensional images of Mickey Mouse—toy dolls, or
the papier-mâché heads the grotesque Disneyland Mickeys wear—make us
uneasy, since the ears inevitably exist edgewise as well as frontally. These
ears properly belong not to three-dimensional space but to an ideal realm
of notation, of symbolization, of cartoon resilience and indestructibility. In
drawings, when Mickey is in profile, one ear is at the back of his head like
a spherical ponytail, or like a secondary bubble in a computer-generated
Mandelbrot set. We accept it, as we accepted Li'l Abner's hair always being

parted on the side facing the viewer. A surreal optical consistency is part of the cartoon world, halfway between our world and the plane of pure signs, of alphabets and trademarks.

In the sixty-four years since Mickey Mouse's image was promulgated, the ears, though a bit more organically irregular and flexible than the classic 1930s appendages, have not been essentially modified. Many other modifications have, however, overtaken that first crude cartoon, born of an era of starker stylizations. White gloves, like the gloves worn in minstrel shows, appeared after those first, to cover the black hands. The infantile bare chest and shorts with two buttons were phased out in the forties. The eyes have undergone a number of changes, most drastically in the late thirties, when, some historians mistakenly claim, they acquired pupils. Not so: the old eyes, the black oblongs that acquired a nick of reflection in the sides, *were* the pupils; the eye whites filled the entire space beneath Mickey's cap of black, its widow's peak marking the division between these enormous oculi. This can be seen clearly in the face of the classic Minnie; when she bats her eyelids, their lashed shades cover over the full width of what might be thought to be her brow. But all the old animated animals were built this way from Felix the Cat on; Felix had lower lids, and the Mickey of *Plane Crazy* also. So it was an evolutionary misstep that, beginning in 1938, replaced the shiny black pupils with entire oval eyes, containing pupils of their own. No such mutation has overtaken Pluto, Goofy, or Donald Duck. The change brought Mickey closer to us humans, but also took away something of his vitality, his alertness, his bugeyed cartoon readiness for adventure. It made him less abstract, less iconic, more merely cute and dwarfish. The original Mickey, as he scuttles and bounces through those early animated shorts, was angular and wiry, with much of the impudence and desperation of a true rodent. He was gradually rounded to the proportions of a child, a regression sealed by his fifties manifestation as the genius of the children's television show *The Mickey Mouse Club,* with its live Mouseketeers. Most of the artists who depict Mickey today, though too young to have grown up, as I did, with his old form, have instinctively reverted to it; it is the bare-chested basic Mickey, with his yellow shoes and oval buttons on his shorts, who is the icon, beside whom his modified later version is a mere mousy trousered pipsqueak.

His first, iconic manifestation had something of Chaplin to it; he was the little guy, just over the border of the respectable. His circular ears, like two minimal cents, bespeak the smallest economic unit, the overlookable democratic man. His name has passed into the language as a byword for the small, the weak—a "Mickey Mouse operation" means an undercapitalized company or minor surgery. Children of my generation—wearing our Mickey Mouse watches, prying pennies from our Mickey Mouse piggy banks (I won one in a third-grade spelling bee, my first intellectual triumph), following his running combat with Pegleg Pete in the daily funnies, going to the local movie-house movies every Saturday afternoon and cheering when his smiling visage burst onto the screen to introduce a cartoon—

felt Mickey was one of us, a bridge to the adult world of which Donald
Duck was, for all of his childish sailor suit, an irascible, tyrannical member.
Mickey didn't seek trouble, and he didn't complain; he rolled with the
punches, and surprised himself as much as us when, as in *The Little Tailor,* he
showed warrior resourcefulness and won, once again, a blushing kiss from
dear, all but identical Minnie. His minimal, decent nature meant that he
would yield, in the Disney animated cartoons, the starring role to combat-
ive, sputtering Donald Duck and even to Goofy, with his "gawshes" and
Gary Cooper–like gawkiness. But for an occasional comeback like the "Sorcerer's Apprentice" episode of *Fantasia,* and last year's rather souped-up *The
Prince and the Pauper,* Mickey was through as a star by 1940. But as with
Marilyn Monroe when her career was over, his life as an icon gathered
strength. The American that is not symbolized by that imperial Yankee
Uncle Sam is symbolized by Mickey Mouse. He is America as it feels to
itself—plucky, put-on, inventive, resilient, good-natured, game.

Like America, Mickey has a lot of black blood. This fact was revealed   5
to me in conversation by Saul Steinberg, who, in attempting to depict the
racially mixed reality of New York streets for the supersensitive and race-
blind *New Yorker* of the sixties and seventies, hit upon scribbling numerous
Mickeys as a way of representing what was jauntily and scruffily and un-
ignorably there. From just the way Mickey swings along in his classic, trademark pose, one three-fingered gloved hand held on high, he is jiving.
Along with round black ears and yellow shoes, Mickey has soul. Looking
back to such early animations as the early Looney Tunes' Bosko and Honey
series (1930–36) and the Arab figures in Disney's own *Mickey in Arabia* of
1932, we see that blacks were drawn much like cartoon animals, with round
button noses and great white eyes creating the double arch of the curious peaked skullcaps. Cartoon characters' rubberiness, their jazziness, their
cheerful buoyance and idleness, all chimed with popular images of African
Americans, earlier embodied in minstrel shows and in Joel Chandler Harris's
tales of Uncle Remus, which Disney was to make into an animated feature,
Song of the South, in 1946.

Up to 1950, animated cartoons, like films in general, contained carica-
tures of blacks that would be unacceptable now; in fact, *Song of the South*
raised objections from the NAACP when it was released. In recent reissues
of *Fantasia,* two Nubian centaurettes and a pickaninny centaurette who
shines the others' hooves have been edited out. Not even the superb crows
section of *Dumbo* would be made now. But there is a sense in which all
animated cartoon characters are more or less black. Steven Spielberg's hectic
tribute to animation, *Who Framed Roger Rabbit?,* has them all, from the singing trees of Silly Symphonies to Daffy Duck and Woody Woodpecker, living in a Los Angeles ghetto, Toonville. As blacks were second-class citizens
with entertaining qualities, so the animated shorts were second-class movies,
with unreal actors who mocked and illuminated from underneath the real
world, the live-actor cinema. Of course, even in a ghetto there are class
distinctions. Porky Pig and Bugs Bunny have homes that they tend and

defend, whereas Mickey started out, like those other raffish stick figures and dancing blots from the twenties, as a free spirit, a wanderer. As Richard Schickel has pointed out, "The locales of his adventures throughout the 1930s ranged from the South Seas to the Alps to the deserts of Africa. He was, at various times, a gaucho, teamster, explorer, swimmer, cowboy, fireman, convict, pioneer, taxi driver, castaway, fisherman, cyclist, Arab, football player, inventor, jockey, storekeeper, camper, sailor, Gulliver, boxer," and so forth. He was, in short, a rootless vaudevillian who would play any part that the bosses at Disney Studios assigned him. And though the comic strip, which still persists, has fitted him with all of a white man's household comforts and headaches, it is as an unencumbered drifter whistling along on the road of hard knocks, ready for whatever adventure waits at the next turning, that he lives in our minds.

Cartoon characters have soul as Carl Jung defined it in his *Archetypes and the Collective Unconscious:* "soul is a life-giving demon who plays his elfin game above and below human existence." Without the "leaping and twinkling of the soul," Jung says, "man would rot away in his greatest passion, idleness." The Mickey Mouse of the thirties shorts was a whirlwind of activity, with a host of unsuspected skills and a reluctant heroism that rose to every occasion. Like Chaplin and Douglas Fairbanks and Fred Astaire, he acted out our fantasies of endless nimbleness, of perfect weightlessness. Yet withal, there was nothing aggressive or self-promoting about him, as there was about Popeye. Disney, interviewed in the thirties, said, "Sometimes I've tried to figure out why Mickey appealed to the whole world. Everybody's tried to figure it out. So far as I know, nobody has. He's a pretty nice fellow who never does anybody any harm, who gets into scrapes through no fault of his own, but always manages to come up grinning." This was perhaps Disney's image of himself: for twenty years he did Mickey's voice in the films, and would often say, "There's a lot of the Mouse in me." Mickey was a character created with his own pen, and nurtured on Disney's memories of his mouse-ridden Kansas City studio and of the Missouri farm where his struggling father tried for a time to make a living. Walt's humble, scrambling beginnings remained embodied in the mouse, whom the Nazis, in a fury against the Mickey-inspired Allied legions (the Allied code word on D-Day was "Mickey Mouse"), called "the most miserable ideal ever revealed . . . mice are dirty."

But was Disney, like Mickey, just "a pretty nice fellow"? He was until crossed in his driving perfectionism, his Napoleonic capacity to marshal men and take risks in the service of an artistic and entrepreneurial vision. He was one of those great Americans, like Edison and Henry Ford, who invented themselves in terms of a new technology. The technology—in Disney's case, film animation—would have been there anyway, but only a few driven men seized the full possibilities and made empires. In the dozen years between *Steamboat Willie* and *Fantasia,* the Disney studios took the art of animation to heights of ambition and accomplishment it would never have reached otherwise, and Disney's personal zeal was the animating force. He created an empire of the mind, and its emperor was Mickey Mouse.

The thirties were Mickey's conquering decade. His image circled the globe. In Africa, tribesmen painfully had tiny mosaic Mickey Mouses inset into their front teeth, and a South African tribe refused to buy soap unless the cakes were embossed with Mickey's image, and a revolt of some native bearers was quelled when the safari masters projected some Mickey Mouse cartoons for them. Nor were the high and mighty immune to Mickey's elemental appeal—King George V and Franklin Roosevelt insisted that all film showings they attended include a dose of Mickey Mouse. But other popular phantoms, like Felix the Cat, have faded, where Mickey has settled into the national collective consciousness. The television program revived him for my children's generation, and the theme parks make him live for my grandchildren's. Yet survival cannot be imposed through weight of publicity; Mickey's persistence springs from something unhyped, something timeless in the image that has allowed it to pass in status from a fad to an icon.

To take a bite out of our imaginations, an icon must be simple. The ears, the wiggly tail, the red shorts, give us a Mickey. Donald Duck and Goofy, Bugs Bunny and Woody Woodpecker are inextricably bound up with the draftsmanship of the artists who make them move and squawk, but Mickey floats free. It was Claes Oldenburg's pop art that first alerted me to the fact that Mickey Mouse had passed out of the realm of commercially generated image into that of artifact. A new Disney gadget, advertised on television, is a camera-like box that spouts bubbles when a key is turned; the key consists of three circles, two mounted on a larger one, and the image is unmistakably Mickey. Like yin and yang, like the Christian cross and the star of Israel, Mickey can be seen everywhere—a sign, a rune, a hieroglyphic trace of a secret power, an electricity we want to plug into. Like totem poles, like African masks, Mickey stands at that intersection of abstraction and representation where magic connects.

Usually cartoon figures do not age, and yet their audience does age, as generation succeeds generation, so that a weight of allusion and sentimental reference increases. To the movie audiences of the early thirties, Mickey Mouse was a piping-voiced live wire, the latest thing in entertainment; by the time of *Fantasia* he was already a sentimental figure, welcomed back. *The Mickey Mouse Club,* with its slightly melancholy pack leader, Jimmie Dodd, created a Mickey more removed and marginal than in his first incarnation. The generation that watched it grew up into the rebels of the sixties, to whom Mickey became camp, a symbol of U.S. cultural fast food, with a touch of the old rodent raffishness. Politically, Walt, stung by the studio strike of 1940, moved to the right, but Mickey remains one of the thirties proletariat, not uncomfortable in the cartoon-rickety, cheerfully verminous crash pads of the counterculture. At the Florida and California theme parks, Mickey manifests himself as a short real person wearing an awkward giant head, costumed as a ringmaster; he is in danger, in these nineties, of seeming not merely venerable kitsch but part of the great trash problem, one more piece of visual litter being moved back and forth by the bulldozers of consumerism.

consumerist danger

But never fear, his basic goodness will shine through. Beyond recall, perhaps, is the simple love felt by us of the generation that grew up with him. He was five years my senior and felt like a playmate. I remember crying when the local newspaper, cutting down its comic pages to help us win World War II, eliminated the Mickey Mouse strip. I was old enough, nine or ten, or write an angry letter to the editor. In fact, the strips had been eliminated by the votes of a readership poll, and my indignation and sorrow stemmed from my incredulous realization that not everybody loved Mickey Mouse as I did. In an account of my boyhood written over thirty years ago, "The Dogwood Tree," I find these sentences concerning another boy, a rival: "When we both collected Big Little Books, he outbid me for my supreme find (in the attic of a third boy), the first Mickey Mouse. I can still see that book. I wanted it so badly, its paper tan with age and its drawings done in Disney's primitive style, when Mickey's black chest is naked like a child's and his eyes are two nicked oblongs." And I once tried to write a short story called "A Sensation of Mickey Mouse," trying to superimpose on adult experience, as a shiver-inducing revenant, that indescribable childhood sensation—a rubbery taste, a licorice smell, a feeling of supernatural clarity and close-in excitation that Mickey Mouse gave me, and gives me, much dimmed by the years, still. He is a "genius" in the primary dictionary sense of "an attendant spirit," with his vulnerable bare black chest, his touchingly big yellow shoes, the mysterious place at the back of his shorts where his tail came out, the little cleft cushion of a tongue, red as a valentine and glossy as candy, always peeping through the catenary curves of his undiscourageable smile. Not to mention his ears.

good shines thru

Questions of Subject and Theme

1. According to Updike, what is the "mystery" of Mickey Mouse? What are the major elements that define that mystery?
2. Summarize the relations that Updike sees between the characteristics of Mickey Mouse and his creator, Walt Disney.

Questions of Method and Strategy

1. Compare and contrast the methods Updike employs in inviting his reader to take Mickey seriously with those used by Gould.
2. Updike is most famous as a novelist. Point to those moments when his writing seems most novelistic to you and describe what elements characterize the style you observe.

WEIRD WORLD OF DISNEY

George Vlahogiannis

> George Vlahogiannis wrote the following essay for the *Inside Beat* section of the *Rutgers Daily Targum,* a section largely devoted to reviews of current popular cultural enthusiasms. Do you find his views representative of student attitudes toward the topic on your campus?

Ever since I was a little kid, I always hated Mickey Mouse and his band of anthropomorphic pals. To a child, Mickey is everywhere on TV, in books, on clothes, on toys and just about everywhere else. Mickey and pals were pushed on you as a child; the name Mickey has become virtually synonymous with images of playfulness and childhood, and is thus used to appease children by placing his image on such child-hated things as toothbrushes and diapers. Whenever you saw Mickey on something other than a toy, you knew it was something that you ordinarily wouldn't want if it didn't have little ears on it.

I personally never understood the appeal of the Disney characters. Mickey, Minnie, Donald and all the other characters were cartoons which served no function in the cartoon world: they never did anything that would make them likable. The 'Disney Pals' as they were coined, weren't like Underdog who rescued damsels in distress while high on pills, or Courageous Cat and Minit Mouse who had cool theme music, or even Inspector Gadget who had all kinds of gimmicks. The only thing Mickey and his friends had were moronic, blank stares and empty smiles, while performing stupid tasks that would seem mindless to the average individual such as chasing a dog or driving a car. Some wore clothes and costumes—stupid ones at that— which served as weak indicators of their cartoon status. Without his clothes, little would separate Mickey from a naked rat, and Donald would be nothing but a foul [sic] with a speech impediment. Furthermore, these creatures resembled humans in all ways but one: they were sexless, with the exception of Minnie who was identical to Mickey but was gendered, by a dress and a bow in her hair. The Disney Pals bumbled about like sexless eunuchs, (which accounted for the hollow eyes and blank stares) finding bliss in the most mundane of all daily tasks. As a child, these characters frightened me, and I often wondered what it was that people found so great about the Disney world that I found so ridiculous.

We can learn a lot about the Disney mentality by examining the creator himself: Mr. Walt Disney. Walt was a sick man, who lived in a fantasy world of his own. Obsessed by the fact that there was no official record of his birth, Walt spent his whole life trying to formulate a forgotten childhood and past. Disney used his art as a tool to create the family background and childhood he could not recall, and created a fantasy world based on his imagined past. From this past he held a set of lofty ideals of decency and order which he sought to maintain and impose in the lives of others. As a domestic spy for the US government in the 1940s, he became a member of the HUAC and was one of the members of the board in charge of blacklisting many in Hollywood. During his stint as guardian of the American way, Disney became close to president and fellow lunatic, Herbert Hoover, and supported his red-scare paranoia.

imposing Disney "order"

A middle class man from the midwest, Disney surrounded his house with small figurines, statues of his rodent characters, and a miniaturized train he would ride to get inspiration for his drawings. Disney found the world around him to be "indecent and immoral" so he created characters through which he represented his ideals. Popular forms of commercialized leisure were distasteful in his eyes as they were filled with "dirty" immigrants and subscribed to "low brow" tastes. Disney sought to create a world where people could go and spend their leisure-time and dollars and not have to deal with the "filth" that made up commercialized leisure at that time. Located in Anaheim California, Disneyland offered(s) rides and amusements based upon his characters and themes which he considered to be decent and wholesome entertainment (ie: Mr. Toad's Wild Ride.) The structures built in Disneyworld were modeled after actual buildings that existed on the Main Street in the small Kansas town he grew up in, at 5/12ths the size of the real buildings. Disney also had an apartment in one of the buildings on Main Street USA that he lived in for weeks at a time (it was red and had all kinds of furry stuff on the walls.) This kept his deranged mind busy for a while, but Disney still sought for something greater. Inspired by the displays of French architect/planner Le Corbusier's neo-fascist 'Radiant City' at the 1933 World Expo, Disney looked for opportunities to create an even larger place that would represent his ideals. The Radiant City was a model of the "perfect" city of tomorrow, free from the overcrowding, diversity and street-culture of the urban landscape. This vision of uniformity and bleak cleanliness inspired Walt Disney to aim high in his aspirations to create the perfect society. The product of this dream was Disneyworld.

Disney Morality

Disneyworld was to be a place where mice wore clothes and ducks with lisps could come and go as they pleased. It was to be a shrine and a place to praise the greatness of Mickey Mouse and his congenial friends. By the time the design and construction for Disneyworld began, Disney was too sick to run the company and turned it over to a board to oversee its operation. With the corporation out of his hands, Disney grew angry at the direction his corporation was headed. The Disney corporation was steering away from the family-like company he sought to create and was becoming a money-making machine. Walt's vision of a Disneyworld based on his dream world became subject to the criteria of investors and their demands for money-making concessions. This angered Walt and only worsened his health.

5

As his health declined, Walt Disney developed a fascination with the results of cryogenic research being done at the University of California. He knew that his health was failing (lung disease) and was desperately seeking some sort of cure or alternative to death, making the thought of being frozen very attractive to him. Finally in December of 1969, Walt Disney allegedly died in his sleep. A very exclusive funeral was held and he was allegedly cremated and buried, but no records exist of his cremation. To this day, his burial site is highly protected and access is very limited. Makes you wonder . . .

Today, the world of Disney exists under the names of Buena Vista, Touchstone, SBK and so on. However, when Walt Disney is thawed out and revived, I don't believe he'll be very happy with what has become of his creations. The man is coming back and we will all feel his wrath. Think *The Cat From Outer Space* was moronic? Imagine *Herbie, The Love Bug* all over again. Sure Beauty and The Beast was offensively idiotic in its simpleminded romanticism, but wait till Walt comes back to give us something to really fear. Michael Eisners's deranged, mindless productions like *My Father, The Hero* and *Blank Check* will sit in the shadows of the many reinterpretions of Walt Disney's lost past to come.

 ### Questions of Subject and Theme

1. List the reasons Vlahogiannis gives for hating Mickey Mouse. Which seems the most important? Explain what makes it seem most important to you.
2. What does the author think of Mickey's creator, Walt Disney? What relations between creature and creator does Vlahogiannis claim?

Questions of Method and Strategy

1. The author makes his general attitude clear from the title and first sentence. What else about his style contributes to your sense of the author as straightforward and candid in his views?
2. The author emphasizes what he finds "weird" or "deranged" in the fantasies he examines. Besides using these words, how does he emphasize what he considers abnormal?

———

Suggestions for Writing on the Juxtapositions

1. Walt Disney describes Mickey as, among other things, "loveable"; Stephen Jay Gould says the mouse is a "symbol of insipidity"; George Vlahogiannis goes even further. Write an essay in which you analyze, compare, and contrast the differing meanings each writer sees in the character of Mickey Mouse.
2. John Updike says that other cartoon characters have faded but Mickey remains. Does Mickey Mouse seem dated to you or not? Write an essay in which you compare and contrast your sense of Mickey to a more recent creature from cartoons or comic books.

3. Pick another fictional figure from popular culture (Bart Simpson, for example) and, using the techniques of the essayists here for models or inspiration, write an essay that gives a sense of the meaning of a cultural icon.
4. Have you visited Disney World or Disneyland? If so, write an essay in which you show how that enterprise manifests the spirit of Walt Disney as described in this section's essays.

14   *Why Is Weight So Weighty?*

Anne Hollander, "Why It's Fashionable to Be Thin"
Sallie Tisdale, "A Weight That Women Carry"
Joseph Epstein, "A Fat Man Struggles to Get Out"

Cookbooks and diet books are among the biggest sellers in the United States today. Why do eating and body weight have such impact on the modern imagination? Consider the following questions as you read the three essays here:

1. Two of the authors are women and one is a man. Do they assume that their gender influences their attitudes toward the topic? Discuss the issue with examples.

2. Both Epstein and Tisdale discuss the idea that food and weight are somehow related to morality. Compare and contrast the ways in which each author creates the relations.

3. To what degree do you think Tisdale would agree with Hollander on the issue of clothing styles? Explain your answer with supporting evidence.

4. Epstein says that while he doesn't want to be fat, "stout" doesn't seem so bad to him. Compare and contrast the ways in which at least two writers find that language is interwoven with the topic of thinness.

WHY IT'S FASHIONABLE TO BE THIN

Anne Hollander

Anne Hollander is an art historian whose particular specialty is the history of costume and design. She is the author of numerous essays in national magazines and of *Seeing Through Clothes* (1978), a book on the importance of clothing in Western civilization and the meaning of its changes in fashion.

The strong appeal of female slimness in the twentieth century is usually *1* accounted for by social and economic changes rather than through a purely aesthetic development of style. Feminine emancipation from many physical and moral restraints, the increasing popularity of sport for women, together with new possibilities for gainful employment and political power, all eventually contributed to the new physical ideal. Good sense and good health, mental and physical, were seen to be properly served by freedom and activity, and feminine clothing evolved so as to allow for these and (more importantly) for the look of these. What is meant by "modern" looks developed after the First World War with the aid of clothing that expressed (although it did not always provide) an ideal of comfort and the possibility of action.

The most important expressive element in this new visual conception of female dress was not the uncorseted torso but the shortened skirt. After women's skirts had risen off the ground, any given clothed woman was perceptibly smaller in scale than formerly. Hair was shortened, as well as skirts, and worn close to the head. Hats shrank. During most of the nineteenth century a fashionable woman's dress, including coiffure, headgear, and a possible muff, handbag, and parasol, had consisted of an extensive, complicated system with many different sections (sleeves, bodice, skirt, collar, train). These were all separately conceived and embellished and all tended to enlarge the total volume of the clothed body, partly by being difficult to perceive all at once. After the First World War a woman's dress came more and more to present a compact and unified visual image. This is what men's clothes had already succeeded in doing a century before. The new simplified and reduced clothes for women, although they were designed and made absolutely differently from men's clothes and out of different fabrics, nevertheless expressed the new sense of the equality of the sexes—an equality, that is, with respect to the new character of their important differences.

Female sexual submissiveness, either meek or wanton, was no longer modish and no longer avowed by elements of dress. Feminine sexuality had to abandon the suggestion of plump, hidden softness and find expression in exposed, lean hardness. Women strove for the erotic appeal inherent in the racehorse and the sports car, which might be summed up as a mettlesome challenge: a vibrant, somewhat unaccountable readiness for action but only under expert guidance. This was naturally best offered in a self-contained, sleekly composed physical format: a thin body, with few layers of covering. Immanent sexuality, best expressed in a condition of stasis, was no longer the foundation of female allure. The look of possible movement became a necessary element in fashionable female beauty, and all women's clothing, whatever other messages it offered, consistently incorporated visible legs and feet into the total female image. Women, once thought to glide, were seen to walk. Even vain or fruitless or nervous activity, authorized by fashionable morbid aestheticism, came to seem preferable to immobility, idleness, passivity. The various dance crazes of the first quarter of the century undoubtedly were an expression of this restless spirit, but its most important vehicle was the movies.

The rapid advance of the movies as the chief popular art made the public increasingly aware of style in feminine physical movement. Movies taught everyone how ways of walking and dancing, of using the hands and moving the head and shoulders, could be incorporated into the conscious ways of wearing clothes. After about 1920 the fact that women's clothes showed such a reduction in overall volume was undoubtedly partly due to the visual need for the completely clothed body to be satisfactorily seen *in motion*. Perfect feminine beauty no longer formed a still image, ideally wrought by a Leonardo da Vinci or a Titian into an eternal icon. It had become transmuted into a photograph, a single instant that represented a sequence of instants—an ideally moving picture, even if it were momentarily still. For this kind of mobile beauty, thinness was a necessary condition.

The still body that is nevertheless perceived as ideally in motion seems to present a blurred image—a perpetual suggestion of all the other possible moments at which it might be seen. It seems to have a dynamic, expanding outline. The actual physical size of a human body is made apparently larger by its movements, and if its movements are what constitute its essential visual reality, they must be what gives it its visual substance. Even if a body is perceived at a motionless instant, the possibility of enlargement by movement is implicit in the image. Before consciousness had been so much affected by photography, a body perceived as ideally still could be visually enlarged by layers of fat or clothing with aesthetic success, but a body that is perceived to be about to move must apparently replace those layers with layers of possible space to move in. The camera eye seems to fatten the figure; human eyes, trained by camera vision, demand that it be thin to start with, to allow for the same effect in direct perception. The thin female body, once considered visually meager and unsatisfying without the suggestive expansions of elaborate clothing (or of flesh, which artists sometimes had to provide), has become substantial, freighted with potential action.

It came about that all the varieties of female desirability conceived by the twentieth century seemed ideally housed in a thin, resilient, and bony body. Healthy innocence, sexual restlessness, creative zest, practical competence, even morbid but poetic obsessiveness and intelligence—all seemed appropriate in size ten. During the six decades following the First World War, styles in gesture, posture, and erotic emphasis have undergone many changes, but the basically slim female ideal has been maintained. Throughout all the shifting levels of bust and waist and the fluctuating taste in gluteal and mammary thrust, the bodies of women have been conceived as ideally slender, and clearly supported by bones.

Questions of Subject and Theme

1. In her first sentence Hollander distinguishes between aesthetic explanations and others. Where do you find her making only an aesthetic analysis in her essay? Where does she link social and economic explanations with aesthetics?
2. Hollander writes at the end of "six decades" of the twentieth century. Do you find her analysis fits fashions since that time? Explain with examples.

Questions of Method and Strategy

1. What point of view does Hollander adopt toward thinness? Is she, in your view, suspicious, opposed, in favor, objective? Explain with examples how her uses of language create her point of view.
2. Hollander's paragraphs are long compared to some of the other writers you have read in this book. How does she structure them? Do they seem well formed to you? Discuss the issue of her paragraphing with examples.

A WEIGHT THAT WOMEN CARRY

Sallie Tisdale

Sallie Tisdale was trained as a nurse and continues part-time in her profession. She is also a prolific essayist with four collections published in book form since 1986. The following essay originally appeared in *Harper's*.

I don't know how much I weigh these days, though I can make a good   *1*
guess. For years I'd known that number, sometimes within a quarter pound,
known how it changed from day to day and hour and hour. I want to weigh
myself now; I lean toward the scale in the next room, imagine standing
there, lining up the balance. But I don't do it. Going this long, starting to
break the scale's spell—it's like waking up suddenly sober.

By the time I was sixteen years old I had reached my adult height of five
feet six inches and weighed 164 pounds. I weighed 164 pounds before and
after a healthy pregnancy. I assume I weigh about the same now; nothing
significant seems to have happened to my body, this same old body I've had
all these years. I usually wear a size 14, a common clothing size for American
women. On bad days I think my body looks lumpy and misshapen. On my
good days, which are more frequent lately, I think I look plush and strong;
I think I look like a lot of women whose bodies and lives I admire.

I'm not sure when the word "fat" first sounded pejorative to me, or
when I first applied it to myself. My grandmother was a petite woman, the
only one in my family. She stole food from other people's plates, and hid the
debris of her own meals so that no one would know how much she ate. My
mother was a size 14, like me, all her adult life; we shared clothes. She fretted
endlessly over food scales, calorie counters, and diet books. She didn't want
to quit smoking because she was afraid she would gain weight, and she worried about her weight until she died of cancer five years ago. Dieting was
always in my mother's way, always there in the conversations above my head,
the dialogue of stocky women. But I was strong and healthy and didn't pay
too much attention to my weight until I was grown.

It probably wouldn't have been possible for me to escape forever. It
doesn't matter that whole human epochs have celebrated big men and
women, because the brief period in which I live does not; since I was born,
even the voluptuous calendar girl has gone. Today's models, the women
whose pictures I see constantly, unavoidably, grow more minimal by the day.
When I berate myself for not looking like—whomever I think I should look
like that day, I don't really care that no one looks like that. I don't care that
Michelle Pfeiffer doesn't look like the photographs I see of Michelle Pfeiffer,
I want to look—think I should look—like the photographs. I want her little
miracles; the makeup artists, photographers, and computer imagers who can

add a mole, remove a scar, lift the breasts, widen the eyes, narrow the hips, flatten the curves. The final product is what I see, have seen my whole adult life. And I've seen this: Even when big people become celebrities, their weight is constantly remarked upon and scrutinized; their successes seem always to be *in spite of* their weight. I thought my successes must be, too.

I feel myself expand and diminish from day to day, sometimes from hour to hour. If I tell someone my weight, I change in their eyes: I become bigger or smaller, better or worse, depending on what that number, my weight, means to them. I know many men and women, young and old, gay and straight, who look fine, whom I love to see and whose faces and forms I cherish, who despise themselves for their weight. For their ordinary, human bodies. They and I are simply bigger than we think we should be. We always talk about weight in terms of gains and losses, and don't wonder at the strangeness of the words. In trying always to lose weight, we've lost hope of simply being seen for ourselves.

My weight has never affected anything—it's never seemed to mean anything one way or the other to how I lived. Yet for the last ten years I've felt quite bad about it. After a time, the number on the scale became my totem, more important than my experience—it was layered, metaphorical, *metaphysical,* and it had bewitching power. I thought if I could change that number I could change my life.

In my mid-twenties I started secretly taking diet pills. They made me feel strange, half-crazed, vaguely nauseated. I lost about twenty-five pounds, dropped two sizes, and bought new clothes. I developed rituals and taboos around food, ate very little, and continued to lose weight. For a long time afterward I thought it only coincidental that with every passing week I also grew more depressed and irritable.

I could recite the details, but they're remarkable only for being so common. I lost more weight until I was rather thin, and then I gained it all back. It came back slowly, pound by pound, in spite of erratic and melancholy and sometimes frantic dieting, dieting I clung to even though being thin had changed nothing, had meant nothing to my life except that I was thin. Looking back, I remember blinding moments of shame and lightning-bright moments of clearheadedness, which inevitably gave way to rage at the time I'd wasted—rage that eventually would become, once again, self-disgust and the urge to lose weight. So it went, until I weighed exactly what I'd weighed when I began.

I used to be attracted to the sharp angles of the chronic dieter—the caffeine-wild, chain-smoking, skinny women I see sometimes. I considered them a pinnacle not of beauty but of will. Even after I gained back my weight, I wanted to be like that, controlled and persevering, live that underfed life so unlike my own rather sensual and disorderly existence. I felt I should always be dieting, for the dieting of it; dieting had become a rule, a given, a constant. Every ordinary value is distorted in this lens. I felt guilty for not being completely absorbed in my diet, for getting distracted, for not caring enough all the time. The fat person's character flaw is a lack of narcissism. She's let herself go.

So I would begin again—and at first it would all seem so . . . easy. *10* Simple arithmetic. After all, 3,500 calories equal one pound of fat—so the books and articles by the thousands say. I would calculate how long it would take to achieve the magic number on the scale, to succeed, to win. All past failures were suppressed. If 3,500 calories equal one pound, all I needed to do was cut 3,500 calories out of my intake every week. The first few days of a new diet would be colored with a sense of control—organization and planning, power over the self. Then the basic futile misery took over.

I would weigh myself with foreboding, and my weight would determine how went the rest of my day, my week, my life. When 3,500 calories didn't equal one pound lost after all, I figured it was my body that was flawed, not the theory. One friend, who had tried for years to lose weight following prescribed diets, made what she called "an amazing discovery." The real secret to a diet, she said, was that you had to be willing to be hungry *all the time.* You had to eat even less than the diet allowed.

I believed that being thin would make me happy. Such a pernicious, enduring belief. I lost weight and wasn't happy and saw that elusive happiness disappear in a vanishing point, requiring more—more self-disgust, more of the misery of dieting. Knowing all that I know now about the biology and anthropology of weight, knowing that people naturally come in many shapes and sizes, knowing that diets are bad for me and won't make me thin—sometimes none of this matters. I look in the mirror and think: Who am I kidding? *I've got to do something about myself.* Only then will this vague discontent disappear. Then I'll be loved.

For ages humans believed that the body helped create the personality, from the humors of Galen to W. H. Sheldon's somatotypes. Sheldon distinguished between three templates—endomorph, mesomorph, and ectomorph—and combined them into hundreds of variations with physical, emotional, and psychological characteristics. When I read about weight now, I see the potent shift in the last few decades: The modern culture of dieting is based on the idea that the personality creates the body. Our size must be in some way voluntary, or else it wouldn't be subject to change. A lot of my misery over my weight wasn't about how I looked at all. I was miserable because I believed *I* was bad, not my body. I felt truly reduced then, reduced to being just a body and nothing more.

Fat is perceived as an *act* rather than a thing. It is antisocial, and curable through the application of social controls. Even the feminist revisions of dieting, so powerful in themselves, pick up the theme: the hungry, empty heart; the woman seeking release from sexual assault, or the man from the loss of the mother, through food and fat. Fat is now a symbol not of the personality but of the soul—the cluttered, neurotic, and immature soul.

Fat people eat for "mere gratification," I read, as though no one else *15* does. Their weight is *intentioned,* they simply eat "too much," their flesh is lazy flesh. Whenever I went on a diet, eating became cheating. One pretzel was cheating. Two apples instead of one was cheating—a large potato instead of a small, carrots instead of broccoli. It didn't matter which diet I was on; diets have failure built in, failure is in the definition. Every substitution—even carrots for broccoli—was a triumph of desire over will. When I dieted, I didn't feel pious just for sticking to the rules. I felt condemned for the act of eating itself, as though my hunger were never normal. My penance was to not eat at all.

My attitude toward food became quite corrupt. I came, in fact, to subconsciously believe food itself was corrupt. Diet books often distinguish between "real" and "unreal" hunger, so that *correct* eating is hollowed out, unemotional. A friend of mine who thinks of herself as a compulsive eater says she feels bad only when she eats for pleasure. "Why?" I ask, and she says, "Because I'm eating food I don't need." A few years ago I might have admired that. Now I try to imagine a world where we eat only food we need, and it seems inhuman. I imagine a world devoid of holidays and wedding feasts, wakes and reunions, a unique shared joy. "What's wrong with eating a cookie because you like cookies?" I ask her, and she hasn't got an answer. These aren't rational beliefs, any more than the unnecessary pleasure of ice cream is rational. Dieting presumes pleasure to be an insignificant, or at least malleable, human motive.

I felt no joy in being thin—it was just work, something I had to do. But when I began to gain back the weight, I felt despair. I started reading about the "recidivism" of dieting. I wondered if I had myself to blame not only for needing to diet in the first place but for dieting itself, the weight inevitably regained. I joined organized weight-loss programs, spent a lot of money, listened to lectures I didn't believe on quack nutrition, ate awful, processed diet foods. I sat in groups and applauded people who'd lost a half pound, feeling smug because I'd lost a pound and a half. I felt ill much of the time, found exercise increasingly difficult, cried often. And I thought that if I could only lose a little weight, everything would be all right.

When I say to someone, "I'm fat," I hear, "Oh, no! You're not *fat!* You're just—" What? Plump? Big-boned? Rubenesque? I'm just *not thin.* That's crime enough. I began this story by stating my weight. I said it all at once, trying to forget it and take away its power; I said it to be done being scared. Doing so, saying it out loud like that, felt like confessing a mortal sin. I have to bite my tongue not to seek reassurance, not to defend myself, not to plead. I see an old friend for the first time in years, and she comments on how much my fourteen-year-old son looks like me—"except, of course, he's not chubby." "Look who's talking," I reply, through clenched teeth. This pettiness is never far away; concern with my weight evokes the smallest, meanest parts of me. I look at another woman passing on the street and think, "At least I'm not *that* fat."

Recently I was talking with a friend who is naturally slender about a mutual acquaintance who is quite large. To my surprise my friend reproached this woman because she had seen her eating a cookie at lunchtime.

"How is she going to lose weight that way?" my friend wondered. When you are as fat as our acquaintance is, you are primarily, fundamentally, seen as fat. It is your essential characteristic. There are so many presumptions in my friend's casual, cruel remark. She assumes that this woman should diet all the time—and that she *can*. She pronounces whole categories of food to be denied her. She sees her unwillingness to behave in this externally prescribed way, even for a moment, as an act of rebellion. In his story "A Hunger Artist," Kafka writes that the guards of the fasting man were "usually butchers, strangely enough." Not so strange, I think.

I know that the world, even if it views me as overweight (and I'm not sure it really does), clearly makes a distinction between me and this very big woman. I would rather stand with her and not against her, see her for all she is besides fat. But I know our experiences aren't the same. My thin friend assumes my fat friend is unhappy because she is fat: Therefore, if she loses weight she will be happy. My fat friend has a happy marriage and family and a good career, but insofar as her weight is a source of misery, I think she would be much happier if she could eat her cookie in peace, if people would shut up and leave her weight alone. But the world never lets up when you are her size; she cannot walk to the bank without risking insult. Her fat is seen as perverse bad manners. I have no doubt she would be rid of the fat if she could be. If my left-handedness invited the criticism her weight does, I would want to cut that hand off.

In these last several years I seem to have had an infinite number of conversations about dieting. They are really all the same conversation— weight is lost, then weight is gained back. This repetition finally began to sink in. Why did everyone sooner or later have the same experience? (My friend who had learned to be hungry all the time gained back all the weight she had lost and more, just like the rest of us.) Was it really our bodies that were flawed? I began reading the biology of weight more carefully, reading the fine print in the endless studies. There is, in fact, a preponderance of evidence disputing our commonly held assumptions about weight.

The predominant biological myth of weight is that thin people live longer than fat people. The truth is far more complicated. (Some deaths of fat people attributed to heart disease seem actually to have been the result of radical dieting.) If health were our real concern, it would be dieting we questioned, not weight. The current ideal of thinness has never been held before, except as a religious ideal; the underfed body is the martyr's body. Even if people can lose weight, maintaining an artificially low weight for any period of time requires a kind of starvation. Lots of people are naturally thin, but for those who are not, dieting is an unnatural act; biology rebels. The metabolism of the hungry body can change inalterably, making it ever harder and harder to stay thin. I think chronic dieting made me gain weight—not only pounds, but fat. This equation seemed so strange at first that I couldn't believe it. But the weight I put back on after losing was much more stubborn than the original weight. I had lost it by taking diet pills and not eating much of anything at all for quite a long time. I haven't touched the pills again, but not eating much of anything no longer works.

When Oprah Winfrey first revealed her lost weight, I didn't envy her. I thought, She's in trouble now. I knew, I was certain, she would gain it back; I believed she was biologically destined to do so. The tabloid headlines blamed it on a cheeseburger or mashed potatoes, they screamed OPRAH PASSES 200 POUNDS, and I cringed at her misery and how the world wouldn't let up, wouldn't leave her alone, wouldn't let her be anything else. How dare the world do this to anyone? I thought, and then realized I did it to myself.

The "Ideal Weight" charts my mother used were at their lowest acceptable-weight ranges in the 1950s, when I was a child. They were based on sketchy and often inaccurate actuarial evidence, using, for the most part, data on northern Europeans and allowing for the most minimal differences in size for a population of less than half a billion people. I never fit those weight charts, I was always just outside the pale. As an adult, when I would join an organized diet program, I accepted their version of my Weight Goal as gospel, knowing it would be virtually impossible to reach. But reach I tried; that's what one does with gospel. Only in the last few years have the weight tables begun to climb back into the world of the average human. The newest ones distinguish by gender, frame, and age. And suddenly I'm not off the charts anymore. I have a place.

A man who is attracted to fat women says, "I actually have less specific   25
physical criteria than most men. I'm attracted to women who weigh 170 or 270 or 370. Most men are only attracted to women who weigh between 100 and 135. So who's got more of a fetish?" We look at fat as a problem of the fat person. Rarely do the tables get turned, rarely do we imagine that it might be the viewer, not the viewed, who is limited. What the hell is wrong with *them,* anyway? Do they believe everything they see on television?

My friend Phil, who is chronically and almost painfully thin, admitted that in his search for a partner he finds himself prejudiced against fat women. He seemed genuinely bewildered by this. I didn't jump to reassure him that such prejudice is hard to resist. What I did was bite my tongue at my urge to be reassured by him, to be told that I, at least, wasn't fat. That over the centuries humans have been inclined to prefer extra flesh rather than the other way around seems unimportant. All we see now tells us otherwise. Why does my kindhearted friend criticize another woman for eating a cookie when she would never dream of commenting in such a way on another person's race or sexual orientation or disability? Deprivation is the dystopian idea.

My mother called her endless diets "reducing plans." Reduction, the diminution of women, is the opposite of feminism, as Kim Chernin points out in *The Obsession.* Smallness is what feminism strives against, the smallness that women confront everywhere. All of women's spaces are smaller than those of men, often inadequate, without privacy. Furniture designers distinguish between a man's and a woman's chair, because women don't spread out like men. (A sprawling woman means only one thing.) Even our voices are kept down. By embracing dieting I was rejecting a lot I held dear, and the emotional dissonance that created just seemed like one more necessary evil.

A fashion magazine recently celebrated the return of the "well-fed" body; a particular model was said to be "the archetype of the new womanly woman . . . stately, powerful." She is a size 8. The images of women presented to us, images claiming so maliciously to be the images of women's whole lives, are not merely social fictions. They are *absolute* fictions; they can't exist. How would it feel, I began to wonder, to cultivate my own real womanliness rather than despise it? Because it was my fleshy curves I wanted to be rid of, after all. I dreamed of having a boy's body, smooth, hipless, lean. A body rapt with possibility, a receptive body suspended before the storms of maturity. A dear friend of mine, nursing her second child, weeps at her newly voluptuous body. She loves her children and hates her own motherliness, wanting to be unripened again, to be a bud and not a flower.

Recently I've started shopping occasionally at stores for "large women," where the smallest size is a 14. In department stores the size 12 and 14 and 16 clothes are kept in a ghetto called the Women's Department. (And who would want that, to be the size of a woman? We all dream of being "juniors" instead.) In the specialty stores the clerks are usually big women and the customers are big, too, big like a lot of women in my life—friends, my sister, my mother and aunts. Not long ago I bought a pair of jeans at Lane Bryant and then walked through the mall to the Gap, with its shelves of generic clothing. I flicked through the clearance rack and suddenly remembered the Lane Bryant shopping bag in my hand and its enormous weight, the sheer heaviness of that brand name shouting to the world. The shout is that I've let myself go. I still feel like crying out sometimes: Can't I feel *satisfied?* But I am not supposed to be satisfied, not allowed to be satisfied. My discontent fuels the market; I need to be afraid in order to fully participate.

American culture, which has produced our dieting mania, does more *30* than reward privation and acquisition at the same time: it actually associates them with each other. Read the ads: the virtuous runner's reward is a new pair of $180 running shoes. The fat person is thought to be impulsive, indulgent, but insufficiently or incorrectly greedy, greedy for the wrong thing. The fat person lacks ambition. The young executive is complimented for being "hungry"; he is "starved for success." We are teased with what we will *have* if we are willing to *have not* for a time. A dieting friend, avoiding the food on my table, says, "I'm just dying for a bite of that."

Dieters are the perfect consumers: They never get enough. The dieter wistfully imagines food without substance, food that is not food, that begs the definition of food, because food is the problem. Even the ways we *don't eat* are based in class. The middle class don't eat in support groups. The poor can't afford not to eat at all. The rich hire someone to not eat with them in private. Dieting is an emblem of capitalism. It has a venal heart.

The possibility of living another way, living without dieting, began to take root in my mind a few years ago, and finally my second trip through Weight Watchers ended dieting for me. This last time I just couldn't stand the details, the same kind of details I'd seen and despised in other programs, on other diets: the scent of resignation, the weighing-in by the quarter pound, the before and after photographs of group leaders prominently displayed. Jean Nidetch, the founder of Weight Watchers, says, "Most fat people need to be hurt badly before they do something about themselves." She mocks every aspect of our need for food, of a person's sense of entitlement to food, of daring to *eat what we want.* Weight Watchers refuses to release its own weight charts except to say they make no distinction for frame size; neither has the organization ever released statistics on how many people who lose weight on the program eventually gain it back. I hated the endlessness of it, the turning of food into portions and exchanges, everything measured out, permitted, denied. I hated the very idea of "maintenance." Finally I realized I didn't just hate the diet. I was sick of the way I acted on a diet, the way I whined, my niggardly, penny-pinching behavior. What I liked in myself seemed to shrivel and disappear when I dieted. Slowly, slowly I saw these things. I saw that my pain was cut from whole cloth, imaginary, my own invention. I saw how much time I'd spent on something ephemeral, something that simply wasn't important, didn't matter. I saw the real point of dieting is dieting—to not be done with it, ever.

I looked in the mirror and saw a woman, with flesh, curves, muscles, a few stretch marks, the beginnings of wrinkles, with strength and softness in equal measure. My body is the one part of me that is always, undeniably, here. To like myself means to be, literally, shameless, to be wanton in the pleasures of being inside a body. I feel *loose* this way, a little abandoned, a little dangerous. That first feeling of liking my body—not being resigned to it or despairing of change, but actually *liking* it—was tentative and guilty and frightening. It was alarming, because it was the way I'd felt as a child, before the world had interfered. Because surely I was wrong; I knew, I'd known for so long, that my body wasn't all right this way. I was afraid even to act as though I were all right: I was afraid that by doing so I'd be acting a fool.

For a time I was thin, I remember—and what I remember is nothing special—strain, a kind of hollowness, the same troubles and fears, and no magic. So I imagine losing weight again. If the world applauded, would this comfort me? Or would it only compromise whatever approval the world gives me now? What else will be required of me besides thinness? What will happen to me if I get sick, or lose the use of a limb, or, God forbid, grow old?

By fussing endlessly over my body, I've ceased to inhabit it. I'm trying to reverse this equation now, to trust my body and enter it again with   *35* a whole heart. I know more now than I used to about what constitutes "happy" and "unhappy," what the depths and textures of contentment are like. By letting go of dieting, I free up mental and emotional room. I have more space, I can move. The pursuit of another, elusive body, the body someone else says I should have, is a terrible distraction, a sidetracking that might have lasted my whole life long. By letting myself go, I go places.

Each of us in this culture, this twisted, inchoate culture, has to choose between battles: one battle is against the cultural ideal, and the other is against ourselves. I've chosen to stop fighting myself. Maybe I'm tilting at windmills; the cultural ideal is ever-changing, out of my control. It's not a cerebral journey, except insofar as I have to remind myself to stop counting, to stop thinking in terms of numbers. I know, even now that I've quit dieting and eat what I want, how many calories I take in every day. If I eat as I please, I eat a lot one day and very little the next; I skip meals and snack at odd times. My nourishment is good—as far as nutrition is concerned. I'm in much better shape than when I was dieting. I know that the small losses and gains in my weight over a period of time aren't simply related to the number of calories I eat. Someone asked me not long ago how I could possibly know my calorie intake if I'm not dieting (the implication being, perhaps, that I'm dieting secretly). I know because calorie counts and grams of fat and fiber are embedded in me. I have to work to *not* think of them, and I have to learn to not think of them in order to really live without fear.

When I look, *really* look, at the people I see every day on the street, I see a jungle of bodies, a community of women and men growing every which way like lush plants, growing tall and short and slender and round, hairy and hairless, dark and pale and soft and hard and glorious. Do I look around at the multitudes and think all these people—all these people who are like me and not like me, who are various and different—are not loved or lovable? Lately, everyone's body interests me, every body is desirable in some way. I see how muscles and skin shift with movement; I sense a cornucopia of flesh in the world. In the midst of it I am a little capacious and unruly.

I repeat with Walt Whitman, "I dote on myself . . . there is that lot of me, and all so luscious." I'm eating better, exercising more, feeling fine— and then I catch myself thinking, *Maybe I'll lose some weight.* But my mood changes or my attention is caught by something else, something deeper, more lingering. Then I can catch a glimpse of myself by accident and think only: That's me. My face, my hips, my hands. Myself.

Questions of Subject and Theme

1. Tisdale's first sentence is of two parts connected by a comma. How do the two parts represent two of the major themes she explores in the essay as a whole? Explain with examples.
2. Speaking of Oprah Winfrey, Tisdale writes: "How dare the world do this

to anyone? I thought, and then realized I did it to myself." How does this passage represent two of the major themes in the essay? Explain with examples.

Questions of Method and Strategy

1. What point of view does Tisdale adopt toward thinness? Is she, in your view, suspicious, opposed, in favor, objective? Explain with examples how her uses of language create her point of view.

2. Tisdale says that she doesn't find it strange that the guards of the fasting man in Kafka's story "A Hunger Artist" were butchers. Where and how does she use other paradoxes to make her points in the essay? Pick some examples of apparent paradoxes and explain what they seem to mean to the author.

A FAT MAN STRUGGLES TO GET OUT

Joseph Epstein

Joseph Epstein is an essayist with many collections to his credit, including *Once More Around the Block* (1987) from which the following selection comes. He is also the long-standing editor of *The American Scholar,* the journal of the Phi Beta Kappa Society.

How do things stand with you and the seven deadly sins? Here is my scorecard: Sloth I fight—to a draw. I surrendered to Pride long ago. Anger I tend to give in to so often that it makes me angry. Lust I'd rather not discuss. I haven't thus far done well enough in the world to claim Avarice as anything more than a theoretical sin. I appear to be making some headway against Envy, though I realize that it's touch and go. Of the seven deadly sins, the only one that has a continuing interest for me is Gluttony. But "continuing interest" is a euphemism; by it I mean that Gluttony is the last deadly sin that excites me in a big way—so much so that, though I am prepared to admit that Gluttony can be deadly, I am not all that prepared to say it is a sin. As soon as I pop this chocolate-chip cookie in my mouth, I shall attempt to explain what I mean.

I am not beautiful and I am probably not very fit, but I am, at least in a rough geometrical sense, in shape. I weigh what the charts say I ought to weigh. To some people I may seem slender. For the most part, I am not displeased with my physique. Certainly I have no wish to be fat; flabby I should heartily dislike; portly is a touch more than I should prefer—but, let me confess it, stout, solid dignified stout, doesn't sound that bad to me. Was it Cyril Connolly who said that within every fat man a thin man struggles to get out? With me the reverse condition obtains: I am a relatively thin man in whom a fat man struggles, sometimes quite desperately, to get out.

That fat man is no gourmet. He cannot claim to be a gourmand, which A. J. Liebling, a fat man who did get out, once defined as someone who loves delicacies and plenty of 'em. My fat man is less discriminating. He longs for quantities of sandwiches and great mounds of rather greasy french fried potatoes followed by great hunks of cake, a little snack washed down with tankards of soda pop (with Pepsi-Cola, to be specific, and not the no-calorie, caffeine-free, unleaded kind, either). Ribs, pizza, raw oysters, servings of ice cream that cover the entire surface of dinner plates—these are the names of some of my fat man's desires. He is always on the lookout for inexpensive restaurants that serve in impressive tonnage—restaurants out of which he dreams of walking, a toothpick clamped in his mouth, remarking to himself, "Yes, indeed, a slap-up meal; they did me very well in there."

You can see why this fat man cannot be turned loose. I do on occasion let him out for a weekend or a holiday, in what I suppose is the

gastronomical equivalent of a work-release program. But set scot-free, left
to forage full-time for himself, this man would kill me with his teeth and
bury me with a fork. Clearly a dangerous character, he must be held under
lock and key and, when let out, kept under the strictest surveillance. Mod-
eration is a principle he does not recognize, deferred gratification is a phrase
of whose meaning he remains ignorant, compromise he won't even consider. All this being the case, I can only say to him, as I frequently do, "Sorry,
Tons-of-Fun, it's the slammer for you."

Perhaps I would be better off in the condition of a friend who one day   5
told me that, as the result of a boyhood fistfight in which his nose was so
badly smashed it had to be remade, he had lost roughly eighty percent of his
sense of taste. To him food was now almost sheerly a matter of fuel. I greeted
this announcement with a mixture of envy for his release from a troubling
passion and sadness at his deprivation. I have known others who could eat
until the cows come home, and then slaughter the cows for a steak sandwich—all without the least effect on girth or chin or limb. These, in my
view, are among the favorites of the gods. To me the gods have dealt differently, bestowing upon me an appetite that is matched only by my vanity. I
wish to live fat but be thin.

I was not bred for the kind of careful abstinence that is the admired
eating standard of our day. A finicky child, I was catered to in my extreme
fussiness. (Freud says that a man who as a child feels assured of his mother's
love is likely to think himself a conqueror; I say this same conqueror is likely
to have a weight problem.) Whatever Joseph wanted, Joseph got—in my
mother's kitchen, Lola had nothing on me. In adolescence, my tastes in food
broadened and my appetite deepened. Ours was always an impressive larder.
I can recall many a night, before settling in to sleep, fixing myself a little
snack that might consist of, say, a dozen or so cookies, a pint of butter-pecan
ice cream, a gross or so of grapes, and four fingers of salami. Nor was sleep
after such a repast in any way a problem. Today, of course, this kind of snack,
attempted at my age, could only be construed as a suicide attempt.

My mother knew I ate huge portions at home, but she could not know
that the ample meals she served me were perhaps half my daily ration. She
could not know because I did not tell her. As a serious eater I hadn't, you
might say, come out of the pantry. But out of the pantry I surely emerged.
After a breakfast at home of orange juice, eggs, and toast, I would, upon
arrival at high school, generally plunge into a smoke-filled school store
called Harry's, where, to fortify myself for the strenuous mental effort that
lay ahead, I engorged something known as a chocolate square (approximate
weight: one-third pound), a small stein of root beer, and the smoke of two
Lucky Strike cigarettes. Often with friends I would take tiffin at a nearby
Jewish delicatessen called Ashkenaz; the meal usually consisted of soup,
corned-beef sandwiches, and other of those Jewish foods that, as one sour-
stomached Jewish gentleman I know has put it, have caused more difficulties
for the Jews than Pharaoh himself. After lunch it was back to the classroom,
where, on a full stomach, I was easily able to ignore what should have been

the rudiments of my education. After school, a *flâneur du gastronomique,* I might knock back a small bag of french fries liberally slathered with ketchup, which, most afternoons, along with perhaps a banana and six or seven cookies, would see me through to dinner.

Proust famously used food—his little fluted madeleine cake—to beckon memory; working at things the other way round, I beckon memory to recall food. I remember a Rumanian Jewish restaurant to which my parents used to take us where the waiters seemed to have stepped out of Jewish jokes. Once, as a small boy, when I asked one of them if the restaurant had any soda pop, he, towel over his shoulder, pencil poised over his order pad, sourly replied, "Yeh, ve gots two kinds. Ve gots red and ve gots brown." I remember when a small chain of rather deluxe hamburger restaurants named Peter Pan was caught serving its customers horse meat and, in a gesture to return to the public's good graces, gave away free hamburgers for a day, thus creating a living fantasy in which every boy could be his own Wimpy. In the autumn of 1952, Dwight David Eisenhower was elected president, elaborate peace negotiations were under way in Korea, François Mauriac won the Nobel Prize for literature, and I, a freshman in high school, tasted pizza for the first time and thought I had died and gone to heaven.

That same year, in an episode of shame, I recall walking along the avenue with my faithful companion Robert Ginsburg, who, always the tempter, suggested we buy and share and dispatch a cake. Dispatch it we did, but I cannot say neatly. As in so many of our combined enterprises, an element of planning was missing. In this instance, the cake now purchased, we noted the absence of utensils for cutting it—a large chocolate affair with a combined chocolate and pistachio frosting—and, once cut, for conveying it to our mouths. We could have brought the cake home, there to have an ample slice in his or my mother's kitchen. But we did not want a slice of cake, however ample—we wanted an entire cake. So we ate it, walking along side streets, prying great fistfuls away from the cake and stuffing them into our mouths in the style we designated "one billion B.C." We are talking about two reasonably well brought up middle-class boys here, you understand, but true hunger, to the truly craving, will turn even a middle-class lad into a savage.

Middle-class and middle western, I should have added, for when I think of the ideal middle-class meal of my youth, eaten in a restaurant, it comprises the following plain but to me, then as now, quite pleasing Middle Western menu: it begins with a shrimp cocktail; followed by a wedge of iceberg lettuce with thousand island dressing; followed by a rather thick slab of medium-rare prime rib of beef, with a baked potato (not cooked in aluminum foil) lavished with butter and sour cream with chives; and concluded with strawberry shortcake and coffee. This is, you will recognize, almost an entirely prelapsarian meal; it could only have been eaten in good conscience before the vile knowledge that certain foods can clog arteries, set tumors growing, send up blood pressure. If you are someone who would like to get to ninety-six or ninety-seven, and hence someone attentive to death by cancer, heart attack, or stroke, what you are permitted from that meal I have described, once the calories, the cholesterol, and the caffeine are removed, is a plain baked potato on a bed of undressed lettuce with a few strawberries atop it nicely garnished with chives. Dig in.

I mock such curtailment of pleasure—I hate it, truth to tell—yet I am myself victim to it. Far from always but still all too often, I look down at the plate set before me to find potential death through possible heart disease or cancer lurking there—and if not death, social disgrace through overweight. Until roughly twenty-five years ago, those of us born into industrially developed countries, though we may not have known it, were all living in the kitchen of Eden. The snake responsible for casting us out is named Diet: today few are the people who are not dieting for health, for beauty, for longevity. *Eat to Win* is the title of a recent best-seller that supplies diets and menus for people who wish to stay young and athletically competitive. The well-named *Self* magazine calls it "the eating wave of the future." *Eat to Win?* Whatever happened to, eat to eat?

Not that I am above diet. I spend a serious portion of my life attempting to lose the extra four or five pounds that clearly wishes to adhere to me. I gain it, I drop it off, I gain it, I drop it off—we are, those four or five pounds and I, like a couple who cannot agree to live peaceably together but who refuse to separate permanently. I need no reminder when they have returned: when the press of my flesh rubs the waist of my trousers, it is time to miss a meal, hold the fries, play strong defense generally. Aggravation makes the best diet, in my view, and once, in a troubled time in my life, I dropped off fifteen pounds without consciously attempting to do so. Another time I set out to lose twenty pounds; I did it, and I wish to report that the feeling upon having succeeded in doing so is one I describe as "fatness of soul." One is so splendidly well pleased with oneself. An element of fanaticism slides in. One has lost twenty-pounds—why not twenty-five? A friend described my play on the racquetball court as quicker than a sperm. I thought I looked wonderfully well when I had lost all that weight: so lithe, so elegant, so youthful. Apparently this was not the effect I everywhere conveyed, for more than one person, during this period, asked my wife straight-out if I were suffering from a wasting disease.

Because of this little experience I believe I can understand something of what goes on in the mind of the anorexic. The anorexic is the reverse of the glutton, but it is well to remember that the anorexic is the other side of the same coin. (The currently accepted definition of anorexia nervosa is "a serious illness of deliberate self-starvation with profound psychiatric and physical components.") As food excites the glutton, so does it repel the anorexic (most of whom are adolescent girls or youngish women). The glutton's idea of a jolly fine time is precisely the anorexic's idea of hell. As the glutton in extreme cases will have to have his jaw wired to prevent him from eating, the anorexic will in equally extreme cases have to be hospitalized and force-fed through tubes.

For the true glutton, as for the true anorexic, food may well not be the real problem; the love and hatred of food, when they take on such obsessive energy, doubtless mask deeper problems, distinctive in individual cases. But it is interesting that reactions to food can be a significant symptom in serious psychological disorders. Freud, that suspicious Viennese, thought that a great deal more was going on at the table than met the fork. Unquestionably there sometimes is. But I prefer to stand on this question with Cyril Connolly, who put the mouth of a character in this story "Shade Those Laurels" the lines: "They say that food is a substitute for love. Well, it's certainly a bloody good one."

Questions of Subject and Theme

1. What does Epstein's title mean to you after you have finished the essay? In a few sentences, describe as clearly as you can what his title means.
2. Epstein often moves between observations about himself and more general claims about contemporary attitudes. Pick an example of each mode and explain how it is related to the theme of his essay as a whole.

Questions of Method and Strategy

1. What point of view does Epstein adopt toward thinness? Is he, in your view, suspicious, opposed, in favor, objective? Explain with examples how his uses of language create his point of view.
2. In his first paragraph, Epstein says that "Gluttony is the last deadly sin that excites me in a big way." Does he convey that excitement to his reader? Pick some examples and show how his writing does or does not convey excitement about his subject.

Suggestions for Writing on the Juxtapositions

1. Using notes from your answers to the discussion questions on the individual authors, write an essay in which you compare and contrast the attitudes taken by the different writers on the subject of thinness.
2. What is your attitude toward thinness? Write an essay in which you use personal and cultural evidence to analyze what the topic means to you.
3. Epstein says of gluttons more or less what Tisdale says of dieters: They never get enough. Write an essay in which you compare and contrast the ideas of gluttony and dieting explored by the two authors.
4. An earlier section dealt with the language of food. Using that section for models or inspiration, write an essay in which you describe the "language of thinness." Find your evidence in your own experience as well as in the essays of this section.

15 *Meaning on the Mall*

Bob Greene, "15"

Joyce Carol Oates, "Shopping"

William Geist, "Sport Shopping in Suburbia"

"Going to the mall" is one of the most common activities of modern suburban life. But what does it mean to those who go there? Consider the following questions as you read the analyses and explanations in this section:

1. What does *shopping* mean to the three groups described? What does *the mall* mean to them? Do the authors of their accounts share their definitions?

2. One description focuses on a mall in the early eighties. The others describe scenes of the late eighties and nineties. Do the different times reflect different notions of malls, or are they essentially the same? Compare and contrast the malls described from the point of view of recent history.

3. Money is a topic in all three essays. When, if ever, do the authors share their subjects' points of view on money? When, if ever, do they differ? Discuss the topic with examples.

4. In each essay age seems to be a factor that defines a given person's attitude toward the mall. Compare and contrast the values and assumptions dramatized in the three essays that seem attributable to their subjects' ages.

15

Bob Greene

Bob Greene started writing for the *Chicago Sun-Times* in his early twenties and went on to become a syndicated columnist and a contributing correspondent to ABC's *Nightline*. A specialist in the human-interest story, Greene favors offbeat and out-of-the-way subjects.

"This would be excellent, to go in the ocean with this thing," says Dave Gembutis, fifteen.   1

He is looking at a $170 Sea Cruiser raft.

"Great," says his companion, Dan Holmes, also fifteen.

This is at Herman's World of Sporting Goods, in the middle of the Woodfield Mall in Schaumburg, Illinois.

The two of them keep staring at the raft. It is unlikely that they will   5
purchase it. For one thing, Dan has only twenty dollars in his pocket, Dave five dollars. For another thing—ocean voyages aside—neither of them is even old enough to drive. Dave's older sister, Kim, has dropped them off at the mall. They will be taking the bus home.

Fifteen. What a weird age to be male. Most of us have forgotten about it, or have idealized it. But when you are fifteen . . . well, things tend to be less than perfect.

You can't drive. You are only a freshman in high school. The girls your age look older than you and go out with upperclassmen who have cars. You probably don't shave. You have nothing to do on the weekends.

So how do you spend your time? In 1982, most likely at a mall. Woodfield is an enclosed shopping center sprawling over 2.25 million square feet in northern Illinois. There are 230 stores at Woodfield, and on a given Saturday those stores are cruised in and out of by thousands of teenagers killing time. Today two of those teenagers are Dave Gembutis and Dan Holmes.

Dave is wearing a purple Rolling Meadows High School Mustangs Windbreaker over a gray M★A★S★H T-shirt, jeans, and Nike running shoes. He has a red plastic spoon in his mouth, and will keep it there for most of the afternoon. Dan is wearing a white Ohio State Buckeyes T-shirt, jeans, and Nike running shoes.

We are in the Video Forum store. Paul Simon and Art Garfunkel are   10
singing "Wake Up Little Susie" from their Central Park concert on four television screens. Dave and Dan have already been wandering around Woodfield for an hour.

"There's not too much to do at my house," Dan says to me.

"Here we can at least look around," Dave says. "At home I don't know what we'd do."

"Play catch or something," Dan says. "Here there's lots of things to see."

"See some girls or something, start talking," Dave says.

I ask them how they would start a conversation with girls they had   15
never met.

"Ask them what school they're from," Dan says. "Then if they say Arlington Heights High School or something, you can say, 'Oh, I know somebody from there.'"

I ask them how important meeting girls is to their lives.

"About forty-five percent," Dan says.

"About half your life." Dave says.

"Half is girls," Dan says. "Half is going out for sports."   20

An hour later, Dave and Dan have yet to meet any girls. They have seen a girl from their own class at Rolling Meadows High, but she is walking with an older boy, holding his hand. Now we are in the Woodfield McDonald's. Dave is eating a McRib sandwich, a small fries, and a small Coke. Dan is eating a cheeseburger, a small fries, and a medium root beer.

In here, the dilemma is obvious. The McDonald's is filled with girls who are precisely as old as Dave and Dan. The girls are wearing eye shadow, are fully developed, and generally look as if they could be dating the Green Bay Packers. Dave and Dan, on the other hand . . . well, when you're a fifteen-year-old boy, you look like a fifteen-year-old boy.

"They go with the older guys who have the cars," Dan says.

"It makes them more popular," Dave says.

"My ex-girlfriend is seeing a junior," Dan says.   25

I ask him what happened.

"Well, I was in Florida over spring vacation," he says. "And when I got back I heard that she was at Cinderella Rockefella one night, and she was dancing with this guy, and she liked him, and he drove her home and stuff."

"She two-timed him," Dave says.

"The guy's on the basketball team," Dan says.

I ask Dan what he did about it.   30

"I broke up with her," he says, as if I had asked the stupidest question in the world.

I ask him how he did it.

"Well, she was at her locker," he says. "She was working the combination. And I said, 'Hey, Linda, I want to break up.' And she was opening her locker door and she just nodded her head yes. And I said, 'I hear you had a good time while I was gone, but I had a better time in Florida.'"

I ask him if he feels bad about it.

"Well, I feel bad," he says. "But a lot of guys told me, 'I heard you broke   35
up with her. Way to be.'"

"It's too bad the Puppy Palace isn't open," Dan says.

"They're remodeling," Dave says.

We are walking around the upper level of Woodfield. I ask them why they would want to go to the Puppy Palace.

"The dogs are real cute and you feel sorry for them," Dan says.

We are in a fast-food restaurant called the Orange Bowl. Dave is eating   *40* a frozen concoction called an O-Joy. They still have not met any girls.

"I feel like I'd be wasting my time if I sat at home," Dan says. "If it's Friday or Saturday and you sit home, it's considered . . . low."

"Coming to the mall is about all there is," Dave says. "Until we can drive."

"Then I'll cruise," Dan says. "Look for action a little farther away from my house, instead of just riding my bike around."

"When you're sixteen, you can do anything," Dave says. "You can go all the way across town."

"When you have to ride your bike . . ." Dan says. "When it rains, it   *45* ruins everything."

In the J. C. Penney store, the Penney Fashion Carnival is under way. Wally the Clown is handing out favors to children, but Dave and Dan are watching the young female models parade onto a stage in bathing suits.

"Just looking is enough for me," Dan says.

Dave suggests that they head out back into the mall and pick out some girls to wave to. I ask why.

"Well, see, even if they don't wave back, you might see them later in the day," Dan says. "And then they might remember that you waved at them, and you can meet them."

We are at the Cookie Factory. These guys eat approximately every   *50* twenty minutes.

It is clear that Dan is attracted to the girl behind the counter. He walks up, and his voice is slower and about half an octave lower than before.

The tone of voice is going to have to carry the day, because the words are not all that romantic:

"Can I have a chocolate-chip cookie?"

The girl does not even look up as she wraps the cookie in tissue paper.

Dan persists. The voice might be Clark Gable's: *55*

"What do they cost?"

The girl is still looking down.

"Forty-seven," she says and takes his money, still looking away, and we move on.

Dave and Dan tell me that there are lots of girls at Woodfield's indoor ice-skating rink. It costs money to get inside, but they lead me to an exit door, and when a woman walks out we slip into the rink. It is chilly in here, but only three people are on the ice.

"It's not time for open skating yet," Dan says. "This is all private lessons." 60

"Not much in here," Dave says.

We sit on benches. I ask them if they wish they were older.

"Well," Dan says, "when you get there, you look back and you remember. Like I'm glad that I'm not in the fourth or fifth grade now. But I'm glad I'm not twenty-five, either."

"Once in a while I'm sorry I'm not twenty-one," Dave says. "There's not much you can do when you're fifteen. This summer I'm going to caddy and try to save some money."

"Yeah," Dan says. "I want to save up for a dirt bike." 65

"Right now, being fifteen is starting to bother me a little bit," Dave says. "Like when you have to get your parents to drive you to Homecoming with a girl."

I ask him how that works.

"Well, your mom is in the front seat driving," he says. "And you're in the back seat with your date."

I ask him how he feels about that.

"It's embarrassing," he says. "Your date understands that there's nothing 70 you can do about it, but it's still embarrassing."

Dave says he wants to go to Pet World.

"I think they closed it down," Dan says, but we head in that direction anyway.

I ask them what the difference is between Pet World and the Puppy Palace.

"They've got snakes and fish and another assortment of dogs," Dan says. "But not as much as the Puppy Palace."

When we arrive, Pet World is, indeed, boarded up. 75

We are on the upper level of the mall. Dave and Dan have spotted two girls sitting on a bench directly below them, on the mall's main level.

"Whistle," Dan says. Dave whistles, but the girls keep talking.

"Dave, wave to them and see if they look," Dan says.

"They aren't looking," Dave says.

"There's another one over there," Dan says. 80

"Where?" Dave says.

"Oh, that's a mother," Dan says. "She's got her kid with her."

They return their attention to the two downstairs.

Dan calls to them: "Would you girls get the dollar I just dropped?"

The girls look up. 85

"Just kidding," Dan says.

The girls resume their conversation.

"I think they're laughing," Dan says.

"What are you going to do when the dumb girls won't respond," Dave says.

"At least we tried," Dan says.   *90*

I ask him what response would have satisfied him.

"The way we would have known that we succeeded," he says, "they'd have looked up here and started laughing."

The boys keep staring at the two girls.

"Ask her to look up," Dan says. "Ask her what school they go to."

"I did," Dave says. "I did."   *95*

The two boys lean over the railing.

"Bye, girls," Dave yells.

"See you later," Dan yells.

The girls do not look up.

"Too hard," Dan says. "Some girls are stuck on themselves, if you know   *100* what I mean by that."

We go to a store called the Foot Locker, where all the salespeople are dressed in striped referee's shirts.

"Dave!" Dan says. "Look at this! Seventy bucks!" He holds up a pair of New Balance running shoes. Both boys shake their heads.

We move on to a store called Passage to China. A huge stuffed tiger is placed by the doorway. There is a PLEASE DO NOT TOUCH sign attached to it. Dan rubs his hand over the tiger's back. "This would look so great in my room," he says.

We head over to Alan's TV and Stereo. Two salesmen ask the boys if they are interested in buying anything, so they go back outside and look at the store's window. A color television set is tuned to a baseball game between the Chicago Cubs and the Pittsburgh Pirates.

They watch for five minutes. The sound is muted, so they cannot hear   *105* the announcers.

"I wish they'd show the score," Dave says.

They watch for five minutes more.

"Hey, Dave," Dan says. "You want to go home?"

"I guess so," Dave says.

They do. We wave goodbye. I watch them walk out of the mall toward   *110* the bus stop. I wish them girls, dirt bikes, puppies, and happiness.

Questions of Subject and Theme

1. At the beginning of the essay, Greene says that, when you are fifteen, "things tend to be less than perfect." What are some of the "things" that his account shows are less than perfect for Dave and Dan?
2. How do the attitudes of the girls in the essay differ from those of the boys? In your view, are the differences accurately observed? Discuss with examples.

Questions of Method and Strategy

1. The first words in the essay use the conditional verb form: "That would be excellent. . . ." How does "the conditional" pervade the spirit of the account in more than grammatical ways?

2. Greene seems a sympathetic observer on the whole. What does he do and not do, both as a writer and as a character within the account, to establish his emotional attitude toward Dave and Dan?

SHOPPING

Joyce Carol Oates

Since the 1960s, Joyce Carol Oates has been a prolific writer of novels, short stories, essays, and reviews. She has even done a book on boxing, and as a professor at Princeton University she is vocal in current critical debates. The following sketch of the relations of a mother and daughter illustrates her abiding fictional interest in the emotional lives of contemporary women.

An old ritual, Saturday morning shopping. Mother and daughter. Mrs. Dietrich and Nola. Shops in the village, stores and boutiques at the splendid Livingstone Mall on Route 12. Bloomingdale's, Saks, Lord & Taylor, Bonwit's, Neiman-Marcus: and the rest. Mrs. Dietrich would know her way around the stores blindfolded but there is always the surprise of lavish seasonal displays, extraordinary holiday sales, the openings of new stores at the Mall like Laura Ashley, Paraphernalia. On one of their Mall days Mrs. Dietrich and Nola would try to get there at midmorning, have lunch around 1 P.M. at one or another of their favorite restaurants, shop for perhaps an hour after lunch, then come home. Sometimes the shopping trips were more successful than at other times but you have to have faith, Mrs. Dietrich tells herself. Her interior voice is calm, neutral, free of irony. Ever since her divorce her interior voice has been free of irony. You have to have faith.

Tomorrow morning Nola returns to school in Maine; today will be a day at the Mall. Mrs. Dietrich has planned it for days. At the Mall, in such crowds of shoppers, moments of intimacy are possible as they rarely are at home. (Seventeen-year-old Nola, home on spring break for a brief eight days, seems always to be *busy,* always out with her *friends*—the trip to the Mall has been postponed twice.) But Saturday, 10:30 A.M., they are in the car at last headed south on Route 12, a bleak March morning following a night of freezing rain, there's a metallic cast to the air and no sun anywhere in the sky but the light hurts Mrs. Dietrich's eyes just the same. "Does it seem as if spring will ever come?—it must be twenty degrees colder up in Maine," she says. Driving in heavy traffic always makes Mrs. Dietrich nervous and she is overly sensitive to her daughter's silence, which seems deliberate, perverse, when they have so little time remaining together—not even a full day.

Nola asks politely if Mrs. Dietrich would like her to drive and Mrs. Dietrich says no, of course not, she's fine, it's only a few more miles and maybe traffic will lighten. Nola seems about to say something more, then thinks better of it. So much between them that is precarious, chancy—but they've been kind to each other these past seven days. Mrs. Dietrich loves Nola with a fierce unreasoned passion stronger than any she felt for the man who had been her husband for thirteen years, certainly far stronger than any she ever felt for her own mother. Sometimes in weak despondent moods, alone, lonely, self-pitying, when she has had too much to drink, Mrs. Dietrich thinks she is in love with her daughter—but this is a thought she can't contemplate for long. And how Nola would snort in amused contempt, incredulous, mocking—"Oh *Mother!*"—if she were told.

Mrs. Dietrich tries to engage her daughter in conversation of a harmless sort but Nola answers in monosyllables, Nola is rather tired from so many nights of partying with her friends, some of whom attend the local high school, some of whom are home for spring break from prep schools— Exeter, Lawrenceville, Concord, Andover, Portland. Late nights, but Mrs. Dietrich doesn't consciously lie awake waiting for Nola to come home: they've been through all that before. Now Nola sits beside her mother looking wan, subdued, rather melancholy. Thinking her private thoughts. She is wearing a bulky quilted jacket Mrs. Dietrich has never liked, the usual blue jeans, black calfskin boots zippered tightly to mid-calf. Mrs. Dietrich must resist the temptation to ask, "Why are you so quiet, Nola? What are you thinking?" They've been through all that before.

Route 12 has become a jumble of small industrial parks, high-rise office   5 and apartment buildings, torn-up landscapes—mountains of raw earth, uprooted trees, ruts and ditches filled with muddy water. There is no natural sequence to what you see—buildings, construction work, leveled woods, the lavish grounds owned by Squibb. Though she has driven this route countless times, Mrs. Dietrich is never quite certain where the Mall is and must be prepared for a sudden exit. She remembers getting lost the first several times, remembers the excitement she and her friends felt about the grand opening of the Mall, stores worthy of serious shopping at last. Today is much the same. No, today is worse. Like Christmas when she was a small child, Mrs. Dietrich thinks. She'd hoped so badly to be happy she'd felt actual pain, a constriction in her throat like crying.

"*Are* you all right, Nola?—you've been so quiet all morning," Mrs. Dietrich asks, half-scolding. Nola stirs from her reverie, says she's fine, a just perceptible edge to her reply, and for the remainder of the drive there's some stiffness between them. Mrs. Dietrich chooses to ignore it. In any case she is fully absorbed in driving—negotiating a tricky exit across two lanes of traffic, then the hairpin curve of the ramp, the numerous looping drives of the Mall. Then the enormous parking lot, daunting to the inexperienced, but Mrs. Dietrich always heads for the area behind Lord & Taylor on the far side of the Mall, Lot D; her luck holds and she finds a space close in. "Well—we made it," she says, smiling happily at Nola. Nola laughs in reply—what does a seventeen-year-old's laughter *mean?*—but she remembers, getting out, to lock both doors on her side of the car. The smile Nola gives Mrs. Dietrich across the car's roof is careless and beautiful and takes Mrs. Dietrich's breath away.

The March morning tastes of grit with an undercurrent of something acrid, chemical; inside the Mall, beneath the first of the elegant brass-buttressed glass domes, the air is fresh and tonic, circulating from invisible vents. The Mall is crowded, rather noisy—it *is* Saturday morning—but a feast for the eyes after that long trip on Route 12. Tall slender trees grow out of the mosaic-tiled pavement, there are beds of Easter lilies, daffodils, jonquils, tulips of all colors. Mrs. Dietrich smiles with relief. She senses that Nola too is relieved, cheered. It's like coming home.

The shopping excursions began when Nola was a small child but did not acquire their special significance until she was twelve or thirteen years old and capable of serious, sustained shopping with her mother. This was about the time when Mr. Dietrich moved out of the house and back into their old apartment in the city—a separation, he'd called it initially, to give them perspective—though Mrs. Dietrich had no illusions about what "perspective" would turn out to entail—so the shopping trips were all the more significant. Not that Mrs. Dietrich and Nola spent very much money—they really didn't, *really* they didn't, when compared to friends and neighbors.

At seventeen Nola is shrewd and discerning as a shopper, not easy to please, knowledgeable as a mature woman about certain aspects of fashion, quality merchandise, good stores. Her closets, like Mrs. Dietrich's, are crammed, but she rarely buys anything that Mrs. Dietrich thinks shoddy or merely faddish. Up in Portland, at the Academy, she hasn't as much time to shop but when she is home in Livingstone it isn't unusual for her and her girlfriends to shop nearly every day. Like all her friends she has charge accounts at the better stores, her own credit cards, a reasonable allowance. At the time of their settlement Mr. Dietrich said guiltily that it was the least he could do for them—if Mrs. Dietrich wanted to work part-time, she could (she was trained, more or less, in public relations of a small-scale sort); if not, not. Mrs. Dietrich thought, It's the most you can do for us too.

Near Bloomingdale's entrance mother and daughter see a disheveled $_{10}$ woman sitting by herself on one of the benches. Without seeming to look at her, shoppers are making a discreet berth around her, a stream following a natural course. Nola, taken by surprise, stares. Mrs. Dietrich has seen the woman from time to time at the Mall, always alone, smirking and talking to herself, frizzed gray hair in a tangle, puckered mouth. Always wearing the same black wool coat, a garment of fairly good quality but shapeless, rumpled, stained, as if she sleeps in it. She might be anywhere from forty to sixty years of age. Once Mrs. Dietrich saw her make menacing gestures at children who were teasing her, another time she'd seen the woman staring belligerently at *her*. A white paste had gathered in the corners of her mouth. . . . "My God, that poor woman," Nola says. "I didn't think there were people like her here—I mean, I didn't think they would allow it."

"She doesn't seem to cause any disturbance," Mrs. Dietrich says. "She just sits—Don't stare, Nola, she'll see you."

"You've seen her here before? Here?"

"A few times this winter."

"Is she always like that?"

"I'm sure she's harmless, Nola. She just *sits*."

Nola is incensed, her pale blue eyes like washed glass. "I'm sure *she's* harmless, Mother. It's the harm the poor woman has to endure that is the tragedy."

Mrs. Dietrich is surprised and a little offended by her daughter's passionate tone but she knows enough not to argue. They enter Bloomingdale's, taking their habitual route. So many shoppers!—so much merchandise! Nola speaks of the tragedy of women like that woman—the tragedy of the homeless, the mentally disturbed—bag ladies out on the street—outcasts of an affluent society—but she's soon distracted by the busyness on all sides, the attractive items for sale. They take the escalator up to the third floor, to the Juniors department where Nola often buys things. From there they will move on to Young Collector, then to New Impressions, then to Petites, then one or another boutique and designer—Liz Claiborne, Christian Dior, Calvin Klein, Carlos Falchi, and the rest. And after Bloomingdale's the other stores await, to be visited each in turn. Mrs. Dietrich checks her watch and sees with satisfaction that there's just enough time before lunch but not *too* much time. She gets ravenously hungry, shopping at the Mall.

Nola is efficient and matter-of-fact about shopping, though she acts solely upon instinct. Mrs. Dietrich likes to watch her at a short distance— holding items of clothing up to herself in the three-way mirrors, modeling things she thinks especially promising. A twill blazer with rounded shoulders and blouson jacket, a funky zippered jumpsuit in white sailcloth, a pair of straight-leg Evan-Picone pants, a green leather vest: Mrs. Dietrich watches her covertly. At such times Nola is perfectly content, fully absorbed in the task at hand; Mrs. Dietrich knows she isn't thinking about anything that would distress her. (Like Mr. Dietrich's betrayal. Like Nola's difficulties with her friends. Like her difficulties at school—as much as Mrs. Dietrich knows of them.) Once, at the Mall, perhaps in this very store in this very department, Nola saw Mrs. Dietrich watching her and walked away angrily and when Mrs. Dietrich caught up with her she said, "I can't stand it, Mother." Her voice was choked and harsh, a vein prominent in her forehead. "Let me go. For Christ's sake will you let me go." Mrs. Dietrich didn't dare touch her though she could see Nola was trembling. For a long terrible moment mother and daughter stood side by side near a display of bright brash Catalina beachwear while Nola whispered, "Let me go. *Let me go.*"

Difficult to believe that girl standing so poised and self-assured in front of the three-way mirror was once a plain, rather chunky, unhappy child. She'd been unpopular at school. Overly serious. Anxious. Quick to tears. Aged eleven she hid herself away in her room for hours at a time, reading, drawing pictures, writing little stories she could sometimes be prevailed upon to read aloud to her mother, sometimes even to her father, though she dreaded his judgment. She went through a "scientific" phase a while later— Mrs. Dietrich remembers an ambitious bas-relief map of North America, meticulous illustrations for "photosynthesis," a pastel drawing of an eerie ball of fire labeled "Red Giant" (a dying star?) which won a prize in a state competition for junior high students. Then for a season it was stray facts Nola confronted them with, often at the dinner table. Interrupting her parents' conversation to say brightly: "Did you know that Nero's favorite color was green?—he carried a giant emerald and held it up to his eye to watch Christians being devoured by lions." And once at a large family gathering: "Did you know that last week downtown a little baby's nose was chewed off by rats in his crib?—a little *black* baby?" Nola meant only to call attention to herself but you couldn't blame her listeners for being offended. They stared at her, not knowing what to say. What a strange child! What queer glassy-pale eyes! Mr. Dietrich told her curtly to leave the table—he'd had enough of the game she was playing and so had everyone else.

Nola stared at him, her eyes filling with tears. Game?   20

When they were alone Mr. Dietrich said angrily to Mrs. Dietrich: "Can't you control her in front of other people, at least?" Mrs. Dietrich was angry too, and frightened. She said "I *try*."

They sent her off aged fourteen to the Portland Academy up in Maine and without their help she matured into a girl of considerable beauty. A heart-shaped face, delicate features, glossy red-brown hair scissor-cut to her shoulders. Five feet seven inches tall, weighing less than one hundred pounds—the result of constant savage dieting. (Mrs. Dietrich, who has weight problems herself, doesn't dare to inquire as to details. They've been through that already.) Thirty days after they'd left her at the Portland Academy Nola telephoned home at 11:00 P.M. one Sunday giggly and high telling Mrs. Dietrich she adored the school she adored her suite mates she adored most of her teachers particularly her riding instructor Terri, Terri the Terrier they called the woman because she was so fierce, such a character, eyes that bore right through your skull, wore belts with the most amazing silver buckles! Nola loved Terri but she wasn't *in* love—there's a difference!

Mrs. Dietrich broke down weeping, *that* time.

Now of course Nola has boyfriends. Mrs. Dietrich has long since given up trying to keep track of their names. There is even one "boy"—or young man—who seems to be married: who seems to be, in fact, one of the junior instructors at the school. (Mrs. Dietrich does not eavesdrop on her daughter's telephone conversations but there are things she cannot help overhearing.) Is your daughter on the Pill? the women in Mrs. Dietrich's circle asked one another for a while, guiltily, surreptitiously. Now they no longer ask.

But Nola has announced recently that she loathes boys—she's fed up.   25

She's never going to get married. She'll study languages in college, French, Italian, something exotic like Arabic, go to work for the American foreign service. Unless she drops out of school altogether to become a model.

"Do you think I'm fat, Mother?" she asks frequently, worriedly, standing in front of the mirror twisted at the waist to reveal her small round belly which, it seems, can't help being round: she bloats herself on diet Cokes all day long. "Do you think it *shows?*"

When Mrs. Dietrich was pregnant with Nola she'd been twenty-nine years old and she and Mr. Dietrich had tried to have a baby for nearly five years. She'd lost hope, begun to despise herself, then suddenly it happened: like grace. Like happiness swelling so powerfully it can barely be contained. I can hear its heartbeat! her husband exclaimed. He'd been her lover then, young, vigorous, dreamy. Caressing the rock-hard belly, splendid white tight-stretched skin. Mr. Dietrich gave Mrs. Dietrich a reproduction on stiff glossy paper of Dante Gabriel Rossetti's *Beata Beatrix,* embarrassed, apologetic, knowing it was sentimental and perhaps a little silly but that was how he thought of her—so beautiful, rapturous, pregnant with their child. She told no one but she knew the baby was to be a girl. It would be herself again, reborn and this time perfect.

"Oh, Mother—isn't it *beautiful?*" Nola exclaims.

It is past noon. Past twelve-thirty. Mrs. Dietrich and Nola have made 30 the rounds of a half-dozen stores, traveled countless escalators, one clothing department has blended into the next and the chic smiling saleswomen have become indistinguishable and Mrs. Dietrich is beginning to feel the urgent need for a glass of white wine. Just a glass. "Isn't it beautiful?—it's *perfect,*" Nola says. Her eyes glow with pleasure, her smooth skin is radiant. As Nola models in the three-way mirror a queer little yellow-and-black striped sweater with a ribbed waist, punk style, mock-cheap, Mrs. Dietrich feels the motherly obligation to register a mild protest, knowing that Nola will not hear. She must have it and will have it. She'll wear it a few times, then retire it to the bottom of a drawer with so many other novelty sweaters, accumulated since sixth grade. (She's like her mother in that regard—can't bear to throw anything away.)

"*Isn't* it beautiful?" Nola demands, studying her reflection in the mirror.

Mrs. Dietrich pays for the sweater on her charge account.

Next, they buy Nola a good pair of shoes. And a handbag to go with them. In Paraphernalia, where rock music blasts overhead and Mrs. Dietrich stands to one side, rather miserable, Nola chats companionably with two girls—tall, pretty, cutely made up—she'd gone to public school in Livingstone with, says afterward with an upward rolling of her eyes, "God, I was afraid they'd latch on to us!" Mrs. Dietrich has seen women friends and acquaintances of her own in the Mall this morning but has shrunk from being noticed, not wanting to share her daughter with anyone. She has a sense of time passing ever more swiftly, cruelly.

She watches Nola preening in a mirror, watches other shoppers watching her. My daughter. Mine. But of course there is no connection between them—they don't even resemble each other. A seventeen-year-old, a forty-seven-year-old. When Nola is away she seems to forget her mother entirely—doesn't telephone, certainly doesn't write. It's the way all their daughters are, Mrs. Dietrich's friends tell her. It doesn't *mean* anything. Mrs. Dietrich thinks how when she was carrying Nola, those nine long months, they'd been completely happy—not an instant's doubt or hesitation. The singular weight of the body. A trancelike state you are tempted to mistake for happiness because the body is incapable of thinking, therefore incapable of anticipating change. Hot rhythmic blood, organs, packed tight and moist, the baby upside down in her sac in her mother's belly, always present tense, always *now*. It was a shock when the end came so abruptly but everyone told Mrs. Dietrich she was a natural mother, praised and pampered her. For a while. Then of course she'd had her baby, her Nola. Even now Mrs. Dietrich can't really comprehend the experience. *Giving birth. Had a baby. Was born.* Mere words, absurdly inadequate. She knows no more of how love ends than she knew as a child, she knows only of how love begins—in the belly, in the womb, where it is always present tense.

The morning's shopping has been quite successful but lunch at La Crêperie doesn't go well for some reason. La Crêperie is Nola's favorite Mall restaurant—always amiably crowded, bustling, a simulated sidewalk café with red-striped umbrellas, wrought-iron tables and chairs, menus in French, music piped in overhead. Mrs. Dietrich's nerves are chafed by the pretense of gaiety, the noise, the openness onto one of the Mall's busy promenades where at any minute a familiar face might emerge, but she is grateful for her glass of chilled white wine. She orders a small tossed salad and a creamed-chicken crepe and devours it hungrily—she *is* hungry. While Nola picks at her seafood crepe with a disdainful look. A familiar scene: mother watching while daughter pushes food around on her plate. Suddenly Nola is tense, moody, corners of her mouth downturned. Mrs. Dietrich wants to ask, What's wrong? She wants to ask, Why are you unhappy? She wants to smooth Nola's hair back from her forehead, check to see if her forehead is overly warm, wants to hug her close, hard. Why, why? What did I do wrong? Why do you hate me?

Calling the Portland Academy a few weeks ago Mrs. Dietrich suddenly lost control, began crying. She hadn't been drinking and she hadn't known she was upset. A girl unknown to her, one of Nola's suite mates, was saying, "Please, Mrs. Dietrich, it's all right. I'm sure Nola will call you back later tonight, or tomorrow, Mrs. Dietrich?—I'll tell her you called, all right?—Mrs. Dietrich?" as embarrassed as if Mrs. Dietrich had been her own mother.

How love begins. How love ends.

Mrs. Dietrich orders a third glass of wine. This is a celebration of sorts isn't it?—their last shopping trip for a long time. But Nola resists, Nola isn't sentimental. In casual defiance of Mrs. Dietrich she lights up a cigarette— yes, Mother, Nola has said ironically, since *you* stopped smoking *everybody* is supposed to stop—and sits with her arms crossed, watching streams of shoppers pass. Mrs. Dietrich speaks lightly of practical matters, tomorrow morning's drive to the airport, and will Nola telephone when she gets to Portland to let Mrs. Dietrich know she has arrived safely?

Then with no warning—though of course she'd been planning this all along—Nola brings up the subject of a semester in France, in Paris and Rouen, the fall semester of her senior year it would be; she has put in her application, she says, and is waiting to hear if she's been accepted. She smokes her cigarette calmly, expelling smoke from her nostrils in a way Mrs. Dietrich thinks particularly coarse. Mrs. Dietrich, who believed that particular topic was finished, takes care to speak without emotion. "I just don't think it's a very practical idea right now, Nola," she says. "We've been through it haven't we? I—"

"I'm going," Nola says.   40

"The extra expense, for one thing. Your father—"

"If I get accepted, I'm going."

"Your father—"

"The hell with him too."

Mrs. Dietrich would like to slap her daughter's face. Bring tears to those   45
steely eyes. But she sits stiff, turning her wine glass between her fingers, patient, calm, she's heard all this before; she says, "Surely this isn't the best time to discuss it, Nola."

Mrs. Dietrich is afraid her daughter will leave the restaurant, simply walk away, that has happened before and if it happens today she doesn't know what she will do. But Nola sits unmoving; her face closed, impassive. Mrs. Dietrich feels her quickened heartbeat. Once after one of their quarrels Mrs. Dietrich told a friend of hers, the mother too of a teenage daughter, "I just don't know her any longer, how can you keep living with someone you don't know?" and the woman said, "Eventually you can't."

Nola says, not looking at Mrs. Dietrich: "Why don't we talk about it, Mother?"

"Talk about what?" Mrs. Dietrich asks.

"You know."

"The semester in France? Again?"   50

"No."

"What, then?"

"You *know*."

"I don't know, really. Really!" Mrs. Dietrich smiles, baffled. She feels the corners of her eyes pucker white with strain.

Nola says, sighing, "How exhausting it is."   55

"How *what?*"

"How exhausting it is."

"What is?"

"You and me—"

"What?"   60

"Being together—"

"Being together how—?"

"The two of us, like this—"

"But we're hardly ever together, Nola," Mrs. Dietrich says.

Her expression is calm but her voice is shaking. Nola turns away, cov-   65
ering her face with a hand, for a moment she looks years older than her
age—in fact exhausted. Mrs. Dietrich sees with pity that her daughter's skin
is fair and thin and dry—unlike her own, which tends to be oily—it will
wear out before she's forty. Mrs. Dietrich reaches over to squeeze her hand.
The fingers are limp, ungiving. "You're going back to school tomorrow,
Nola," she says. "You won't come home again until June 12. And you probably will go to France—if your father consents."

Nola gets to her feet, drops her cigarette to the flagstone terrace and
grinds it beneath her boot. A dirty thing to do, Mrs. Dietrich thinks, considering there's an ashtray right on the table, but she says nothing. She dislikes La Crêperie anyway.

Nola laughs, showing her lovely white teeth. "Oh, the hell with him,"
she says. "Fuck Daddy, right?"

They separate for an hour, Mrs. Dietrich to Neiman-Marcus to buy a
birthday gift for her elderly aunt, Nola to the trendy new boutique Pour
Vous. By the time Mrs. Dietrich rejoins her daughter she's quite angry,
blood beating hot and hard and measured in resentment, she has had time
to relive old quarrels between them, old exchanges, stray humiliating memories of her marriage as well, these last-hour disagreements are the cruelest
and they are Nola's specialty. She locates Nola in the rear of the boutique
amid blaring rock music, flashing neon lights, chrome-edged mirrors, her
face still hard, closed, prim, pale. She stands beside another teenage girl
looking in a desultory way through a rack of blouses, shoving the hangers
roughly along, taking no care when a blouse falls to the floor. As Nola
glances up, startled, not prepared to see her mother in front of her, their
eyes lock for an instant and Mrs. Dietrich stares at her with hatred. Cold
calm clear unmistakable hatred. She is thinking, Who are *you?* What have
I to do with *you?* I don't know *you,* I don't love *you,* why should I?

Has Nola seen, heard?—she turns aside as if wincing, gives the blouses
a final dismissive shove. Her eyes look tired, the corners of her mouth downturned. Anxious, immediately repentant, Mrs. Dietrich asks if she has found
anything worth trying on. Nola says with a shrug, "Not a thing, Mother."

On their way out of the Mall Mrs. Dietrich and Nola see the disheveled   70
woman in the black coat again, this time sitting prominently on a concrete
ledge in front of Lord & Taylor's busy main entrance. Shopping bag at her
feet, shabby purse on the ledge beside her. She is shaking her head in a series
of annoyed twitches as if arguing with someone but her hands are loose,
palms up, in her lap. Her posture is unfortunate—she sits with her knees
parted, inner thighs revealed, fatty, dead white, the tops of cotton stockings
rolled tight cutting into the flesh. Again, streams of shoppers are making a
careful berth around her. Alone among them Nola hesitates, seems about to

approach the woman—Please don't, Nola! please! Mrs. Dietrich thinks—then changes her mind and keeps on walking. Mrs. Dietrich murmurs isn't it a pity, poor thing, don't you wonder where she lives, who her family is, but Nola doesn't reply. Her pace through the first door of Lord & Taylor is so rapid that Mrs. Dietrich can barely keep up.

But Nola's upset. Strangely upset. As soon as they are in the car, packages and bags in the backseat, she begins crying.

It's childish helpless crying, as though her heart is broken. But Mrs. Dietrich knows it isn't broken, she has heard these very sobs before. Many times before. Still she comforts her daughter, embraces her, hugs her hard, hard. A sudden fierce passion. Vehemence. "Nola honey. Nola dear, what's wrong, dear, everything will be all right, dear," she says, close to weeping herself. She would embrace Nola even more tightly except for the girl's quilted jacket, that bulky L. L. Bean thing she has never liked, and Nola's stubborn lowered head. Nola has always been ashamed, crying, frantic to hide her face. Strangers are passing close by the car, curious, staring. Mrs. Dietrich wishes she had a cloak to draw over her daughter and herself, so that no one else would see.

 Questions of Subject and Theme

1. In what senses is "Shopping" an appropriate title for what you have read? In what senses might the story be said not to be about shopping at all? Discuss what you think the story is really "about."
2. When are mother and daughter happiest together? When are they most at odds? What seems to be the rationale of cause and effect in each case?

Questions of Method and Strategy

1. Going in and out of the mall, the mother and daughter meet a disheveled woman. What does this figure contribute to your sense of the mother and daughter? How does it do so?
2. Though not present, Mr. Dietrich is an important figure in the story. Discuss with examples the ways in which Oates employs the theme of "Mr. Dietrich."

SPORT SHOPPING IN SUBURBIA

William Geist

William Geist worked as a newspaperman and wrote the column "About New York" for the *New York Times* before shifting to television. He became a commentator and feature reporter for CBS news and was featured on several shows. He often focuses on the suburban scene.

"I have one thing to say to that gray fox," says Fran. "I want you, I need you, I love you." She takes a bite of her tuna-pecan water chestnut on croissant.   *1*

"Think of the money you'd be saving Steve," Jackie says with a note of sarcasm, taking a bite of her avocado-chicken salad sandwich.

Steve is Fran's husband. Fran and Jackie are friends. The gray fox is a $7,500 coat that is marked down on Neiman-Marcus's fur sale to $6,000— a potentially handsome $1,500 saving for Steve. The fabulous fox is poised for sale not far from where they are having lunch, the Zodiac restaurant in the Neiman-Marcus store in the Northbrook Court mall in Chicago's northern suburbs.

They sit in a mecca of conspicuous consumption. It is rumored that anyone entering Northbrook Court with less than two designer labels showing on his or her person will be wrestled to the ground by Security. Shopping here is a sport; Fran and Jackie would seem to be world class competitors.

It is said that shopping was once done of necessity. An example might   *5* be shopping to buy a pair of shoes without big holes in the bottoms. Now we go shopping for entertainment, to get out of the house, to see those new things that are making those people in the television commercials so remarkably happy, and to mingle with people. Where else in the suburbs can we see people stripped of their cars?

The better sport shoppers at Northbrook Court would seem to be women in their thirties or forties, traveling most often in twos, and either thin or divorced. They have chic hair styles; and their faces represent the state of the art in cosmetology. Many wear "fun furs" and designer tops with designer jeans. The jeans may be tucked into new low-cut cowboy (if you will) boots. If Designer Jeans Are Not Tucked In, They Shall Be Stylishly Rolled Up—The Management.

Fran is tucked; Jackie, rolled. One wonders if this places a strain on their relationship. They are not wearing coats. Really good sport shoppers know that there are places in malls to drop off coats. The two seem as comfortable as if they were at home, which to some extent they are.

They are here at Northbrook Court nearly the entire day. They were here yesterday. The day before that they went into the city, to Watertower Place, one of the vertical shopping malls that cities are building to emulate the suburban malls that have been stealing away all of their business. Once Fran and Jackie even spent the night at Watertower Place, in the Ritz Hotel. They may spend more time shopping than they do at home. They aren't sure.

They are carrying shopping bags but say they haven't bought anything. "This is just something for my daughter [nine years old] to knock around in," Fran says, holding open a bag containing a Givenchy terry cloth top ($20) and Gloria Vanderbilt jeans ($32) purchased at I. Magnin, an up-scale store that just opened at the mall. "It changed my life," Fran says with a smirk about the store opening. Jackie has a one-pound box of Godiva chocolates that have crossed chocolate tennis racquets on their tops ($12).

After lunch they glide through this clean, climate-controlled shopping   10 womb, through Ann Taylor and Lord & Taylor before stopping in Stanley Korshak to buy Fran a bikini ($58) for an upcoming Palm Springs vacation. Jackie buys a pound of freshly ground coffee—make that Ethiopian Harrar coffee—at The Coffee Factory ($5.25). Fran returns to I. Magnin to inspect a plain black piece of luggage about the size of a gym bag—but with Ralph Lauren's name on it—priced at $550. The two shoppers stop at the cosmetics department to talk with the clerks about Erno Laszlo skin care programs and to buy some cosmetics. It is a minor purchase ($9), yet still a purchase, complete with attendant conversation and salesclerks fawning a bit over these preferred customers.

Jackie takes a serious look at a Bottega Veneta Italian lambskin shoulder bag ($185) that looks to have about enough room in it for half a tuna-pecan water chestnut on croissant. It is almost time for the children to come home on the school bus. Jackie feels rushed.

She tells the clerk that she will "sleep on it." Tomorrow is another day.

At Roosevelt Field shopping mall on Long Island, Lisa D'Amico drifts through the corridors like a fish in a comfortably familiar aquarium, needing nothing in particular other than to shop. "I didn't really come today to buy anything," says the thirty-two-year-old Garden City housewife.

Roosevelt Field, a 180-store, 2.2 million-square-foot enclosed shopping center (that argues with the Woodfield Mall in suburban Chicago about which is the world's largest), was considered a risky undertaking when it was built in 1956. But now, during the celebration of its twenty-fifth anniversary, it is viewed as a visionary prototype of the mega-malls that have transformed the country's landscape and spawned a generation of shoppers such as Mrs. D'Amico.

"Shopping has become a mode of entertainment," says Frieda Stangler,   15 a spokesperson for the mall. Shoppers describe Roosevelt Field as "pleasant," "fun," and "exciting." There are frequent special events, such as antique shows, fashion shows, car shows, boat shows, and appearances by film, sports, and soap opera stars.

"We believe that if we can get them to the mall," Mrs. Stangler says, "there will be purchases."

The purchases of 275,000 visitors a week total about $230 million a year. An assortment of restaurants and such things as lockers for coats and other belongings encourage them to stay, as do the benches and tables outside the stores, where shoppers can relax with no pressure to buy. There are no clocks or windows.

The country's more than two thousand enclosed malls are overwhelmingly successful, finely tuned selling machines, in which everything from climate to clientele has always been closely controlled to produce an impeccably pleasant shopping environment. Retailers not fitting the total marketing concept are not allowed into most malls, and the ones that are let in usually have their hours set and their store designs approved by mall management.

In malls it never rains or snows. There are no puddles to jump, no unpleasant aromas to smell, no crummy bars or people who frequent them. There are no Hare Krishnas or protestors or anyone to introduce unpleasantness of any kind. Such people have no rights here; this is private property.

Of late, however, many shopping mall managers say they have had the uncomfortable feeling that the outside world is seeping in. In suburban Hartford, for example, there is grave concern over a group of women that wants to put up a little folding card table in Westfarms Mall. *20*

Attorneys for the 127-store mall have been battling in court for more than two years to keep out the card table where two representatives of the National Organization for Women would collect signatures on petitions supporting the Equal Rights Amendment. The women's organization argues that even though such malls are private property, they have become the nation's "new downtowns," public places where individuals and groups have as much right to collect signatures on petitions and hand out literature as on any street corner. Moreover, argues Martin Margulies, the group's attorney, "malls are the place, the only place, to see people in the suburbs anymore." The women's organization won the first round in its court battle with Westfarms Mall early last year.

Court battles on this point are being waged across the country. In Paramus, New Jersey, sometimes referred to as the shopping center capital of the country, because of its five major centers, a political candidate has sued for the right to distribute campaign literature in Bergen Mall.

The attorney for the candidate argues, "There is no real downtown Paramus. Areas of the mall outside the stores are the town's public sidewalks." He noted that community events were held at the mall and that it contained a meeting hall, a post office, and a Roman Catholic chapel.

"We in the industry are quite concerned about a loss of control," says Peter Hollis, senior vice president for the Taubman Company, one of the nation's largest mall developers and the management concern for Westfarms

Mall. "The hassle-free environment is the whole basis of shopping mall development."

Mrs. D'Amico says she comes to the Roosevelt Field mall about three 25 times a week, twice on weekday trips with friends and once on the weekend with her husband and two children. When she comes with her friends, they browse, make a few small purchases, and have lunch at a new restaurant in the mall called Houlihan's Old Place, which is decorated with old-fashioned tin ceilings and reproductions of memorabilia and has a menu awash with frothy frozen strawberry daiquiris, piña coladas, nacho platters, and Huevos California. "It's a fun place," she says.

Donna Shapiro, who is seventeen years old and says she has been coming here all her life, is at the mall after school with two friends, looking for just the right pair of jeans at such stores as Jeans West, Just Jeans, Jeans Only, and Pants Place Plus. They also meander into such places as Just Shirts and Just Cards and make purchases of opportunity as they go: one pound of very cherry jelly beans at Fanny Farmer Candies, one Bob Seger double album at Record World, and a bag of Bruce's Chunky Chocolate Chip Cookies.

They have some laughs trying on hairpieces at Wig Allure but become serious when the clerk turns the discussion to the shop's acrylic fingernails. They have also come here to troll for friends in general, boys to be more specific, and Jim in particular. As one of Donna's friends says, "This is where you see everybody."

"A lot of young people come here on shopping dates," Mrs. Stangler says. "There are not the cultural activities for young people in the suburbs that there are in the city. It is a very expensive proposition to keep teenagers amused these days, and they can come here free, where it is safe and warm. I don't think that it's bad for them."

There are many elderly people at the mall, one of whom explains that they come regularly to get out of the house without having to worry about crime or inclement weather.

They all say they can get anything they want at the 180 stores and other 30 businesses at Roosevelt Field. Visitors to the mall can see a movie, take out a life insurance policy, have their television sets and cars repaired, have their hair styled, have their income taxes prepared, attend "jazz-ercise" classes at the health spa or weight loss classes at Weight Watchers, mail a package at the mall's post office, visit the optometrist, or have a cavity filled at Dental World. They can buy a dog or buy a Florida retirement home in a six-thousand-house development populated primarily by former Roosevelt Field shoppers.

There is a waiting list of seven to ten years for businesses to get into Roosevelt Field, and those not on the inside line every roadway to the mall, attempting to lure motorists headed for the mall's 12,300-space parking lot. Office buildings, banks, and corporate headquarters have built on the periphery. The mass, the gravitational pull of Roosevelt Field, seems to have drawn everything from miles around into its orbit, and officials of surrounding suburbs bemoan the loss of stores, jobs (with six thousand employees, the mall is Long Island's fourth-largest employer), sales, and taxes.

The downtowns of older suburbs often go out of business when malls are built. Newer suburbs often have no downtowns, just roadways to the mall.

Asked why he comes to Roosevelt Field, one shopper replies, "Everything is here now." Others say that they have not been to Manhattan for months or even years. Their most recent shopping trips there, they report, were "a hassle," "a little scary at times," or "too expensive."

Donna Shapiro and her friends are passing by Just Cards, heading toward Just Shirts. She has found the pants she was looking for, and they have seen a number of "cute boys." They have not seen Jim, but they fear not. "School's out," one of Donna's friends says. "He's got to be here someplace."

Questions of Subject and Theme

1. In what senses does the author present shopping as a sport? Discuss the issue with examples.
2. The author quotes a developer as saying: "The hassle-free environment is the whole basis of shopping mall development." What "hassles" does the author's account show people to be "free" of in malls? How do they differ? How are they related? Discuss the issue with examples.

Questions of Method and Strategy

1. The author often seems ironic about what he observes. Pick some examples and analyze what values and assumptions the irony criticizes and what values and assumptions it supports as a basis from which to make that criticism.
2. The author describes many types of people in many malls. Could all have been found in the same mall? What effect is created by the constant movement of attention to another mall?

——————

Suggestions for Writing on the Juxtapositions

1. What has the mall meant to you? Write an essay that analyzes your experience with family or friends.
2. In your view, which author likes malls the most? Which least? Why do they do so? Write an essay in which you analyze the ways in which your two authors implicitly or explicitly present their own views in the course of describing the experience of others.
3. In "Sport Shopping in Suburbia," Martin Margulies is quoted as saying that "malls are the place, the only place, to see people in the sub-

urbs anymore." Write an essay that discusses what you think of this proposition.

4. Consider the following proposition: The first essay seems to report real observations; the second seems fictional; the third some combination of reporting and fiction. Write an essay that analyzes the differing writing techniques presented to defend or refute the proposition.

16 Reimagining a Fairy Tale

Jakob and Wilhelm Grimm, "Red Riding Hood"

James Finn Garner, "Little Red Riding Hood"

Russell Baker, "Little Red Riding Hood Revisited"

Bruno Bettelheim, "Fairy Tale versus Myth: Optimism versus Pessimism"

Fairy tales continue to stimulate modern imaginations—those of adults as well as those of children. As you read the original, two updated versions of "Little Red Riding Hood," and an essay on the psychic power of fairy tales and myths, consider the following questions:

1. In Bettelheim's terms, why would the traditional "Little Red Riding Hood" be classified as a fairy tale rather than a myth?

2. Both Garner and Baker make fun of some aspects of contemporary language. But how, if at all, does what Garner makes fun of differ from what Baker makes fun of? Explain with examples.

3. A famous novelist once said that "satire is a lesson; parody is a game." According to this distinction, has Garner written a satire or a parody? What about Baker? Explain your reasoning.

4. Would Bettelheim include the "modernized" versions in the terms of his classifications? In your opinion, do the processes of modernizing enacted by Garner and Baker strive for anything like the goals that Bettelheim says fairy tales and myths serve? For example, how do they make you feel about your command of language? Do they aid in any "rites of passage" involved in your life?

RED RIDING HOOD
from Grimms' Fairy Tales

Jakob and Wilhelm Grimm

The tale of Red Riding Hood was collected by the German
brothers Grimm and published by them, with more than two hundred
other tales, in 1819. The story, a favorite both in the United States and
elsewhere, is reinterpreted in the selections that follow it here.

Once upon a time there was a sweet little maiden who was loved by all   1
who knew her, but she was especially dear to her grandmother, who did
not know how to make enough of the child. Once she gave her a little red
velvet cloak. It was so becoming and she liked it so much that she would
never wear anything else, and so she got the name of Red Riding Hood.

One day her mother said to her, "Come here, Red Riding Hood! Take
this cake and bottle of wine to grandmother. She is weak and ill, and they
will do her good. Go quickly, before it gets hot. Don't loiter by the way,
nor run, or you will fall and break the bottle, and there will be no wine for
grandmother. When you get there, don't forget to say 'Good morning' pret-
tily, without staring about you."

"I will do just as you tell me," Red Riding Hood promised her mother.

Her grandmother lived away in the wood, a good half hour from the
village. When she got to the wood she met a wolf, but Red Riding Hood
did not know what a wicked animal he was, so she was not a bit afraid
of him.

"Good morning, Red Riding Hood," he said.   5

"Good morning, wolf," she answered.

"Whither away so early, Red Riding Hood?"

"To grandmother's."

"What have you got in your basket?"

"Cake and wine. We baked yesterday, so I'm taking a cake to her. She   10
wants something to make her well."

"Where does she live, Red Riding Hood?"

"A good quarter of an hour farther into the wood. Her house stands
under three big oak trees, near a hedge of nut trees which you must know,"
said Red Riding Hood.

The wolf thought, "This tender little creature will be a plump morsel!
She will be nicer than the old woman. I must be cunning and snap them
both up."

He walked along with Red Riding Hood for a while. Then he said,
"Look at the pretty flowers, Red Riding Hood. Why don't you look about

you? I don't believe you even hear the birds sing. You are as solemn as if you were going to school. All else is so gay out here in the woods."

Red Riding Hood raised her eyes, and when she saw the sunlight danc-   *15* ing through the trees, and all the bright flowers, she thought, "I'm sure grandmother would be pleased if I took her a bunch of fresh flowers. It is still quite early. I shall have plenty of time to pick them."

So she left the path and wandered off among the trees to pick the flow-ers. Each time she picked one, she always saw another prettier one farther on. So she went deeper and deeper into the forest.

In the meantime the wolf went straight off to the grandmother's cottage and knocked at the door.

"Who is there?"

"Red Riding Hood, bringing you a cake and some wine. Open the door!"

"Lift the latch," called out the old woman. "I am too weak to get up."   *20*

The wolf lifted the latch and the door sprang open. He went straight in and up to the bed without saying a word, and ate up the poor old woman. Then he put on her nightdress and cap, got into bed and drew the curtains.

Red Riding Hood picked flowers till she could carry no more, and then she remembered her grandmother again. She was astonished when she got to the house to find the door open, and when she entered the room every-thing seemed so strange. She felt quite frightened but she did not know why. "Generally I like coming to see grandmother so much," she thought. "Good morning, grandmother," she cried. But she received no answer.

Then she went up to the bed and drew the curtain back. There lay her grandmother, but she had drawn her cap down over her face and she looked very odd.

"Oh grandmother, what big ears you have," she said.

"The better to hear you with, my dear."   *25*

"Grandmother, what big eyes you have."

"The better to see you with, my dear."

"What big hands you have, grandmother."

"The better to catch hold of you with, my dear."

"But grandmother, what big teeth you have."   *30*

"The better to eat you with, my dear."

Hardly had the wolf said this than he made a spring out of bed and swallowed poor little Red Riding Hood. When the wolf had satisfied him-self he went back to bed, and he was soon snoring loudly.

A huntsman went past the house and thought, "How loudly the old lady is snoring. I must see if there is anything the matter with her."

So he went into the house and up to the bed, where he found the wolf fast asleep. "Do I find you here, you old sinner!" he said. "Long enough have I sought you!"

He raised his gun to shoot, when it just occurred to him that perhaps   *35* the wolf had eaten up the old lady, and that she might still be saved. So he took a knife and began cutting open the sleeping wolf. At the first cut he saw the little red cloak, and after a few more slashes, the little girl sprang out and cried, "Oh, how frightened I was! It was so dark inside the wolf." Next the old grandmother came out, alive but hardly able to breathe.

Red Riding Hood brought some big stones with which they filled the wolf. He woke up and tried to spring away, but the stones dragged him back and he fell down dead.

They were all quite happy now. The huntsman skinned the wolf and took the skin home. The grandmother ate the cake and drank the wine which Red Riding Hood had brought, and she soon felt quite strong. Red Riding Hood thought to herself, "I will never again wander off into the forest as long as I live, when my mother forbids it."

moral lesson

LITTLE RED RIDING HOOD
from Politically Correct Bedtime Stories

James Finn Garner

James Finn Garner is a writer and performer based in Chicago. His work has been published in the *Chicago Tribune Magazine* and has appeared on Chicago Public Radio. His first book, *Politically Correct Bedtime Stories* became a national bestseller very quickly after its publication.

There once was a young person named Red Riding Hood who lived   *1*
with her mother on the edge of a large wood. One day her mother asked her to take a basket of fresh fruit and mineral water to her grandmother's house—not because this was womyn's work, mind you, but because the deed was generous and helped engender a feeling of community. Furthermore, her grandmother was *not* sick, but rather was in full physical and mental health and was fully capable of taking care of herself as a mature adult.

So Red Riding Hood set off with her basket through the woods. Many people believed that the forest was a foreboding and dangerous place and never set foot in it. Red Riding Hood, however, was confident enough in her own budding sexuality that such obvious Freudian imagery did not intimidate her.

On the way to Grandma's house, Red Riding Hood was accosted by a wolf, who asked her what was in her basket. She replied, "Some healthful snacks for my grandmother, who is certainly capable of taking care of herself as a mature adult."

The wolf said, "You know, my dear, it isn't safe for a little girl to walk through these woods alone."

Red Riding Hood said, "I find your sexist remark offensive in the ex-   *5*
treme, but I will ignore it because of your traditional status as an outcast from society, the stress of which has caused you to develop your own, entirely valid, worldview. Now, if you'll excuse me, I must be on my way."

Red Riding Hood walked on along the main path. But, because his status outside society had freed him from slavish adherence to linear, Western-style thought, the wolf knew a quicker route to Grandma's house. He burst into the house and ate Grandma, an entirely valid course of action for a carnivore such as himself. Then, unhampered by rigid, traditionalist notions of what was masculine or feminine, he put on Grandma's night-clothes and crawled into bed.

Red Riding Hood entered the cottage and said, "Grandma, I have brought you some fat-free, sodium-free snacks to salute you in your role of a wise and nurturing matriarch."

From the bed, the wolf said softly, "Come closer, child, so that I might see you."

Red Riding Hood said, "Oh, I forgot you are as optically challenged as a bat. Grandma, what big eyes you have!"

"They have seen much, and forgiven much, my dear."   10

"Grandma, what a big nose you have—only relatively, of course, and certainly attractive in its own way."

"It has smelled much, and forgiven much, my dear."

"Grandma, what big teeth you have!"

The wolf said, "I am happy with *who* I am and *what* I am," and leaped out of bed. He grabbed Red Riding Hood in his claws, intent on devouring her. Red Riding Hood screamed, not out of alarm at the wolf's apparent tendency toward cross-dressing, but because of his willful invasion of her personal space.

Her screams were heard by a passing woodchopper-person (or log-fuel   15
technician, as he preferred to be called). When he burst into the cottage, he saw the melee and tried to intervene. But as he raised his ax, Red Riding Hood and the wolf both stopped.

"And just what do you think you're doing?" asked Red Riding Hood.

The woodchopper-person blinked and tried to answer, but no words came to him.

"Bursting in here like a Neanderthal, trusting your weapon to do your thinking for you!" she exclaimed. "Sexist! Speciesist! How dare you assume that womyn and wolves can't solve their own problems without a man's help!"

When she heard Red Riding Hood's impassioned speech, Grandma jumped out of the wolf's mouth, seized the woodchopper-person's ax, and cut his head off. After this ordeal, Red Riding Hood, Grandma, and the wolf felt a certain commonality of purpose. They decided to set up an alternative household based on mutual respect and cooperation, and they lived together in the woods happily ever after.

Questions of Subject and Theme

1. If the grandmother provides jokes about "ageism," what other "isms" does Garner address in the course of the story? Make a list with examples.
2. Pick a moment in the story where you think Garner tries to amuse you. What are the values and assumptions that underlie the uses of language he ridicules? What is assumed to be "politically correct" about the language? Are you amused? Why or why not?

Questions of Method and Strategy

1. How does Garner make use of the Woodchopper character in his version of the story? What advantages do you think he gains by his changes in that aspect of the traditional tale?
2. Garner changes the traditional ending to the story. Do you think that the change in plot is like or unlike the changes in language that he makes throughout? Explain your answer.

LITTLE RED RIDING HOOD REVISITED

Russell Baker

Russell Baker is a columnist for *The New York Times* who writes as
a humorist and as a serious political commentator. An example of his
humor is presented here, and one of his more serious essays appears in
the next section.

In an effort to make the classics accessible to contemporary readers, I
am translating them into the modern American language. Here is the translation of "Little Red Riding Hood":

Once upon a point in time, a small person named Little Red Riding
Hood initiated plans for the preparation, delivery and transportation of
foodstuffs to her grandmother, a senior citizen residing at a place of residence in a forest of indeterminate dimension.

In the process of implementing this program, her incursion into the
forest was in midtransportation process when it attained interface with an
alleged perpetrator. This individual, a wolf, made inquiry as to the whereabouts of Little Red Riding Hood's goal as well as inferring that he was
desirous of ascertaining the contents of Little Red Riding Hood's foodstuffs
basket, and all that.

"It would be inappropriate to lie to me," the wolf said, displaying his
huge jaw capability. Sensing that he was a mass of repressed hostility intertwined with acute alienation, she indicated.

"I see you indicating," the wolf said, "but what I don't see is whatever
it is you're indicating at, you dig?"

Little Red Riding Hood indicated more fully, making one thing perfectly clear—to wit, that it was to her grandmother's residence and with
a consignment of foodstuffs that her mission consisted of taking her to
and with.

At this point in time the wolf moderated his rhetoric and proceeded to
grandmother's residence. The elderly person was then subjected to the disadvantages of total consumption and transferred to residence in the perpetrator's stomach.

"That will raise the old woman's consciousness," the wolf said to himself. He was not a bad wolf, but only a victim of an oppressive society, a
society that not only denied wolves' rights, but actually boasted of its capacity for keeping the wolf from the door. An interior malaise made itself manifest inside the wolf.

"Is that the national malaise I sense within my digestive tract?" wondered the wolf. "Or is it the old person seeking to retaliate for her consumption by telling wolf jokes to my duodenum?" It was time to make a

judgment. The time was now, the hour had struck, the body lupine cried out for decision. The wolf was up to the challenge. He took two stomach powders right away and got into bed.

The wolf had adopted the abdominal-distress recovery posture when   *10*
Little Red Riding Hood achieved his presence.

"Grandmother," she said, "your ocular implements are of an extraordinary order of magnitude."

"The purpose of this enlarged viewing capability," said the wolf, "is to enable your image to register a more precise impression upon my sight systems."

"In reference to your ears," said Little Red Riding Hood, "it is noted with the deepest respect that far from being underprivileged, their elongation and enlargement appear to qualify you for unparalleled distinction."

"I hear you loud and clear, kid," said the wolf, "but what about these new choppers?"

"If it is not inappropriate," said Little Red Riding Hood, "it might be   *15*
observed that with your new miracle masticating products you may even be able to chew taffy again."

This observation was followed by the adoption of an aggressive posture on the part of the wolf and the assertion that it was also possible for him, due to the high efficiency ratio of his jaw, to consume little persons, plus, as he stated, his firm determination to do so at once without delay and with all due process and propriety, notwithstanding the fact that the ingestion of one entire grandmother had already provided twice his daily recommended cholesterol intake.

There ensued flight by Little Red Riding Hood accompanied by pursuit in respect to the wolf and a subsequent intervention on the part of a third party, heretofore unnoted in the record.

Due to the firmness of the intervention, the wolf's stomach underwent ax-assisted aperture with the result that Red Riding Hood's grandmother was enabled to be removed with only minor discomfort.

The wolf's indigestion was immediately alleviated with such effectiveness that he signed a contract with the intervening third party to perform with grandmother in a television commercial demonstrating the swiftness of this dramatic relief for stomach discontent.

"I'm going to be on television," cried grandmother.   *20*

And they all joined her happily in crying, "What a phenomena!"

Questions of Subject and Theme

1. Judging from his jokes, what are some of the things that Baker thinks ridiculous about "the modern American language?"
2. Point to some places where the styles of Little Red Riding Hood and the wolf differ. What different kinds of contemporary talk is being made fun of in each case?

Questions of Method and Strategy

1. Baker refers to the woodchopper only as "a third party." Can you imagine any advantages to this strategy? Disadvantages?

2. All the characters say the same words at the end: "What a phenomena!" What does Baker make fun of in this instance? Does it sum up anything about his earlier ridicule? In your opinion what are its advantages and disadvantages as an ending?

FAIRY TALE VERSUS MYTH
Optimism versus Pessimism

Bruno Bettelheim

> Bruno Bettelheim is a psychologist who has written on many sub-
> jects connected with the mental lives and health of children. A long-
> time worker with the emotionally disturbed, he seeks in the following
> essay to understand how traditional stories have helped ease some of
> the psychic strains that are part of growing up.

Plato—who may have understood better what forms the mind of man   *1*
than do some of our contemporaries who want their children exposed only
to "real" people and everyday events—knew what intellectual experiences
make for true humanity. He suggested that the future citizens of his ideal
republic begin their literary education with the telling of myths, rather than
with mere facts or so-called rational teachings. Even Aristotle, master of
pure reason, said: "The friend of wisdom is also a friend of myth."

Modern thinkers who have studied myths and fairy tales from a philosophical or psychological viewpoint arrive at the same conclusion, regardless
of their original persuasion. Mircea Eliade, for one, describes these stories as
"models for human behavior [that,] by that very fact, give meaning and
value to life." Drawing on anthropological parallels, he and others suggest
that myths and fairy tales were derived from, or give symbolic expression to,
initiation rites or other *rites de passage*—such as metaphoric death of an old,
inadequate self in order to be reborn on a higher plane of existence. He feels
that this is why these tales meet a strongly felt need and are carriers of such
deep meaning.

Other investigators with a depth-psychological orientation emphasize
the similarities between the fantastic events in myths and fairy tales and
those in adult dreams and daydreams—the fulfillment of wishes, the win-
ning out over all competitors, the destruction of enemies—and conclude
that one attraction of this literature is its expression of that which is normally
prevented from coming to awareness.

There are, of course, very significant differences between fairy tales and
dreams. For example, in dreams more often than not the wish fulfillment is
disguised, while in fairy tales much of it is openly expressed. To a considerable degree, dreams are the result of inner pressures which have found no
relief, of problems which beset a person to which he knows no solution and
to which the dream finds none. The fairy tale does the opposite: it projects
the relief of all pressures and not only offers ways to solve problems but
promises that a "happy" solution will be found.

We cannot control what goes on in our dreams. Although our inner
censorship influences what we may dream, such control occurs on an

unconscious level. The fairy tale, on the other hand, is very much the result of common conscious and unconscious content having been shaped by the conscious mind, not of one particular person, but the consensus of many in regard to what they view as universal human problems and what they accept as desirable solutions. If all these elements were not present in a fairy tale, it would not be retold by generation after generation. Only if a fairy tale met the conscious and unconscious requirements of many people was it repeatedly retold, and listened to with great interest. No dream of a person could arouse such persistent interest unless it was worked into a myth, as was the story of the pharaoh's dreams as interpreted by Joseph in the Bible.

tales told
& retold
(as solutions)

There is general agreement that myths and fairy tales speak to us in the language of symbols representing unconscious content. Their appeal is simultaneously to our conscious and unconscious mind, to all three of its aspects—id, ego, and superego—and to our need for ego-ideals as well. This makes it very effective; and in the tales' content, inner psychological phenomena are given body in symbolic form.

symbols

Freudian psychoanalysts concern themselves with showing what kind of repressed or otherwise unconscious material underlies myths and fairy tales, and how these relate to dreams and daydreams.

Jungian psychoanalysts stress in addition that the figures and events of these stories conform to and hence represent archetypical psychological phenomena, and symbolically suggest the need for gaining a higher state of selfhood—an inner renewal which is achieved as personal and racial unconscious forces become available to the person.

There are not only essential similarities between myths and fairy tales; there are also inherent differences. Although the same exemplary figures and situations are found in both and equally miraculous events occur in both, there is a crucial difference in the way these are communicated. Put simply, the dominant feeling a myth conveys is: this is absolutely unique; it could not have happened to any other person or in any other setting; such events are grandiose, awe-inspiring, and could not possibly happen to an ordinary mortal like you or me. The reason is not so much that what takes place is miraculous, but that it is described as such. By contrast, although the events which occur in fairy tales are often unusual and most improbable, they are always presented as ordinary, something that could happen to you or me or the person next door when out on a walk in the woods. Even the most remarkable encounters are related in casual, everyday ways in fairy tales.

difference
in tales &
myth

myth:
absolutely
unique;
non-ordinary

tale:
ordinary
(even if
improbable)

An even more significant difference between these two kinds of story is the ending, which in myths is nearly always tragic, while always happy in fairy tales. For this reason, some of the best-known stories found in collections of fairy tales don't really belong in this category. For example, Hans Christian Andersen's "The Little Match Girl" and "The Steadfast Tin Soldier" are beautiful but extremely sad; they do not convey the feeling of consolation characteristic of fairy tales at the end. Andersen's "The Snow Queen," on the other hand, comes quite close to being a true fairy tale.

10

myth: tragic
tale: happy

The myth is pessimistic, while the fairy story is optimistic, no matter how terrifyingly serious some features of the story may be. It is this decisive difference which sets the fairy tale apart from other stories in which equally fantastic events occur, whether the happy outcome is due to the virtues of the hero, chance, or the interference of supernatural figures.

Myths typically involve superego demands in conflict with id–motivated action, and with the self-preserving desires of the ego. A mere mortal is too frail to meet the challenges of the gods. Paris, who does the bidding of Zeus as conveyed to him by Hermes, and obeys the demand of the three goddesses in choosing which shall have the apple, is destroyed for having followed these commands, as are untold other mortals in the wake of this fateful choice.

Try as hard as we may, we can never live up fully to what the superego, as represented in myths by the gods, seems to require of us. The more we try to please it, the more implacable its demands. Even when the hero does not know that he gave in to the proddings of his id, he is still made to suffer horribly for it. When a mortal incurs the displeasure of a god without having done anything wrong, he is destroyed by these supreme superego representations. The pessimism of myths is superbly exemplified in the paradigmatic myth of psychoanalysis, the tragedy of Oedipus.

The myth of Oedipus, particularly when well performed on the stage, arouses powerful intellectual and emotional reactions in the adult—so much so, that it may provide a cathartic experience, as Aristotle taught all tragedy does. After watching Oedipus, a viewer may wonder why he is so deeply moved; and in responding to what he observes as his emotional reaction, ruminating about the mythical events and what these mean to him, a person may come to clarify his thoughts and feelings. With this, certain inner tensions which are the consequence of events long past may be relieved; previously unconscious material can then enter one's awareness and become accessible for conscious working through. This can happen if the observer is deeply moved emotionally by the myth, and at the same time strongly motivated intellectually to understand it.

Vicariously experiencing what happened to Oedipus, what he did and what he suffered, may permit the adult to bring his mature understanding to what until then had remained childish anxieties, preserved intact in infantile form in the unconscious mind. But this possibility exists only because the myth refers to events which happened in the most distant times, as the adult's oedipal longings and anxieties belong to the dimmest past of his life. If the underlying meaning of a myth were spelled out and presented as an event that could have happened in the person's adult conscious lifetime, then this would vastly increase old anxieties, and result in deeper repression.

A myth is not a cautionary tale like a fable which, by arousing anxiety, prevents us from acting in ways which are described as damaging to us. The myth of Oedipus can never be experienced as warning us not to get caught in an oedipal constellation. If one is born and raised as a child of two parents, oedipal conflicts are inescapable.

The oedipus complex is the crucial problem of childhood—unless a child remains fixated at an even earlier stage of development, such as the oral stage. A young child is completely caught up in oedipal conflicts as the inescapable reality of his life. The older child, from about age five on, is struggling to extricate himself by partly repressing the conflict, partly solving it by forming emotional attachments to others besides his parents, and partly sublimating it. What such a child needs least of all is to have his oedipal conflicts activated by such a myth. Suppose that the child still actively wishes, or has barely repressed the desire, to rid himself of one parent in order to have the other exclusively; if he is exposed—even though only in symbolic form—to the idea that by chance, unknowingly, one may murder a parent and marry the other, then what the child has played with only in fantasy suddenly assumes gruesome reality. The consequence of this exposure can only be increased anxiety about himself and the world.

A child not only dreams about marrying his parent of the other sex, but actively spins fantasies around it. The myth of Oedipus tells what happens if that dream becomes reality—and still the child cannot yet give up the wishful fantasies of marrying the parent at some future time. After hearing the myth of Oedipus, the conclusion in the child's mind could only be that similar horrible things—the death of a parent and mutilation of himself—will happen to him.

At this age, from four until puberty, what the child needs most is to be presented with symbolic images which reassure him that there is a happy solution to his oedipal problems—though he may find this difficult to believe—provided that he slowly works himself out of them. But reassurance about a happy outcome has to come first, because only then will the child have the courage to labor confidently to extricate himself from his oedipal predicament.

In childhood, more than in any other age, all is becoming. As long as we have not yet achieved considerable security within ourselves, we cannot engage in difficult psychological struggles unless a positive outcome seems certain to us, whatever the chances for this may be in reality. The fairy tale offers fantasy materials which suggest to the child in symbolic form what the battle to achieve self-realization is all about, and it guarantees a happy ending. Mythical heroes offer excellent images for the development of the superego, but the demands they embody are so rigorous as to discourage the child in his fledgling strivings to achieve personality integration. While the mythical hero experiences a transfiguration into eternal life in heaven, the central figure of the fairy tale lives happily ever after on earth, right among the rest of us. Some fairy tales conclude with the information that if perchance he has not yet died, the hero may be still alive. Thus, a happy though ordinary existence is projected by fairy tales as the outcome of the trials and tribulations involved in the normal growing-up process.

True, these psychosocial crises of growing up are imaginatively embroidered and symbolically represented in fairy tales as encounters with fairies, witches, ferocious animals, or figures of superhuman intelligence or cunning—but the essential humanity of the hero, despite his strange experiences, is affirmed by the reminder that he will have to die like the rest of us. Whatever strange events the fairy-tale hero experiences, they do not make him superhuman, as is true for the mythical hero. This real humanity suggests to the child that, whatever the content of the fairy tale, it is but fanciful elaborations and exaggerations of the tasks he has to meet, and of his hopes and fears.

Though the fairy tale offers fantastic symbolic images for the solution of problems, the problems presented in them are ordinary ones: a child's suffering from the jealousy and discrimination of his siblings, as is true for Cinderella; a child being thought incompetent by his parent, as happens in many fairy tales—for example, in the Brothers Grimm's story "The Spirit in the Bottle." Further, the fairy-tale hero wins out over these problems right here on earth, not by some reward reaped in heaven.

The psychological wisdom of the ages accounts for the fact that every myth is the story of a particular hero: Theseus, Hercules, Beowulf, Brunhild. Not only do these mythical characters have names, but we are also told the names of their parents, and of the other major figures in a myth. It just wouldn't do to name the myth of Theseus "The Man Who Slew the Bull," or that of Niobe "The Mother Who Had Seven Daughters and Seven Sons."

The fairy tale, by contrast, makes clear that it tells about everyman, people very much like us. Typical titles are "Beauty and the Beast," "The Fairy Tale of One Who Went Forth to Learn Fear." Even recently invented stories follow this pattern—for example, "The Little Prince," "The Ugly Duckling," "The Steadfast Tin Soldier." The protagonists of fairy tales are referred to as "a girl," for instance, or "the youngest brother." If names appear, it is quite clear that these are not proper names, but general or descriptive ones. We are told that "Because she always looked dusty and dirty, they called her Cinderella," or: "A little red cap suited her so well that she was always called 'Little Red Cap.'" Even when the hero is given a name, as in the Jack stories, or in "Hansel and Gretel," the use of very common names makes them generic terms, standing for any boy or girl.

This is further stressed by the fact that in fairy stories nobody else has a name; the parents of the main figures in fairy tales remain nameless. They are referred to as "father," "mother," "stepmother," though they may be described as "a poor fisherman" or "a poor woodcutter." If they are "a king" and "a queen," these are thin disguises for father and mother, as are "prince" and "princess" for boy and girl. Fairies and witches, giants and godmothers remain equally unnamed, thus facilitating projections and identifications.

Mythical heroes are of obviously superhuman dimensions, an aspect which helps to make these stories acceptable to the child. Otherwise the child would be overpowered by the implied demand that he emulate the hero in his own life. Myths are useful in forming not the total personality, but only the superego. The child knows that he cannot possibly live up to the hero's virtue, or parallel his deeds; all he can be expected to do is emulate the hero to some small degree; so the child is not defeated by the discrepancy between this ideal and his own smallness.

[handwritten margin note: hist. heroes show child's insignificance (inferiority)]

The real heros of history, however, having been people like the rest of us, impress the child with his own insignificance when compared with them. Trying to be guided and inspired by an ideal that no human can fully reach is at least not defeating—but striving to duplicate the deeds of actual great persons seems hopeless to the child and creates feelings of inferiority: first, because one knows one cannot do so, and second, because one fears others might.

[handwritten margin note: pessimist superego myth; optimist, id tale]

Myths project an ideal personality acting on the basis of superego demands, while fairy tales depict an ego integration which allows for appropriate satisfaction of id desires. This difference accounts for the contrast between the pervasive pessimism of myths and the essential optimism of fairy tales.

Questions of Subject and Theme

1. According to Bettelheim what are the differences and similarities of fairy tales and myths?
2. Recall to yourself the "traditional" version of "Little Red Riding Hood." Bettelheim says that fairy tales give symbolic expression to initiation rites or rites of passage "such as metaphoric death of an old, inadequate self in order to be reborn on a higher plane of existence." He also says: "The fairy tale offers fantasy materials which suggest to the child in symbolic form what the battle to achieve self-realization is all about, and it guarantees a happy ending." In your view, do Bettelheim's definitions fit the traditional tale? Do they fit the "modernized" versions you have read here in similar or different ways? Explain your answers.

Questions of Method and Strategy

1. Suppose Bettelheim had begun with his final paragraph. What, if anything, about the essay would be changed for you? Explain your answer.
2. Bettelheim often uses terms of Freudian psychology with its struggle between superego, ego, and id. Does he treat this struggle itself as like a fairy tale or a myth for the purposes of organizing his essay? Explain your answer with examples.

———

Suggestions for Writing on the Juxtapositions

1. Using Garner and Baker as models or sources of inspiration, write a "modernized" version of another traditional story—"The Three Little Pigs," for example.
2. Write an essay in which you compare and contrast the apparent goals of

Garner and Baker. Where are they alike in what they do? Where un-alike? What might each find to say about the other's work?

3. A book on writing style divides the area of diction or word choice into three levels: Tough, Sweet, and Stuffy. Write an essay in which you analyze the writing styles displayed in the three essays here, finding examples of words and phrases that fit these categories.

4. What do you think Bettelheim would have to say about the parodies or satires you have read? Write an essay in which you attempt to apply his method of analysis to what Garner and Baker attempt.

Advocacy and Argument

17 Language and Manners

Thomas H. Middleton, "Freshman Class?"

Ellen Goodman, "Vulgarity May Be Common,
  but It's Not Okay"

Barbara Lawrence, "Four-Letter Words Can Hurt You"

Private language such as slang is often used not to communicate with listeners but to separate the speakers from some parts of their audience. What happens when slang goes public? Consider these questions as you read:

1. In what ways do the three arguments about the proper uses of language differ from the satires or parodies on a similar subject in the preceding section? Explain your answer with examples.

2. All the writers seem opposed to "vulgar" language. What similarities and differences do you see among the reasons given by the authors for their opposition? Which two would most agree? Which two would most disagree?

3. Middleton and Goodman distinguish implicitly or explicitly between private and public uses of language. What position does Lawrence implicitly or explicitly take on this issue?

4. In examining sexual language, all the writers give varying degrees of attention to politically charged speech as well. What differences and similarities does each author find between the two areas of discourse?

FRESHMAN CLASS?

Thomas H. Middleton

Thomas Middleton's work often focuses on the topics of words and writing. His essays have appeared in national publications, including *The Saturday Review,* where the column "On Language" first featured the following selection.

A few years ago, my wife and I were in Vermont on one of our soul-refreshing trips from Southern California back to our Eastern origins. We were with two friends, native Californians who, we had learned to our astonishment, had never experienced New York or New England. This was in early October, and the Vermont foliage was coming into its full autumnal splendor.

In Woodstock, we saw a poster announcing that Princeton and Dartmouth would be playing football in Hanover, New Hampshire, that coming Saturday. We decided to go.

The day of the game barely dawned at all: lowering skies, pregnant storm clouds, no sun. Nevertheless, we drove over to New Hampshire, buying foul-weather gear at an Army-Navy store on the way.

The gods were with us, and the sky cleared spectacularly, leaving a few drifting clouds for dramatic effect. It was the sort of great football day I remembered from my youth: chilly, breezy, with those glorious gold and russet leaves swirling all over the ground. Our friends were delighted, and so, of course, were we. Hanover was gorgeous, Dartmouth proved to be quintessentially Ivy League—a refreshingly far cry from the mammoth UCLA—and I was relishing the anticipated casual elegance of an Ivy League football afternoon.

We took our seats on the visitors' side of the stadium, appreciating the crisp air and the fresh faces of the young men and women. In my day, there were no female students at Dartmouth or Princeton; I'm glad they're finally there.

Then, as the Princeton team came romping out onto the field, a classic picture of exuberant amateurism, a large portion of the Dartmouth freshman class started shouting in chorus "Princeton sucks! Princeton sucks!"

It was a depressing moment. Here were these 17- and 18-year-old boys and girls, just embarking on their higher education, shouting what struck us as an obscenity.

Later, I talked to young people of the approximate age of those Dartmouth freshmen, and I asked them about expressions like "Princeton sucks." It turns out that *sucks* isn't an obscenity at all to the younger generation. "Princeton sucks" is just about the same as "Princeton stinks."

Words do, indeed, change their meanings and their flavors, and what was unprintable and unsayable a few years ago is printed and said with some regularity this year.

In 1980, a play by Bill C. Davis called *Mass Appeal* opened in New York. It involves a middle-aged priest and a young seminarian. The seminarian prepares a sermon, and the priest criticizes it, at first referring to it as a "kick-ass" sermon. That's a phrase that would have shocked at least some members of a New York audience thirty-five years ago. The priest later tells the young seminarian "Mark, your sermon sucks."

I guess *sucks* has indeed taken on the connotation of *stinks*. Still, "Princeton sucks!" is a lousy thing for a bunch of kids to yell at a football game, and if I'd heard a bunch of Princeton freshmen yelling "Dartmouth sucks!"—as I am now reasonably certain they might—I'd have been embarrassed and a bit angry.

Language changes, and words that were once considered to be ultimately taboo are now out in the open. Cultured young ladies now freely use language that, thirty years ago, a young man would have been ostracized for using, had he done so in mixed company. I am ambivalent about this sort of thing.

The acceptability of certain words and phrases is dependent in large part upon social mores, and social mores are, in turn, influenced to a great degree by words and phrases. Vast numbers of people sincerely believe that many of the problems of the modern world—the high divorce rate, illegitimate births, abortions, prostitution, and crime in the streets—can be pegged directly to the Berkeley "free-speech" movement of the Sixties. That was actually less of a free-speech movement than an insistence upon students' rights to scream obscenities at anyone they disagreed with, drowning out the offending speech.

Some sort of release of the power of obscenity was inevitable, especially given the enormous social pressures of the Sixties. In some ways, that release has been welcome.

Remember the Hollywood films made during and about World War II in which, with bullets whining and crashing, bombs screaming and exploding, death and pandemonium everywhere, our G.I. Joes said things like "Heck!" and "Darn!"? To those of us who were in the service or, indeed, to anyone who knew anything at all about human behavior, this sort of dialogue was not simply laughable, it was embarrassing. I for one was delighted to see some of those absurd taboos fall.

I'm sure freshman classes will continue to captivate us older people at times and to infuriate us at others, not least in their use of language. I pray fervently that they will very quickly learn richer aspersions than "Princeton (or anyone) sucks!" That's just too infra dig.

Questions of Subject and Theme

1. When he records the central scene of his essay, Middleton says: "It was a depressing moment." Considering the essay as a whole, what was he

depressed about? Why did he feel that emotion and not another—resentment, say? Summarize the causes of his feeling in a sentence or two.

2. Middleton says that words depend on social mores, but that social mores are influenced by words. Does he take this point for granted or support it by argument or evidence in the essay? Explain your answer.

Questions of Method and Strategy

1. Of the changes in public speech by young people Middleton says: "I am ambivalent about this sort of thing." How does the organization of his essay work to support this assertion. Consider the organization of his sentences and paragraphs as well as of the essay as a whole.

2. Middleton ends his essay with a Latin tag meaning "beneath one's dignity." How does the style and content of this ending contribute to his argument as a whole?

VULGARITY MAY BE COMMON, BUT IT'S NOT OKAY

Ellen Goodman

> Ellen Goodman is a nationally syndicated columnist whose essays focus on the political implications of cultural events and issues. She has won the Pulitzer Prize for Commentary with essays like the following selection.

It is a miserable day on the planet, or at least on this part of it, and CBS begins the evening news with a report on the relentless cold. The camera homes in on a young, neat, specimen of the Chicago tundra. The man is asked his opinion of the winter wonderland and he answers cheerily: "It sucks."

My sentiments exactly. But not my language.

The next night, another of the cameras endlessly stalking Tonya Harding films her while she practices her routine. When she slips up, the camera zooms in.

You don't have to be a lip reader to recognize the outline of the word. S--t.

I don't flinch at this language. Nor do I purse my lips into some variation of "tsk, tsk."

Nevertheless, I am fascinated at what's happened to words. We seem to be in this fluid era where formerly dirty words are being washed clean. At the same time, formerly acceptable terms have become fighting words.

The traffic light of language, the signal that says what does and doesn't go in public, is operated by a button labeled "Offensive." Offensive language is usually given the red light.

For a long time there was a single standard of such words, a community threshold of sensitivity. But now the definition of what is offensive and who is offended changes as often as the venue.

Consider the anatomically correct speech that makes its way into the daily news. Remember when various male television anchors faced with reporting toxic-shock syndrome had to practice saying the word "tampons" into the mirror before they could get it out over the airwaves?

By the time the Bobbitt case ended, American journalists were talking and writing about penises with more clinical objectivity than even their seventh-grade hygiene teachers. And few people were offended.

We have also had multicultural revisions. I'm not talking about basic Farrakhan-speak. I'm talking about what is often hostilely described as politically correct speech. When The Los Angeles Times offered up some guidelines on ethnic, racial and gender terms last November they asked reporters to ask themselves: "Are they (these terms) likely to be considered offensive?"

Among those words the newspaper labeled most likely to be offensive were babe, Bible-thumper, bitch, crippled, dyke, gal, hick, Oriental and white trash.

But at the same time we're minding our p's and q's in one part of the media culture, we have Howard Stern, expletiving all over the radio and Snoop Doggy Dogg singing "For All My Niggaz and Bitches" on a CD.

Indeed it is entirely possible to find people who will not deign to speak or write of the Washington Redskins or the Cleveland Indians, but will feel perfectly comfortable telling you that the teams suck.

In general, I agree with anatomically correct speech. It would be absurd   15
to speak of John Bobbitt's "private parts," let alone his "peepee." Anatomy isn't vulgarity.

I also think it's correct—politically or otherwise—to be careful about the names we call people. Yes, some folks are too sensitive. On the other hand, I wish teen-agers who buy rap music were *more* sensitive.

I understand as well that sometimes we have to use words to discuss their use (see all of the above). And, yes, the weight of words changes. On the offensiveness scale they may move from felony to misdemeanor. The traffic signal changes from red to yellow, stop to slow. But does everything go?

Maybe those of us who still use words like "vulgar" should align ourselves as an ethnic group. Those of us who prefer that people keep their profanity private could declare ourselves offended. We could offer alternative sentences to the verbally impoverished.

As for the weather report and the state of the language: It's a bone-chilling, horrific, brain-numbing, ice-forming, seasonal-affecting-disordering sort of winter that makes a person long for global warming. But it doesn't s--k.

Questions of Subject and Theme

1. In her second paragraph Goodman says: "My sentiments exactly. But not my language." What distinctions does she make between these two categories in the rest of her essay?
2. Goodman says that "Anatomy isn't vulgarity." According to her essay as a whole, what *is* vulgarity, and how is it reflected in differing uses of language?

Questions of Method and Strategy

1. Goodman begins and ends by mentioning a weather report. What does this device contribute to the organization of her essay as a whole? What is the implicit argument of her ending?
2. Goodman says that "formerly dirty words are being washed clean" and that "formerly acceptable terms have become fighting words." Throughout the essay, where and how does she divide her attention between the two topics?

FOUR-LETTER WORDS CAN HURT YOU

Barbara Lawrence

Barbara Lawrence wrote this essay originally as an op-ed piece for the *New York Times*. She is a professor of language and literature at the State University of New York at Old Westbury, and has frequently written on questions of language for professional and general audiences.

Why should any words be called obscene? Don't they all describe natu-   *1*
ral human functions? Am I trying to tell them, my students demand, that the "strong, earthy, gut-honest"—or, if they are fans of Norman Mailer, the "rich, liberating, existential"—language they use to describe sexual activity isn't preferable to "phony-sounding, middle-class words like 'intercourse' and 'copulate'?" "Cop You Late!" they say with fancy inflections and gagging grimaces. "Now, what is *that* supposed to mean?"

Well, what is it supposed to mean? And why indeed should one group of words describing human functions and human organs be acceptable in ordinary conversation and another, describing presumably the same organs and functions, be tabooed—so much so, in fact, that some of these words still cannot appear in print in many parts of the English-speaking world?

The argument that these taboos exist only because of "sexual hangups" (middle-class, middle-age, feminist), or even that they are a result of class oppression (the contempt of the Norman conquerors for the language of their Anglo-Saxon serfs), ignores a much more likely explanation, it seems to me, and that is the sources and functions of the words themselves.

The best known of the tabooed sexual verbs, for example, comes from the German *ficken,* meaning "to strike"; combined, according to Partridge's etymological dictionary *Origins,* with the Latin sexual verb *futuere;* associated in turn with the Latin *fustis,* "a staff or cudgel"; the Celtic *buc,* "a point, hence to pierce"; the Irish *bot,* "the male member"; the Latin *battuere,* "to beat"; the Gaelic *batair,* "a cudgeller"; the Early Irish *bualaim,* "I strike"; and so forth. It is one of what etymologists sometimes call "the sadistic group of words for the man's part in copulation."

The brutality of this word, then, and its equivalents ("screw," "bang,"   *5*
etc.), is not an illusion of the middle class or a crotchet of Women's Liberation. In their origins and imagery these words carry undeniably painful, if not sadistic, implications, the object of which is almost always female. Consider, for example, what a "screw" actually does to the wood it penetrates; what a painful, even mutilating, activity this kind of analogy suggests. "Screw" is particularly interesting in this context, since the noun, according to Partridge, comes from words meaning "groove," "nut," "ditch," "breeding sow," "scrofula" and "swelling," while the verb, besides its explicit

imagery, has antecedent associations to "write on," "scratch," "scarify," and so forth—a revealing fusion of a mechanical or painful action with an obviously denigrated object.

Not all obscene words, of course, are as implicitly sadistic or denigrating to women as these, but all that I know seem to serve a similar purpose: to reduce the human organism (especially the female organism) and human functions (especially sexual and procreative) to their least organic, most mechanical dimension; to substitute a trivializing or deforming resemblance for the complex human reality of what is being described.

Tabooed male descriptives, when they are not openly denigrating to women, often serve to divorce a male organ or function from any significant interaction with the female. Take the word "testes," for example, suggesting "witnesses" (from the Latin *testis*) to the sexual and procreative strengths of the male organ; and the obscene counterpart of this word, which suggests little more than a mechanical shape. Or compare almost any of the "rich," "liberating" sexual verbs, so fashionable today among male writers, with that much-derided Latin word "copulate" ("to bind or join together") or even that Anglo-Saxon phrase (which seems to have had no trouble surviving the Norman Conquest) "make love."

How arrogantly self-involved the tabooed words seem in comparison to either of the other terms, and how contemptuous of the female partner. Understandably so, of course, if she is only a "skirt," a "broad," a "chick," a "pussycat" or a "piece." If she is, in other words, no more than her skirt, or what her skirt conceals; no more than a breeder, or the broadest part of her; no more than a piece of human being or a "piece of tail."

The most severely tabooed of all the female descriptives, incidentally, are those like a "piece of tail," which suggest (either explicitly or through antecedents) that there is no significant difference between the female channel through which we are all conceived and born and the anal outlet common to both sexes—a distinction that pornographers have always enjoyed obscuring.

This effort to deny women their biological identity, their individuality, their humanness, is such an important aspect of obscene language that one can only marvel at how seldom, in an era preoccupied with definitions of obscenity, this fact is brought to our attention. One problem, of course, is that many of the people in the best position to do this (critics, teachers, writers) are so reluctant today to admit that they are angered or shocked by obscenity. Bored, maybe, unimpressed, aesthetically displeased, but— no matter how brutal or denigrating the material—never angered, never shocked. *10*

And yet how eloquently angered, how piously shocked many of these same people become if denigrating language is used about any minority group other than women; if the obscenities are racial or ethnic, that is, rather than sexual. Words like "coon," "kike," "spic," "wop," after all, deform identity, deny individuality and humanness in almost exactly the same way that sexual vulgarisms and obscenities do.

No one that I know, least of all my students, would fail to question the values of a society whose literature and entertainment rested heavily on racial or ethnic pejoratives. Are the values of a society whose literature and entertainment rest as heavily as ours on sexual pejoratives any less questionable?

 Questions of Subject and Theme

1. In her second paragraph Lawrence asks the question that defines her topic. What arguments does she list in the course of her essay that propose answers to this question? Where does she herself stand with regard to each of these arguments?
2. Lawrence says that all obscene words serve a similar purpose. According to her, what is that purpose? In your view do her examples all support her claim? Explain your answer with examples.

 Questions of Method and Strategy

1. What general argumentative use does Lawrence make of her research into the histories of words? What particular argument does that research make in response to the "honest" versus "phony" distinction made by her students, as recorded in the first paragraph?
2. At the end of her essay Lawrence compares two kinds of pejorative language. How does that comparison support her earlier claims?

––––––––

Suggestions for Writing on the Juxtapositions

1. What is your position on the use of "vulgar" speech? Write an essay in which you defend your views, while taking into account (whether for support or refutation) the arguments you have read in this section.
2. It is notoriously difficult to discuss the issues presented here without awkwardness or embarrassment. In your view, which writer succeeds best in overcoming this difficulty? Write an essay defending your choice by comparing and contrasting evidence from all three essays.
3. Each writer makes a distinction between older and younger generations with regard to their assumptions about language. Write an essay in which you argue for or against this distinction, using evidence from your own experience as well as from your reading.
4. Lawrence does not analyze the particular word that the first two writers focus on. Write an essay on that word in which you make use of Lawrence's techniques of analysis to argue for or against its proper inclusion in public speech.

18   The Power of Naming

Itabari Njeri, "What's in a Name?"
Richard Crasta, "What's in a Name?"

Most people have a "given name," but what issues arise when you decide to choose your own or to "give" one to a child? Consider the following questions as you read two responses to Shakespeare's famous question.

1. Briefly summarize your sense of the answer each author gives to the question "What's in a name?"

2. Each of the authors is sometimes witty and sometimes serious about the topic of names. Pick an example of each mode from each author and discuss the similarities and differences with particular regard to how the combination of styles contributes to the advancement of the author's position on the issue.

3. Each writer records opposition from people who share his or her ancestry. How, if at all, does such opposition differ from that of people who represent the society to which the author now belongs? Explain your answer with examples.

4. Compare and contrast the concerns with naming raised by these two authors to those raised by Anna Quindlen's essay "The Name Is Mine" earlier in the book. Which author here is most like Quindlen in her attitude toward social pressure?

WHAT'S IN A NAME?

Itabari Njeri

Itabari Njeri has worked as a reporter for the *Miami Herald* and for the *Los Angeles Times*. She won a National Book Award for the family memoir, *Every Goodbye Ain't Gone,* from which the following selection is taken.

The decade was about to end when I started by first newspaper job. The seventies might have been the disco generation for some, but it was a continuation of the Black Power, post–civil rights era for me. Of course in some parts of America it was still the pre–civil rights era. And that was the part of America I wanted to explore. As a good reporter I needed a sense of the whole country, not just the provincial Northeast Corridor in which I was raised.

I headed for Greenville ("Pearl of the Piedmont"), South Carolina.

"*Wheeere,*" some people snarled, their nostrils twitching, their mouths twisted so their top lips went slightly to the right, the bottom ones way down and to the left, "did you get *that* name from?"

Itabiddy, Etabeedy. Etabeeree. Eat a berry. Mata Hari. Theda Bara. And one secretary in the office of the Greenville Urban League told her employer: "It's Ms. Idi Amin."

Then, and now, there are a whole bunch of people who greet me with: "Hi, Ita." They think "Bari" is my last name. Even when they don't, they still want to call me "Ita." When I tell them my first name is Itabari, they say, "Well, what do people call you for short?"

"They don't call me anything for short," I say. "The name is Itabari."

Sophisticated white people, upon hearing my name, approach me as would a cultural anthropologist finding a piece of exotica right in his own living room. This happens a lot, still, at cocktail parties.

"Oh, what an unusual and beautiful name. Where are you from?"

"Brooklyn," I say. I can see the disappointment in their eyes. Just another home-grown Negro.

Then there are other white people who, having heard my decidedly northeastern accent, will simply say, "What a lovely name," and smile knowingly, indicating that they saw *Roots* and understand.

Then there are others, black and white, who for different reasons take me through this number:

"What's your *real* name?"

"Itabari Njeri is my real, legal name," I explain.

"Okay, what's your *original* name?" they ask, often with eyes rolling, exasperation in their voices.

After Malcolm X, Muhammad Ali, Kareem Abdul-Jabbar, Ntozake *15*
Shange, and Kunta Kinte, who, I ask, should be exasperated by this
question-and-answer game?

Nevertheless, I explain, "Because of slavery, black people in the Western
world don't usually know their original names. What you really want to
know is what my slave name was."

Now this is where things get tense. Four hundred years of bitter history,
culture, and politics between blacks and whites in America is evoked by this
one term, "slave name."

Some white people wince when they hear the phrase, pained and embarrassed by this reminder of their ancestors' inhumanity. Further, they
quickly scrutinize me and conclude that mine was a post–Emancipation
Proclamation birth. "You were never a slave."

I used to be reluctant to tell people my slave name unless I surmised that
they wouldn't impose their cultural values on me and refuse to use my African name. I don't care anymore. When I changed my name, I changed my
life, and I've been Itabari for more years now than I was Jill. Nonetheless,
people will say: "Well, that's your *real* name, you were born in America and
that's what I am going to call you." My mother tried a variation of this on
me when I legalized my traditional African name. I respectfully made it clear
to her that I would not tolerate it. Her behavior, and subsequently her attitude, changed.

But many black folks remain just as skeptical of my name as my *20*
mother was.

"You're one of those black people who changed their name, huh," they
are likely to begin. "Well, I still got the old slave master's Irish name," said
one man named O'Hare at a party. This man's defensive tone was a reaction
to what I call the "blacker than thou" syndrome perpetrated by many black
nationalists in the sixties and seventies. Those who reclaimed their African
names made blacks who didn't do the same thing feel like Uncle Toms.

These so-called Uncle Toms couldn't figure out why they should use an
African name when they didn't know a thing about Africa. Besides, many of
them were proud of their names, no matter how they had come by them.
And it should be noted that after the Emancipation Proclamation in 1863,
four million black people changed their names, adopting surnames such as
Freeman, Freedman, and Liberty. They eagerly gave up names that slave
masters had imposed upon them as a way of identifying their human chattel.

Besides names that indicated their newly won freedom, blacks chose
common English names such as Jones, Scott, and Johnson. English was their
language. America was their home, and they wanted names that would allow
them to assimilate as easily as possible.

Of course, many of our European surnames belong to us by birthright.
We are the legal as well as "illegitimate" heirs to the names Jefferson, Franklin, Washington, et al., and in my own family, Lord.

Still, I consider most of these names to be by-products of slavery, if not *25* actual slave names. Had we not been enslaved, we would not have been cut off from our culture, lost our indigenous languages, and been compelled to use European names.

The loss of our African culture is a tragic fact of history, and the conflict it poses is a profound one that has divided blacks many times since Emancipation: Do we accept the loss and assimilate totally or do we try to reclaim our culture and synthesize it with our present reality?

A new generation of black people in America is reexamining the issues raised by the cultural nationalists and Pan-Africanists of the sixties and seventies: What are the cultural images that appropriately convey the "new" black aesthetic in literature and art?

The young Afro-American novelist Trey Ellis has asserted that the "New Black Aesthetic shamelessly borrows and reassembles across both race and class lines." It is not afraid to embrace the full implications of our hundreds of years in the New World. We are a new people who need not be tied to externally imposed or self-inflicted cultural parochialism. Had I understood that as a teenager, I might still be singing today.

Even the fundamental issue of identity and nomenclature, raised by Baraka and others twenty years ago, is back on the agenda: Are we to call ourselves blacks or African Americans?

In reality, it's an old debate. "Only with the founding of the American Colonization Society in 1816 did blacks recoil from using the term African in referring to themselves and their institutions," the noted historian and author Sterling Stuckey pointed out in an interview with me. They feared that using the term "African" would fuel white efforts to send them back to Africa. But they felt no white person had the right to send them back when they had slaved to build America.

Many black institutions retained their African identification, most notably the African Methodist Episcopal Church. Changes in black self-identification in America have come in cycles, usually reflecting the larger dynamics of domestic and international politics.

The period after World War II, said Stuckey, "culminating in the Cold War years of Roy Wilkins's leadership of the NAACP," was a time of "frenzied integrationism." And there was "no respectable black leader on the scene evincing any sort of interest in Africa—neither the NAACP or the Urban League."

This, he said, "was an example of historical discontinuity, the likes of which we, as a people, had not seen before." Prior to that, for more than a century and a half, black leaders were Pan-Africanists, including Frederick Douglass. "He recognized," said Stuckey, "that Africa was important and that somehow one had to redeem the motherland in order to be genuinely respected in the New World."

The Reverend Jesse Jackson has, of course, placed on the national agenda the importance of blacks in America restoring their cultural, historical, and political links with Africa.

But what does it really mean to be called an African American?

"Black" can be viewed as a more encompassing term, referring to all people of African descent. "Afro-American" and "African American" refer to a specific ethnic group. I use the terms interchangeably, depending on the context and the point I want to emphasize.

But I wonder: As the twenty-first century breathes down our necks—prodding us to wake up to the expanding mélange of ethnic groups immigrating in record numbers to the United States, inevitably intermarrying, and to realize the eventual reshaping of the nation's political imperatives in a newly multicultural society—will the term "African American" be as much of a racial and cultural obfuscation as the term "black"? In other words, will we be the only people, in a society moving toward cultural pluralism, viewed to have no history and no culture? Will we just be a color with a new name: African American?

Or will the term be—as I think it should—an ethnic label describing people with a shared culture who descended from Africans, were transformed in (as well as transformed) America, and are genetically intertwined with myriad other groups in the United States?

Such a definition reflects the historical reality and distances us from the fallacious, unscientific concept of separate races when there is only one: *Homo sapiens.*

But to comprehend what should be an obvious definition requires knowledge and a willingness to accept history. *40*

When James Baldwin wrote *Nobody Knows My Name,* the title was a metaphor—at the deepest level of the collective African-American psyche—for the blighting of black history and culture before the nadir of slavery and since.

The eradication or distortion of our place in world history and culture is most obvious in the popular media. Liz Taylor—and, for an earlier generation, Claudette Colbert—still represent what Cleopatra—a woman of color in a multiethnic society, dominated at various times by blacks—looks like.

And in American homes, thanks to reruns and cable, a new generation of black kids grow up believing that a simpleton shouting "Dy-no-mite!" is a genuine reflection of Afro-American culture, rather than a white Hollywood writer's stereotype.

More recently, *Coming to America,* starring Eddie Murphy as an African prince seeking a bride in the United States, depicted traditional African dancers in what amounted to a Las Vegas stage show, totally distorting the nature and beauty of real African dance. But with every burlesque-style pelvic thrust on the screen, I saw blacks in the audience burst into applause. They think that's African culture, too.

And what do Africans know of us, since blacks don't control the organs of communication that disseminate information about us? *45*

"No!" screamed the mother of a Kenyan man when he announced his engagement to an African-American woman who was a friend of mine. The mother said marry a European, marry a white American. But please, not one of those low-down, ignorant, drug-dealing, murderous black people she had seen in American movies. Ultimately, the mother prevailed.

In Tanzania, the travel agent looked at me indignantly. "Njeri, that's Kikuyu. What are you doing with an African name?" he demanded.

I'd been in Dar es Salaam about a month and had learned that Africans assess in a glance the ethnic origins of the people they meet.

Without a greeting, strangers on the street in Tanzania's capital would comment, "Oh, you're an Afro-American or West Indian."

"Both."

"I knew it," they'd respond, sometimes politely, sometimes not.

Or, people I got to know while in Africa would mention, "I know another half-caste like you." Then they would call in the "mixed-race" person and say, "Please meet Itabari Njeri." The darker-complected African, presumably of unmixed ancestry, would then smile and stare at us like we were animals in the zoo.

Of course, this "half-caste" (which I suppose is a term preferable to "mulatto," which I hate, and which every person who understands its derogatory meaning—"mule"—should never use) was usually the product of a mixed marriage, not generations of ethnic intermingling. And it was clear from most "half-castes" I met that they did not like being compared to so mongrelized and stigmatized a group as Afro-Americans.

I had minored in African studies in college, worked for years with Africans in the United States, and had no romantic illusions as to how I would be received in the motherland. I wasn't going back to find my roots. The only thing that shocked me in Tanzania was being called, with great disdain, a "white woman" by an African waiter. Even if the rest of the world didn't follow the practice, I then assumed everyone understood that any known or perceptible degree of African ancestry made one "black" in America by law and social custom.

But I was pleasantly surprised by the telephone call I received two minutes after I walked into my Dar es Salaam hotel room. It was the hotel operator. "Sister, welcome to Tanzania. . . . Please tell everyone in Harlem hello for us." The year was 1978, and people in Tanzania were wearing half-foot-high platform shoes and dancing to James Brown wherever I went.

Shortly before I left, I stood on a hill surrounded by a field of endless flowers in Arusha, near the border of Tanzania and Kenya. A toothless woman with a wide smile, a staff in her hand, and two young girls at her side, came toward me on a winding path. I spoke to her in fractured Swahili and she to me in broken English.

"I know you," she said smiling. "Wa-Negro." "Wa" is a prefix in Bantu languages meaning people. "You are from the lost tribe," she told me. "Welcome," she said, touching me, then walked down a hill that lay in the shadow of Mount Kilimanjaro.

I never told her my name, but when I told other Africans, they'd say: "*Emmmm,* Itabari. Too long. How about I just call you Ita."

50

55

Questions of Subject and Theme

1. Name the implicit and explicit arguments that the author makes for choosing her name.
2. Name the implicit and explicit arguments of those who question her choice. What implicit and explicit rejoinders does she offer them?

Questions of Method and Strategy

1. Compare and contrast the context in which a shortened name is used at the end of the essay to the context surrounding the same shortened name in the beginning. What effect does the repetition of the issue create? What implicit argument does the author make with the repetition?
2. The author interweaves personal narrative with a discussion of general issues. Pick an example of such interweaving and discuss the ways in which the personal and the general are related at that point.

WHAT'S IN A NAME?

Richard Crasta

As his essay makes clear, Richard Crasta was born in India. He has lived in the United States since 1980 and studied at American University and Columbia University. A freelance writer, Crasta has completed a novel entitled *The Revised Kama-Sutra*.

No wonder a newborn baby cries. It is hungry, naked, and—if it is an American—already owes the government $12,010.57, its approximate share of the U.S. national debt.

But if that baby happens to be, like mine, the American-born child of recent immigrant parents from Asia or Africa, it has all the more reason to cry, because its parents must face the genuine problem of whether to give the child a name from their old country or their new.

And until an adventurer named James M. Fail came along, the burden weighed even more heavily on me, a three-time father who had always regarded with utmost seriousness, with almost somber awe, the responsibility of naming a child.

Let me clarify. Though my name is Richard, I am, from my history to my abject dependence on regular injections of red pepper, a real Indian from the real India. Living in a part-Catholic, innocent corner of South India—the multiethnic town of Mangalore—I had always been proud of my name (Richard the Lionhearted was big in my childhood storybooks).

Of course, when I went to work in North India, I did encounter chauvinist people ignorant of the fact that Christianity, dating from the first century, was India's third most populous religion, and who implied, with exaggerated smiles and pseudo-British accents, that my name was not quite Indian. It was also at the time that Richard "Tricky Dick" Nixon was spreading his notoriety, and there were moments when my name was called out in public and I wanted to duck.

But when I came to the United States I decided I would, despite my history, give my child a name that was more recognizably "Indian."

And then, five years later, my first child, a son, was born.

Give him an American name, advised many of my friends (meaning, of course, give him an Anglo-European name), passionately. He'll have enough problems in school with his looks without an extra oral reminder to bring attention to them, without having to battle teasers and mispronouncers, without being scarred by it all for life. So said (among others) a white American father who had named his two adopted Korean girls Jacqueline and Susan.

I know what it is like to have a foreign face and an "American" name. Americans will often ask, when I introduce myself, "But what is your *real*, your *Indian* name?" Sometimes, peeved, I will answer with "Abdul the Bull Bull Abbasid"—something tongue-twisting—and I am amazed at how credulously most people will accept my Abdul bull.

On the other hand, I thought, any child born here is going to be an outright American no matter what name I give him. America is so addicting. Now, at age five, my son is already a perfect consumer of American television and its commercial offerings, parroting with an innocently straight face their sale pitches as infallible fact. Unless we move back to India before he reaches the age of unreason (between seven and seventeen)—that is, well beyond the age of sweet unreason—he is unlikely ever to choose to adopt his parents' country. So why not leave him some little stamp of his heritage—a little memory aid—an Indian name? So long as one doesn't go overboard with tongue-twisting ethnicity, calling one's children Mbongo Bow-wow or Mu Mu Zwbingli or Venkatagiri Pillaiswamy, isn't an ethnic name your vote (and your child's) for the principle and future of cultural diversity and well-exercised tongues in the America of the twentieth century?

But then, what is permanent about a name that my son could easily change when he grows up—as indeed adult immigrant Indians (and others) under the assault of massacred and mispronounced names are constantly doing in America—from Balwinder to Billy, from Subramaniam to Sam, from Saraswati to Sarah, from Krishna to Chris?

I have often, woolly-headedly, wished for a world where names and national origins didn't matter. Until then, however, we finally decided out of concern for our child's well-being and happiness to choose an "American" name.

At the time, I was under the spell of James Joyce's *Ulysses;* and Bertrand Russell had always been my kind of philosopher, passionate and caring, not cold and academic. And, moved by novelist Ralph Ellison's admission that his being named after Ralph Waldo Emerson had been the formative influence in his life, we named our son James Russell. But by the time of his christening party, a month later, his name was expanded, like the federal budget, to accommodate a variety of special and parochial interests, such as in-laws, Indian pride, and my sense of humorous resignation. The name on the cake read: James Russell Charles Ashok Prabhu Crasta.

That longer name was a christening party joke, of course, incorporating my original Indian surname of "Prabhu" and my favorite Indian king, the pacifist Ashoka. Still, my narrow, chauvinistic Indianness began to rebel at my choice of James Russell, and not in the least because a snooty friend of mine informed me that Russell had long ago been knocked out by Wittgenstein in the philosophical prize fights. When our next child arrived—another son—we went through whole lists of Indian names looking for possible cruel tricks that might be played by teasers ("Anil" was mercilessly ruled out), gleefully striking out the names of boys we had disliked in school. Finally, we were lucky to stumble upon Dev, not only a name we liked, but a name that, being almost identical to the American "Dave" in its

Indian pronunciation, passed with flying colors at the maternity ward's nurses' station.

Our third son was born in March—and with the gun of the hospital   15
bureaucracy at our heads, we quickly decided on the Indian name Rohan Arjun. Or so I thought, until I found out that my wife, still disoriented from the anesthetic and lack of sleep, had told the hospital people it was Rohit Zubin—one of ten finalists from our initial list of two hundred names.

For a while, this caused us some concern. Then we read about a man named James M. Fail who, despite his failure-prone last name, had *succeeded* wildly—having, with an absurd thousand-dollar personal investment (and the right connections), raked in a dizzying $1.8 billion in American government subsidies to build up a savings and loan empire. Wow! For a miserable fraction of that amount, a measly half-million, I'd be willing to change my name to Genghis H. Hoolamoola and still be so ecstatic that I'd spent half my remaining days lying on my back, wiggling my arms and legs in the air, and gurgling with pleasure like a baby just stuffed with infant formula. Hadn't I put myself through a lot of unnecessary agony?

But seriously, I realize that, with each child, I've become more confident and trusting of my heritage, more attached to my roots. Was it that, as I get more Americanized, more sucked into the Mass Society, I need to cling more strongly to the frail raft of my identity (however dubious in the first place)? Is it that, to take a statistical and mechanistic view of human behavior, I am just part of the current American trend of returning to ethnic names? Or maybe I have realized that Americans—especially the new Americans, the ones headed for the Twenty-first Century, are kinder and more tolerant than their detractors first made me believe. (And if they're not: tough luck!)

And so, the names are going to stay the way they are. If my family roster now sounds like a miniature United Nations, so be it.

And if the whole internal brouhaha was a personal sorting out of a personal identity crisis, its result is a small squeak of protest against those Indians who pretend that their name encapsulates the exclusive, inalienable essence of Indianness; who spit out your name at you; who preach internationalism, then practice cultural chauvinism; who say on the one hand that Hinduism is a way of life, an inclusive, absorptive, and tolerant religion, and on the other hand, dressed in tight pants and pointy shoes with Pantene heads, Mac Fast Foods burger in hand, speak amongst themselves with mild scorn of Indians with names different from their own. Once, I had seriously considered changing to a more "Indian" name, but had been stopped by the bureaucratic work. Now I ask, "What's in a name? A Narayana Nambudiri by any other name is often as ridiculous."

Questions of Subject and Theme

1. Describe the implicit and explicit arguments the author gives for favoring "American" names for his children. Describe the implicit and explicit arguments for favoring "Indian" names.

2. Describe the implicit and explicit arguments raised against both "American" and "Indian" names by other people in the author's life.

Questions of Method and Strategy

1. The author writes about his decisions in a style that is often serious and often lighthearted. Pick an example where one manner turns into the other and explain what point the author makes by the change.
2. At the end of the essay, the author plays on the phrase "A rose by any other name would smell as sweet." What argumentative point made by his essay as a whole does this pun seek to support?

Suggestions for Writing on the Juxtapositions

1. Where do you stand on the issue of your own name? Write an essay in which you explain your reasons for wanting to keep or to change your name.
2. Where do you stand on the issue of naming children? Write an essay that argues for your views on a parent's responsibility in naming a child.
3. In your opinion, which author makes the weakest case? Write an essay in which you show how and why the author's arguments fail in force for you.
4. The names we are known by are often outside not only our own control but also the control of our parents. Can we escape our nicknames? From your experience, pick two examples of nicknames, one derogatory and the other affectionate. Write an essay that analyzes the implicit powers present in the act of giving a nickname.

19 Two Visions of Freedom

Martin Luther King, Jr., "I Have a Dream"
Malcolm X, "The Ballot or the Bullet"

Two famous leaders of the civil rights movement give their historic visions of the way to bring racial equality to American society. Consider these questions in your reading:

1. While Martin Luther King, Jr., speaks of a dream, Malcolm X speaks of a nightmare. How do their styles reflect a dream and a nightmare, respectively?

2. Compare the attitudes of the two men toward government and the society it governs. How powerful is that government for good or ill? What are the powers of society? Can one change the other?

3. Each man repeatedly speaks of time, and each often uses words that refer to time. What kind of history does each implicitly assume? For example, is history seen as progress? As a fall from grace? A tragedy? Explain your answer with examples.

4. Each man speaks of violence and nonviolence. Compare and contrast each man's views on those issues.

I HAVE A DREAM

Martin Luther King, Jr.

Martin Luther King, Jr., delivered the following speech from the steps of the Lincoln Memorial in 1963 on the hundredth anniversary of the Emancipation Proclamation. He received the Nobel Peace Prize in 1964. Four years later he was assassinated in Memphis, Tennessee.

I am happy to join with you today in what will go down in history as *1* the greatest demonstration for freedom in the history of our nation.

Five score years ago, a great American, in whose symbolic shadow we stand today, signed the Emancipation Proclamation. This momentous decree came as a great beacon light of hope to millions of Negro slaves who had been seared in the flames of withering injustice. It came as a joyous daybreak to end the long night of their captivity. But one hundred years later, the Negro still is not free. One hundred years later, the life of the Negro is still sadly crippled by the manacles of segregation and the chains of discrimination. One hundred years later, the Negro lives on a lonely island of poverty in the midst of a vast ocean of material prosperity. One hundred years later, the Negro is still anguished in the corners of American society and finds himself in exile in his own land. And so we have come here today to dramatize a shameful condition.

In a sense we have come to our nation's capital to cash a check. When the architects of our republic wrote the magnificent words of the Constitution and the Declaration of Independence, they were signing a promissory note to which every American was to fall heir. This note was the promise that all men—yes, black men as well as white men—would be guaranteed the inalienable rights of life, liberty, and the pursuit of happiness.

It is obvious today that America has defaulted on this promissory note insofar as her citizens of color are concerned. Instead of honoring this sacred obligation, America has given the Negro people a bad check, a check which has come back marked "insufficient funds." But we refuse to believe that the bank of justice is bankrupt. We refuse to believe that there are insufficient funds in the great vaults of opportunity of this nation; and so we have come to cash this check, a check that will give us upon demand the riches of freedom and the security of justice.

We have also come to his hallowed spot to remind America of the fierce *5* urgency of *now.* This is no time to engage in the luxury of cooling off or to take the tranquilizing drug of gradualism. *Now* is the time to make real the promises of democracy. *Now* is the time to rise from the dark and desolate valley of segregation to the sunlit path of racial justice. *Now* is the time to lift our nation from the quicksands of racial injustice to the solid rock of brotherhood. *Now* is the time to make justice a reality for all of God's children.

It would be fatal for the nation to overlook the urgency of the moment. This sweltering summer of the Negro's legitimate discontent will not pass until there is an invigorating autumn of freedom and equality. Nineteen sixty-three is not an end, but a beginning. And those who hope that the Negro needed to blow off steam and will now be content will have a rude awakening if the nation returns to business as usual. There will be neither rest nor tranquility in America until the Negro is granted his citizenship rights. The whirlwinds of revolt will continue to shake the foundations of our nation until the bright day of justice emerges.

But there is something that I must say to my people who stand on the warm threshold which leads into the palace of justice. In the process of gaining our rightful place, we must not be guilty of wrongful deeds. Let us not seek to satisfy our thirst for freedom by drinking from the cup of bitterness and hatred. We must forever conduct our struggle on the high plane of dignity and discipline. We must not allow our creative protest to degenerate into physical violence. Again and again we must rise to the majestic heights of meeting physical force with soul force. And the marvelous new militancy which has engulfed the Negro community must not lead us to a distrust of all white people; for many of our white brothers, as evidenced by their presence here today, have come to realize that their destiny is tied up with our destiny, and they have come to realize that their freedom is inextricably bound to our freedom.

We cannot walk alone. And as we walk we must make the pledge that we shall always march ahead. We cannot turn back. There are those who are asking the devotees of civil rights, "When will you be satisfied?" We can never be satisfied as long as the Negro is the victim of the unspeakable horrors of police brutality. We can never be satisfied as long as our bodies, heavy with the fatigue of travel, cannot gain lodging in the motels of the highways and the hotels of the cities. We cannot be satisfied as long as the Negro's basic mobility is from a smaller ghetto to a larger one. We can never be satisfied as long as our children are stripped of their selfhood and robbed of their dignity by signs stating "For Whites Only." We cannot be satisfied as long as the Negro in Mississippi cannot vote and a Negro in New York believes he has nothing for which to vote. No, no, we are not satisfied, and we will not be satisfied until justice rolls down like waters and righteousness like a mighty stream.

I am not unmindful that some of you have come here out of great trials and tribulations. Some of you have come fresh from narrow jail cells. Some of you have come from areas where your quest for freedom left you battered by the storms of persecution and staggered by the winds of police brutality. You have been the veterans of creative suffering. Continue to work with the faith that unearned suffering is redemptive.

Go back to Mississippi, and go back to Alabama. Go back to South Carolina. Go back to Georgia. Go back to Louisiana. Go back to the slums and ghettos of our Northern cities, knowing that somehow this situation can and will be changed. Let us not wallow in the valley of despair.

10

I say to you today, my friends, even though we face the difficulties of today and tomorrow, I still have a dream. It is a dream deeply rooted in the American dream. I have a dream that one this nation will rise up and live out the true meaning of its creed: "We hold these truths to be self-evident, that all men are created equal." I have a dream that one day, on the red hills of Georgia, sons of former slaves and the sons of former slave owners will be able to sit down together at the table of brotherhood. I have a dream that one day even the state of Mississippi, a state sweltering with the heat of injustice, sweltering with the heat of oppression, will be transformed into an oasis of freedom and justice. I have a dream that my four little children will one day live in a nation where they will not be judged by the color of their skin, but by the content of their character.

I have a dream today. I have a dream that one day down in Alabama—with its vicious racists, with its governor's lips dripping with the words of interposition and nullification—one day right there in Alabama, little black boys and black girls will be able to join hands with little white boys and white girls as sisters and brothers.

I have a dream today. I have a dream that one day every valley shall be exalted and every hill and mountain shall be made low, the rough places will be made plain and the crooked places will be made straight, and the glory of the Lord shall be revealed, and all flesh shall see it together.

This is our hope. This is the faith that I go back to the South with. And with this faith we will be able to hew out of the mountain of despair a stone of hope. With this faith we will be able to transform the jangling discords of our nation into a beautiful symphony of brotherhood. With this faith we will be able to work together, to play together, to struggle together, to go to jail together, to stand up for freedom together, knowing that we will be free one day.

And this will be the day—this will be the day when all of God's children   *15* will be able to sing with new meaning:

> My country, 'tis of thee,
> Sweet land of liberty,
>   Of thee I sing;
> Land where my fathers died,
> Land of the Pilgrims' pride,
> From every mountainside
>   Let freedom ring.

And if America is to be a great nation, this must become true.

And so let freedom ring from the prodigious hilltops of New Hampshire. Let freedom ring from the mighty mountains of New York. Let freedom ring from the heightening Alleghenies of Pennsylvania. Let freedom ring from the snow-capped Rockies of Colorado. Let freedom ring from the curvaceous slopes of California.

Questions of Subject and Theme

1. Where and how does King appeal to patriotism as a method of criticizing his country? What kind of language expresses the patriotism? How, if at all, does it differ from the kind of language usually used in criticism?
2. Find a moment where King appeals to his audience's emotions. Name the emotions and describe the implicit argument they affirm.

Questions of Method and Strategy

1. King focuses on the past, the present, and the future. What proportion of his attention does he devote to each? In your opinion, what rationale controls this aspect of his organization?
2. King often repeats words or phrases. Pick an example and rewrite the passage without the repetition. Compare your result with the original and discuss the difference in effect.

THE BALLOT OR THE BULLET

Malcolm X

While in prison for burglary, Malcolm X (born Malcolm Little), taught himself to read and write and became a convert to Islam. He delivered the following speech early in 1964. Not quite a year later, he was assassinated in New York City.

If we don't do something real soon, I think you'll have to agree that we're going to be forced either to use the ballot or the bullet. It's one or the other in 1964. It isn't that time is running out—time has run out! 1964 threatens to be the most explosive year America has ever witnessed. The most explosive year. Why? It's also a political year. It's the year when all of the white politicians will be back in the so-called Negro community jiving you and me for some votes. The year when all of the white political crooks will be right back in your and my community with their false promises, building up our hopes for a letdown, with their trickery and their treachery, with their false promises which they don't intend to keep. As they nourish these dissatisfactions, it can only lead to one thing, an explosion; and now we have the type of black man on the scene in America today—I'm sorry, Brother Lomax—who just doesn't intend to turn the other cheek any longer.

Don't let anybody tell you anything about the odds are against you. If they draft you, they send you to Korea and make you face 800 million Chinese. If you can be brave over there, you can be brave right here. These odds aren't as great as those odds. And if you fight here, you will at least know what you're fighting for.

I'm not a politician, not even a student of politics; in fact, I'm not a student of much of anything. I'm not a Democrat, I'm not a Republican, and I don't even consider myself an American. If you and I were Americans, there'd be no problem. Those Hunkies that just got off the boat, they're already Americans; Polacks are already Americans; the Italian refugees are already Americans. Everything that came out of Europe, every blue-eyed thing, is already an American. And as long as you and I have been over here, we aren't Americans yet.

Well, I am one who doesn't believe in deluding myself. I'm not going to sit at your table and watch you eat, with nothing on my plate, and call myself a diner. Sitting at the table doesn't make you a diner, unless you eat some of what's on that plate. Being here in America doesn't make you an American. Being born here in America doesn't make you an American. Why, if birth made you American, you wouldn't need any legislation, you wouldn't need any amendments to the Constitution, you wouldn't be faced with civil-rights filibustering in Washington, D.C., right now. They don't have to pass civil-rights legislation to make a Polack an American.

No, I'm not an American. I'm one of the 22 million black people who   5
are the victims of Americanism. One of the 22 million black people who
are the victims of democracy, nothing but disguised hypocrisy. So, I'm not
standing here speaking to you as an American, or a patriot, or a flag-saluter,
or a flag-waver—no, not I. I'm speaking as a victim of this American system.
And I see America through the eyes of the victim. I don't see any American
dream; I see an American nightmare. . . .

Last but not least, I must say this concerning the great controversy over
rifles and shotguns. The only thing that I've ever said is that in areas where
the government has proven itself either unwilling or unable to defend the
lives and the property of Negroes, it's time for Negroes to defend themselves. Article number two of the constitutional amendments provides you
and me the right to own a rifle or a shotgun. It is constitutionally legal to
own a shotgun or a rifle. This doesn't mean you're going to get a rifle and
form battalions and go out looking for white folks, although you'd be within
your rights—I mean, you'd be justified; but that would be illegal and we
don't do anything illegal. If the white man doesn't want the black man buying rifles and shotguns, then let the government do its job. That's all. And
don't let the white man come to you and ask you what you think about what
Malcolm says—why, you old Uncle Tom. He would never ask you if you
thought you were going to say, "Amen!" No, he is making a Tom out
of you.

So, this doesn't mean forming rifle clubs and going out looking for
people, but it is time, in 1964, if you are a man, to let that man know. If
he's not going to do his job in running the government and providing you
and me with the protection that our taxes are supposed to be for, since he
spends all those billions for his defense budget, he certainly can't begrudge
you and me spending $12 or $15 for a single-shot, or double-action. I hope
you understand. Don't go out shooting people, but any time, brothers and
sisters, and especially the men in this audience—some of you wearing
Congressional Medals of Honor, with shoulders this wide, chests this big,
muscles that big—any time you and I sit around and read where they bomb
a church and murder in cold blood, not some grownups, but four little girls
while they were praying to the same god the white man taught them to pray
to, and you and I see the government go down and can't find who did it.

Why, this man—he can find Eichmann hiding down in Argentina
somewhere. Let two or three American soldiers, who are minding somebody else's business way over in South Vietnam, get killed, and he'll send
battleships, sticking his nose in their business. He wanted to send troops
down to Cuba and make them have what he calls free elections—this old
cracker who doesn't have free elections in his own country. No, if you never
see me another time in your life, if I die in the morning, I'll die saying one
thing: the ballot or the bullet, the ballot or the bullet.

If a Negro in 1964 has to sit around and wait for some cracker senator
to filibuster when it comes to the rights of black people, why, you and I

should hang our heads in shame. You talk about a march on Washington in 1963, you haven't seen anything. There's some more going down in '64. And this time they're not going like they went last year. They're not going singing "We Shall Overcome." They're not going with white friends. They're not going with placards already painted for them. They're not going with round-trip tickets. They're going with one-way tickets.

And if they don't want that non–nonviolent army going down there, tell   10 them to bring the filibuster to a halt. The black nationalists aren't going to wait. Lyndon B. Johnson is the head of the Democratic Party. If he's for civil rights, let him go into the Senate next week and declare himself. Let him go in there right now and declare himself. Let him go in there and denounce the Southern branch of his party. Let him go in there right now and take a moral stand—right now, not later. Tell him, don't wait until election time. If he waits too long, brothers and sisters, he will be responsible for letting a condition develop in this country which will create a climate that will bring seeds up out of the ground with vegetation on the end of them looking like something these people never dreamed of. In 1964, it's the ballot or the bullet. Thank you.

Questions of Subject and Theme

1. Where and how does Malcolm X appeal to the principles of the United States to criticize the country?
2. Malcolm X says, "If you and I were Americans, there'd be no problem." Explain the arguments made elsewhere that are summarized by this phrase.

Questions of Method and Strategy

1. This selection, like that by Dr. King, is taken from a speech. What evidence seems to point to its having been written for oral presentation?
2. What is the implicit argument made by the repetition of the key phrase "the ballot or the bullet?"

———

Suggestions for Writing on the Juxtapositions

1. Each writer makes arguments appealing to emotions and arguments appealing to rationality. Write an essay comparing and contrasting the ways in which each writer combines these methods.
2. In your view, what would each man say about the other's speech? Write an essay in which you give what you imagine as a rejoinder to one writer from the other.
3. What are your views on the violence versus nonviolence issue today? Write an essay that argues for your position, being sure to take into ac-

count, whether to refute or support him, the relevant arguments represented here.

4. Each writer talks about what it means to be an "American." What does
   it mean to you? Write an essay that argues for your definition, being sure
   to take into account the arguments of King and Malcolm X.

20   *Einstein's Brain*

Steven Levy, "My Search for Einstein's Brain"
Roland Barthes, "The Brain of Einstein"

How do other minds imagine Einstein's mind? An investigative reporter and a literary theorist come up with radically different answers. Compare the essays by considering the following questions:

1. How does his journalistic profession affect the questions that Levy asks and seeks to answer? How does Barthes's identity as a literary critic affect his mode of inquiry?

2. In your view does Levy believe in what Barthes calls a myth? Does he achieve "euphoric security" through paradoxes? Explain your answer with examples from each essay.

3. Barthes makes distinctions between the physical and the spiritual. Does Levy make such distinctions? Point to some examples and explain what each writer means by *brain*. Does the term include *mind*?

4. Compare Barthes's ideas about "myth" to those of Bruno Bettleheim in "Fairy Tale versus Myth" in an earlier section. How, if at all, do the two men agree in arguing what myth does? How, if at all, do they disagree?

MY SEARCH FOR EINSTEIN'S BRAIN

Steven Levy

As his essay makes clear, Steven Levy is an investigative reporter who brings excitement and energy to his investigations. With much of the spirit of a detective novel, he describes a quest that took him over much of the country and some twenty years back in time.

The mystery of the world is its comprehensibility.

—ALBERT EINSTEIN

Albert Einstein lived in Princeton. A small house, address 112 Mercer Street. He was a familiar figure in the town, usually walking around in a ragged sweater and tennis shoes, thin gray hair awry, thoughts entangled in a complex mathematical labyrinth. Children loved him; he would occasionally help them with their homework.

In 1955, he was working on a theory of gravitation that he would never perfect. He had turned down the presidency of Israel three years earlier, and was now involved in drafting a letter with Bertrand Russell imploring the nations of the world to abolish war. He was noted as the greatest thinker in the world. He had changed our conception of time and space. But at 76, his health was failing.

The doctors called it a hardened aorta. It leaked blood. He had known about the fault in his heart for several years. When first hearing that the artery might develop an aneurysm that could burst, he said, "Let it burst." On April 13, it looked as if it might.

His physician, Dr. Guy K. Dean, called in two consultants, and the three doctors concluded that unless surgery was attempted, the outlook was grim. The creator of the theory of relativity refused. On Friday, April 15, Einstein was persuaded to move his sickbed from Mercer Street to the Princeton Hospital.

During the weekend, things began to look better. Einstein's son, Hans Albert, flew in from California. His stepdaughter Margot was already in the hospital, being treated for a minor illness. On Sunday, it looked as if the aneurysm might heal temporarily. Dr. Dean took a look at his patient at eleven P.M. He was sleeping peacefully.

The nurse assigned to Einstein was named Alberta Roszel. After midnight, she noticed some troubled breathing in her patient. She went to get help. The bed was cranked up. Pale and emaciated, Albert Einstein was muttering something in German, a language Alberta Roszel did not understand. He took two deep breaths and died.

Princeton Hospital in 1955 was not the major facility it would become in later years. A major mobilization was needed to handle publicity on the occasion of the death of such a well-known international figure. Almost seven hours after the death, the hospital announced it and set up a news conference at 11:15. During the hours between the death and the release of details, the Einstein family, their friends, and the hospital officials worked in concert to deny the reporters then flooding to Princeton any scenes to witness, any physical evidence to describe to the millions who craved more than cold facts. Einstein had specifically asked that he not become the subject of a "personality cult." He did not want 112 Mercer Street to become a museum. He did not want his remains available to admirers making pilgrimages. His family shared his zeal for privacy. By the time the news conference began, an autopsy had been performed. The hospital pathologist, Dr. Thomas S. Harvey, had presided. He worked alone, under the eyes of Dr. Otto Nathan, a friend and colleague of the deceased who was the designated executor of the Einstein literary estate. For a period of time, Dr. Dean was also in the autopsy room. It was Dr. Dean who signed the death certificate. Official Cause: rupture of the arteriosclerotic. Birthplace: Ulm, Germany. Citizen of: U.S.A. Occupation: scientist.

If the assembled reporters hoped for any details of the autopsy, they were disappointed; they learned only the cause of Einstein's death. The body was not available for viewing. It was taken to the Mather Funeral Home in Princeton, where it sat for an hour and a half, until it was driven to the Ewing Crematory in Trenton. At four-thirty in the afternoon, the body was cremated. Later, Dr. Nathan took the ashes and dispersed them in a river, presumably the Delaware.

But part of the remains was spared. Einstein had requested his brain be removed for posthumous study, and his family bid it be done at the autopsy. It was placed in a jar. A *New York Times* reporter on April 20 wrote an article headlined "KEY SOUGHT IN EINSTEIN BRAIN." It talked of a study to be performed on the brain and the possible implications. The study, said the story, "may shed light on one of nature's greatest mysteries—the secret of genius." More details were to be released on how the study would be performed. Another press conference was scheduled for the following week.

The Einstein family was upset by the article and told the doctors entrusted with the brain that there was to be no publicity whatsoever concerning the study. The press conference never took place. Einstein's brain had gone into hiding.   10

"I want you to find Einstein's brain."

Of course I know who Albert Einstein was. I knew, like most people, about the theory of relativity, but could provide little detail. Something about e equaling mc², and something about atomic energy, and something about how time and space differed depending on your point of view. I knew it changed the world, and I knew that although it was responsible for nuclear weapons, the theory itself was a step forward, and Einstein was recognized as a humanitarian as well as a genius. I didn't know that his brain was still around.

Neither, really, did my editor. He had done some work on the subject of the brain and had wondered what had happened to this brain of brains, this organic masterpiece of gray matter and cerebral cortex. He had read the last pages of Ronald Clark's *Einstein: The Life and Times,* where the author says of Einstein, "He had insisted his brain be used for research . . ." and then drops the subject. And my editor had heard all sorts of rumors. Einstein's brain was lost. Einstein's brain was examined and found to be normal. Einstein's brain was examined and found to be extraordinary. Einstein's brain was hidden in a vault, frozen for cloning. And so on.

So the editor had written to Clark, asking him what happened to the brain. The author of Einstein's standard biography wrote back saying, "I'm afraid I don't know the answer, but have a recollection that it *was* preserved somewhere." He suggested contacting Otto Nathan, the executor of the Einstein estate. Nathan replied promptly. His one-paragraph letter confirmed that the brain had been removed before cremation, and stated that the pathologist in charge had been a Dr. Thomas Harvey. "As far as I know," Nathan concluded, "he is no longer with the hospital."

The letter was a year old. Now my editor wanted to know where the brain was. And he wanted me to find it.   15

"Sure," I said.

I had to wait a long time. Then a voice came over the phone. "Mr. Seligman will be right with you," it said. While someone in the hospital paged him, I read some more of a book explaining relativity. My reading habits had changed drastically. This was the third "layman's" book on Einstein's theories I had been through. In each book I did fine until the mathematical formulas, "easily handled by the average high school graduate," began a relentless progression of incremental obliqueness. I would plod onward, and though I didn't grasp the intricacies of relativity, I now at least misunderstood it clearly. I could see how Einstein convinced the scientific community that neither time nor space was absolute. According to my books, this applied chiefly to someone walking to the bathroom on a moving train while simultaneously comparing fixed points with a friend on a moving supersonic transport. Or, failing that, it would become obvious at speeds approaching the speed of light (the famous *c*), the velocity of some subatomic particles. It is only at these speeds that we can perceive that the universe is not as it seemed to Isaac Newton. It all sounds quite irrelevant until you consider that applications of the theory of relativity have given us everything from nuclear energy to laser beams and have helped explain many major astronomical discoveries in the past few decades. The brain I was looking for had changed our perception of the universe, and since Walter Seligman was a vice-president of the Princeton Medical Center, where the brain had been removed from the highly recognizable head of Albert Einstein, I hoped for a clue.

Finally, he reached a phone. "Yes, the operation took place here," he conceded. "But there are no records." He paused. "The only person who would know anything about it would be the pathologist who performed the operation. Doctor Thomas Harvey."

Where would Dr. Harvey be found?

"I'm afraid I don't know. He left here years ago."   20

Would your personnel department have any records?

"No. He moved several times since, I've heard. He's out of the state, I'm sure."

What about records of the autopsy itself? Exact time? Who worked there with Harvey? Which operating room? Anyone who might know if. . . .

"No. He was the only one working on it and he took all records with him. We have nothing on file here. All this, of course, was before my time."

It was before many of our times—it was twenty-three years ago. The   25 world was gloomy, worried about a cold war that threatened to heat into a nuclear disaster. No one was more concerned than Albert Einstein. All his life he had tried to nudge mankind toward a pacifist ideal. His efforts were inconstant because his pacifism was always subordinated to his physics; he knew it was by his mental labors that he could make his greatest contributions. So while he worked for peace, he worked harder at his formulas, even as his heart leaked blood and a blister on his aorta verged on a fatal rupture. During his short final stay in Princeton Hospital, he had requested pencil and paper to continue his calculations. With these he could work—"My brain is my laboratory," he once said.

And the whereabouts of his brain? God knows where. I had spent hours of library work and found items of negative value. The brain, it seemed, had been sectioned soon after his death (this I learned from the article that led Einstein's family to impose secrecy on the project), and would never be able to regain its original form. Pieces had still been under study as late as 1963 (this from a minor biography of Einstein). And, according to all available indices of scientific research, *nothing had been published concerning studies of Einstein's brain.* Nothing.

Reading about Einstein, and about the workings of the human brain, I began thinking about the subject more than was reasonable. I would create uneasy silences in editorial lunches by remarking how the timing of the Michelson-Morley experiments paved the way for Einstein's work on relativity. I carried on barroom seminars on the relation between brain size and human intelligence (little—scientists have found that a moron's brain can be larger than a genius's). I learned that current theories postulate that intelligence is probably a function of the speed with which electrical impulses jump through the synapses between the billions of cells in the brain, and that these impulses are triggered by enzymes in a process still not totally understood. I had no idea how quickly impulses had jumped through the gray matter of Albert Einstein. I wanted to know. Above all, I wanted my eyes to allow light to trigger off impulses in my optic nerve that would excite sensations in my own brain, and that through some magical process I hope we will never understand, these sensations would thrill me and edify me, seeing the brain that all brains aspire to.

My growing obsession distracted me. One night I drove to a friend's house in Princeton. The hour was late and I was two drinks silly. I missed a turn off Hodge Road, and somewhere along the line made a left, thinking it the right direction. It wasn't, so I made a U-turn. I felt an itchy discomfort as I veered toward town; checking a road sign I saw I was traveling on Mercer Street. In half a block, I saw it, a common white frame house, no different than any other of the common single houses on Mercer Street. Lights were on. I could see plants in the window. Einstein had lived here.

"You're looking for Einstein's brain?" said a coworker. "I have a friend who saw a picture of it."

What?   30

"She's a medical student in California. Her teacher had slides of it. Here's her number."

I called. The woman, it seemed, had not seen the slide, but had once been invited to by her instructor, a Dr. Moore. Supposedly he had in his possession slides that pictured Einstein's brain. She wasn't sure how he got them. She gave me his number.

Dr. Moore was willing to talk.

"I worked on the study of the brain," he said. "In Chicago. Sets of the section were sent to various experts for analysis. The man I was working for, Dr. Sidney Schulman, specialized in the thalamus, and we got portions of Einstein's thalamus, sectioned and stained for microscopic study."

The thalamus is a part of the brain which transmits impulses to the cere-   35
bral cortex.

"As far as the thalamus is concerned," said Dr. Moore, "Einstein's brain cells were like anyone else's at that age. If you showed the slides blind to someone, he would say that they came from any old man. Even so, I took Kodachromes of a couple slides to show to my students."

I wondered if Dr. Moore knew where the brain section came from and whether he knew of parts of the brain that might still be around.

"I'm not sure. I think the stuff we got was from some pathologist from Princeton."

Dr. Sidney Schulman seemed surprised that someone was calling him about Einstein's brain at this late date, and he told me to wait while he got his files. I hoped he wouldn't change his mind before he got back to the phone.

"I couldn't find the file," he said after a nearly interminable hiatus. "All   *40*
it really would have for you is the name of the pathologist who was doing
the study. He was the man who performed the autopsy on Einstein."

A Dr. Thomas Harvey?

"*That's* the name. He came to me soon after Einstein's death. He had
heard about my interest in the thalamus and had sent me some microscopic
slides with material from the brain. Later he visited me and took back the
slides. I did keep a few for my own use."

What came of the studies?

"Well, Dr. Harvey was interested in finding out if the brain varied from
the norm. Using the methods then available I found no variation. But the
problem was that methods used today weren't available back then. And even
if they were, they couldn't have been used in this case.

"You see, today studies like these are done with electron microscopes.   *45*
But they can only be used with samples fixed directly after removal from a
live body. In something like Einstein's case, the delay between death and
fixation (the use of a substance like formaldehyde) causes post-mortem
changes. Partially because of this, there *are* no established standards of nor-
mality in cells like these.

"Dr. Harvey wanted me to do a more intensive study, to count the cells
and cell types, but I didn't think it would be worthwhile. I suggested another
expert, a Dr. Kuhlenbeck of Philadelphia. I don't know whether he took
my advice."

Have you heard anything from Doctor Harvey? Do you know where
he is?

"No, I haven't heard from him since he took back the samples. And I
have never seen anything published. Do *you* know where to reach him?"

No, I didn't know where to reach him. But I had one last idea. Since
my man was a doctor, he must be a member of the American Medical Association. Surely they keep track of their members.

The AMA is headquartered in Chicago. They told me that they don't   *50*
give out members' whereabouts over the phone. But I'm a reporter on a
deadline, I insisted. They transferred me to several people before someone,
apparently exasperated enough to bend a regulation, asked me the name of
the person I sought.

I told her. A silence. Did I hear the rustling of pages while I waited?

"What's the middle initial? And how old would he be?" the woman
asked.

"S," I said. "And he'd be up in years by now."

"Well, there's a Thomas S. Harvey, born 1912, in Wichita, Kansas."

Wichita? So be it. But please, please, give me the number.   *55*

"We don't have a number," she said. "How about an address?"

Fine. As I wrote it down, I wondered—was this the address of Albert
Einstein's brain?

Since Dr. Harvey was the obvious key to my search, I was nervous before calling him. If he hung up on me, I would never see the brain. On the other hand, he might be very nice. We might have a pleasant conversation and he might tell me that he did study the brain, found nothing, and tossed the pieces into a Jiffy Bag. Or, just as bad, the man I called might not be the Dr. Harvey I sought. In the twenty-three years since taking out Albert Einstein's brain, Dr. Thomas S. Harvey might well have died and taken with him whatever secrets Einstein's brain held.

There was a tense pause when I asked the man who came to the phone whether he was the same Dr. Harvey who had worked at Princeton Hospital in the mid-1950s. Almost as if he had been considering a denial, he slowly said yes. I told him I was interested in Einstein's brain and I was willing to visit him to talk about it. I didn't mention the obsessive character my search had begun to take on.

He told me that there had been an agreement not to talk to anyone   60
about the study of the brain. He was sorry, but. . . .

I was more than sorry. I persisted, telling him about the impeccable reputation of my publication, and how the letter from Dr. Nathan giving Harvey's name (though not where to find him) was an implicit go-ahead from the Einstein estate. The doctor finally agreed to see me, on the condition that he not be bound to tell me any scientific information that might yet be published.

Throughout the conversation, Dr. Harvey had sounded very uncomfortable. I felt as if the wrong question would lead him to dismiss any idea of dealing with me. So I hadn't asked him some obvious questions. Like why nothing had been published. Like why the subject was still so touchy. Like whether he still had any of the brain in his possession.

These questions I would ask in Wichita.

As far as I can ascertain, Albert Einstein never visited Wichita during his three-quarters century of life. I quickly saw why. Kansas is about as appealing as a day-old wheat pancake. The Kansas headquarters for my search was the Wichita Plaza Holiday Inn, at twenty-six stories the tallest building in the state.

The twenty-fifth story housed the Penthouse Club. The view at mid-   65
night is not breathtaking—many streetlights illuminating vacant sidewalks. I was visiting the Penthouse Club as a new member—signing up was the requirement for buying a drink in Kansas, a "dry" state. Albert Einstein would not have appreciated that. He enjoyed a good glass of wine. When his doctors eventually forbade him his drink, he would sniff at a full glass and remark, in a tone of mock tragedy, that the sniff was the extent of the pleasures the medical establishment allowed him. They probably would have made him join the Penthouse Club to sniff wine in Wichita.

My wakeup call came at seven, two hours before my appointment with Dr. Harvey. It was a miserable morning, blackened by rainclouds that looked intent on dropping great volumes of water on Wichita. The torrent began about the time I started looking for a taxi to the residential area of town where Dr. Harvey worked as a medical supervisor in a bio-testing lab. In no time, the streets were pocked with puddles the size of bomb craters. The cabdriver thought nothing of nosing the taxi into one of these instant lakes. All I was concerned about was making my appointment. Especially if it meant finding Einstein's brain.

Only a few minutes late, I was met by Dr. Harvey. To get to his corner office, he ushered me through a maze of noisy computers and silent medical technicians working on blood and urine samples. He seemed a gentle man. His hair was gray, but there was spunk in his blue eyes. He wore a pastel shirt and patterned tie. In his shirt pocket was the kind of pen capable of writing three different colors. He smiled as we shook hands. He seemed somewhat embarrassed at the situation.

Some small talk disposed of, we got down to the subject I was yearning to discuss—Albert Einstein.

Dr. Harvey had met Einstein several times. He had been to Einstein's house to take samples for lab tests. "He was very informal and cordial," Dr. Harvey recalled. "A very kind sort of man."

Then came Einstein's fatal illness. It changed the life of Thomas Harvey, who had come to Princeton by way of Yale Medical School, Philadelphia General Hospital, and Pepper Laboratories. By virtue of his job as hospital pathologist, it was up to him to conduct the autopsy on Einstein and to take the brain out. And somehow it fell to him to conduct the study on this exceptional brain. 70

It made sense to appoint a regular hospital pathologist to make sure the task of studying the brain would be done properly—Harvey apparently was eager to take on a large project that could be, as he put it, "one of my major professional contributions." Harvey confirmed that it was luck that led him to conduct the study. "By being there, I felt that I had a responsibility to do an adequate and complete examination," he said in a friendly but nervous tone. He was still talking as if he expected some buzzer to ring and a voice from the heavens to boom down and say, "That's quite enough." But as he told the story of Einstein's brain, his voice took on confidence. At times, it took on a tone of awe.

What the reporters weren't told in 1955 was that Dr. Harvey was enlisting some brain experts to assist him in studying the most significant chunk of "gross material," as Harvey put it, ever to become available to medical science. Dr. Harvey himself had a special interest in neuropathology (the study of disorders of the nervous system), but he realized that he needed specialists to help him in his marathon task of searching for the clues to genius. One of the initial specialists he contacted was Dr. Harry Zimmerman in New York, and eventually he lined up Percival Bailey of Chicago and Hartwig Kuhlenbeck of Philadelphia. There were others, but Dr. Harvey was reluctant to give their names.

The first step in the process was an exacting measurement and complete photographing of the whole brain. This was done at Princeton Hospital, which had agreed to partially fund the study. From these measurements, there was apparently no difference between Einstein's brain and a "normal" one. Certainly it was no bigger, and at two and sixty-four hundredths pounds, it was no heavier. This was no surprise; the real work would take place in microscopic studies of the dissected brain.

So sometime in the early fall of 1955, Dr. Harvey packed up the brain of Albert Einstein, made sure it was well cushioned in its formaldehyde-filled jar, and drove—very, very carefully—from Princeton to Philadelphia, where the brain would be sectioned in a laboratory at the University of Pennsylvania.

"They had a big lab there," Dr. Harvey recalled. "They had equipment for sectioning whole brains, including a microtome used only for brain work. Those particular microtomes are very scarce, and special technicians are needed to operate them. Dr. Erich, who ran the laboratory, had such a technician, and though it took six months to do, we did a beautiful job of sectioning the brain."

From there, the sections of the brain, some in small chunks preserved in celloidin (a gelatinous material), some on microscopic slides, went off to various parts of the country to be studied by specialists. "I usually delivered the pieces myself," said Harvey. "It could have been handled by mail, I guess, but I wanted to meet these men."

The idea was that the specialists would eventually publish papers on the brain parts they studied. Meanwhile, Harvey would perform his own tests, some paralleling the other work and some that no one was duplicating.

"In order to do a study like this," said Dr. Harvey, "you have to have seen enough of the normal brain to have a pretty good idea what would be extraordinary. Unfortunately, not a lot of brains have been studied completely. Less than a dozen. Of course, when it comes to genius . . . not even that many. It really is a mammoth task. There's a tremendous number of cells in the brain. You don't examine every one of them in detail, but you look at an awful lot of sections. Almost all the brain now is in sections. There's a little left as brain tissue, but very little."

How little, I wondered to myself. And where was it? All this history had been fascinating, but I wanted to *view* the damn thing. Of course, you couldn't just bust in on a guy and demand to see a brain. Somehow I had to steer things toward the "gross material" itself. I asked Dr. Harvey if it might be possible to see . . . a slide, perhaps.

"I don't really have any slides here in this office," he said. "So I can't do it here."

Where are the slides? At your home?

"No, they're not there. . . ." He was shifting uncomfortably in his chair. "I really don't think it'll be of much help to you to see one of the slides. I can show you a slide of something else, to show you what they're *like* . . . as I say, I don't have any of the brain here."

My heart sank. "Is any of it in Wichita?" I asked.

"Um, yes. But not in the office here. Aren't you familiar with microscopic slides?"

"Yes, but—"

85

"Well, I don't want to say any more about it," he said with an air of finality.

Perhaps I could have accepted not seeing the brain if I knew that it didn't exist, or that it existed only in an unreachable place—like the ocean bottom. But to leave Wichita knowing that there might well be some brain to see? Unthinkable. Dr. Harvey noted my obvious dismay, and almost as a consolation asked me if I had any more questions about the study.

Well, all right. Why had things been taking so long?

"We had no urgency to publish. And the actual examination didn't take this long, of course. Though there is some work still to be done. You see, my career since I did the autopsy has been sort of interrupted. I left Princeton Hospital in 1960 and moved to Freehold. And for the past few years, I've been here in Wichita. I don't work on it as much as I used to. But we're getting closer to publication. I'd say we're perhaps a year away."

Has the study found the brain to be . . . different?

90

Dr. Harvey thought a bit before answering. "So far it's fallen within normal limits for a man his age. There are changes that occur within the brain with age. And his brain showed these. No more so than the average man. The anatomical variations," he said, "are within normal limits."

Another uneasy silence followed. Dr. Harvey shifted in his seat. He seemed to have something he wanted to say, but was agonizing whether to voice it or not.

"Do you have a *photograph* of it here?" I blurted out.

"No, I don't," he said. "I don't have any material here." Then he paused. A shy grin came over his face. "I *do* have a little bit of the gross here," he said, almost apologetically.

Pardon?

95

"Gross material. Unsectioned. But that's all."

Here? *In this office we're sitting in?*

I looked around. Dr. Harvey was sitting across from me, behind a large desk piled with papers and magazines. On one side of the room was a bookshelf brimming with books and journals; on the other, a small clutter of cardboard boxes and a cooler one might take on a fishing trip. Certainly no temperature-controlled vaults such as I imagined would hold such a scientific treasure.

Without another word, Dr. Harvey rose from his seat and walked around the desk, crossing in front of me to get to the corner of the room. He bent down over the clutter on the floor, stopping at the red plastic cooler. He picked it up and put it on a chair next to me. It didn't fit between the arms of the chair. Moving slowly, he placed it on the floor.

Einstein's brain in a beer cooler?

100

No. He turned away from the cooler, going back to the corner. Of the two cardboard boxes stacked there, he picked up the top one and moved it to the side. Then he bent down over the bottom box, which had a logo reading COSTA CIDER on the side. There was no top to the box, and it looked filled with crumpled newspapers. Harvey, still wearing a sheepish grin, thrust his hand into the newspapers and emerged with a large mason jar. Floating inside the jar, in a clear liquid solution, were several pieces of matter. A conch shell–shaped mass of wrinkly material the color of clay after kiln firing. A fist-sized chunk of grayish, lined substance, the apparent consistency of sponge. And in a separate pouch, a mass of pinkish-white strings resembling bloated dental floss. All the material was recognizably brain matter.

Dr. Harvey pointed out that the conch-shaped mass was Einstein's cerebellum, the gray blob a chunk of cerebral cortex, and the stringy stuff a group of aortic vessels.

"It's all in sections, except for this," he said. I had risen up to look into the jar, but now I was sunk in my chair, speechless. My eyes were fixed upon that jar as I tried to comprehend that these pieces of gunk bobbing up and down had caused a revolution in physics and quite possibly changed the course of civilization. *There it was!* Before I could regain my wits, Dr. Harvey had reached back into the box for another jar. This one was larger, and since it was not a mason jar, the top had been fixed in place by yellowed masking tape. Inside it were dozens of rectangular translucent blocks, the size of Goldenberg's Peanut Chews, each with a little sticker reading CEREBRAL CORTEX and bearing a number. Encased in every block was a shriveled blob of gray matter.

Dr. Harvey explained the fixative process, and told me what part of the brain the chunks were from. Not a word penetrated my own gray cells. I made no objection as he placed the jars back in the newspaper-filled cider box and moved the cooler back to its original position. Doctor Harvey didn't know it, but I had accomplished my mission. I was too stunned, though, for self-congratulation. We made some more perfunctory conversation, he said he was sorry he couldn't show me his laboratory or give me scientific data, and he offered to write to Dr. Nathan of Einstein's estate to see if I could be authorized to receive some more information. I nodded, but my heart was not in it. Having seen the object of my search, the scientific details seemed superfluous.

A few weeks later, writing this, the scientific details do not seem so superfluous. It would be nice to know all the scientists who worked with Dr. Harvey. It would be nice to know the exact nature of the tests performed on the brain. It would be nice to know if there were any technical qualifiers to Dr. Harvey's generalization that, as of now, it looks as if Einstein's brain is essentially no different from that of a nongenius. But for that, we'll have to wait the year or so that Dr. Harvey said remains between now and the publication of the study that's been twenty-three years in the making.

When Dr. Harvey contacted Otto Nathan about giving me the scientific information, Nathan apparently became upset that Harvey had talked to me at all—I had penetrated a secret that the Einstein trust wished preserved.

All along, I had feared that if I ever did get to see Einstein's brain, the experience would be a terrific letdown. I had suspected that the inevitable lifelessness of the material would make looking at the brain matter as interesting as viewing a dead jellyfish. My fears were unjustified. For a moment, with the brain before me, I had been granted a rare peek into an organic crystal ball. Swirling in formaldehyde was the power of the smashed atom, the mystery of the universe's black holes, the utter miracle of human achievement.

I could see why the effects of Einstein before his death, and of his family and estate afterwards, had been directed toward keeping the brain out of the limelight. It was powerful, capable of refocusing attention on the mystical aspects of Einstein that his family always tried to understate. But as much as a family has a right to privacy, I think a case can be made for discarding the shroud that surrounds this "gross material." Whether you see it or merely contemplate it, there is something very awesome in the post-mortem remains of Albert Einstein's brain. It is something of ourselves at our best, or something of what we humans can be—using our own awesome powers to work out the relation between ourselves and our surroundings. The fact that twenty-three years of study indicate that Einstein's brain is physiologically no different from yours or mine seems to bear this out. "God does not play dice with the Universe," Albert Einstein liked to say, and he spent the bulk of his life trying to prove it. I think that he would be happy to find that, with no better a roll than most of us, he managed to beat the house. What we do with our own dice rolls is up to us, and not chance. There are no better lessons to extract from Albert Einstein's brain.

Questions of Subject and Theme

1. What is it that Levy says he seeks in trying to find Einstein's brain? Find a passage where he states his goal and rewrite it in your own words.
2. Toward the end of his essay Levy says: "Having seen the object of my search, the scientific details seemed superfluous." What happened to him when he saw parts of the brain? Why are scientific details now superfluous?

Questions of Method and Strategy

1. Levy tells the story of his quest with a beginning, a middle, and an end. Where would you divide these parts? What do you think are the advantages of the division?

2. Toward the end of his essay, Levy says: "I had penetrated a secret that the Einstein trust wished preserved." What implicit arguments about "secrets" does Levy depend on here? What does he expect his reader to agree with?

THE BRAIN OF EINSTEIN

Roland Barthes

Roland Barthes was a leading intellectual in France until his accidental death in 1980. As his essay shows, he brought some of the skills of literary criticism to the investigation of popular culture and much of the excitement of popular culture to literary criticism. This section is from a collection of brief essays called *Mythologies*.

Einstein's brain is a mythical object: paradoxically, the greatest intelligence of all provides an image of the most up-to-date machine, the man who is too powerful is removed from psychology, and introduced into a world of robots; as is well known, the supermen of science-fiction always have something reified about them. So has Einstein: he is commonly signified by his brain, which is like an object for anthologies, a true museum exhibit. Perhaps because of his mathematical specialization, superman is here divested of every magical character; no diffuse power in him, no mystery other than mechanical: he is a superior, a prodigious organ, but a real, even a physiological one. Mythologically, Einstein is matter, his power does not spontaneously draw one towards the spiritual, it needs the help of an independent morality, a reminder about the scientist's 'conscience' (*Science without conscience,* they said . . .).

Einstein himself has to some extent been a party to the legend by bequeathing his brain, for the possession of which two hospitals are still fighting as if it were an unusual piece of machinery which it will at last be possible to dismantle. A photograph shows him lying down, his head bristling with electric wires: the waves of his brain are being recorded, while he is requested to 'think of relativity'. (But for that matter, what does 'to think of' mean, exactly?) What this is meant to convey is probably that the seismograms will be all the more violent since 'relativity' is an arduous subject. Thought itself is thus represented as an energetic material, the measurable product of a complex (quasi-electrical) apparatus which transforms cerebral substance into power. The mythology of Einstein shows him as a genius so lacking in magic that one speaks about his thought as of a functional labour analogous to the mechanical making of sausages, the grinding of corn or the crushing of ore: he used to produce thought, continuously, as a mill makes flour, and death was above all, for him, the cessation of a localized function: '*the most powerful brain of all has stopped thinking*'.

What this machine of genius was supposed to produce was equations. Through the mythology of Einstein, the world blissfully regained the image of knowledge reduced to a formula. Paradoxically, the more the genius of the man was materialized under the guise of his brain, the more the product of his inventiveness came to acquire a magical dimension, and gave a new incarnation to the old esoteric image of a science entirely contained in a few letters. There is a single secret to the world, and this secret is held in one word; the universe is a safe of which humanity seeks the combination: Einstein almost found it, this is the myth of Einstein. In it, we find all the Gnostic themes: the unity of nature, the ideal possibility of a fundamental reduction of the world, the unfastening power of the word, the age-old struggle between a secret and an utterance, the idea that total knowledge can only be discovered all at once, like a lock which suddenly opens after a thousand unsuccessful attempts. The historic equation $E = mc^2$, by its unexpected simplicity,, almost embodies the pure idea of the key, bare, linear, made of one metal, opening with a wholly magical ease a door which had resisted the desperate efforts of centuries. Popular imagery faithfully expresses this: *photographs* of Einstein show him standing next to a blackboard covered with mathematical signs of obvious complexity; but *cartoons* of Einstein (the sign that he has become a legend) show him chalk still in hand, and having just written on an empty blackboard, as if without preparation, the magic formula of the world. In this way mythology shows an awareness of the nature of the various tasks: research proper brings into play clockwork-like mechanisms and has its seat in a wholly material organ which is monstrous only by its cybernetic complication; discovery, on the contrary, has a magical essence, it is simple like a basic element, a principial substance, like the philosophers' stone of hermetists, tar-water for Berkeley, or oxygen for Schelling.

But since the world is still going on, since research is proliferating, and on the other hand since God's share must be preserved, some failure on the part of Einstein is necessary: Einstein died, it is said, without having been able to verify '*the equation in which the secret of the world was enclosed*'. So in the end the world resisted; hardly opened, the secret closed again, the code was incomplete. In this way Einstein fulfils all the conditions of myth, which could not care less about contradictions so long as it establishes a euphoric security: at once magician and machine, eternal researcher and unfulfilled discoverer, unleashing the best and the worst, brain and conscience. Einstein embodies the most contradictory dreams, and mythically reconciles the infinite power of man over nature with the 'fatality' of the sacrosanct, which man cannot yet do without.

Questions of Subject and Theme

1. In his first sentence, Barthes mentions a paradox. Explain what is paradoxical about it and what Barthes's view of the paradox is.
2. In his last paragraph Barthes says that myths provide "euphoric security." According to the essay as a whole, what security does the "myth" of Einstein's brain provide for those who believe in that myth? Why is the security "euphoric?"

Questions of Method and Strategy

1. Starting with one paradox, Barthes goes on to point to several others in his essay. Make a list of the paradoxes and describe how they are related to one another and to Barthes's idea of "myth."
2. In your view, what is Barthes's main point about myth? Does he argue that it is foolish? Bad? Necessary? Explain his position as clearly as you can, and show how it becomes clear through examples.

Suggestions for Writing on the Juxtapositions

1. Levy says he searched for a secret. In this third paragraph Barthes claims that part of the myth of Einstein is "the age-old struggle between a secret and an utterance." Write an essay in which you argue that Levy's essay does or does not enact this and other aspects of what Barthes calls the myth of Einstein.
2. In your opinion, which writer most fully understands the relation of the spiritual and the physical aspects of Einstein's brain? Write an essay in which you argue for the justice of your view, being sure to take into account the views of both essayists.
3. In his third paragraph Barthes speaks of "the image of knowledge reduced to a formula." What are some other "formulas," whether scientific or otherwise, that seem to you to operate in the same way? "You can't turn back the clock," for example, or the "law" of gravity. Write an essay in which you argue that your formula does or does not fit Barthes's definition of myth.
4. What relation of Einstein to the Atomic Bomb does each writer see? Do you think Einstein should have contributed to its development? Write an essay in which you argue for the proper relations between scientific research and morality.

21 When the Earth Shook

William James, "On Some Mental Effects of the
  Earthquake"

Susanna Styron, "Risk Management: Men versus
  Women in the L.A. Earthquake"

Isak Dinesen, "The Earthquake"

In the following selections three major earthquakes raise related but differing issues for the writers who experience them. As you read, consider the following questions:

1. For both William James and Isak Dinesen the major emotions that an earthquake awakes are quite positive. How do they differ from one another in their responses, and how do they each differ from the responses of Susanna Styron? How do you imagine you would respond?

2. William James notices that he immediately personified his earthquake, thinking of it as if it were alive. What other people within the readings do as James does? What more "scientific" views do still others adopt toward the phenomenon?

3. In what ways does Styron's analysis of differences between men and women seem supported by the other readings? In what ways do they not? Explain with examples.

4. William James reports that "seriousness" was the most apparent general characteristic of the survivors. Does this seriousness also seem characteristic of the three writers in this section? Compare and contrast the ways in which each does or does not convey the seriousness with which he or she responds to the experience of an earthquake.

ON SOME MENTAL EFFECTS
OF THE EARTHQUAKE[1]

William James

> Brother of the novelist Henry James, William James became fa-
> mous as a psychologist and philosopher at Harvard in the late nine-
> teenth and early twentieth centuries. While visiting the West in 1906,
> he was a witness to the great San Francisco earthquake and immedi-
> ately turned his experiences into an occasion for psychological and
> philosophical research.

When I departed from Harvard for Stanford University last December,
almost the last good-by I got was that of my old Californian friend B: "I
hope they'll give you a touch of earthquake while you're there, so that you
may also become acquainted with *that* Californian institution."

Accordingly, when, lying awake at about half past five on the morning
of April 18 in my little "flat" on the campus of Stanford, I felt the bed begin
to waggle, my first consciousness was one of gleeful recognition of the nature of the movement. "By Jove," I said to myself, "here's B's old earthquake, after all!" And then, as it went *crescendo,* "And a jolly good one it is,
too!" I said.

Sitting up involuntarily, and taking a kneeling position, I was thrown
down on my face as it went *fortior* shaking the room exactly as a terrier shakes
a rat. Then everything that was on anything else slid off to the floor, over
went bureau and chiffonier with a crash, as the *fortissimo* was reached; plaster
cracked, an awful roaring noise seemed to fill the outer air, and in an instant
all was still again, save the soft babble of human voices from far and near that
soon began to make itself heard, as the inhabitants in costumes *négligés* in
various degrees sought the greater safety of the street and yielded to the
passionate desire for sympathetic communication.

The thing was over, as I understand the Lick Observatory to have declared, in forty-eight seconds. To me it felt as if about that length of time,
although I have heard others say that it seemed to them longer. In my case,
sensation and emotion were so strong that little thought, and no reflection
or volition, were possible in the short time consumed by the phenomenon.

The emotion consisted wholly of glee and admiration; glee at the vividness which such an abstract idea or verbal term as "earthquake" could put
on when translated into sensible reality and verified concretely; and admi-

---

1. At the time of the San Francisco earthquake the author was at Leland Stanford University
nearby. He succeeded in getting into San Francisco on the morning of the earthquake, and
spent the remainder of the day in the city. These observations appeared in the *Youth's Companion* for June 7, 1906.

ration at the way in which the frail little wooden house could hold itself together in spite of such a shaking. I felt no trace whatever of fear; it was pure delight and welcome.

"*Go it*," I almost cried aloud, "and go it *stronger!*"

I ran into my wife's room, and found that she, although awakened from sound sleep, had felt no fear, either. Of all the persons whom I later interrogated, very few had felt any fear while the shaking lasted, although many had had a "turn," as they realized their narrow escapes from bookcases or bricks from chimney-breasts falling on their beds and pillows an instant after they had left them.

As soon as I could think, I discerned retrospectively certain peculiar ways in which my consciousness had taken in the phenomenon. These ways were quite spontaneous, and, so to speak, inevitable and irresistible.

First, I personified the earthquake as a permanent individual entity. It was *the* earthquake of my friend B's augury, which had been lying low and holding itself back during all the intervening months, in order, on that lustrous April morning, to invade my room, and energize the more intensely and triumphantly. It came, moreover, directly to *me*. It stole in behind my back, and once inside the room, had me all to itself, and could manifest itself convincingly. Animus and intent were never more present in any human action, nor did any human activity ever more definitely point back to a living agent as its source and origin.

All whom I consulted on the point agreed as to this feature in their experience. "It expressed intention," "It was vicious," "It was bent on destruction," "It wanted to show its power," or what not. To me, it wanted simply to manifest the full meaning of its *name*. But what was this "It"? To some, apparently, a vague demonic power; to me an individualized being, B's earthquake, namely.

One informant interpreted it as the end of the world and the beginning of the final judgment. This was a lady in a San Francisco hotel, who did not think of its being an earthquake till after she had got into the street and some one had explained it to her. She told me that the theological interpretation had kept fear from her mind, and made her take the shaking calmly. For "science," when the tensions of the earth's crust reach the breaking-point, and strata fall into an altered equilibrium, earthquake is simply the collective *name* of all the cracks and shakings and disturbances that happen. They *are* the earthquake. But for me *the* earthquake was the *cause* of the disturbances, and the perception of it as a living agent was irresistible. It had an overpowering dramatic convincingness.

I realize now better than ever how inevitable were men's earlier mythologic versions of such catastrophes, and how artificial and against the grain of our spontaneous perceiving are the later habits into which science educates us. It was simply impossible for untutored men to take earthquakes into their minds as anything but supernatural warnings or retributions.

A good instance of the way in which the tremendousness of a catastrophe may banish fear was given me by a Stanford student. He was in the fourth story of Encina Hall, an immense stone dormitory building. Awakened from sleep, he recognized what the disturbance was, and sprang from the bed, but was thrown off his feet in a moment, while his books and furniture fell round him. Then, with an awful, sinister, grinding roar, everything gave way, and with chimneys, floor-beams, walls and all, he descended through the three lower stories of the building into the basement. "This is my end, this is my death," he felt; but all the while no trace of fear. The experience was too overwhelming for anything but passive surrender to it. (Certain heavy chimneys had fallen in, carrying the whole centre of the building with them.)

Arrived at the bottom, he found himself with rafters and *débris* round him, but not pinned in or crushed. He saw daylight, and crept toward it through the obstacles. Then, realizing that he was in his nightgown, and feeling no pain anywhere, his first thought was to get back to his room and find some more presentable clothing. The stairways at Encina Hall are at the ends of the building. He made his way to one of them, and went up the four flights, only to find his room no longer extant. Then he noticed pain in his feet, which had been injured, and came down the stairs with difficulty. When he talked with me ten days later he had been in hospital a week, was very thin and pale, and went on crutches, and was dressed in borrowed clothing.

So much for Stanford, where all our experiences seem to have been very similar. Nearly all our chimneys went down, some of them disintegrating from top to bottom; parlor floors were covered with bricks; plaster strewed the floors; furniture was everywhere upset and dislocated; but the wooden dwellings sprang back to their original position, and in house after house not a window stuck or a door scraped at top or bottom. Wood architecture was triumphant! Everybody was excited, but the excitement at first, at any rate, seemed to be almost joyous. Here at last was a *real* earthquake after so many years of harmless waggle! Above all, there was an irresistible desire to talk about it, and exchange experiences.

Most people slept outdoors for several subsequent nights, partly to be safer in case of a recurrence, but also to work off their emotion, and get the full unusualness out of the experience. The vocal babble of early-waking girls and boys from the gardens of the campus, mingling with the birds' songs and the exquisite weather, was for three or four days a delightful sunrise phenomenon.

Now turn to San Francisco, thirty-five miles distant, from which an automobile ere long brought us the dire news of a city in ruins, with fires beginning at various points, and the water-supply interrupted. I was fortunate enough to board the only train of cars—a very small one—that got up to the city; fortunate enough also to escape in the evening by the only train that left it. This gave me and my valiant feminine escort some four hours of observation. My business is with "subjective" phenomena exclusively; so I will say nothing of the material ruin that greeted us on every hand—the daily papers and the weekly journals have done full justice to that topic. By

15

midday, when we reached the city, the pall of smoke was vast and the dynamite detonations had begun, but the troops, the police and the firemen seemed to have established order, dangerous neighborhoods were roped off everywhere and picketed, saloons closed, vehicles impressed, and every one at work who *could* work.

It was indeed a strange sight to see an entire population in the streets, busy as ants in an uncovered ant-hill scurrying to save their eggs and larvæ. Every horse, and everything on wheels in the city, from hucksters' wagons to automobiles, was being loaded with what effects could be scraped together from houses which the advancing flames were threatening. The sidewalks were covered with well-dressed men and women, carrying baskets, bundles, valises, or dragging trunks to spots of greater temporary safety, soon to be dragged farther, as the fire kept spreading!

In the safer quarters, every doorstep was covered with the dwelling's tenants, sitting surrounded with their more indispensable chattels, and ready to flee at a minute's notice. I think every one must have fasted on that day, for I saw no one eating. There was no appearance of general dismay, and little of chatter or of inco-ordinated excitement.

Every one seemed doggedly bent on achieving the job which he had set   20
himself to perform; and the faces, although somewhat tense and set and grave, were inexpressive of emotion. I noticed only three persons overcome, two Italian women, very poor, embracing an aged fellow countrywoman, and all weeping. Physical fatigue and *seriousness* were the only inner states that one could read on countenances.

With lights forbidden in the houses, and the streets lighted only by the conflagration, it was apprehended that the criminals of San Francisco would hold high carnival on the ensuing night. But whether they feared the disciplinary methods of the United States troops, who were visible everywhere, or whether they were themselves solemnized by the immensity of the disaster, they lay low and did not "manifest," either then or subsequently.

The only very discreditable thing to human nature that occurred was later, when hundreds of lazy "bummers" found that they could keep camping in the parks, and make alimentary storage-batteries of their stomachs, even in some cases getting enough of the free rations in their huts or tents to last them well into the summer. This charm of pauperized vagabondage seems all along to have been Satan's most serious bait to human nature. There was theft from the outset, but confined, I believe, to petty pilfering.

Cash in hand was the only money, and millionaires and their families were no better off in this respect than any one. Whoever got a vehicle could have the use of it; but the richest often went without, and spent the first two nights on rugs on the bare ground, with nothing but what their own arms had rescued. Fortunately, those nights were dry and comparatively warm, and Californians are accustomed to camping conditions in the summer, so suffering from exposure was less great than it would have been elsewhere. By the fourth night, which was rainy, tents and huts had brought most campers under cover.

I went through the city again eight days later. The fire was out, and about a quarter of the area stood unconsumed. Intact skyscrapers dominated the smoking level majestically and superbly—they and a few walls that had survived the overthrow. Thus has the courage of our architects and builders received triumphant vindication!

The inert elements of the population had mostly got away, and those that remained seemed what Mr. H. G. Wells calls "efficients." Sheds were already going up as temporary starting-points of business. Every one looked cheerful, in spite of the awful discontinuity of past and future, with every familiar association with material things dissevered; and the discipline and order were practically perfect. 25

As these notes of mine must be short, I had better turn to my more generalized reflections.

Two things in retrospect strike me especially, and are the most emphatic of all my impressions. Both are reassuring as to human nature.

The first of these was the rapidity of the improvisation of order out of chaos. It is clear that just as in every thousand human beings there will be statistically so many artists, so many athletes, so many thinkers, and so many potentially good soldiers, so there will be so many potential organizers in times of emergency. In point of fact, not only in the great city, but in the outlying towns, these natural ordermakers, whether amateurs or officials, came to the front immediately. There seemed to be no possibility which there was not some one there to think of, or which within twenty-four hours was not in some way provided for.

A good illustration is this: Mr. Keith is the great landscape-painter of the Pacific slope, and his pictures, which are many, are artistically and pecuniarily precious. Two citizens, lovers of his work, early in the day diverted their attention from all other interests, their own private ones included, and made it their duty to visit every place which they knew to contain a Keith painting. They cut them from their frames, rolled them up, and in this way got all the more important ones into a place of safety.

When they then sought Mr. Keith, to convey the joyous news to him, they found him still in his studio, which was remote from the fire, beginning a new painting. Having given up his previous work for lost, he had resolved to lose no time in making what amends he could for the disaster. 30

The completeness of organization at Palo Alto, a town of ten thousand inhabitants close to Stanford University, was almost comical. People feared exodus on a large scale of the rowdy elements of San Francisco. In point of fact, very few refugees came to Palo Alto. But within twenty-four hours, rations, clothing, hospital, quarantine, disinfection, washing, police, military, quarters in camp and in houses, printed information, employment, all were provided for under the care of so many volunteer committees.

Much of this readiness was American, much of it Californian; but I believe that every country in a similar crisis would have displayed it in a way to astonish the spectators. Like soldiering, it lies always latent in human nature.

The second thing that struck me was the universal equanimity. We soon got letters from the East, ringing with anxiety and pathos; but I now know fully what I have always believed, that the pathetic way of feeling great disasters belongs rather to the point of view of people at a distance than to the immediate victims. I heard not a single really pathetic or sentimental word in California expressed by any one.

The terms "awful," "dreadful" fell often enough from people's lips, but always with a sort of abstract meaning, and with a face that seemed to admire the vastness of the catastrophe as much as it bewailed its cuttingness. When talk was not directly practical, I might almost say that it expressed (at any rate in the nine days I was there) a tendency more toward nervous excitement than toward grief. The hearts concealed private bitterness enough, no doubt, but the tongues disdained to dwell on the misfortunes of self, when almost everybody one spoke to had suffered equally.

Surely the cutting edge of all our usual misfortunes comes from their character of loneliness. We lose our health, our wife or children die, our house burns down, or our money is made way with, and the world goes on rejoicing, leaving us on one side and counting us out from all its business. In California every one, to some degree, was suffering, and one's private miseries were merged in the vast general sum of privation and in the all-absorbing practical problem of general recuperation. The cheerfulness, or, at any rate, the steadfastness of tone, was universal. Not a single whine or plaintive word did I hear from the hundred losers whom I spoke to. Instead of that there was a temper of helpfulness beyond the counting. 35

It is easy to glorify this as something characteristically American, or especially Californian. Californian education has, of course, made the thought of all possible recuperations easy. In an exhausted country, with no marginal resources, the outlook on the future would be much darker. But I like to think that what I write of is a normal and universal trait of human nature. In our drawing-rooms and offices we wonder how people ever *do* go through battles, sieges and shipwrecks. We quiver and sicken in imagination, and think those heroes superhuman. Physical pain, whether suffered alone or in company, is always more or less unnerving and intolerable. But mental pathos and anguish, I fancy, are usually effects of distance. At the place of action, where all are concerned together, healthy animal insensibility and heartiness take their place. At San Francisco the need will continue to be awful, and there will doubtless be a crop of nervous wrecks before the weeks and months are over, but meanwhile the commonest men, simply because they *are* men, will go on, singly and collectively, showing this admirable fortitude of temper.

Questions of Subject and Theme

1. What does James say his experience did for him with regard to the term *earthquake?* How and in what ways did the term become redefined for him?

2. James says: "I realize now better than ever how inevitable were men's earlier mythologic versions of such catastrophes, and how artificial and against the grain of our spontaneous perceiving are the later habits into which science educates us." What evidence and what arguments does he bring to support this claim in his essay?

Questions of Method and Strategy

1. In describing the responses of others, James gives only a few details. What are the similarities and differences among the details in each case? What do the details seem designed to illustrate? What kinds of details does he seem to have ignored?
2. James says that at the time he was filled with "glee" and "cheerfulness" during his experience. Do these emotions justly characterize for you the spirit of his written *account* of the experience? Pick a passage that you think fairly represents his general tone and attitude and explain how James uses language to create the tone and the attitude that you perceive in his writing.

RISK MANAGEMENT
Men versus Women in the L.A. Earthquake

Susanna Styron

Susanna Styron survived the great Los Angeles earthquake of 1994. She reflected on her own reactions and those of other members of her family in an essay printed in the "About Women" column of the *Sunday New York Times Magazine*.

In the endless dark minutes and hours following the recent earthquake, which I still cannot believe was not The Big One, my husband was a picture of calm and comfort, telling us everything was fine, checking the gas, getting flashlights and shoes for everyone and being strong and consoling while our two daughters and I huddled on the couch, trembling.

As the days have passed and we've picked up the pieces, my husband has remained relatively even, confident, optimistic. I was at first elated: We survived! After a day or so, the adrenaline began to recede and I became listless and aimless; then, with every aftershock, I became progressively more depressed. When my daughter's school reopened and they played a recording of Cat Stevens's soupily sentimental "Morning Has Broken" at the morning meeting, I began to weep uncontrollably.

Another mother came and wrapped her arms around me. Later we talked about our earthquake experiences and our feelings, as we have endlessly, repeatedly, since Jan. 17. And she said to me what, almost without exception, every married mother of small children has said at some point in those conversations: "My husband thinks I'm crazy."

My husband thinks I'm crazy. This means: "I am hysterically afraid for the safety of my children and I can't let them out of my sight and I can't sleep and I want to move as far away from Los Angeles as I can get—and for this my husband thinks I'm crazy."

My own husband, probably because he knows I'm just crazy enough to kill him if he questions the validity of my fears and anxiety, has refrained from stating the obvious. But all over Los Angeles men are in the throes of what women can only see as denial, scoffing at their wives' fears while desperately trying to maintain perspective in the face of the realization that their families could disintegrate before their eyes in one violent shrug of the earth's shoulders. And there's not a thing they can do to stop it.

Women—traditionally the vulnerable sex, in whose bodies these little lives form and through whose pain they come into life—feel as powerless as the men and deal with it by clinging to the children day and night and calling real-estate agents in North Carolina.

But the difference in the calibration of the safety meter in men and women extends beyond natural disasters. In my own family, it is a source of constant conflict.

The most vivid example was probably the time my husband left our daughters, then not quite 3 and 5, in a bathtub with an 8-year-old friend, the water running and the door to the bathroom shut, while he took a shower a hundred yards away, across the lawn outside another house. I came upon the scene and was immediately filled with horror, disbelief and a murderous rage. His response to my point that a 3-year-old could fall, hit her head and drown in three inches of water before an 8-year-old could run a hundred yards to get him out of the shower and back to our daughter was: "Oh, the chances of that are one in a million."

We fought about it for days, but he never seemed to understand that even if the chances *were* one in a million (though it's probably more like one in a hundred), that's one chance too many for my baby.

And it's not just fathers who are subject to this peculiarly male attitude. Not long after the bathtub episode, I heard my husband's words echoed by our 16-year-old son when he took his father's car and drove to a friend's house before he was properly insured. When I realized what he'd done, I called to say he couldn't drive home because he wasn't insured.

"It's only a couple of miles," he said. "What if you have an accident?" I asked. "The chances of that," he said, "are about 1 in 20,000." I made my husband pick him up that night. A week later, the 1 chance in 20,000: Our son got insurance, borrowed his father's car and totaled it going 30 miles an hour.

What is it that makes men look at a risk factor and see the 19,999 chances that something bad won't happen and women see only the 1 chance that it will? Are women overly protective, projecting fear and creating fearful children? Are men needlessly endangering their offspring because they refuse to admit that the world is not a safe place for human beings? Can we teach our children to be safe without teaching them to be afraid?

I hope that my behavior as a mother will not be dictated by fear and that I will always protect my children from reasonably preventable risks. I will not leave them alone in a bathtub (well, maybe when they're 18). I will, however, let them ride in a car, even though the risk of an accident is terrifyingly high, because to do otherwise would prevent them from leading normal, productive lives. But they must always wear seat belts.

Whether or not we will continue to live in Los Angeles is a more complicated issue.

Sometimes it seems that what men really fear is the act of being afraid (wasn't it a man, after all, who told us we had nothing to fear but fear itself?), as if to admit fear is to allow it to have control over you. My husband does not fit any macho stereotype. He is a poet who cries easily, knows and cares nothing about cars and would rather buy a dress for one of his daughters than attend a Lakers game. And yet he did not want to install a burglar alarm in our house when I did, because he said it would be living with a "fear mentality." It's not macho; it's just male.

I know what it's like to be brave for my children, to pretend I'm not   15
afraid when I am. Is that what it's like to be a man? Or is it that men don't
feel afraid in the same way because they simply do not feel as vulnerable as
women do? Perhaps women feel so vulnerable because we *are* more vulnerable than men to forces outside ourselves—rape, abuse—for physical and
biological reasons.

Or perhaps our hypersensitivity to potential danger comes from another
tradition born of biology: The mother's role lies within the home as creator
of the protective nest we build around our children; the father's role is to
take the children out of the house and into the world. To do so, he must
brave the forces out there and believe he can guide his children through
them safely without being paralyzed by fear.

After a disaster of the magnitude of our recent earthquake, anyone who
does *not* feel vulnerable is crazy. The fact is we are all vulnerable, and always
have been, but suddenly we're shockingly aware of it. We were jolted out
of our sleep into the realization that we simply *cannot protect our children,* not
totally, not ultimately.

But what we do with that realization, and the fear it brings, seems to
break down pretty much along gender lines. Are women really that fearful
and men that fearless? Or are women realistic and men in denial? The truth
probably lies somewhere in between. But there's no Richter scale to measure such things.

Questions of Subject and Theme

1. Styron says that "the difference in the calibration of the safety meter in
   men and women extends beyond natural disasters. In my own family, it
   is a source of constant conflict." What, according to Styron, makes for
   the conflict?
2. Styron speaks of both "vulnerability" and "fear" throughout the essay.
   What relations between the two concepts exist for her?

Questions of Method and Strategy

1. Styron often moves easily between personal anecdotes and general explanations. Pick a moment when she does so, and analyze the ways in which
   she makes her transitions between these modes of writing.
2. In her next-to-last paragraph, Styron says that "anyone who does *not* feel
   vulnerable is crazy." Explain the ways in which her essay as a whole does
   or does not support her analysis here.

THE EARTHQUAKE

Isak Dinesen

Isak Dinesen was the pen name of Karen Blixen, the Danish play-wright, novelist, essayist, and short story writer. As a young woman she moved to Kenya. Her experiences became the basis of her most famous book, *Out of Africa* (1937), from which the following selection is taken.

One year, about Christmas, we had an earthquake; it was strong enough   *1*
to turn over a number of native huts, it was probably of the power of an angry elephant. It came in three shocks, each of them lasted a few seconds, and there was a pause of a few seconds in between them. These intervals gave people time to form their ideas of the happening.

Denys Finch-Hatton, who was at the time camped in the Masai Reserve, and was sleeping in his lorry, told me when he came back, that as he was woken up by the shock he thought, "A rhino has got underneath the lorry." I myself was in my bedroom going to bed when the earthquake came. At the first tug I thought, "A leopard has got up on the roof." When the second shock came, I thought, "I am going to die, this is how it feels to die." But in the short stillness between the second and the third shock, I realized what it was, it was an earthquake, and I had never thought that I should live to see that. For a moment now I believed that the earthquake was over. But when the third and last shock of it came, it brought with it such an overwhelming feeling of joy that I do not remember ever in my life to have been more suddenly and thoroughly transported.

The heavenly bodies, in their courses, have it in their power to move human minds to unknown heights of delight. We are not generally conscious of them; when their idea is suddenly brought back, and actualized to us, it opens up a tremendous perspective. Kepler writes of what he felt when, after many years' work, he at last found the laws of the movements of the planets:

"I give myself over to my rapture. The die is cast. Nothing I have ever felt before is like this. I tremble, my blood leaps. God has waited six thousand years for a looker-on to his work. His wisdom is infinite, that of which we are ignorant is contained in him, as well as the little that we know."

Indeed it was exactly the same transport which took hold of me and   *5*
shook me all through, at the time of the earthquake.

The feeling of colossal pleasure lies chiefly in the consciousness that something which you have reckoned to be immovable, has got it in it to move on its own. That is probably one of the strongest sensations of joy and hope in the world. The dull globe, the dead mass, the Earth itself, rose and stretched under me. It sent me out a message, the slightest touch, but of unbounded significance. It laughed so that the Native huts fell down and cried: *Eppur si muove.*

Early next morning, Juma brought me my tea and said: "The King of England is dead."

I asked him how he knew.

"Did you not, Memsahib," he said, "feel the earth toss and shake last night? That means that the King of England is dead."

But luckily the King of England lived for many years after the earthquake.   10

Questions of Subject and Theme

1. As opposed to her own feelings, what about the earthquake itself does Dinesen describe? How does the manner of her description of physical details contribute to her descriptions of her feelings?
2. How does the logic of Dinesen's analysis work to explain why the earthquake produced "probably one of the strongest sensations of joy and hope in the world?"

Questions of Method and Strategy

1. How does Dinesen's use of the astronomer Kepler help to define more particularly the kind of "joy" and "transport" she felt?
2. Dinesen ends with a superstitious explanation of the earthquake. Does she distinguish between the "scientific" and the "untutored" views of earthquakes in the same way William James does? Explain.

Suggestions for Writing on the Juxtapositions

1. Have you ever experienced a moment of disaster and danger? If so, did the responses of any of the three writers here coincide with and help explain yours? Write an essay in which you give your own explanation of your reactions, being sure to comment on the explanations advanced by the writers you have read.
2. In your view, which writer best links personal experience to general analysis and explanation? Which writer does so least well? Write an essay of your own to support the justice of your distinction.
3. Do you agree with Styron on the different responses of men and women to danger? Write an essay in which you support, refute, or modify her analysis and explanation.
4. Dinesen says that her joy and sense of transport came from the sense of something fixed and stable becoming fluid and mobile, and she compares her feeling to that of scientific discovery. Write an essay in which you analyze the relations of the emotional to the intellectual in Dinesen's arguments or in those of any other writer in the section.

22   Regulating Speech

Russell Baker, "Don't Mention It"
David G. Savage, "Forbidden Words on Campus"
Gloria Naylor, "A Question of Language"

All too often, one person's "free speech" is another's "hate speech." Consider three views on this contemporary issue, keeping the following questions in mind:

1. What views of history seem to underlie each writer's position? For example, to a given writer is recent history an improvement? A movement toward fragmentation and chaos? A series of tragedies and crises? Using particular examples, analyze the ways in which each writer assumes a general view of history that illuminates his or her particular views of offensive speech.

2. Russell Baker makes fun of other aspects of contemporary language in an earlier essay, "Little Red Riding Hood Revisited." What similarities and differences do you find between his humorous and serious modes of writing?

3. In keeping with journalistic tradition, Savage seems to attempt objectivity and balance in his report. Yet the other writers here seem to try to present themselves as fair-minded in spite of their clear positions. Analyze some of the techniques of writing through which each attempts to appear able to examine the issue calmly and fairly. Compare these techniques with those Savage employs.

4. In Naylor's view of offensive speech what function do individual words play? According to her, what besides words are needed to define the meaning of speech for her? How is she like and unlike the other writers in her view of individual words? Given your understanding of her views, how do you think she might respond to Baker's contention about *racist*—a word he calls "the ultimate epithet from which there is no appeal?" What might she say to the college administrator reported by Savage who claimed not to know the meaning of *redneck?*

DON'T MENTION IT

Russell Baker

Russell Baker is a columnist for the *New York Times* who writes both as a humorist and as a serious political commentator. An example of his political commentary is selected here, and one of his more humorous essays appears earlier in the book.

The racial diversity of Americans creates a lot of funny language problems, but you can't laugh about them, of course, because it's dangerous these days to laugh about anything that touches on our racial diversity. When the subject is race and somebody laughs, that somebody is inviting denunciation for "insensitivity."

"Insensitivity" is the latest jawbreaker in the ever growing mushmouth vocabulary Americans use to talk about race without, well, without quite talking about race. Laughter at the wrong time is only one of a hundred ways of committing "insensitivity" in talking race. All are to be skirted like minefields.

One may commit an occasional "insensitivity" and escape deadly abuse, but frequent violations can bring down the ultimate epithet from which there is no appeal: "racist."

"Racist" now has a punishing power similar to the power of "Communist" in Red-hunting days when a politician calling you "Communist" expected your boss to fire you immediately. In two recent New York media incidents—involving Andy Rooney and Jimmy Breslin—blacks, gays and Asian-Americans behaved precisely like the old Red hunters by urging that Rooney and Breslin be punished by firings.

Is it amusing to find the forces of liberal egalitarianism carrying on like old-fashioned, bad-guy conservative Joe McCarthy? If so, don't smile too broadly. Being amused here could get you charged with "insensitivity."

It's safer to shift to another target and berate CBS and Newsday because, in briefly benching Rooney and Breslin, both knuckled to the liberals' use of the old Red-hunting tactic. Nothing there to shock anybody, is there? The McCarthy era taught us to expect feeble spines in the media.

"Insensitivity," however, is not so damning as "racism." It may suggest only that the offender is not viciously benighted, but only a dolt too witless to know the score or a geezer perhaps, too old and set in his ways to know what's new in the world.

Such persons may need re-education. If this sounds like the mercy of Chairman Mao, in racial matters it is an old and honorable American custom. In the past generation alone, the country has submitted to immense re-education in the courtesies necessary if it is to flourish in a racially diverse world.

The old ethnic slang terms that were common American household words 40 years ago have almost disappeared from the speech of all but the most primitive citizenry. There was no great problem in getting rid of this old vocabulary; the problem has been in creating new terminology.

Just now, for instance, there is another disagreement about the socially   10
acceptable term for Americans of African ancestry. The term "African-Americans," endorsed by Jesse Jackson, is getting a good bit of use as a replacement for "blacks," which since 1960 has been the word preferred by—well, what shall we call them?

We Americans have re-educated ourselves in racial matters so success-fully, you see, that a white (ridiculous word, by the way) may even hesitate to speak of them until supplied with a word officially certified civilized by the parties he wants to discuss.

The old term "people of color," once considered demeaning, is surfac-ing again in respectable forums. It showed up Monday in the *New York Times* with the chairman of the City University Student Senate saying university enrollment was "65 percent people of color."

Since this number includes students of both African and Hispanic an-cestry, "people of color" is obviously an effort to produce a term that will embrace both. But will Hispanics submit to the embrace? It would probably invite charges of "insensitivity" for whites (pinks, tans and grays, actually) to start calling Hispanics "people of color" until we get a more authoritative pronunciamento than a student senate chairman can issue.

What is remarkable is the extreme care almost everybody willingly takes to avoid language that could offend anybody. The bright side of this is that it shows, all the other evidence of our society notwithstanding, that there is still some desire among us to treat each other with common courtesy.

There is also a not-so-bright side. This is the tendency of pressure   15
groups that police the language to insist that it conform to whatever the current orthodoxy may be on racial matters. Trying to destroy noncon-formers as heretics can drive the real bigots underground. Under ground is where people like that thrive and multiply.

Questions of Subject and Theme

1. At what point do you first suspect what position Baker himself takes on the issue of offensive language? At what point do you first feel certain? Cite your evidence and explain your reasoning in each instance.
2. In paragraph 14 Baker finds that "What is remarkable is the extreme care almost everyone willingly takes to avoid language that could offend any-body." Where, if at all, in the essay do you find evidence of any kind to support this assertion? What, for example, does he claim as a frame of reference? What does he say has changed in his view in the last forty years?

Questions of Method and Strategy

1. From the first paragraph Baker often uses quotation marks to set off terms he examines. Analyze a few examples of the ways in which quotation marks work in the essay as a writing strategy. Have you ever used a similar technique? What were your aims? Does Baker achieve similar aims in his essay?

2. Baker compares the use of the term *racist* to an earlier use of the term *Communist*. What function does his analogy perform in giving you a sense of his position on the issue of hate speech?

FORBIDDEN WORDS ON CAMPUS

David G. Savage

David Savage reports on the Supreme Court for the Washington bureau of the *Los Angeles Times*. Before becoming a legal reporter, he wrote on educational issues for five years and thus is well qualified to present the issue of hate speech from both points of view.

Campus humor can be a risky business these days. *1*

In December, the editors of the Connector, the student newspaper at the state-run University of Lowell in Massachusetts, published a cartoon mocking what they considered overzealous protestors—both those who favor animal rights and those who favor the death penalty.

One side showed a drawing of an animal rights activist, with the caption: "Some of my best friends are laboratory rats." On the other was a big-bellied death-penalty advocate. "None of his best friends are young, black males," said the legend underneath.

But black students didn't find the cartoon funny and neither did university officials. They promptly charged the student editors with violating the student code by creating a "hostile environment" on campus and other "civil rights" abuses. Eventually, the editors found themselves facing university sanctions that included six months probation and 30 hours of community service and removal from the newspaper's staff.

For decades, denial of free speech has provoked protests on campus. But *5* these days the complaints are on the other side. Today, many students and liberal academics are urging limits on free speech—at least when the topic involves racial or sexual issues.

From Massachusetts to California, more than 200 colleges and universities—many of them the nation's most elite—have either revised their student codes of conduct or enacted new "speech codes" designed to prevent utterances on race, sex, religion, national origin or sexual preference that might offend some students.

"This is the new liberal *cause celebre*," says U.C. Berkeley law professor Robert C. Post. "It has forced a wedge between those devoted to civil rights and civil liberties."

University of Colorado Law School Dean Gene Nichol calls himself an "old-fashioned, free speech liberal" but now finds his views unpopular. "It is no longer 'politically correct' to take the free speech position," Nichol laments.

Examples abound:

- The University of Michigan has warned that it will discipline students for comments that "stigmatize or victimize" others based on race, sex, sexual orientation, ancestry or religion—including joke-telling or making fun of someone.

- The University of Wisconsin has revised its code of conduct to prohibit "discriminatory harassment"—including comments that "demean" another student or "create an intimidating, hostile or demeaning environment."

- The University of California's code prohibits students from making "personally abusive epithets" that are "inherently likely to provoke a violent reaction." These include "derogatory references" to race, ethnic origin, religion, sex or other characteristics.

Faculties and student bodies alike have split over whether the new limits are needed or wise.   10

Supporters of the new policies including many law professors, say that the new codes are needed to prevent the spread of "hate-speech" on campus—a fear prompted by growing reports of racist incidents including cross-burnings, anonymous hate-mailings and fraternity parties in which white students carried out mock "slave auctions," which onlookers found offensive.

University of Houston law professor Michael Olivas concedes that colleges ideally should be "enclaves for discussion and free speech" but argues that racial slurs can prevent young black or Latino students from pursuing their studies.

"These students are extremely vulnerable." Olivas contends. "These comments humiliate and threaten. They don't have anything to do with free speech. The traditional liberals refuse to see that racism warrants special treatment."

Law professors Mari Matsuda of UCLA and Richard Delgado of the University of Colorado contend that racist comments are a form of assault that can and should be banned on campus.

But others argue that free speech must be protected, even when it is offensive to some listeners. "I think it is a dangerous precedent to start banning particular words," says University of Virginia Prof. Robert O'Neil.   15

To some, the growth of such "speech codes" is part of a historic shift in political attitudes.

In the 1960s, the protesters most often were leftists, who campaigned for civil rights and against the Vietnam War. Conservatives talked of "law and order" and of stifling anti-war dissent.

But today, the most vehement street protesters oppose legalized abortion. And it is conservatives who have most visibly taken up the free speech banner.

Whether it is tobacco ads, children's television, anti-abortion demonstrations or racist utterances, "it is the people on the left who want to regulate speech," says University of Chicago law professor Michael McConnell.

What troubles some critics of the new codes is the lengths to which they go in attempting to define improper behavior. Though spurred by in-   20 cidents of blatant racism, the codes have been used to discipline those whose sins are not as clear-cut.

When the University of Michigan first enacted its speech code, in 1988, it also published a brochure citing examples of "violations."

Among the activities that were included: making jokes about homosexual men and lesbians, displaying a Confederate flag in a dormitory, laughing at a joke about someone who stutters, making derogatory comments about a person's physical appearance, sponsoring entertainment in which a comedian makes jokes about Latinos and uttering classroom remarks such as "Women just aren't as good as men in this field."

Initially, Michigan enforced its new code actively. In 1989, a student hearing board found a graduate student guilty of violations for having publicly characterized homosexuality as a "disease"—though it later refused to impose sanctions, which could have ranged from a formal apology to expulsion from the university.

Later, a black dental student was charged with violating the code for having told a minority instructor that she had heard "minority students had a difficult time in the course" and that they "were not treated fairly."

The instructor filed a complaint of her own because, she said, the student's comment could threaten her chances for tenure. The student eventually was required to write an apology.

In another case, a business student who read "an allegedly homophobic limerick" aloud was required to attend "an educational 'gay rap' session" and write a letter of apology to the campus newspaper.

Still another student was charged with anti-Semitism for having voiced the opinion in class that "Jews used the Holocaust" to justify repression of Palestinians. The case eventually was dismissed, but it provoked protest from free speech advocates.

When several students filed suit, challenging the university's speech code on grounds that it violated the 1st Amendment, U.S. District Judge Avern Cohn struck down the Michigan code as unconstitutional.

As a legal matter, the issue mainly affects state-run universities. Although private schools, such as Stanford University, sometimes impose speech codes as well, they aren't subject to challenge under the 1st Amendment, which only bars the government from restricting free speech and so far has not been applied to private universities.

Dartmouth University recently was the subject of nationwide headlines when it suspended several students who edited an off-campus weekly newspaper that ran articles criticizing a black music professor. Over the years, the publication, the Dartmouth Review, has been castigated for its attacks on women, homosexuals, blacks and Indians.

The U.S. Supreme Court has not spoken on whether racist or sexist comments are protected as free speech. In a 1942 case, Chaplinsky vs. New Hampshire, the high court upheld the conviction of a man who shouted into the face of a policeman that he was a "goddamned racketeer and a damned fascist." Such "fighting words" are not protected by the 1st Amendment, the court declared. More recently, the court has whittled down the "fighting words" exception, but not overruled it.

Two years ago, as many state universities were declaring "demeaning" comments illegal, the Supreme Court declared that burning an American flag, while offensive, was nonetheless legal. "If there is a bedrock principle underlying the 1st Amendment, it is that the government may not prohibit the expression of an idea simply because society finds the idea itself offensive or disagreeable," Justice William J. Brennan Jr. wrote for the court in Texas vs. Johnson.

Judge Cohn cited the flag-burning ruling in striking down the Michigan code.

Since then, universities such as Wisconsin, Stanford and the University of California have revised their codes to punish only the use of so-called "fighting words." They also have decided not to provide examples of words or comments that would violate the codes.

When three Wisconsin students complained that they had been called   35
"rednecks," university officials informed them that the code did not cover that word.

"Redneck is not a demeaning term. It does not have a common meaning," said Roger Howard, an assistant dean of students in Madison.

University of California officials in Berkeley and Los Angeles refused to say definitively whether calling a fellow student names ranging from "nigger" to "nerd" would violate the campus codes.

"We don't have a list of good and bad words," says Raymond Goldstone, dean of students at UCLA. "It is a case-by-case situation." Although the University of California's new code took effect in September, 1989, no student has been disciplined because of it.

For traditional liberals, the issue has become a thorny one.

After much hesitation, the American Civil Liberties Union has decided   40
to oppose the new campus codes. Torn between potentially conflicting desires to combat racism and to protect free speech, the ACLU agonized for several years over the issue. But last autumn, the organization issued a new policy statement condemning the new speech codes, while adding that universities are certainly free to punish students for "acts of harassment, intimidation or invasion of privacy."

Nadine Strossen, a New York Law School professor who is ACLU's new president, said that the campus speech issue has proved as diverse as championing the rights of neo-Nazis in 1977 to march through a Jewish community of Skokie, Ill.

But Strossen still disparages the new speech codes. "They are undermining free speech, and they are doing nothing to stop racism and bigotry," she says. "For university administrators, they are a cheap solution to a complex problem."

Meanwhile, back in Lowell, the controversy continues. Last week, after consulting its attorneys, the university said through a spokesman that it was dropping the charges against the student editors—though it had not yet informed them about the decision.

"We sought a second legal opinion and on the basis of that we're discontinuing any kind of action," says Thomas C. Taylor, assistant dean of students, who had signed the initial letters outlining the prescribed punishment.

"We were trying to weigh a lot of issues," he explains. "It was an envi-   45
ronmental issue really. We didn't want to have a hostile environment for black students and an atmosphere that would degrade women. That was our intent."

Ironically, some onlookers believe the black students may have misinterpreted the intent of the cartoon. Although the drawing seems on its face to support claims that they were disproportionately victimized by the death penalty, the students accused the paper of "racial insensitivity" for having "very boldly compared young, black males to laboratory animals, in particular, rats."

But Patty Janice, editor of the student newspaper in Lowell, says that she believes her fellow students were made scapegoats for the university's seeming difficulty in attracting black students.

"They have had problems in the past with recruiting black students—the administration has been under the gun," she says. "Attacking us was the easiest way to make it look like they were doing something on that issue."

Questions of Subject and Theme

1. Savage is an editor and a reporter. Do you find any evidence of his journalistic role in the theme of "forbidden words?" Point to some examples and explain how the theme is or is not influenced by its journalistic medium.
2. How well do college administrators come off in this report? Pick some examples and explain what you see as implicit and explicit evaluations.

Questions of Method and Strategy

1. Why, according to Savage, do private and public universities differ on the issue of speech codes? What aspects of power differ in each case? More generally, what does Savage show about the relations of power and speech codes throughout the piece? What is it that each side claims should be "enforced?"
2. Savage organizes his piece as a narrative, and terms of time abound as openings to new topics and as transitions—*December, for decades,* and *meanwhile* are some examples. Find some others. What does the sense of time and history do for Savage's writing besides providing him with an organization?

A QUESTION OF LANGUAGE

Gloria Naylor

Gloria Naylor earned a graduate degree in Afro-American Studies from Yale before working for the *New York Times*. She has gone on to write an award-winning novel and to teach at several leading universities. The following selection comes from a piece first published in the *Times*.

Language is the subject. It is the written form with which I've managed   1
to keep the wolf away from the door and, in diaries, to keep my sanity. In spite of this, I consider the written word inferior to the spoken, and much of the frustration experienced by novelists is the awareness that whatever we manage to capture in even the most transcendent passages falls far short of the richness of life. Dialogue achieves its power in the dynamics of a fleeting moment of sight, sound, smell, and touch.

I'm not going to enter the debate here about whether it is language that shapes reality or vice versa. That battle is doomed to be waged whenever we seek intermittent reprieve from the chicken and egg dispute. I will simply take the position that the spoken word, like the written word, amounts to a nonsensical arrangement of sounds or letters without a consensus that assigns "meaning." And building from the meanings of what we hear, we order reality. Words themselves are innocuous; it is the consensus that gives them true power.

I remember the first time I heard the word *nigger*. In my third-grade class, our math tests were being passed down the rows, and as I handed the papers to a little boy in back of me, I remarked that once again he had received a much lower mark than I did. He snatched his test from me and spit out that word. Had he called me a nymphomaniac or a necrophiliac, I couldn't have been more puzzled. I didn't know what a nigger was, but I knew that whatever it meant, it was something he shouldn't have called me. This was verified when I raised my hand, and in a loud voice repeated what he had said and watched the teacher scold him for using a "bad" word. I was later to go home and ask the inevitable question that every black parent must face—"Mommy, what does 'nigger' mean?"

And what exactly did it mean? Thinking back, I realize that this could not have been the first time the word was used in my presence. I was part of a large extended family that had migrated from the rural South after World War II and formed a close-knit network that gravitated around my maternal grandparents. Their ground-floor apartment in one of the buildings they owned in Harlem was a weekend mecca for my immediate family, along with countless aunts, uncles, and cousins who brought along assorted friends. It was a bustling and open house with assorted neighbors and tenants popping in and out to exchange bits of gossip, pick up an old quarrel or referee the ongoing checkers game in which my grandmother cheated shamelessly. They were all there to let down their hair and put up their feet after a week of labor in the factories, laundries, and shipyards of New York.

Amid the clamor, which could reach deafening proportions—two or three conversations going on simultaneously, punctuated by the sound of a baby's crying somewhere in the back rooms or out on the street—there was still a rigid set of rules about what was said and how. Older children were sent out of the living room when it was time to get into the juicy details about "you-know-who" up on the third floor who had gone and gotten herself "p-r-e-g-n-a-n-t!" But my parents, knowing that I could spell well beyond my years, always demanded that I follow the others out to play. Beyond sexual misconduct and death, everything else was considered harmless for our young ears. And so among the anecdotes of the triumphs and disappointments in the various workings of our lives, the word *nigger* was used in my presence, but it was set within contexts and inflections that caused it to register in my mind as something else.

In the singular, the word was always applied to a man who had distinguished himself in some situation that brought their approval for his strength, intelligence, or drive:

"Did Johnny really do that?"

"I'm telling you, that nigger pulled in $6,000 of overtime last year. Said he got enough for a down payment on a house."

When used with a possessive adjective by a woman—"my nigger"—it became a term of endearment for husband or boyfriend. But it could be more than just a term applied to a man. In their mouths it became the pure essence of manhood—a disembodied force that channeled their past history of struggle and present survival against the odds into a victorious statement of being: "Yeah, that old foreman found out quick enough—you don't mess with a nigger."

In the plural, it became a description of some group within the community that had overstepped the bounds of decency as my family defined it: Parents who neglected their children, a drunken couple who fought in public, people who simply refused to look for work, those with excessively dirty mouths or unkempt households were all "trifling niggers." This particular circle could forgive hard times, unemployment, the occasional bout of depression—they had gone through all of that themselves—but the unforgivable sin was lack of self-respect.

A woman could never be a *nigger* in the singular, with its connotation of confirming worth. The noun *girl* was its closest equivalent in that sense, but only when used in direct address and regardless of the gender doing the addressing. *Girl* was a token of respect for a woman. The one-syllable word was drawn out to sound like three in recognition of the extra ounce of wit, nerve or daring that the woman had shown in the situation under discussion.

"G-i-r-l, stop. You mean you said that to his face?"

But if the word was used in a third-person reference or shortened so that it almost snapped out of the mouth, it always involved some element of communal disapproval. And age became an important factor in these exchanges. It was only between individuals of the same generation, or from an older person to a younger (but never the other way around), that "girl" would be considered a compliment.

I don't agree with the argument that use of the word *nigger* at this social stratum of the black community was an internalization of racism. The dynamics were the exact opposite: the people in my grandmother's living room took a word that whites used to signify worthlessness or degradation and rendered it impotent. Gathering there together, they transformed *nigger* to signify the varied and complex human beings they knew themselves to be. If the word was to disappear totally from the mouths of even the most liberal of white society, no one in that room was naïve enough to believe it would disappear from white minds. Meeting the word head-on, they proved it had absolutely nothing to do with the way they were determined to live their lives.

So there must have been dozens of times that the word *nigger* was spoken in front of me before I reached the third grade. But I didn't "hear" it until it was said by a small pair of lips that had already learned it could be a way to humiliate me. That was the word I went home and asked my mother about. And since she knew that I had to grow up in America, she took me in her lap and explained.

Questions of Subject and Theme

1. Paraphrase Naylor's views on the differences between the written and the spoken word as argued in the beginning of her essay. Test some examples of your own. They needn't be taken from the vocabulary of hatred, but they should be words that carry emotional resonances and that require what Naylor calls a "consensus" to be heard properly.

2. In paragraph 14, what do you think is meant by the term *internalization?* Why doesn't Naylor agree that the use of the word *nigger,* as she has described it within the black community, implies an "internalization of racism?"

Questions of Method and Strategy

1. What is the effect of Naylor's use of the word *simply* in the third sentence of her second paragraph? Have you ever used the word in a similar way? What do you hope or expect to achieve by its use?

2. What does Naylor achieve by ending as she does? What advantages or disadvantages come from not telling us what her mother explained to her? Would you have ended the essay this way? Explain why or why not.

Suggestions for Writing on the Juxtapositions

1. Using the information provided by the essays here and your own experience, write a short essay that argues for your own views on the issue of speech codes.
2. Offensive speech is an emotionally charged issue. Which writer do you think best deals with the emotional issues involved? Write an essay in which you analyze some of the techniques of writing through which that writer attempts to face firmly and deal clearly with emotional issues. As a start, you might try comparing Russell Baker's style here with his more lighthearted "Little Red Riding Hood Revisited" (p. 312).
3. Savage quotes people who claim that the motives of those who form and administer speech codes are self-serving and opportunistic. Write an essay in which you analyze what seem to you some of the less-than-noble motives of those who argue for "free speech" or against "hate speech."
4. Baker claims that being labeled a "racist" is a charge hard to answer. What makes it so in his view? In yours? The critic Kenneth Burke has called some political words (like *freedom*) "God words" and other words (like *racist*) "Devil words." Make a list of contemporary words that might fit these categories. Pick one of each and write an essay about the difficulty of discussion when such words define the topic.

23 Language as Power

Frederick Douglass, "Learning to Read and Write"

Amy Tan, "Mother Tongue"

Leonard Q. Ross, "Mr. K★A★P★L★A★N, the Comparative, and the Superlative"

Most people take reading and writing for granted, but we all need to be reminded of the immense power conferred by those abilities. While reading the following essays keep these questions in mind:

1. Douglass compares his lack of learning to being shut up in "mental darkness." Do the other accounts in this section share his view of the limitations of illiteracy? Support your opinion with examples.

2. Amy Tan says that she spends a great deal of time "thinking about the power of language." What does she believe is the power of language? What views of linguistic power do the other selections take? Explain with examples.

3. Unlike Frederick Douglass, both Hyman Kaplan and Amy Tan's mother speak nonstandard forms of English. Compare and contrast the strengths and weakness of such forms of English as recorded in the last two selections.

4. Mr. Parkhill takes a dim view of Kaplan's desire to express his "Inner Self." What relations between the self and linguistic limitations do the other two essays show? What might each author say to Mr. Parkhill?

LEARNING TO READ AND WRITE

Frederick Douglass

Frederick Douglass was born of a white man he never identified and a black mother he barely knew. Escaping slavery in Maryland at the age of twenty-one, he lectured in New England and Great Britain for the abolitionist cause. He published his *Narrative of the Life of Frederick Douglass* in 1845, sixteen years before the start of the Civil War.

I lived in Master Hugh's family about seven years. During this time, I succeeded in learning to read and write. In accomplishing this, I was compelled to resort to various stratagems. I had no regular teacher. My mistress, who had kindly commenced to instruct me, had, in compliance with the advice and direction of her husband, not only ceased to instruct, but had set her face against my being instructed by any one else. It is due, however, to my mistress to say of her, that she did not adopt this course of treatment immediately. She at first lacked the depravity indispensable to shutting me up in mental darkness. It was at least necessary for her to have some training in the exercise of irresponsible power, to make her equal to the task of treating me as though I were a brute.

My mistress was, as I have said, a kind and tender-hearted woman; and in the simplicity of her soul she commenced, when I first went to live with her, to treat me as she supposed one human being ought to treat another. In entering upon the duties of a slaveholder, she did not seem to perceive that I sustained to her the relation of a mere chattel, and that for her to treat me as a human being was not only wrong, but dangerously so. Slavery proved as injurious to her as it did to me. When I went there, she was a pious, warm, and tenderhearted woman. There was no sorrow or suffering for which she had not a tear. She had bread for the hungry, clothes for the naked, and comfort for every mourner that came within her reach. Slavery soon proved its ability to divest her of these heavenly qualities. Under its influence, the tender heart became stone, and the lamblike disposition gave way to one of tiger-like fierceness. The first step in her downward course was in her ceasing to instruct me. She now commenced to practise her husband's precepts. She finally became even more violent in her opposition than her husband himself. She was not satisfied with simply doing as well as he had commanded; she seemed anxious to do better. Nothing seemed to make her more angry than to see me with a newspaper. She seemed to think that here lay the danger. I have had her rush at me with a face made all up of fury, and snatch from me a newspaper, in a manner that fully revealed her apprehension. She was an apt woman; and a little experience soon demonstrated, to her satisfaction, that education and slavery were incompatible with each other.

From this time I was most narrowly watched. If I was in a separate room any considerable length of time, I was sure to be suspected of having a book, and was at once called to give an account of myself. All this, however, was too late. The first step had been taken. Mistress, in teaching me the alphabet, had given me the *inch,* and no precaution could prevent me from taking the *ell.*

The plan which I adopted, and the one by which I was most successful, was that of making friends of all the little white boys whom I met in the street. As many of these as I could, I converted into teachers. With their kindly aid, obtained at different times and in different places, I finally succeeded in learning to read. When I was sent on errands, I always took my book with me, and by going one part of my errand quickly, I found time to get a lesson before my return. I used also to carry bread with me, enough of which was always in the house, and to which I was always welcome; for I was much better off in this regard than many of the poor white children in our neighborhood. This bread I used to bestow upon the hungry little urchins, who, in return, would give me that more valuable bread of knowledge. I am strongly tempted to give the names of two or three of those little boys, as a testimonial of the gratitude and affection I bear them; but prudence forbids;—not that it would injure me, but it might embarrass them; for it is almost an unpardonable offence to teach slaves to read in this Christian country. It is enough to say of the dear little fellows, that they lived on Philpot Street, very near Durgin and Bailey's ship-yard. I used to talk this matter of slavery over with them. I would sometimes say to them, I wished I could be as free as they would be when they got to be men. "You will be free as soon as you are twenty-one, *but I am a slave for life!* Have not I as good a right to be free as you have?" These words used to trouble them; they would express for me the liveliest sympathy, and console me with the hope that something would occur by which I might be free.

I was now about twelve years old, and the thought of being *a slave for*   5
life began to bear heavily upon my heart. Just about this time, I got hold of a book entitled "The Columbian Orator." Every opportunity I got, I used to read this book. Among much of other interesting matter, I found in it a dialogue between a master and his slave. The slave was represented as having run away from his master three times. The dialogue represented the conversation which took place between them, when the slave was retaken the third time. In this dialogue, the whole argument in behalf of slavery was brought forward by the master, all of which was disposed of by the slave. The slave was made to say some very smart as well as impressive things in reply to his master—things which had the desired though unexpected effect; for the conversation resulted in the voluntary emancipation of the slave on the part of the master.

In the same book, I met with one of Sheridan's mighty speeches on and in behalf of Catholic emancipation: These were choice documents to me. I read them over and over again with unabated interest. They gave tongue to interesting thoughts of my own soul, which had frequently flashed through my mind, and died away for want of utterance. The moral which I gained from the dialogue was the power of truth over the conscience of even a slaveholder. What I got from Sheridan was a bold denunciation of slavery, and a powerful vindication of human rights. The reading of these documents enabled me to utter my thoughts, and to meet the arguments brought forward to sustain slavery; but while they relieved me of one difficulty, they brought on another even more painful than the one of which I was relieved. The more I read, the more I was led to abhor and detest my enslavers. I could regard them in no other light than a band of successful robbers, who had left their homes, and gone to Africa, and stolen us from our homes, and in a strange land reduced us to slavery. I loathed them as being the meanest as well as the most wicked of men. As I read and contemplated the subject, behold! that very discontentment which Master Hugh had predicted would follow my learning to read had already come, to torment and sting my soul to unutterable anguish. As I writhed under it, I would at times feel that learning to read had been a curse rather than a blessing. It had given me a view of my wretched condition, without the remedy. It opened my eyes to the horrible pit, but to no ladder upon which to get out. In moments of agony, I envied my fellow-slaves for their stupidity. I have often wished myself a beast. I preferred the condition of the meanest reptile to my own. Any thing, no matter what, to get rid of thinking! It was this everlasting thinking of my condition that tormented me. There was no getting rid of it. It was pressed upon me by every object within sight or hearing, animate or inanimate. The silver trump of freedom had roused my soul to eternal wakefulness. Freedom now appeared, to disappear no more forever. It was heard in every sound, and seen in every thing. It was ever present to torment me with a sense of my wretched condition. I saw nothing without seeing it, I heard nothing without hearing it, and felt nothing without feeling it. It looked from every star, it smiled in every calm, breathed in every wind, and moved in every storm.

I often found myself regretting my own existence, and wishing myself dead; and but for the hope of being free, I have no doubt but that I should have killed myself, or done something for which I should have been killed. While in this state of mind, I was eager to hear any one speak of slavery. I was a ready listener. Every little while, I could hear something about the abolitionists. It was some time before I found what the word meant. It was always used in such connections as to make it an interesting word to me. If a slave ran away and succeeded in getting clear, or if a slave killed his master, set fire to a barn, or did any thing very wrong in the mind of a slaveholder, it was spoken of as the fruit of *abolition*. Hearing the word in this connection very often, I set about learning what it meant. The dictionary afforded me little or no help. I found it was "the act of abolishing"; but then I did not know what was to be abolished. Here I was perplexed. I did not dare to ask any one about its meaning, for I was satisfied that it was something they wanted me to know very little about. After a patient waiting, I got one of our city papers, containing an account of the number of petitions from the north, praying for the abolition of slavery in the District of Columbia, and of the slave trade between the States. From this time I understood the words *abolition* and *abolitionist,* and always drew near when that word was spoken, expecting to hear something of importance to myself and fellow-slaves. The light broke in upon me by degrees. I went one day down to the wharf of Mr. Waters; and seeing two Irishmen unloading a scow of stone, I went, unasked, and helped them. When we had finished, one of them came to me and asked me if I were a slave. I told him I was. He asked, "Are ye a slave for life?" I told him that I was. The good Irishman seemed to be deeply affected by the statement. He said to the other that it was a pity so fine a little fellow as myself should be a slave for life. He said it was a shame to hold me. They both advised me to run away to the north; that I should find friends there, and that I should be free. I pretended not to be interested in what they said, and treated them as if I did not understand them; for I feared they might be treacherous. White men have been known to encourage slaves to escape, and then, to get the reward, catch them and return them to their masters. I was afraid that these seemingly good men might use me so; but I nevertheless remembered their advice, and from that time I resolved to run away. I looked forward to a time at which it would be safe for me to escape. I was too young to think of doing so immediately; besides, I wished to learn how to write, as I might have occasion to write my own pass. I consoled myself with the hope that I should one day find a good chance. Meanwhile, I would learn to write.

The idea as to how I might learn to write was suggested to me by being in Durgin and Bailey's ship-yard, and frequently seeing the ship carpenters, after hewing, and getting a piece of timber ready for use, write on the timber the name of that part of the ship for which it was intended. When a piece of timber was intended for the larboard side, it would be marked thus—"L." When a piece was for the starboard side, it would be marked thus—"S." A piece for the larboard side forward, would be marked thus— "L. F." When a piece was for starboard side forward, it would be marked thus—"S. F." For larboard aft, it would be marked thus—"L. A." For starboard aft, it would be marked thus—"S. A." I soon learned the names of these letters, and for what they were intended when placed upon a piece of timber in the ship-yard. I immediately commenced copying them, and in a short time was able to make the four letters named. After that, when I met with any boy who I knew could write, I would tell him I could write as well as he. The next word would be, "I don't believe you. Let me see you try it." It would then make the letters which I had been so fortunate as to learn, and ask him to beat that. In this way I got a good many lessons in writing, which it is quite possible I should never have gotten in any other way. During this time, my copy-book was the board fence, brick wall, and pavement; my pen and ink was a lump of chalk. With these, I learned mainly how to write. I then commenced and continued copying the Italics in Webster's Spelling Book, until I could make them all without looking on the book. By this time, my little Master Thomas had gone to school, and learned how to write, and had written over a number of copy-books. These had been brought home, and shown to some of our near neighbors, and then laid aside. My mistress used to go to class meeting at the Wilk Street meeting-house every Monday afternoon, and leave me to take care of the house. When left thus, I used to spend the time in writing in the spaces left in Master Thomas's copy-book, copying what he had written. I continued to do this until I could write a hand very similar to that of Master Thomas. Thus, after a long, tedious effort for years, I finally succeeded in learning how to write.

Questions of Subject and Theme

1. According to Douglass, why did his owners oppose his learning to read and write? How well grounded was their attitude?
2. According to Douglass, what were the positive and negative results to him of his having learned to read?

Questions of Method and Strategy

1. Douglass's style shows how well he had "learned to write." Pick a moment where the power and dignity of his style contrasts with the helplessness and shame that makes his content. What uses of language heighten this contrast?
2. Douglass says ironically of his mistress: "She was an apt woman; and a little experience soon demonstrated, to her satisfaction, that education and slavery were incompatible with each other." Pick another moment when Douglass uses irony. Compare the moment with the one quoted and explain as clearly as you can the duality of meaning that operates in each case.

MOTHER TONGUE

Amy Tan

Amy Tan was born in California, where her Chinese family had recently settled. After college she worked for years as a freelance business writer until the success of her novel, *The Joy Luck Club* (1989). Her essay here was selected for *The Best American Essays 1991*.

I am not a scholar of English or literature. I cannot give you much more than personal opinions on the English language and its variations in this country or others.

I am a writer. And by that definition, I am someone who has always loved language. I am fascinated by language in daily life. I spend a great deal of my time thinking about the power of language—the way it can evoke an emotion, a visual image, a complex idea, or a simple truth. Language is the tool of my trade. And I use them all—all the Englishes I grew up with.

Recently, I was made keenly aware of the different Englishes I do use. I was giving a talk to a large group of people, the same talk I had already given to half a dozen other groups. The nature of the talk was about my writing, my life, and my book, *The Joy Luck Club*. The talk was going along well enough, until I remembered one major difference that made the whole talk sound wrong. My mother was in the room. And it was perhaps the first time she had heard me give a lengthy speech, using the kind of English I have never used with her. I was saying things like, "The intersection of memory upon imagination" and "There is an aspect of my fiction that relates to thus-and-thus"—a speech filled with carefully wrought grammatical phrases, burdened, it suddenly seemed to me, with nominalized forms, past perfect tenses, conditional phrases, all the forms of standard English that I had learned in school and through books, the forms of English I did not use at home with my mother.

Just last week, I was walking down the street with my mother, and I again found myself conscious of the English I was using, the English I do use with her. We were talking about the price of new and used furniture and I heard myself saying this: "Not waste money that way." My husband was with us as well, and he didn't notice any switch in my English. And then I realized why. It's because over the twenty years we've been together I've often used that same kind of English with him, and sometimes he even uses it with me. It has become our language of intimacy, a different sort of English that relates to family talk, the language I grew up with.

So you'll have some idea of what this family talk I heard sounds like, I'll quote what my mother said during a recent conversation which I videotaped and then transcribed. During this conversation, my mother was talking about a political gangster in Shanghai who had the same last name as her family's, Du, and how the gangster in his early years wanted to be adopted by her family, which was rich by comparison. Later, the gangster became more powerful, far richer than my mother's family, and one day showed up at my mother's wedding to pay his respects. Here's what she said in part:

"Du Yusong having business like fruit stand. Like off the street kind. He is Du like Du Zong—but not Tsung-ming Island people. The local people call putong, the river east side, he belong to that side local people. That man want to ask Du Zong father take him in like become own family. Du Zong father wasn't look down on him, but didn't take seriously, until that man big like become a mafia. Now important person, very hard to inviting him. Chinese way, came only to show respect, don't stay for dinner. Respect for making big celebration, he shows up. Mean gives lots of respect. Chinese custom. Chinese social life that way. If too important won't have to stay too long. He come to my wedding. I didn't see, I heard it. I gone to boy's side, they have YMCA dinner. Chinese age I was nineteen."

You should know that my mother's expressive command of English belies how much she actually understands. She reads the *Forbes* report, listens to *Wall Street Week,* converses daily with her stockbroker, reads all of Shirley MacLaine's books with ease—all kinds of things I can't begin to understand. Yet some of my friends tell me they understand 50 percent of what my mother says. Some say they understand 80 to 90 percent. Some say they understand none of it, as if she were speaking pure Chinese. But to me, my mother's English is perfectly clear, perfectly natural. It's my mother tongue. Her language, as I hear it, is vivid, direct, full of observation and imagery. That was the language that helped shape the way I saw things, expressed things, made sense of the world.

Lately, I've been giving more thought to the kind of English my mother speaks. Like others, I have described it to people as "broken" or "fractured" English. But I wince when I say that. It has always bothered me that I can think of no way to describe it other than "broken," as if it were damaged and needed to be fixed, as if it lacked a certain wholeness and soundness. I've heard other terms used, "limited English," for example. But they seem just as bad, as if everything is limited, including people's perceptions of the limited English speaker.

I know this for a fact, because when I was growing up, my mother's "limited" English limited *my* perception of her. I was ashamed of her English. I believed that her English reflected the quality of what she had to say. That is, because she expressed them imperfectly her thoughts were imperfect. And I had plenty of empirical evidence to support me: the fact that people in department stores, at banks, and at restaurants did not take her seriously, did not give her good service, pretended not to understand her, or even acted as if they did not hear her.

My mother has long realized the limitations of her English as well. 10
When I was fifteen, she used to have me call people on the phone to pretend I was she. In this guise, I was forced to ask for information or even to com-

plain and yell at people who had been rude to her. One time it was a call to her stockbroker in New York. She had cashed out her small portfolio and it just so happened we were going to go to New York the next week, our very first trip outside California. I had to get on the phone and say in an adolescent voice that was not very convincing, "This is Mrs. Tan."

And my mother was standing in the back whispering loudly, "Why he don't send me check, already two weeks late. So mad he lie to me, losing me money."

And then I said in perfect English, "Yes, I'm getting rather concerned. You had agreed to send the check two weeks ago, but it hasn't arrived."

Then she began to talk more loudly. "What he want, I come to New York tell him front of his boss, you cheating me?" And I was trying to calm her down, make her be quiet, while telling the stockbroker, "I can't tolerate any more excuses. If I don't receive the check immediately, I am going to have to speak to your manager when I'm in New York next week." And sure enough, the following week there we were in front of this astonished stockbroker, and I was sitting there red-faced and quiet, and my mother, the real Mrs. Tan, was shouting at his boss in her impeccable broken English.

We used a similar routine just five days ago, for a situation that was far less humorous. My mother had gone to the hospital for an appointment, to find out about a benign brain tumor a CAT scan had revealed a month ago. She said she had spoken very good English, her best English, no mistakes. Still, she said, the hospital did not apologize when they said they had lost the CAT scan and she had come for nothing. She said they did not seem to have any sympathy when she told them she was anxious to know the exact diagnosis, since her husband and son had both died of brain tumors. She said they would not give her any more information until the next time and she would have to make another appointment for that. So she said she would not leave until the doctor called her daughter. She wouldn't budge. And when the doctor finally called her daughter, me, who spoke in perfect English—lo and behold—we had assurances the CAT scan would be found, promises that a conference call on Monday would be held, and apologies for any suffering my mother had gone through for a most regrettable mistake.

I think my mother's English almost had an effect on limiting my possibilities in life as well. Sociologists and linguists probably will tell you that a person's developing language skills are more influenced by peers. But I do think that the language spoken in the family, especially in immigrant families which are more insular, plays a large role in shaping the language of the child. And I believe that it affected my results on achievement tests, IQ tests, and the SAT. While my English skills were never judged as poor, compared to math, English could not be considered my strong suit. In grade school I did moderately well, getting perhaps B's, sometimes B-pluses, in English and scoring perhaps in the sixtieth or seventieth percentile on achievement tests. But those scores were not good enough to override the opinion that my true abilities lay in math and science, because in those areas I achieved A's and scored in the ninetieth percentile or higher.

15

This was understandable. Math is precise; there is only one correct answer. Whereas, for me at least, the answers on English tests were always a judgment call, a matter of opinion and personal experience. Those tests were constructed around items like fill-in-the-blank sentence completion, such as, "Even though Tom was ———, Mary thought he was ———." And the correct answer always seemed to be the most bland combinations of thoughts, for example, "Even though Tom was shy, Mary thought he was charming," with the grammatical structure "even though" limiting the correct answer to some sort of semantic opposites, so you wouldn't get answers like, "Even though Tom was foolish, Mary thought he was ridiculous." Well, according to my mother, there were very few limitations as to what Tom could have been and what Mary might have thought of him. So I never did well on tests like that.

The same was true with word analogies, pairs of words in which you were supposed to find some sort of logical, semantic relationship—for example, "*Sunset* is to *nightfall* as ——— is to ———." And here you would be presented with a list of four possible pairs, one of which showed the same kind of relationship: *red* is to *stoplight, bus* is to *arrival, chills* is to *fever, yawn* is to *boring*. Well, I could never think that way. I knew what the tests were asking, but I could not block out of my mind the images already created by the first pair, "*sunset* is to *nightfall*"—and I would see a burst of colors against a darkening sky, the moon rising, the lowering of a curtain of stars. And all the other pairs of words—red, bus, stoplight, boring—just threw up a mass of confusing images, making it impossible for me to sort out something as logical as saying: "A sunset precedes nightfall" is the same as "a chill precedes a fever." The only way I would have gotten that answer right would have been to imagine an associative situation, for example, my being disobedient and staying out past sunset, catching a chill at night, which turns into feverish pneumonia as punishment, which indeed did happen to me.

I have been thinking about all this lately, about my mother's English, about achievement tests. Because lately I've been asked, as a writer, why there are not more Asian Americans represented in American literature. Why are there few Asian Americans enrolled in creative writing programs? Why do so many Chinese students go into engineering? Well, these are broad sociological questions I can't begin to answer. But I have noticed in surveys—in fact, just last week—that Asian students, as a whole, always do significantly better on math achievement tests than in English. And this makes me think that there are other Asian-American students whose English spoken in the home might also be described as "broken" or "limited." And perhaps they also have teachers who are steering them away from writing and into math and science, which is what happened to me.

Fortunately, I happen to be rebellious in nature and enjoy the challenge of disproving assumptions made about me. I became an English major my first year in college, after being enrolled as pre-med. I started writing nonfiction as a freelancer the week after I was told by my former boss that writing was my worst skill and I should hone my talents toward account management.

But it wasn't until 1985 that I finally began to write fiction. And at first   *20* I wrote using what I thought to be wittily crafted sentences, sentences that would finally prove I had mastery over the English language. Here's an example from the first draft of a story that later made its way into *The Joy Luck Club,* but without this line: "That was my mental quandary in its nascent state." A terrible line, which I can barely pronounce.

Fortunately, for reasons I won't get into today, I later decided I should envision a reader for the stories I would write. And the reader I decided upon was my mother, because these were stories about mothers. So with this reader in mind—and in fact she did read my early drafts—I began to write stories using all the Englishes I grew up with: the English I spoke to my mother, which for lack of a better term might be described as "simple"; the English she used with me, which for lack of a better term might be described as "broken"; my translation of her Chinese, which could certainly be described as "watered down"; and what I imagined to be her translation of her Chinese if she could speak in perfect English, her internal language, and for that I sought to preserve the essence, but neither an English nor a Chinese structure. I wanted to capture what language ability tests can never reveal: her intent, her passion, her imagery, the rhythms of her speech and the nature of her thoughts.

Apart from what any critic had to say about my writing, I knew I had succeeded where it counted when my mother finished reading my book and gave me her verdict: "So easy to read."

Questions of Subject and Theme

1. In her second paragraph, Tan says: "I use them all—all the Englishes I grew up with." How many "Englishes" does she refer to in the essay? Give an example of each and describe the kind of occasion on which Tan employs it.

2. Tan is careful in naming the kind of English her mother speaks. What names does she find? How and why do the names differ in Tan's view?

Questions of Method and Strategy

1. Given the essay as a whole, what strategy does Tan employ with the disavowals of her first paragraph? What focus does the paragraph provide for her essay?

2. In the third paragraph from the end of the essay, Tan gives what she thinks now is "a terrible line." What does she find wrong with the line? Rewrite it as you imagine her mother might. Then rewrite it in the style you find more representative of Tan's usual English throughout the essay.

MR. K★A★P★L★A★N, THE COMPARATIVE, AND THE SUPERLATIVE

Leonard Q. Ross

"Leonard Q. Ross" is the pen name of the author Leo Rosten, who grew up with much closer associations to the New York immigrant English of his character, Hyman Kaplan (whose native language was Yiddish), than to the "correct" English of Kaplan's teacher, Mr. Parkhill. Originally appearing in the *New Yorker,* the tales of Kaplan's love affair with the English language were first collected in *The Education of H★Y★M★A★N★ K★A★P★L★A★N* in 1937, when the idea of bilingual education was yet in the womb of time.

FOR two weeks Mr. Parkhill had been delaying the inescapable: Mr. Kaplan, like the other students in the beginners' grade of the American Night Preparatory School for Adults, would have to present a composition for class analysis. All the students had had their turn writing the assignment on the board, a composition of one hundred words, entitled "My Job." Now only Mr. Kaplan's rendition remained.

It would be more accurate to say Mr. K★A★P★L★A★N's rendition of the assignment remained, for even in thinking of that distinguished student, Mr. Parkhill saw the image of his unmistakable signature, in all its red-blue-green glory. The multicolored characters were more than a trademark; they were an assertion of individuality, a symbol of singularity, a proud expression of Mr. Kaplan's Inner Self. To Mr. Parkhill, the signature took on added meaning because it was associated with the man who had said his youthful ambition had been to become "a physician and sergeant," the Titan who had declined the verb "to fail": "fail, failed, bankrupt."

One night, after the two weeks' procrastination, Mr. Parkhill decided to face the worst. "Mr. Kaplan, I think it's your turn to—er—write your composition on the board."

Mr. Kaplan's great, buoyant smile grew more great and more buoyant. "My!" he exclaimed. He rose, looked around at the class proudly as if surveying the blessed who were to witness a linguistic *tour de force,* stumbled over Mrs. Moskowitz's feet with a polite "Vould you be so kindly?" and took his place at the blackboard. There he rejected several pieces of chalk critically, nodded to Mr. Parkhill—it was a nod of distinct reassurance—and then printed in firm letters:

My Job A Cotter In Dress Faktory
Comp. by
H★Y★

"You need not write your name on the board," interrupted Mr. Parkhill quickly. "Er—to save time . . ."

Mr. Kaplan's face expressed astonishment. "Podden me, Mr. Pockheel. But de name is by me *pot* of mine composition."

"Your name is *part* of the composition?" asked Mr. Parkhill in an anxious tone.

"Yas*sir!*" said Mr. Kaplan with dignity. He printed the rest of H★Y★M★A★N K★A★P★L★A★N for all to see and admire. You could tell it was a disappointment for him not to have colored chalk for this performance. In pale white the elegance of his work was dissipated. The name, indeed, seemed unreal, the letters stark, anemic, almost denuded.

His brow wrinkled and perspiring, Mr. Kaplan wrote the saga of A Cotter In Dress Faktory on the board, with much scratching of the chalk and an undertone of sound. Mr. Kaplan repeated each word to himself softly, as if trying to give to its spelling some of the flavor and originality of his pronunciation. The smile on the face of Mr. Kaplan had taken on something beatific and imperishable: it was his first experience at the blackboard; it was his moment of glory. He seemed to be writing more slowly than necessary as if to prolong the ecstasy of his Hour. When he had finished he said "Hau Kay" with distinct regret in his voice, and sat down. Mr. Parkhill observed the composition in all its strange beauty:

My Job A Cotter In Dress Faktory

Comp. by

H★Y★M★A★N K★A★P★L★A★N

Shakspere is saying what fulls man is and I am feeling
just the same way when I am thinking about mine
job a cotter in Dress Faktory on 38 st. by 7 av. For
why should we slafing in dark place by laktric lights
and all kinds hot for $30 or maybe $36 with overtime,
for Boss who is fat and driving in fency automobil?
I ask! Because we are the deprassed workers of world.
And are being exployted. By Bosses. In mine shop is
no difference. Oh how bad is laktric light, oh how is
all kinds hot. And when I am telling Foreman should
be better conditions he hollers, Kaplan you redical!!

At this point a glazed look came into Mr. Parkhill's eyes, but he read on.   *10*

So I keep still and work by bad light and always hot.
But somday will the workers making Bosses to work!
And then Kaplan will give to them bad laktric and positively
no windows for the air should come in! So they
can know what it means to slafe! Kaplan will make
Foreman a cotter like he is. And give the most bad
dezigns to cot out. Justice.
Mine job is cotting Dress dezigns.

T-H-E E-N-D

Mr. Parkhill read the amazing document over again. His eyes, glazed but a moment before, were haunted now. It was true: spelling, diction, sentence structure, punctuation, capitalization, the use of the present perfect for the present—all true.

"Is planty mistakes, I s'pose," suggested Mr. Kaplan modestly.

"Y-yes . . . yes, there are many mistakes."

"Dat's because I'm tryink to give *dip ideas,*" said Mr. Kaplan with the   *15*
sigh of those who storm heaven.

Mr. Parkhill girded his mental loins. "Mr. Kaplan—er—your composition doesn't really meet the assignment. You haven't described your *job,* what you *do,* what your work *is.*"

"Vell, it's not soch a interastink jop," said Mr. Kaplan.

"Your composition is not a simple exposition. It's more of a—well, an *essay* on your *attitude.*"

"Oh, fine!" cried Mr. Kaplan with enthusiasm.

"No, no," said Mr. Parkhill hastily. "The assignment was *meant* to be a   *20*
composition. You see, we must begin with simple exercises before we try— er—more philosophical essays."

Mr. Kaplan nodded with resignation. "So naxt time should be no ideas, like abot Shaksbeer? Should be only *fects?*"

"Y-yes. No ideas, only—er—facts."

You could see by Mr. Kaplan's martyred smile that his wings, like those of an eagle's, were being clipped.

"And Mr. Kaplan—er—why do you use 'Kaplan' in the body of your composition? Why don't you say '*I* will make the foreman a cutter' instead of '*Kaplan* will make the foreman a cutter?'"

Mr. Kaplan's response was instantaneous. "I'm so glad you eskink me   *25*
dis! Ha! I'm usink 'Keplen' in de composition for plain and tsimple rizzon: becawss I didn't vant de reader should tink I am *prajudiced* aganst de foreman, so I said it more like abot a strenger: '*Keplen* vill make de foreman a cotter!'"

In the face of this subtle passion for objectivity, Mr. Parkhill was silent. He called for corrections. A forest of hands went up. Miss Mitnick pointed out errors in spelling, the use of capital letters, punctuation; Mr. Norman Bloom corrected several more words, rearranged sentences, and said, "Woikers is exployted with an '*i,*' not 'y' as Kaplan makes"; Miss Caravello changed "fulls" to "fools," and declared herself uncertain as to the validity of the word "Justice" standing by itself in "da smalla da sentence"; Mr. Sam Pinsky said he was sure Mr. Kaplan meant "*opprassed* voikers of de voild, not *deprassed,* aldough dey are deprassed *too,*" to which Mr. Kaplan replied, "So ve bote got right, no? Don' *chenge* 'deprassed,' only *add* 'opprassed.'"

Then Mr. Parkhill went ahead with his own corrections, changing tenses, substituting prepositions, adding the definite article. Through the whole barrage Mr. Kaplan kept shaking his head, murmuring "Mine gootness!" each time a correction was made. But he smiled all the while. He seemed to be proud of the very number of errors he had made; of the labor to which the class was being forced in his service; of the fact that his *ideas,* his creation, could survive so concerted an onslaught. And as the composition took more respectable form, Mr. Kaplan's smile grew more expansive.

Questions of Subject and Theme

1. According to Mr. Parkhill, are Kaplan's "errors" all of one sort? Explain your answer with examples.
2. What is Kaplan's reason for writing his essay the way he does? What is his teacher's objection? Kaplan's response? In your opinion, who wins this argument and why?

Questions of Method and Strategy

1. In the second paragraph, the phrase "Inner Self" is capitalized, and we later read about "the ecstasy of his Hour." What is the point of these capitalizations?
2. The narrator seems to adopt Mr. Parkhill's attitude toward Kaplan's uses of language. How would you characterize that attitude? Do you think this is the author's attitude? Explain your view of the author's method and strategy with regard to his narrator's attitude.

———

Suggestions for Writing on the Juxtapositions

1. In your view, which writer does most justice to the power of language? Write an essay in which you defend your choice.
2. Have you grown up with what Amy Tan calls several "Englishes?" At the very least, is the English you speak to your friends the same English that you use in class? What do you think is the proper role of "proper" English? Write an essay in which you defend your opinion.
3. Each writer raises the issue of limitations of language perceived as mental limitations. Write an essay in which you compare and contrast the implicit and explicit arguments on this issue presented in these selections.
4. Bilingual education is one proposed solution to some of the difficulties recorded in these selections. Using your own experience and the evidence here, write an essay in which you argue for or against the use of bilingual instruction.

24 *Mirror, Mirror*

Nathaniel Hawthorne, "The Birth-Mark"
Molly O'Neill, "The Anatomy Lesson"
Marjorie Rosen, "New Face, New Body, New Self"

An old proverb has it that "Human beings are the architects of their bodies." What happens when people act on that proposition? Consider the following questions as you read:

1. In what ways do the different selections view the concepts of the "ideal" (or "perfection") and the "real?"

2. How much does fashion influence David Barton's ideas about the way a body should look? How big a part does changing fashion play in the other selections?

3. In "The Anatomy Lesson" David Barton says "People are concerned with living life, not conquering it." In what ways do the selections in this section confirm or refute this claim?

4. Compare the selections here to those on the idea of body weight presented earlier (p. 260). To what extent are the same values, assumptions, and arguments shared? To what extent do they differ?

THE BIRTH-MARK[1]

Nathaniel Hawthorne

Nathaniel Hawthorne, the great nineteenth-century American
novelist and short story writer, was interested in artistic problems
throughout his career. In the story that follows, a scientist becomes
an artist in an attempt to create an ideal human.

In the latter part of the last century, there lived a man of science—an   *1*
eminent proficient in every branch of natural philosophy—who, not long
before our story opens, had made experience of a spiritual affinity, more
attractive than any chemical one. He had left his laboratory to the care of an
assistant, cleared his fine countenance from the furnace-smoke, washed the
stain of acids from his fingers, and persuaded a beautiful woman to become
his wife. In those days, when the comparatively recent discovery of electricity, and other kindred mysteries of nature, seemed to open paths into the
region of miracle, it was not unusual for the love of science to rival the love
of woman, in its depth and absorbing energy. The higher intellect, the
imagination, the spirit, and even the heart, might all find their congenial
aliment in pursuits which, as some of their ardent votaries believed, would
ascend from one step of powerful intelligence to another, until the philosopher should lay his hand on the secret of creative force, and perhaps make
new worlds for himself. We know not whether Aylmer possessed this degree
of faith in man's ultimate control over nature. He had devoted himself, however, too unreservedly to scientific studies, ever to be weaned from them by
any second passion. His love for his young wife might prove the stronger of
the two; but it could only be by intertwining itself with his love of science,
and uniting the strength of the latter to its own.

Such a union accordingly took place, and was attended with truly remarkable consequences, and a deeply impressive moral. One day, very soon
after their marriage, Aylmer sat gazing at his wife, with a trouble in his
countenance that grew stronger, until he spoke.

"Georgiana," said he, "has it never occurred to you that the mark upon
your cheek might be removed?"

"No, indeed," said she, smiling; but perceiving the seriousness of his
manner, she blushed deeply. "To tell you the truth, it has been so often
called a charm, that I was simple enough to imagine it might be so."

"Ah, upon another face, perhaps it might," replied her husband. "But   *5*
never on yours! No, dearest Georgiana, you came so nearly perfect from
the hand of Nature, that this slightest possible defect—which we hesitate

---

1. First published in the *Pioneer Magazine* in 1843 and included in *Mosses From an Old Manse*
(1846).

whether to term a defect or a beauty—shocks me, as being the visible mark of earthly imperfection."

"Shocks you, my husband!" cried Georgiana, deeply hurt; at first reddening with momentary anger, but then bursting into tears. "Then why did you take me from my mother's side? You cannot love what shocks you!"

To explain this conversation, it must be mentioned, that, in the centre of Georgiana's left cheek, there was a singular mark, deeply interwoven, as it were, with the texture and substance of her face. In the usual state of her complexion,—a healthy, though delicate bloom,—the mark wore a tint of deeper crimson, which imperfectly defined its shape amid the surrounding rosiness. When she blushed, it gradually became more indistinct, and finally vanished amid the triumphant rush of blood, that bathed the whole cheek with its brilliant glow. But, if any shifting emotion caused her to turn pale, there was the mark again, a crimson stain upon the snow, in what Aylmer sometimes deemed an almost fearful distinctness. Its shape bore not a little similarity to the human hand, though of the smallest pigmy size. Georgiana's lovers were wont to say, that some fairy, at her birth-hour, had laid her tiny hand upon the infant's cheek, and left this impress there, in token of the magic endowments that were to give her such sway over all hearts. Many a desperate swain would have risked life for the privilege of pressing his lips to the mysterious hand. It must not be concealed, however, that the impression wrought by this fairy sign-manual varied exceedingly, according to the difference of temperament in the beholders. Some fastidious persons—but they were exclusively of her own sex—affirmed that the Bloody Hand, as they chose to call it, quite destroyed the effect of Georgiana's beauty, and rendered her countenance even hideous. But it would be as reasonable to say, that one of those small blue stains, which sometimes occur in the purest statuary marble, would convert the Eve of Powers to a monster. Masculine observers, if the birth-mark did not heighten their admiration, contented themselves with wishing it away, that the world might possess one living specimen of ideal loveliness, without the semblance of a flaw. After his marriage—for he thought little or nothing of the matter before—Aylmer discovered that this was the case with himself.

Had she been less beautiful—if Envy's self could have found aught else to sneer at—he might have felt his affection heightened by the prettiness of this mimic hand, now vaguely portrayed, now lost, now stealing forth again, and glimmering to-and-fro with every pulse of emotion that throbbed within her heart. But, seeing her otherwise so perfect, he found this one defect grow more and more intolerable, with every moment of their united lives. It was the fatal flaw of humanity, which Nature, in one shape or another, stamps ineffaceably on all her productions, either to imply that they are temporary and finite, or that their perfection must be wrought by toil and pain. The Crimson Hand expressed the ineludible gripe, in which mortality clutches the highest and purest of earthly mould, degrading them into kindred with the lowest, and even with the very brutes, like whom their visible frames return to dust. In this manner, selecting it as the symbol of his wife's liability to sin, sorrow, decay, and death, Aylmer's sombre imagination was not long in rendering the birth-mark a frightful object, causing him more trouble and horror than ever Georgiana's beauty, whether of soul or sense, had given him delight.

At all the seasons which should have been their happiest, he invariably, and without intending it—nay, in spite of a purpose to the contrary—reverted to this one disastrous topic. Trifling as it at first appeared, it so connected itself with innumerable trains of thought, and modes of feeling, that it became the central point of all. With the morning twilight, Aylmer opened his eyes upon his wife's face, and recognized the symbol of imperfection; and when they sat together at the evening hearth, his eyes wandered stealthily to her cheek, and beheld, flickering with the blaze of the wood fire, the spectral Hand that wrote mortality, where he would fain have worshipped. Georgiana soon learned to shudder at his gaze. It needed but a glance, with the peculiar expression that his face often wore, to change the roses of her cheek into a deathlike paleness, amid which the Crimson Hand was brought strongly out, like a bas-relief of ruby on the whitest marble.

Late, one night, when the lights were growing dim, so as hardly to   10
betray the stain on the poor wife's cheek, she herself, for the first time, voluntarily took up the subject.

"Do you remember, my dear Aylmer," said she, with a feeble attempt at a smile—"have you any recollection of a dream, last night, about this odious Hand?"

"None!—none whatever!" replied Aylmer, starting; but then he added in a dry, cold tone, affected for the sake of concealing the real depth of his emotion:—"I might well dream of it; for before I fell asleep, it had taken a pretty firm hold of my fancy."

"And you did dream of it," continued Georgiana, hastily; for she dreaded lest a gush of tears should interrupt what she had to say—"A terrible dream! I wonder that you can forget it. Is it possible to forget this one expression?—Reflect, my husband; for by all means I would have you recall that dream."

The mind is in a sad note, when Sleep, the all-involving, cannot confine her spectres within the dim region of her sway, but suffers them to break forth, affrighting this actual life with secrets that perchance belong to a deeper one. Aylmer now remembered his dream. He had fancied himself, with his servant Aminadab, attempting an operation for the removal of the birth-mark. But the deeper went the knife, the deeper sank the Hand, until at length its tiny grasp appeared to have caught hold of Georgiana's heart; whence, however, her husband was inexorably resolved to cut or wrench it away.

When the dream had shaped itself perfectly in his memory, Aylmer sat   15
in his wife's presence with a guilty feeling. Truth often finds its way to the mind close-muffled in robes of sleep, and then speaks with uncompromising directness of matters in regard to which we practise an unconscious self-deception, during our waking moments. Until now, he had not been aware

of the tyrannizing influence acquired by one idea over his mind, and of the lengths which he might find in his heart to go, for the sake of giving himself peace.

"Aylmer," resumed Georgiana, solemnly, "I know not what may be the cost to both of us, to rid me of this fatal birth-mark. Perhaps its removal may cause cureless deformity. Or, it may be, the stain goes as deep as life itself. Again, do we know that there is a possibility, on any terms, of unclasping the firm grip of this little Hand, which was laid upon me before I came into the world?"

"Dearest Georgiana, I have spent much thought upon the subject," hastily interrupted Aylmer—"I am convinced of the perfect practicability of its removal."

"If there be the remotest possibility of it," continued Georgiana, "let the attempt be made, at whatever risk. Danger is nothing to me; for life— while this hateful mark makes me the object of your horror and disgust— life is a burthen which I would fling down with joy. Either remove this dreadful Hand, or take my wretched life! You have deep science! All the world bears witness of it. You have achieved great wonders! Cannot you remove this little, little mark, which I cover with the tips of two small fingers? Is this beyond your power, for the sake of your own peace, and to save your poor wife from madness?"

"Noblest—dearest—tenderest wife!" cried Aylmer, rapturously. "Doubt not my power. I have already given this matter the deepest thought— thought which might almost have enlightened me to create a being less perfect than yourself. Georgiana, you have led me deeper than ever into the heart of science. I feel myself fully competent to render this dear cheek as faultless as its fellow; and then, most beloved, what will be my triumph, when I shall have corrected what Nature left imperfect, in her fairest work! Even Pygmalion, when his sculptured woman assumed life, felt not greater ecstasy than mine will be."

"It is resolved, then," said Georgiana, faintly smiling,—"And, Aylmer, 20 spare me not, though you should find the birth-mark take refuge in my heart at last."

Her husband tenderly kissed her cheek—her right cheek—not that which bore the impress of the Crimson Hand.

The next day, Aylmer apprized his wife of a plan that he had formed, whereby he might have opportunity for the intense thought and constant watchfulness, which the proposed operation would require; while Georgiana, likewise, would enjoy the perfect repose essential to its success. They were to seclude themselves in the extensive apartments occupied by Aylmer as a laboratory, and where, during his toil-some youth, he had made discoveries in the elemental powers of nature, that had roused the admiration of all the learned societies in Europe. Seated calmly in this laboratory, the pale philosopher had investigated the secrets of the highest cloud-region, and of the profoundest mines; he had satisfied himself of the causes that kindled and kept alive the fires of the volcano; and had explained the mystery of fountains, and how it is that they gush forth, some so bright and pure, and others with such rich medicinal virtues, from the dark bosom of the earth. Here, too, at an earlier period, he had studied the wonders of the human frame, and attempted to fathom the very process by which Nature assimilates all her precious influences from earth and air, and from the spiritual world, to create and foster Man, her masterpiece. The latter pursuit, however, Aylmer had long laid aside, in unwilling recognition of the truth, against which all seekers sooner or later stumble, that our great creative Mother, while she amuses us with apparently working in the broadest sunshine, is yet severely careful to keep her own secrets, and, in spite of her pretended openness, shows us nothing but results. She permits us indeed, to mar, but seldom to mend, and, like a jealous patentee, on no account to make. Now, however, Aylmer resumed these half-forgotten investigations; not, of course, with such hopes or wishes as first suggested them; but because they involved such physiological truth, and lay in the path of his proposed scheme for the treatment of Georgiana.

As he led her over the threshold of the laboratory, Georgiana was cold and tremulous. Aylmer looked cheerfully into her face, with intent to reassure her, but was so startled with the intense glow of the birth-mark upon the whiteness of her cheek, that he could not restrain a strong convulsive shudder. His wife fainted.

"Aminadab! Aminadab!" shouted Aylmer, stamping violently on the floor.

Forthwith, there issued from an inner apartment a man of low stature, but bulky frame, with shaggy hair hanging about his visage, which was grimed with the vapors of the furnace. This personage had been Aylmer's under-worker during his whole scientific career, and was admirably fitted for that office by his great mechanical readiness, and the skill with which, while incapable of comprehending a single principle, he executed all the practical details of his master's experiments. With his vast strength, his shaggy hair, his smoky aspect, and the indescribable earthiness that incrusted him, he seemed to represent man's physical nature; while Aylmer's slender figure, and pale, intellectual face, were no less apt a type of the spiritual element.

"Throw open the door of the boudoir, Aminadab," said Aylmer, "and burn a pastille."

"Yes, master," answered Aminadab, looking intently at the lifeless form of Georgiana; and then he muttered to himself:—"If she were my wife, I'd never part with that birth-mark."

When Georgiana recovered consciousness, she found herself breathing an atmosphere of penetrating fragrance, the gentle potency of which had recalled her from her deathlike faintness. The scene around her looked like enchantment. Aylmer had converted those smoky, dingy, sombre rooms, where he had spent his brightest years in recondite pursuits, into a series of beautiful apartments, not unfit to be the secluded abode of a lovely woman. The walls were hung with gorgeous curtains, which imparted the combination of grandeur and grace, that no other species of adornment can achieve; and as they fell from the ceiling to the floor, their rich and ponderous folds, concealing all angles and straight lines, appeared to shut in the scene from infinite space. For aught Georgiana knew, it might be a pavilion among the clouds. And Aylmer, excluding the sunshine, which would have interfered with his chemical processes, had supplied its place with perfumed lamps, emitting flames of various hue, but all uniting in a soft, empurpled radiance. He now knelt by his wife's side, watching her earnestly, but without alarm; for he was confident in his science, and felt that he could draw a magic circle round her, within which no evil might intrude.

"Where am I?—Ah, I remember!" said Georgiana, faintly; and she placed her hand over her cheek, to hide the terrible mark from her husband's eyes.

"Fear not, dearest!" exclaimed he. "Do not shrink from me! Believe me, Georgiana, I even rejoice in this single imperfection, since it will be such rapture to remove it." 30

"Oh, spare me!" sadly replied his wife—"Pray do not look at it again. I never can forget that convulsive shudder."

In order to soothe Georgiana, and, as it were, to release her mind from the burthen of actual things, Aylmer now put in practice some of the light and playful secrets, which science had taught him among its profounder lore. Airy figures, absolutely bodiless ideas, and forms of unsubstantial beauty, came and danced before her, imprinting their momentary footsteps on beams of light. Though she had some indistinct idea of the method of these optical phenomena, still the illusion was almost perfect enough to warrant the belief, that her husband possessed sway over the spiritual world. Then again, when she felt a wish to look forth from her seclusion, immediately, as if her thoughts were answered, the procession of external existence flitted across a screen. The scenery and the figures of actual life were perfectly represented, but with that bewitching, yet indescribable difference, which always makes a picture, an image, or a shadow, so much more attractive than the original. When wearied of this, Aylmer bade her cast her eyes upon a vessel, containing a quantity of earth. She did so, with little interest at first, but was soon startled, to perceive the germ of a plant, shooting upward from the soil. Then came the slender stalk—the leaves gradually unfolded themselves—and amid them was a perfect and lovely flower.

"It is magical!" cried Georgiana, "I dare not touch it."

"Nay, pluck it," answered Aylmer, "pluck it, and inhale its brief perfume while you may. The flower will wither in a few moments, and leave nothing save its brown seed-vessels—but thence may be perpetuated a race as ephemeral as itself."

But Georgiana had no sooner touched the flower than the whole plant suffered a blight, its leaves turning coal-black, as if by the agency of fire. 35

"There was too powerful a stimulus," said Aylmer thoughtfully.

To make up for this abortive experiment, he proposed to take her portrait by a scientific process of his own invention. It was to be effected by

rays of light striking upon a polished plate of metal. Georgiana assented—
but, on looking at the result, was affrighted to find the features of the portrait blurred and indefinable; while the minute figure of a hand appeared
where the cheek should have been. Aylmer snatched the metallic plate, and
threw it into a jar of corrosive acid.

Soon, however, he forgot these mortifying failures. In the intervals of
study and chemical experiment, he came to her, flushed and exhausted, but
seemed invigorated by her presence, and spoke in glowing language of the
resources of his art. He gave a history of the long dynasty of the Alchemists,
who spent so many ages in quest of the universal solvent, by which the
Golden Principle might be elicted from all things vile and base. Aylmer
appeared to believe, that, by the plainest scientific logic, it was altogether
within the limits of possibility to discover this long-sought medium; but, he
added, a philosopher who should go deep enough to acquire the power,
would attain too lofty a wisdom to stoop to the exercise of it. Not less singular were his opinions in regard to the Elixir Vitæ. He more than inti-
mated, that it was his option to concoct a liquid that should prolong life for
years—perhaps interminably—but that it would produce a discord in nature, which all the world, and chiefly the quaffer of the immortal nostrum,
would find cause to curse.

"Aylmer, are you in earnest?" asked Georgiana, looking at him with
amazement and fear; "it is terrible to possess such power, or even to dream
of possessing it!"

"Oh, do not tremble, my love!" said her husband, "I would not wrong
either you or myself by working such inharmonious effects upon our lives.
But I would have you consider how trifling, in comparison, is the skill req-
uisite to remove this little Hand."

At the mention of the birth-mark, Georgiana, as usual, shrank, as if a
red-hot iron had touched her cheek.

Again Aylmer applied himself to his labors. She could hear his voice in
the distant furnace-room, giving directions to Aminadab, whose harsh, un-
couth, misshapen tones were audible in response, more like the grunt or
growl of a brute than human speech. After hours of absence, Aylmer reappeared, and proposed that she should now examine his cabinets of chemical
products, and natural treasures of the earth. Among the former he showed
her a small vial, in which, he remarked, was contained a gentle yet most
powerful fragrance, capable of impregnating all the breezes that blow across
a kingdom. They were of inestimable value, the contents of that little vial;
and, as he said so, he threw some of the perfume into the air, and filled the
room with piercing and invigorating delight.

"And what is this?" asked Georgiana, pointing to a small crystal globe,
containing a gold-colored liquid. "It is so beautiful to the eye, that I could
image it the Elixir of Life."

"In one sense it is," replied Aylmer, "or rather the Elixir of Immortality.
It is the most precious poison that ever was concocted in this world. By its
aid, I could apportion the lifetime of any mortal at whom you might point

your finger. The strength of the dose would determine whether he were to linger out years, or drop dead in the midst of a breath. No king, on his guarded throne, could keep his life, if I, in my private station, should deem that the welfare of millions justified me in depriving him of it."

"Why do you keep such a terrific drug?" inquired Georgiana in horror.   *45*

"Do not mistrust me, dearest!" said her husband, smiling; "its virtuous potency is yet greater than its harmful one. But, see! here is a powerful cosmetic. With a few drops of this, in a vase of water, freckles may be washed away as easily as the hands are cleansed. A stronger infusion would take the blood out of the cheek, and leave the rosiest beauty a pale ghost."

"Is it with this lotion that you intend to bathe my cheek?" asked Georgiana anxiously.

"Oh, no!" hastily replied her husband—"this is merely superficial. Your case demands a remedy that shall go deeper."

In his interviews with Georgiana, Aylmer generally made minute inquiries as to her sensations, and whether the confinement of the rooms, and the temperature of the atmosphere, agreed with her. These questions had such a particular drift, that Georgiana began to conjecture that she was already subjected to certain physical influences, either breathed in with the fragrant air, or taken with her food. She fancied, likewise—but it might be altogether fancy—that there was a stirring up of her system,—a strange indefinite sensation creeping through her veins, and tingling, half painfully, half pleasurably, at her heart. Still, whenever she dared to look into the mirror, there she beheld herself, pale as a white rose, and with the crimson birth-mark stamped upon her cheek. Not even Aylmer now hated it so much as she.

To dispel the tedium of the hours which her husband found it necessary   *50* to devote to the processes of combination and analysis, Georgiana turned over the volumes of his scientific library. In many dark old tomes, she met with chapters full of romance and poetry. They were the works of the philosophers of the middle ages, such as Albertus Magnus, Cornelius Agrippa, Paracelsus, and the famous friar who created the prophetic Brazen Head. All these antique naturalists stood in advance of their centuries, yet were imbued with some of their credulity, and therefore were believed, and perhaps imagined themselves, to have acquired from the investigation of nature a power above nature, and from physics a sway over the spiritual world. Hardly less curious and imaginative were the early volumes of the Transactions of the Royal Society, in which the members, knowing little of the limits of natural possibility, were continually recording wonders, or proposing methods whereby wonders might be wrought.

But, to Georgiana, the most engrossing volume was a large folio from her husband's own hand, in which he had recorded every experiment of his scientific career, with its original aim, the methods adopted for its development, and its final success or failure, with the circumstances to which either event was attributable. The book, in truth, was both the history and emblem of his ardent, ambitious, imaginative, yet practical and laborious, life. He handled physical details, as if there were nothing beyond them; yet spiritualized them all, and redeemed himself from materialism, by his strong and eager aspiration towards the infinite. In his grasp, the veriest clod of earth assumed a soul. Georgiana, as she read, reverenced Aylmer, and loved him more profoundly than ever, but with a less entire dependence on his judgment than heretofore. Much as he had accomplished, she could not but observe that his most splendid successes were almost invariably failures, if compared with the ideal at which he aimed. His brightest diamonds were the merest pebbles, and felt to be so by himself, in comparison with the inestimable gems which lay hidden beyond his reach. The volume, rich with achievements that had won renown for its author, was yet as melancholy a record as ever mortal hand had penned. It was the sad confession, and continual exemplification, of the short-comings of the composite man—the spirit burthened with clay and working in matter—and of the despair that assails the higher nature, as finding itself so miserably thwarted by the earthly part. Perhaps every man of genius, in whatever sphere, might recognize the image of his own experience in Aylmer's journal.

So deeply did these reflections affect Georgiana, that she laid her face upon the open volume, and burst into tears. In this situation she was found by her husband.

"It is dangerous to read in a sorcerer's books," said he, with a smile, though his countenance was uneasy and displeased. "Georgiana, there are pages in that volume, which I can scarcely glance over and keep my senses. Take heed lest it prove as detrimental to you!"

"It has made me worship you more than ever," said she.

"Ah! wait for this one success," rejoined he, "then worship me if you will. I shall deem myself hardly unworthy of it. But, come! I have sought you for the luxury of your voice. Sing to me, dearest!"

So she poured out the liquid music of her voice to quench the thirst of his spirit. He then took his leave, with a boyish exuberance of gaiety, assuring her that her seclusion would endure but a little longer, and that the result was already certain. Scarcely had he departed, when Georgiana felt irresistibly impelled to follow him. She had forgotten to inform Aylmer of a symptom, which, for two or three hours past, had begun to excite her attention. It was a sensation in the fatal birth-mark, not painful, but which induced a restlessness throughout her system. Hastening after her husband, she intruded, for the first time, into the laboratory.

The first thing that struck her eye was the furnace, that hot and feverish worker, with the intense glow of its fire, which, by the quantities of soot clustered above it, seemed to have been burning for ages. There was a distilling apparatus in full operation. Around the room were retorts, tubes, cylinders, crucibles, and other apparatus of chemical research. An electrical machine stood ready for immediate use. The atmosphere felt oppressively close, and was tainted with gaseous odors, which had been tormented forth by the process of science. The severe and homely simplicity of the apartment, with its naked walls and brick pavement, looked strange, accustomed as Georgiana had become to the fantastic elegance of her boudoir. But what chiefly, indeed almost solely, drew her attention, was the aspect of Aylmer himself.

He was pale as death, anxious, and absorbed, and hung over the furnace as if it depended upon his utmost watchfulness whether the liquid, which it was distilling, should be the draught of immortal happiness or misery. How different from the sanguine and joyous mien that he had assumed for Georgiana's encouragement!

"Carefully now, Aminadab! Carefully, thou human machine! Carefully, thou man of clay!" muttered Aylmer, more to himself than his assistant. "Now, if there be a thought too much or too little, it is all over!"

"Hoh! hoh!" mumbled Aminadab—"look, master, look!"   60

Aylmer raised his eyes hastily, and at first reddened, then grew paler than ever, on beholding Georgiana. He rushed towards her, and seized her arm with a gripe that left the print of his fingers upon it.

"Why did you come hither? Have you no trust in your husband?" cried he impetuously. "Would you throw the blight of that fatal birth-mark over my labors? It is not well done. Go, prying woman, go!"

"Nay, Aylmer," said Georgiana, with the firmness of which she possessed no stinted endowment, "it is not you that have a right to complain. You mistrust your wife! You have concealed the anxiety with which you watch the development of this experiment. Think not so unworthily of me, my husband! Tell me all the risk we run; and fear not that I shall shrink, for my share in it is far less than your own!"

"No, no, Georgiana!" said Aylmer impatiently, "it must not be."

"I submit," replied she calmly. "And, Aylmer, I shall quaff whatever   65
draught you bring me; but it will be on the same principle that would induce me to take a dose of poison, if offered by your hand."

"My noble wife," said Aylmer, deeply moved, "I knew not the height and depth of your nature, until now. Nothing shall be concealed. Know, then, that this Crimson Hand, superficial as it seems, has clutched its grasp into your being, with a strength of which I had no previous conception. I have already administered agents powerful enough to do aught except to change your entire physical system. Only one thing remains to be tried. If that fail us, we are ruined!"

"Why did you hesitate to tell me this?" asked she.

"Because, Georgiana," said Aylmer, in a low voice, "there is danger!"

"Danger? There is but one danger—that this horrible stigma shall be left upon my cheek!" cried Georgiana. "Remove it! remove it!—whatever be the cost—or we shall both go mad!"

"Heaven knows, your words are too true," said Aylmer, sadly. "And   70
now, dearest, return to your boudoir. In a little while, all will be tested."

He conducted her back, and took leave of her with a solemn tenderness, which spoke far more than his words how much was now at stake. After his departure, Georgiana became wrapt in musings. She considered the character of Aylmer, and did it completer justice than at any previous moment.

Her heart exulted, while it trembled, at his honorable love, so pure and lofty that it would accept nothing less than perfection, nor miserably make itself contented with an earthlier nature than he had dreamed of. She felt how much more precious was such a sentiment, than that meaner kind which would have borne with the imperfection for her sake, and have been guilty of treason to holy love, by degrading its perfect idea to the level of the actual. And, with her whole spirit, she prayed, that, for a single moment, she might satisfy his highest and deepest conception. Longer than one moment, she well knew, it could not be; for his spirit was ever on the march—ever ascending—and each instant required something that was beyond the scope of the instant before.

The sound of her husband's footsteps aroused her. He bore a crystal goblet, containing a liquor colorless as water, but bright enough to be the draught of immortality. Aylmer was pale; but it seemed rather the consequence of a highly wrought state of mind, and tension of spirit, than of fear or doubt.

"The concoction of the draught has been perfect," said he, in answer to Georgiana's look. "Unless all my science have deceived me, it cannot fail."

"Save on your account, my dearest Aylmer," observed his wife, "I might wish to put off this birth-mark of mortality by relinquishing mortality itself, in preference to any other mode. Life is but a sad possession of those who have attained precisely the degree of moral advancement at which I stand. Were I weaker and blinder, it might be happiness. Were I stronger, it might be endured hopefully. But, being what I find myself, methinks I am of all mortals the most fit to die."

"You are fit for heaven without tasting death!" replied her husband. 75 "But why do we speak of dying? The draught cannot fail. Behold its effect upon this plant!"

On the window-seat there stood a geranium, diseased with yellow blotches, which had overspread all its leaves. Aylmer poured a small quantity of the liquid upon the soil in which it grew. In a little time, when the roots of the plant had taken up the moisture, the unsightly blotches began to be extinguished in a living verdure.

"There needed no proof," said Georgiana, quietly. "Give me the goblet. I joyfully stake all upon your word."

"Drink then, thou lofty creature!" exclaimed Aylmer, with fervid admiration. "There is no taint of imperfection on thy spirit. Thy sensible frame, too, shall soon be all perfect!"

She quaffed the liquid, and returned the goblet to his hand.

"It is grateful," said she, with a placid smile. "Methinks it is like water 80 from a heavenly fountain; for it contains I know not what of unobtrusive fragrance and deliciousness. It allays a feverish thirst, that had parched me for many days. Now, dearest, let me sleep. My earthly senses are closing over my spirit, like the leaves round the heart of a rose, at sunset."

She spoke the last words with a gentle reluctance, as if it required almost more energy than she could command to pronounce the faint and lingering syllables. Scarcely had they loitered through her lips, ere she was lost in slumber. Aylmer sat by her side, watching her aspect with the emotions proper to a man, the whole value of whose existence was involved in the process now to be tested. Mingled with this mood, however, was the philosophic investigation, characteristic of the man of science. Not the minutest symptom escaped him. A heightened flush of the cheek—a slight irregularity of breath—a quiver of the eyelid—a hardly perceptible tremor through the frame—such were the details which, as the moments passed, he wrote down in his folio volume. Intense thought had set its stamp upon every previous page of that volume; but the thoughts of years were all concentrated upon the last.

While thus employed, he failed not to gaze often at the fatal Hand, and not without a shudder. Yet once, by a strange and unaccountable impulse, he pressed it with his lips. His spirit recoiled, however, in the very act, and Georgiana, out of the midst of her deep sleep, moved uneasily and murmured, as if in remonstrance. Again, Aylmer resumed his watch. Nor was it without avail. The Crimson Hand, which at first had been strongly visible upon the marble paleness of Georgiana's cheek now grew more faintly outlined. She remained not less pale than ever; but the birth-mark, with every breath that came and went, lost somewhat of its former distinctness. Its presence had been awful; its departure was more awful still. Watch the stain of the rainbow fading out of the sky; and you will know how that mysterious symbol passed away.

"By Heaven, it is well nigh gone!" said Aylmer to himself, in almost irrepressible ecstasy. "I can scarcely trace it now. Success! Success! And now it is like the faintest rose-color. The slightest flush of blood across her cheek would overcome it. But she is so pale!"

He drew aside the window-curtain, and suffered the light of natural day to fall into the room, and rest upon her cheek. At the same time, he heard a gross, hoarse chuckle, which he had long known as his servant Aminadab's expression of delight.

"Ah clod! Ah, earthly mass!" cried Aylmer, laughing in a sort of frenzy. 85 "You have served me well! Matter and Spirit—Earth and Heaven—have both done their part in this! Laugh, thing of senses! You have earned the right to laugh."

These exclamations broke Georgiana's sleep. She slowly unclosed her eyes, and gazed into the mirror, which her husband had arranged for that purpose. A faint smile flitted over her lips, when she recognized how barely perceptible was now that Crimson Hand, which had once blazed forth with such disastrous brilliancy as to scare away all their happiness. But then her eyes sought Aylmer's face, with a trouble and anxiety that he could by no means account for.

"My poor Aylmer!" murmured she.

"Poor? Nay, richest! Happiest! Most favored!" exclaimed he. "My peerless bride, it is successful! You are perfect!"

"My poor Aylmer!" she repeated, with a more than human tenderness.

"You have aimed loftily!—you have done nobly! Do not repent, that, with so high and pure a feeling, you have rejected the best that earth could offer. Aylmer—dearest Aylmer—I am dying!"

Alas, it was too true! The fatal Hand had grappled with the mystery of life, and was the bond by which an angelic spirit kept itself in union with a mortal frame. As the last crimson tint of the birth-mark—that sole token of human imperfection—faded from her cheek, the parting breath of the now perfect woman passed into the atmosphere, and her soul, lingering a moment near her husband, took its heavenward flight. Then a hoarse, chuckling laugh was heard again! Thus ever does the gross Fatality of Earth exult in its invariable triumph over the immortal essence, which, in this dim sphere of half-development, demands the completeness of a higher state. Yet, had Aylmer reached a profounder wisdom, he need not thus have flung away the happiness, which would have woven his mortal life of the self-same texture with the celestial. The momentary circumstance was too strong for him; he failed to look beyond the shadowy scope of Time, and living once for all in Eternity, to find the perfect Future in the present.

1843

Questions of Subject and Theme

1. In the second paragraph, the narrator speaks of a "deeply impressive moral" attending on a "union." What union is referred to here? Given the story as a whole, what is the "moral?"
2. What does "The Crimson Hand" express to Aylmer? Paraphrase his views in a sentence or two.

Questions of Method and Strategy

1. In the first paragraph, the narrator opposes the spiritual and the chemical. To what does this opposition specifically refer here? To what does it refer in the story as a whole? What advantages does Hawthorne gain by this method of beginning?
2. The last paragraph of the story contains many temporal words and discusses time. What meaning does the context created by the paragraph as a whole give to the phrase "the now perfect woman?" Explain in a sentence or two.

THE ANATOMY LESSON

Molly O'Neill

Molly O'Neill frequently writes for the *Sunday New York Times Magazine,* where the following selection first appeared. Her account of an "artist" who pursues an ever-changing ideal of beauty by building muscles to fashion's dictates makes, among other things, an odd updating of Hawthorne's tale.

David Barton is a sculptor whose medium is human flesh. A gym owner and trainer (and one pumped-up individual), Barton is looking at nudes at the Metropolitan Museum of Art, as mesmerized by perfection as a young ballplayer by Ted Williams's swing.

Artists of other centuries used marble, clay or paint to depict the idealized human form. Barton builds strategic muscles. It's a question of proportion—accentuating one group to deaccentuate another. One of Barton's favorite techniques is to build the outer thigh to a pearlike bulge. "It deemphasizes the hips and gives the illusion of that straight-up-and-down male line," he says, flexing his own bulbous quadriceps.

Barton has ways of dealing with slope-shouldered men ("Build biceps!") and men with paunches ("Bulk up the chest; it's easier"). He has ways of making the female waist look smaller ("Widen the shoulders") and the bust tauter ("Pecs, pecs, pecs . . . build 'em up and you have a whole new tilt").

Barton also has ways of looking at art.

He's crazy about "Kouros," the museum's best example of the classical ideal. "Great body. Nice, long lines," he says, stroking the lean sweep of the statue's quadriceps and getting reprimanded for it by a guard. Barton can't help himself. "I so rarely see pure athleticism," he sighs. But Kouros's back is another story. "Oh, God, no definition!" he yelps. "Deltoids. What he needs is deltoids. We have machines for that."

Barton is less hopeful about Lombardo's "Adam," a lithe, almost womanly figure from the 15th century who would need "a back, a chest, upper arms, thighs. Real guys are, uh, dense, muscularly speaking." Rodin's "Adam," with its rippling hard body, seems to cheer him. "I'd prefer to think Adam looked like this," he says. And then, yanking up his own T-shirt to reveal a stomach reminiscent of a low-rolling mountain range, he adds, "but he could use some abdominal work."

A white-haired woman in old Chanel stops to take a look. Simply fabulous, she says of the real thing. "Fabulous! Fabulous!" But Barton disagrees.

"No, this stuff is retro," he says, grimacing at the immobile mountain of muscle that rises like dead rock when he flexes his biceps. "During the 80's the whole thing was building up a look. My muscles are cosmetic—they can't *do* anything. Of course, it's my profession; I have to be larger than life . . ."

But Barton is not entirely surprised that the ideal form has moved away from pumping iron to a stringy, more elongated look. "People want me to give them long, skinny muscles," he notes. "They don't want to look like they go to a gym. They want to look like they got a little forearm holding a guitar. People are concerned with living life, not conquering it. And it changes the esthetic."

Ideal form has always been a fickle thing, and like any artist, Barton   10 is fascinated by how his forerunners contended with the flux of popular esthetics.

"Generally, the ideal is a reaction, not a reality," he says, gazing at Courbet's "Young Bather." "When Rubens was painting, people didn't have enough to eat; skinny was ugly, zaftig was a turn-on. Of course, if that bather were around today, she'd be freaked out by the dimples in her hips. But look at her. Perfectly at ease."

Cabanel's "Venus" reminds him of his prom date, "beautiful, but definitely going to run into some thigh problems if she doesn't stop lolling around." But then he slaps his head and announces: "Talk about denial! The fact is, I find her very sexy. She likes who she is, and that's always a turn-on. And she's soft. A woman who works out loses softness and eventually elasticity."

A body sculptor can build the illusion of perfection, but not without sacrifice. "The deliberately developed look is contrary to the essence of living," explains Barton, oblivious, in his black tights and high-top sneakers, to the shocked looks his flexing and posing elicit on this afternoon stroll. "When the esthetic changes," he says, "a sculptor just makes a new work. It's a lot tougher when your medium is muscles."

Questions of Subject and Theme

1. Given the selection as a whole, in what ways does David Barton regard art and life similarly? Make a list.
2. Given the selection as a whole, what does David Barton mean when he says in the last paragraph that "The deliberately developed look is contrary to the essence of living?" What arguments implicitly underlie this claim?

Questions of Method and Strategy

1. Given the selection as a whole, do you think the analogy of Ted Williams's swing in the first paragraph is well chosen to define the kind of "perfection" David Barton discusses?
2. In your view, what effect would be created by switching the first and last paragraphs? What advantages do you imagine Molly O'Neill saw in her strategy?

NEW FACE, NEW BODY, NEW SELF

Marjorie Rosen

A senior writer for *People Weekly,* Marjorie Rosen has written for many popular periodicals. In the following selection, she offers the arguments of individuals in favor of modifying their bodies and opposes them to the general cultural explanations of plastic surgery most widely accepted today.

In high school a teenager's looks can become a life-absorbing obsession,   1
a source of painful and disabling self-consciousness. So what's the problem with using a knife to put right what nature seems to have done all wrong? "Nothing," says Camille Paglia, author of the controversial *Sexual Personae,* a study of cultural decadence, "as long as there is a serious defect which plastic surgery can correct and help a young person feel more confident. But unfortunately the model that has evolved is the Barbie doll."

And that is the problem, agrees Marie Wilson, president of the Ms. Foundation for Women, an organization that supports projects devoted to women and children. "Most of this is about [already] having a face that is just fine and hoping to make it perfect," she says. Susan Faludi, author of the best-selling *Backlash: The Undeclared War Against American Women,* which chronicles the media assault on women during the past decade, is even more critical of our cut-and-stitch-happy society where 87 out of every 100 plastic surgery patients are women. Blaming plastic surgeons for "wanting to play the role of Frankenstein, wanting the power to shape the female form as though it's putty," she observes: "Young women are much less free to come up with individual ideals of beauty than men, and the pressure to conform that causes young girls to have plastic surgery is one more way to confine them."

But apparently teenagers don't all see it that way. The girls—and boy— on the following pages were determined to change their lives through cosmetic surgery, and they did. They share their stories below.

Thinner Thighs in an Hour and a Half— All for Just $10,000

For years, Robyn Notrica, now 21, wore boxer shorts to the beach and bought pants five sizes too big in the waist because otherwise she couldn't squeeze her thighs into them. The pants she *did* wear were frayed between the legs where her flesh rubbed together. "My thighs were humongous," recalls the five-foot two-inch sophomore at the New York School of Design in Manhattan. "I was small in my upper body, but my hips were huge."

And not for lack of dieting. All the while she was growing up in suburban Roslyn, New York, she fought a nonstop battle against lower-body bulge. At one time weighing 175 pounds, she spent five summers at weight-loss camps and even followed the Nutri/System program. But nothing helped.

Thoroughly frustrated, Notrica began to think about a more drastic   5 solution: liposuction. Finally, two-and-a-half years ago, she went to see New York City plastic surgeon Dr. Helen Cohen. "She said she'd never seen a girl my age with so much fat on her legs," says Notrica. Supported by her mother, Marna, a housewife, and her father, Jack, a retired cop, Robyn underwent a one-and-a-half-hour, ten-thousand-dollar procedure, during which fat was suctioned from her hips and thighs. Explains Dr. Cohen, who cautions patients to look for surgeons certified in liposuction techniques: "When the procedure was first done here in 1983, people died from shock because when you remove fat and fluid, you lose electrolytes, too. But if you do it right, there is no problem." In fact, she says, teenagers respond better to liposuction than older women because their skin is more elastic and will shrink back into shape.

Notrica did experience discomfort, though. "For a week it felt as if I'd worked out too much," she says, and her legs remained bruised for a month. These days she can barely recall the unpleasantness. The only telltale signs are twelve fading scars, each the size of a pinky nail, that mark the spots where the liposuction cannula pierced her skin. Notrica, delighted by the new "great shape" of her legs, says the surgery eliminated six inches from her hips. Best of all, she has achieved her "biggest goal": to fit into a pair of Levi's—size 29 waist. "Liposuction," she says, "made me happy."

A New Nose—and a Chin to Match

Growing up in East Brunswick, New Jersey, she was an accident-prone girl who broke her nose badly in ninth-grade gym class when she caught a basketball with her face. So Andrea Rudow visited Dr. Alvin Glasgold, the Highland Park, New Jersey, plastic surgeon who had straightened her older brother Gary's nose when he was sixteen. Since she was only thirteen and still growing, Glasgold advised her to come back in six months. She did— "with a huge red bump on my face. The nasal bone, instead of growing down, was now growing out," she says. Classmates at East Brunswick High School noticed, too, and began calling her Rudolph.

During Andrea's consultation, Dr. Glasgold suggested not only a nose job but an implant to improve her receding chin. "He said that the line of your nose has to fit with your chin," says Rudow, "and I trusted him." According to Glasgold, 25 percent of all rhinoplasty patients also have receding chins. "Sometimes the chin is the real problem and the nose just a minor one," he says.

"Correcting a chin is much simpler than doing rhinoplasty, and the results, using FDA-approved silicone rubber, are extremely consistent." Making an incision either under the chin or in the gums between the chin and the lip, the surgeon slips the implant into place, then anchors it with a surgical stitch to the tissue surrounding the bone. In 1988, when Andrea, now nineteen, had it done, the operation cost her father, Richard, a real estate appraiser, and her mother, Ricki, a medical secretary, thirty-five hundred dollars. (Insurance paid most of the cost because her nasal bone was growing improperly.)

When her bandages came off, "I was laughing and crying at the same time," Rudow says. "Crying because I was so happy and laughing because it didn't look like me."   10

Rudow was so elated with the results that she was inspired to lose weight, too. Back at school, she says, "they looked at me like, 'Oh, did you get a haircut?'" But Rudow felt the difference profoundly. Happier, and feeling prettier, she became less reclusive, making friends and dating regularly. Now a liberal arts student at Middlesex Community College in Edison, New Jersey, she sees only one drawback to her surgery. "Men whistle at me on the street," she says. "At first it was funny, but now it's like, *enough*."

A Teenage Cyrano Divests Himself of a Showpiece

Joe Mann's parents gave him a nose job for his high school graduation present in 1991. The thirty-two-hundred-dollar operation was something that the lanky, six-foot one-inch Houston teenager had contemplated ever since junior high when, he recalls, "kids would tease me by saying things like, 'Is that your real nose?' And once there were these pegs in the locker room for us to hang our clothes on, and someone drew eyes and a mouth around one, like it was supposed to be me."

Even Mann's plastic surgeon, Dr. Charles Bailey, admits, "His was probably the largest nose I've ever seen." But Bailey believes that Mann was a good candidate for surgery for another reason. "Joe seemed very well adjusted," he says. "I'm generally more cautious with young males than young women. Women have a grasp of what they want, but with young men, it's more common to have an underlying problem—something else they don't feel good about." Not Joe. "He was not withdrawn and has a great sense of humor," says Bailey.

When the operation was finished, Mann asked for the pieces of bone and cartilage that were removed from his schnozz and keeps them in a jar of formaldehyde. He loves to show off his *old* nose—now that it's not on his face. "I'm glad I did it," says Mann, nineteen, a freshman at Houston Community College. Although he has no steady these days, he notices that since his transformation, "I have more dates, and I think it's because I look better." That's not all. "People are more courteous," he says. "Like salespeople. They'd rather talk to a good-looking person than a not-so-good-looking one."

Seeking the Perfect Nose:
After Three Strikes, Success

One year ago, after three botched rhinoplasty attempts, Jill Fugler of suburban Houston was beside herself with frustration and disappointment. Today the twenty-two-year-old boasts a perfect profile, thanks both to her own resolute spirit and to Houston plastic surgeon Dr. Benjamin Cohen.

Fugler's odyssey began in 1987 when, at seventeen, she decided to fix the nose she had broken in a neighborhood football game during junior high school. After the surgery the tip had a permanent "swollen" look, she says. When she complained, her surgeon scheduled a second operation. And a third. But the tip remained puffy.

Enter Dr. Cohen, whom Fugler's mom had seen on a local Houston TV show about plastic surgery. Cohen's explanation for the puffiness: "Too much cartilage had been taken from the tip of her nose." Using a new cartilage-graft technique, Cohen removed excess scar tissue and filled out the tip. "Before, I wanted people to look me in the face and not see my profile," says Fugler, who is completing an associate degree at North Harris Montgomery College in Houston. "Now I look at my profile every day."

There Are Times When a Nose Opens Doors

Ever since she was three, Stacy Hirsch had her heart set on becoming an actress. Singing and dancing lessons were part of the plan. So, too, after she turned fourteen, was a nose job. "I had made a real commitment to the profession," says Stacy, sixteen. "I thought having my nose done would give me a new look that would increase my marketability."

Before her surgery, says Stacy, "people weren't really seeing me; they were speaking to me and thinking, 'She's got a big nose.'" Because of Stacy's unhappiness about her appearance, her parents, Larry, a manufacturer's representative, and Linda, a preschool teacher, backed Stacy's decision. "I'd had a nose job myself at sixteen," says Linda. "I never said anything to Stacy about her nose, but she knew I'd had mine done, and maybe that stuck in her mind."

Still, Stacy worried that friends would perceive her as vain and only told   20
those closest to her. "I asked myself, 'Should I not do this because it's not the *good* thing to do?'" she admits. "But I decided I didn't want to ask, 'What if? Would I have gotten that job if I looked different?'"

In July 1991, after her freshman year at Glenbrook North High School in Northbrook, Illinois, Stacy scheduled surgery with Dr. Jack Kerth, who asked Stacy to bring in pictures of noses that she liked. "I looked through my teen magazines and tore off the noses of Julia Roberts and Cindy Crawford," says Stacy. "But I asked Dr. Kerth for a nose that fits my face, that looks natural." And, she believes, she got one. "It was the nose I was born to have and didn't get," she says.

When Hirsch returned to school in September, she says, "boys noticed me." What's more, she got a part on *Energy Express,* a Chicago TV show for teens about sports, which has been picked up nationally for syndication. "I would never have had this response if I had looked a different way," says Hirsch. "When your outside equals your inside, you're going to get twice as much as you already have."

 Questions of Subject and Theme

1. Describe in a sentence or two the theme of the first two paragraphs. Then describe the theme of the rest of the piece in another sentence or two.
2. What does Stacy Hirsch mean at the end of the selection when she talks about her outside equaling her inside? Do the other young people quoted agree with her? Explain your answer with evidence.

Questions of Method and Strategy

1. At the end of the third paragraph, we are told that teenagers are to "share" their stories in the paragraphs to come. What do you think makes the metaphor of "sharing" such a popular one in contexts like the present one? What, for example, does the metaphor imply about potential opposition to what is being "shared?"
2. The selection is sprinkled with subheads, beginning with " *Thinner Thighs in an Hour and a Half—All for Just $10,000.*" What is the general tone of voice employed in the subheads? How is that tone related to the tone in which the teenagers' stories are told? What do you imagine is the argumentative strategy involved?

———

Suggestions for Writing on the Juxtapositions

1. David Barton is quoted as saying of "ideal form" that "Generally, the ideal is a reaction, not a reality." Write an essay in which you argue that the selections in this section do or do not support this contention.
2. Susan Faludi is quoted as saying that "Young women are much less free to come up with individual ideals of beauty than men, and the pressure to conform that causes young girls to have plastic surgery is one more way to confine them." Write an essay in which you argue for or against this contention.
3. In your opinion, which selection did most justice to the relations between the real and the ideal? Write an essay in which you argue for the justice of your choice.
4. All the selections raise the question of right and wrong with regard to modifying the body. Write an essay in which you argue for the proper ethics to be observed in this regard.

Acknowledgments

RUSSELL BAKER, "Little Red Riding Hood Revisited," *The New York Times,* 1979. Copyright © 1979 by The New York Times Company. Reprinted by permission. "Don't Mention It," *The New York Times,* 1990. Copyright © 1990 by The New York Times Company. Reprinted by permission.

ROLAND BARTHES, "The Brain of Einstein," from *Mythologies,* translated by Annette Lavers. Translation copyright © 1972 by Jonathan Cape Ltd. Reprinted by permission of Hill and Wang, a division of Farrar, Straus & Girous, Inc.

BRUNO BETTELHEIM, from *The Uses of Enchantment.* Copyright © 1975, 1976 by Bruno Bettelheim. Reprinted by permission of Alfred A. Knopf, Inc.

RAYMOND CARVER, "Photograph of My Father in His Twenty-Second Year," from *Fires.* Copyright © 1993 by Tess Gallagher. Reprinted by permission of Tess Gallagher.

LUCILLE CLIFTON, "naomi watches as ruth sleeps," from *The Book of Light.* Copyright © 1993 by lucille clifton. Reprinted by permission of Copper Canyon Press, P.O. Box 271, Port Townsend, WA 98368.

ISAK DINESEN, from *Out of Africa.* Copyright © 1937 by Random House, Inc. Copyright renewed 1965 by Rungstedlundfonden. Reprinted by permission of Random House, Inc.

WALT DISNEY, "The Story of Mickey Mouse," from *Walt Disney: A Bio-Bibliography,* by Jackson. Copyright © 1993 by Greenwood Publishing Group Inc. Reprinted with permission of Greenwood Publishing Group, Inc., Westport, CT.

DAVID JAMES DUNCAN, from *The River Why.* Copyright © 1983 by David James Duncan. Reprinted with permission of Sierra Club Books.

JOSEPH EPSTEIN, "A Fat Man Struggles to Get Out." Reprinted from *The American Scholar,* Volume 54, Number 3, Summer 1985. Copyright © 1985 by Joseph Epstein. Reprinted by permission of the publisher.

ZLATA FILIPOVIC, from *Zlata's Diary.* Translation copyright © 1994 Editions Robert Laffont/Fixot. Used by permission of Viking Penguin, a division of Penguin Books USA Inc.

M. F. K. FISHER, "The Indigestible: The Language of Food." Copyright © 1979 by M. F. K. Fisher. Originally appeared in *The New York Review of Books.* Reprinted with permission.

NORMAN MAILER, from *The Executioner's Song.* Copyright © 1979 by Norman Mailer. Reprinted with the permission of Wylie Atiken & Stone, Inc.

MALCOLM X, "The Ballot or the Bullet." Copyright © 1965, 1989 by Betty Shabaz and Pathfinder Press. Reprinted by permission of Pathfinder Press.

H. L. MENCKEN, from *Happy Days.* Copyright © 1939, 1940 by Alfred A. Knopf, Inc. Reprinted by permission of the publisher.

THOMAS H. MIDDLETON, "Freshman Class?" *The Saturday Review,* 1983. Reprinted with the permission of the author.

GLORIA NAYLOR, "A Question of Language." Copyright © 1986 by Gloria Naylor. Reprinted by permission of Sterling Lord Literistic, Inc.

ITABARI NJERI, "What's in a Name?" from *Every Good-bye Ain't Gone.* Copyright © 1990 by Itabari Njeri. Reprinted by permission of the author.

MOLLY O'NEILL, "The Anatomy Lesson," *The New York Times Magazine,* April 1994. Copyright © 1994 by The New York Times Company. Reprinted by permission.

JOYCE CAROL OATES, "Shopping," *Ms.* 1987. Copyright © 1987 by The Ontario Review Inc. Reprinted by permission of John Hawkins & Associates, Inc.

GEORGE ORWELL, "Shooting an Elephant" and "A Hanging," from *Shooting an Elephant and Other Essays.* Copyright © 1950 by Sonioa Brownell Orwell and renewed 1978 by Sonia Pitt-Rivers. Reprinted by permission of Harcourt Brace & Company.

SYLVIA PLATH, "Daddy," from *Ariel.* Copyright © 1963 by Ted Hughes. Copyright renewed. Reprinted by permission of HarperCollins Publishers, Inc.

ANNA QUINDLEN, "The Name is Mine." Reprinted by permission of the author. Anna Quindlen won the Pulitzer Prize for her columns for the *New York Times.* She is a novelist.

THEODORE ROETHKE, "My Papa's Waltz," from *The Collected Poems of Theodore Roethke.* Copyright © 1942 by Hearst Magazines, Inc. Used by permission of Doubleday, a division of Bantam Doubleday Dell Publishing Group, Inc.

MARJORIE ROSEN/VICKI SHEFF-CAHAN, "New Face, New Body, New Self," *People Weekly.* Reprinted by permission of Time Inc.

LEONARD Q. ROSS, excerpt from *The Education of Hyman Kaplan.* Copyright © 1937 by Harcourt Brace & Company and renewed 1964 by Leonard C. Rosten. Reprinted by permission of the publisher.

WILLIAM SAFIRE, "A Bottle of Ketchup," *The New York Times,* October, 1982. Copyright © 1982 by The New York Times Company. Reprinted by permission.

CARL SAGAN, "The Warming of the World." Copyright © 1985 by Carl Sagan. Reprinted by permission from Carl Sagan and *Parade Magazine.*

SCOTT SHUGER, "Who Are the Homeless?" *The Washington Monthly.* Reprinted by permission of the author.

SUSANNE STYRON, "Risk Management," *The New York Times,* April, 1994. Copyright © 1994 by The New York Times Company. Reprinted by permission.

VO THI TAM, "From Vietnam, 1979," from *American Mosaic: The Immigrant Experience in the Words of Those Who Lived It,* by Joan Morrison and Charlotte Fox Zabusky. Copyright © 1980, 1993 by Joan Morrison and Charlotte Fox Zabusky. Reprinted by permission of the University of Pittsburgh Press.

Index to the Readings by Type

Autobiography

DINESEN, ISAK, The Earthquake, 386
DUNCAN, DAVID JAMES, Ma, 108
KINGSTON, MAXINE HONG, Photographs of My Mother, 112
NJERI, ITABARI, What's in a Name? 336
TAM, VO THI, A Boat Person's Story, 170

Bible Story

KING JAMES BIBLE, The Book of Ruth, 152

Diary

FILIPOVIC, ZLATA, from *Zlata's Diary: A Child's Life in Sarajevo*, 27
FRANK, ANNE, from *The Diary of a Young Girl*, 18
HUNTER, LATOYA, from *The Diary of LaToya Hunter*, 37

Essay

BAKER, RUSSELL, Don't Mention It, 390
BARTHES, ROLAND, The Brain of Einstein, 371
BETTELHEIM, BRUNO, Fairy Tale versus Myth: Optimism versus Pessimism, 315
CRASTA, RICHARD, What's in a Name? 342
DICKENS, CHARLES, Among the Condemned, 85
EPSTEIN, JOSEPH, A Fat Man Struggles to Get Out, 275

FISHER, M. F. K., The Indigestible: The Language of Food, 220
GEIST, WILLIAM, Sport Shopping in Suburbia, 298
GOODMAN, ELLEN, Vulgarity May Be Common, but It's Not Okay, 329
GORDON, MARY, More Than Just a Shrine: Paying Homage to the Ghosts of Ellis Island, 166
GOULD, STEPHEN JAY, A Biological Homage to Mickey Mouse, 240
GREENE, BOB, 15, 282
HOLLANDER, ANNE, Why It's Fashionable to Be Thin, 262
HOYLE, SIR FREDERICK, The Next Ice Age, 206
HUGHES, LANGSTON, Salvation, 4
JAMES, WILLIAM, On Some Mental Effects of the Earthquake, 376
LAWRENCE, BARBARA, Four-Letter Words Can Hurt You, 331
LEVY, STEVEN, My Search for Einstein's Brain, 358
LONDON, JACK, Among the London Poor, 178
MENCKEN, H. L., Hangings I Have Known, 92
MIDDLETON, THOMAS H., Freshman Class? 326
NAYLOR, GLORIA, A Question of Language, 398
O'NEILL, MOLLY, The Anatomy Lesson, 433

ORWELL, GEORGE,
   A Hanging, 88
   Shooting an Elephant, 7
QUINDLEN, ANNA, The Name is Mine, 13
ROSEN, MARJORIE, New Face, New Body, New Self, 435
SAFIRE, WILLIAM, A Bottle of Ketchup, 229
SAGAN, CARL, The Warming of the World, 212
SAVAGE, DAVID G., Forbidden Words on Campus, 393
SHUGER, SCOTT, Who Are the Homeless? 186
STYRON, SUSANNA, Risk Management: Men versus Women in the L.A. Earthquake, 383
TAN, AMY, Mother Tongue, 409
TISDALE, SALLIE, A Weight That Women Carry, 265
UPDIKE, JOHN, The Mystery of Mickey Mouse, 250
VLAHOGIANNIS, GEORGE, Weird World of Disney, 256
WALKER, ALICE, In Search of Our Mothers' Gardens, 100
WHITE, E. B., Once More to the Lake, 44

Fairy Tale

GRIMM, JAKOB AND WILHELM, Red Riding Hood, 306

Literary reportage

MAILER, NORMAN, Let's Do It, 94

News account

CRANE, STEPHEN, News Accounts of the Disaster, 122

Poem

CARVER, RAYMOND, Photograph of My Father in His Twenty-Second Year, 53

CLIFTON, LUCILLE, naomi watches as ruth sleeps, 160
FROST, ROBERT, Fire and Ice, 204
HOOD, THOMAS, Ruth, 158
KIZER, CAROLYN, from The Blessing, 118
PLATH, SYLVIA, Daddy, 50
ROETHKE, THEODORE, My Papa's Waltz, 54

Satire

BAKER, RUSSELL, Little Red Riding Hood Revisited, 312
GARNER, JAMES FINN, Little Red Riding Hood, 309

Screenplay

COWEN, RON, screenplay excerpt from *Paul's Case,* 74

Short story

CATHER, WILLA, Paul's Case: A Study in Temperament, 58
CRANE, STEPHEN, The Open Boat, 130
HAWTHORNE, NATHANIEL, The Birth-Mark, 420
KINCAID, JAMAICA, Girl, 116
OATES, JOYCE CAROL, Shopping, 288
ROSS, LEONARD Q., Mr. K★A★P★L★A★N, the Comparative, and the Superlative, 414

Slave narrative

BALL, CHARLES, Slave Ship, 164
DOUGLASS, FREDERICK, Learning to Read and Write, 404

Speech

DISNEY, WALT, The Story of Mickey Mouse, 236
KING, MARTIN LUTHER, JR., I Have a Dream, 348
MALCOLM X, The Ballot or the Bullet, 352

Index of Authors and Titles

Among the Condemned, CHARLES DICKENS, 85

Among the London Poor, JACK LONDON, 178

Anatomy Lesson, The, MOLLY O'NEILL, 433

BAKER, RUSSELL,
   Don't Mention It, 390
   Little Red Riding Hood Revisited, 312
BALL, CHARLES, Slave Ship, 164
Ballot or the Bullet, The, MALCOLM X, 352
BARTHES, ROLAND, The Brain of Einstein, 371
BETTELHEIM, BRUNO, Fairy Tale versus Myth: Optimism versus Pessimism, 315
Biological Homage to Mickey Mouse, A, STEPHEN JAY GOULD, 240
Birth-Mark, The, NATHANIEL HAWTHORNE, 420
Blessing, from The, CAROLYN KIZER, 118
Boat Person's Story, A, VO THI TAM, 170
Book of Ruth, The, KING JAMES BIBLE, 152
Bottle of Ketchup, A, WILLIAM SAFIRE, 229
Brain of Einstein, The, ROLAND BARTHES, 371

CARVER, RAYMOND, Photograph of My Father in His Twenty-Second Year, 53
CATHER, WILLA, Paul's Case: A Study in Temperament, 58

CLIFTON, LUCILLE, naomi watches as ruth sleeps, 160
COWEN, RON, screenplay excerpt from Paul's Case, 74
CRANE, STEPHEN,
   News Accounts of the Disaster, 122
   The Open Boat, 130
CRASTA, RICHARD, What's in a Name? 342

Daddy, SYLVIA PLATH, 50
Diary of LaToya Hunter, from The, LATOYA HUNTER, 37
Diary of a Young Girl, from The, ANNE FRANK, 18
DICKENS, CHARLES, Among the Condemned, 85
DINESEN, ISAK, The Earthquake, 386
DISNEY, WALT, The Story of Mickey Mouse, 236
Don't Mention It, RUSSELL BAKER, 390
DOUGLASS, FREDERICK, Learning to Read and Write, 404
DUNCAN, DAVID JAMES, Ma, 108

Earthquake, The, ISAK DINESEN, 386
EPSTEIN, JOSEPH, A Fat Man Struggles to Get Out, 275

Fairy Tale versus Myth: Optimism versus Pessimism, BRUNO BETTELHEIM, 315
Fat Man Struggles to Get Out, A, JOSEPH EPSTEIN, 275

447

15, BOB GREENE, 282
FILIPOVIC, ZLATA, from *Zlata's Diary: A Child's Life in Sarajevo,* 27
Fire and Ice, ROBERT FROST, 204
FISHER, M. F. K., The Indigestible: The Language of Food, 220
Forbidden Words on Campus, DAVID G. SAVAGE, 393
Four-Letter Words Can Hurt You, BARBARA LAWRENCE, 331
FRANK, ANNE, from *The Diary of a Young Girl,* 18
Freshman Class? THOMAS H. MIDDLETON, 326
FROST, ROBERT, Fire and Ice, 204

GARNER, JAMES FINN, Little Red Riding Hood, 309
GEIST, WILLIAM, Sport Shopping in Suburbia, 298
Girl, JAMAICA KINCAID, 116
GOODMAN, ELLEN, Vulgarity May Be Common, but It's Not Okay, 329
GORDON, MARY, More Than Just a Shrine: Paying Homage to the Ghosts of Ellis Island, 166
GOULD, STEPHEN JAY, A Biological Homage to Mickey Mouse, 240
GREENE, BOB, 15, 282
GRIMM, JAKOB AND WILHELM, Red Riding Hood, 306

Hanging, A, GEORGE ORWELL, 88
Hangings I Have Known, H. L. MENCKEN, 92
HAWTHORNE, NATHANIEL, The Birth-Mark, 420
HOLLANDER, ANNE, Why It's Fashionable to Be Thin, 262
HOOD, THOMAS, Ruth, 158
HOYLE, SIR FREDERICK, The Next Ice Age, 206
HUGHES, LANGSTON, Salvation, 4
HUNTER, LATOYA, from *The Diary of LaToya Hunter,* 37

I Have a Dream, MARTIN LUTHER KING, JR., 348
Indigestible: The Language of Food, The, M. F. K. FISHER, 220

In Search of Our Mothers' Gardens, ALICE WALKER, 100

JAMES, WILLIAM, On Some Mental Effects of the Earthquake, 376

KINCAID, JAMAICA, Girl, 116
KING JAMES BIBLE, The Book of Ruth, 152
KING, MARTIN LUTHER, JR., I Have a Dream, 348
KINGSTON, MAXINE HONG, Photographs of My Mother, 112
KIZER, CAROLYN, from *The Blessing,* 118

LAWRENCE, BARBARA, Four-Letter Words Can Hurt You, 331
Learning to Read and Write, FREDERICK DOUGLASS, 404
Let's Do It, NORMAN MAILER, 94
LEVY, STEVEN, My Search for Einstein's Brain, 358
Little Red Riding Hood, JAMES FINN GARNER, 309
Little Red Riding Hood Revisited, RUSSELL BAKER, 312
LONDON, JACK, Among the London Poor, 178

Ma, DAVID JAMES DUNCAN, 108
MAILER, NORMAN, Let's Do It, 94
MALCOLM X, The Ballot or the Bullet, 352
MENCKEN, H. L., Hangings I Have Known, 92
MIDDLETON, THOMAS H., Freshman Class? 326
Mother Tongue, AMY TAN, 409
More Than Just a Shrine: Paying Homage to the Ghosts of Ellis Island, MARY GORDON, 166
Mr. K★A★P★L★A★N, the Comparative, and the Superlative, LEONARD Q. ROSS, 414
My Papa's Waltz, THEODORE ROETHKE, 54
My Search for Einstein's Brain, STEVEN LEVY, 358
Mystery of Mickey Mouse, The, JOHN UPDIKE, 250

Name Is Mine, The, ANNA QUINDLEN, 13
naomi watches as ruth sleeps, LUCILLE CLIFTON, 160

NAYLOR, GLORIA, A Question of Language, 398

New Face, New Body, New Self, MARJORIE ROSEN, 435

News Accounts of the Disaster, STEPHEN CRANE, 122

Next Ice Age, The, SIR FREDERICK HOYLE, 206

NJERI, ITABARI, What's in a Name? 336

OATES, JOYCE CAROL, Shopping, 288

On Some Mental Effects of the Earthquake, WILLIAM JAMES, 376

Once More to the Lake, E. B. WHITE, 44

O'NEILL, MOLLY, The Anatomy Lesson, 433

Open Boat, The, STEPHEN CRANE, 130

ORWELL, GEORGE,
    A Hanging, 88
    Shooting an Elephant, 7

Paul's Case: A Study in Temperament, WILLA CATHER, 58

Paul's Case, screenplay excerpt from, RON COWEN, 74

Photograph of My Father in His Twenty-Second Year, RAYMOND CARVER, 53

Photographs of My Mother, MAXINE HONG KINGSTON, 112

PLATH, SYLVIA, Daddy, 50

Question of Language, A, GLORIA NAYLOR, 398

QUINDLEN, ANNA, The Name is Mine, 13

Red Riding Hood, JAKOB AND WILHELM GRIMM, 306

Risk Management: Men versus Women in the L.A. Earthquake, SUSANNA STYRON, 383

ROETHKE, THEODORE, My Papa's Waltz, 54

ROSEN, MARJORIE, New Face, New Body, New Self, 435

ROSS, LEONARD Q., Mr. K★A★P★L★A★N, the Comparative, and the Superlative, 414

Ruth, THOMAS HOOD, 158

SAFIRE, WILLIAM, A Bottle of Ketchup, 229

SAGAN, CARL, The Warming of the World, 212

Salvation, LANGSTON HUGHES, 4

SAVAGE, DAVID G., Forbidden Words on Campus, 393

Shooting an Elephant, GEORGE ORWELL, 7

Shopping, JOYCE CAROL OATES, 288

SHUGER, SCOTT, Who Are the Homeless? 186

Slave Ship, CHARLES BALL, 164

Sport Shopping in Suburbia, WILLIAM GEIST, 298

Story of Mickey Mouse, The, WALT DISNEY, 236

STYRON, SUSANNA, Risk Management: Men versus Women in the L.A. Earthquake, 383

TAM, VO THI, A Boat Person's Story, 170

TAN, AMY, Mother Tongue, 409

TISDALE, SALLIE, A Weight That Women Carry, 265

UPDIKE, JOHN, The Mystery of Mickey Mouse, 250

VLAHOGIANNIS, GEORGE, Weird World of Disney, 256

Vulgarity May Be Common, but It's Not Okay, ELLEN GOODMAN, 329

WALKER, ALICE, In Search of Our Mothers' Gardens, 100

Warming of the World, The, CARL SAGAN, 212

Weight That Women Carry, A, SALLIE TISDALE, 265

Weird World of Disney, GEORGE VLAHOGIANNIS, 256

What's in a Name? ITABARI NJERI, 336

What's in a Name? RICHARD CRASTA, 342

WHITE, E. B., Once More to the Lake, 44

Who Are the Homeless? SCOTT SHUGER, 186

Why It's Fashionable to Be Thin, ANNE HOLLANDER, 262

Zlata's Diary: A Child's Life in Sarajevo, from, ZLATA FILIPOVIC, 27